Biological data exploration with Pyth

Set in Latin Modern Roman and Inconsolata

Contents

1 **Introduction**   **6**
   1.1   Motivation 6
     1.1.1   Python's data processing stack 6
     1.1.2   Structure and what's covered 6
     1.1.3   What's not covered 7
   1.2   Your programming environment 7
     1.2.1   Packages and versions 8
   1.3   Formatting conventions 8
     1.3.1   Terminology 9
     1.3.2   Examples 9
   1.4   Example data files 10
     1.4.1   `eukaryotes.tsv` 10
     1.4.2   `common_names.csv` 11
     1.4.3   `contigs.csv` 11
     1.4.4   `weather.csv` 11
     1.4.5   `Berlin_daily_rain.csv` , `London_daily_rain.csv` , `Edinburgh_daily_rain.csv` 11
     1.4.6   `london_rainfall.csv` 11
     1.4.7   `fungi_genomes.csv` 12

2 **Introduction to pandas**   **13**
     2.0.1   Series and dataframe objects 13
     2.0.2   Reading data from files 15
     2.0.3   Investigating a dataframe 16
   2.1   A note about column names 20
   2.2   Wrapping up 22
     2.2.1   Encoding errors 22
     2.2.2   Reading Excel files 22

3 **Working with Series**   **23**
   3.1   Working with columns 23
   3.2   Broadcasting operations on series 26
     3.2.1   Numerical operations 26
     3.2.2   String operations 28
     3.2.3   Selecting multiple columns 29
   3.3   Setting an index 29

4 **Filtering and selecting data**   **34**
   4.1   Selecting rows from dataframes 34
     4.1.1   Selecting things that are in a list 36
     4.1.2   Selecting things based on string properties 37
     4.1.3   Filtering based on multiple conditions 38
   4.2   Filtering on columns with missing data 39
   4.3   Putting it all together 40
     4.3.1   Filtering as a building block 42

5 **Data exploration examples with pandas**   **43**
     5.0.1   How many fungal species have genomes bigger than 100Mb? What are their names? . . . 43
     5.0.2   How many genomes are there for each Kingdom (plants, animals, fungi, protists and other), and how many unique species names? 44
     5.0.3   Make a new dataframe containing just the rows for the *Aquila* genus. 46
     5.0.4   In which assembly status are the most insect genomes? How about the most amphibian genomes? 48
     5.0.5   Which genomes have at least 10% more proteins than genes? 49

6 Introduction to Seaborn   **52**
6.1 Setting up to draw a chart 53
   6.1.1 Plotting distributions 54
   6.1.2 Visualizing relationships between two variables 56

7 Special types of scatter plots   **63**
   7.0.1 Plotting large numbers of points 63
   7.0.2 Plotting regression lines and confidence intervals 73
   7.0.3 Plotting pairwise relationships 75

8 Conditioning charts on categories   **80**

9 Categorical axes with seaborn   **90**
9.1 Types of categorical plots 90
9.2 Categorical scatter plots 90
   9.2.1 Strip plots 91
   9.2.2 Swarm plots 97
9.3 Distribution plots 101
   9.3.1 Box plots 101
   9.3.2 Violin plots 107
   9.3.3 Boxen plots 112
9.4 Point estimate plots 114
   9.4.1 Bar plots 114
   9.4.2 Point plots 118
9.5 Comparing means with statistical tests 122
9.6 Line charts 124
9.7 Count plots 126
   9.7.1 Summary 127

10 Styling figures with seaborn   **128**
10.1 Aesthetic arguments to seaborn functions 128
10.2 Setting styles and contexts 132
10.3 Passing keywords to underlying functions 134
10.4 Editing charts 137

11 Working with color in seaborn   **138**
11.1 Colors and palettes 138
   11.1.1 Setting a color 138
11.2 Working with palettes 141
11.3 Palettes for sequential data 143
11.4 Palettes for categorical data 148
11.5 Diverging palettes 157
11.6 Using color redundantly 161
11.7 Consistency with colors 173
   11.7.1 Reusing palettes for different categories 178

12 Grouping and categories in pandas   **182**
12.1 Types of categories 182
12.2 Grouping 183
   12.2.1 Calculating summaries for groups 185
   12.2.2 Multiple inputs to grouping operations 185
   12.2.3 Filtering based on group properties 195
   12.2.4 Normalizing within groups 198
   12.2.5 Other types of transformation 206
12.3 Iterating over groups 208
12.4 Sorting groups 209

13 Binning and ordered categories   **212**
13.1 Creating a new category 212

13.1.1 Using our new category for visualization 215
13.1.2 More on binning 221
13.2 Binning with `pd.cut` 224
13.2.1 Unequal bins 227
13.3 Custom categories and orders 235

14 Long form and wide form data **241**
14.1 *Long* or *tidy* form 241
14.2 *Wide* or *summary* form 243
14.2.1 Chi squared test 246
14.3 Getting data into tidy form 246
14.3.1 Using `melt` 247
14.3.2 Melting tables with many columns 249
14.3.3 `pivot` and `pivot_table` 253
14.4 A closer look at indices 254
14.4.1 Setting a new index 256
14.4.2 Making a multi index series 257

15 Matrix charts and heatmaps **262**
15.1 Displaying summary tables 262
15.2 Displaying complex summaries 264
15.3 Heatmaps with many categories 267
15.3.1 Diverging palettes with heatmaps 268
15.4 Summary tables, binning and heatmaps 273
15.5 Clustermaps 285
15.6 Complex groups with clustermaps 289
15.7 Bubble grid charts 294

16 Dealing with complicated data files **299**
16.1 Awkward input files 299
16.2 Combining multiple files 308
16.2.1 Concatenation 309
16.2.2 Adding a single column 313
16.3 Merging 316
16.4 Very large datasets 323
16.4.1 Including only the columns we need 326
16.4.2 Using categories 326
16.4.3 Reducing numerical precision 328
16.4.4 Precision with floating point numbers 331
16.4.5 Final memory vs peak memory 333
16.4.6 Chunking input data 333
16.4.7 Other options 336

17 Using `FacetGrid` to lay out small multiples **338**
17.1 Small multiples with arbitrary chart types 338
17.1.1 Using `FacetGrid` directly 339
17.1.2 Mapping with a custom function 342
17.1.3 Mapping using hue 348
17.1.4 Mapping with heatmaps 351

18 Unexpected behaviors **357**
18.1 Missing groups in `groupby` 357
18.1.1 Fixing the problem 361
18.2 Summing a series returns 0 by default if all the values are missing 363
18.2.1 Fixing the problem 366
18.3 Missing points can affect size and hue with seaborn 367
18.3.1 Fixing the problem 370

19 High performance Pandas   **372**

     19.0.1 A note on timing 373

  19.1 Looping vs vectorization 373

  19.2 Looping vs `apply` 375

  19.3 Applying with multiple columns 376

  19.4 Caching a slow function 377

  19.5 Using `sample` before analysing a whole dataset 380

  19.6 Categories and performance 384

  19.7 Indices and performance 385

20 Further reading   **388**

  20.1 Dates and times 388

  20.2 Pandas alternative syntax 392

  20.3 Pandas plotting functions 394

  20.4 Jupyter widgets and interactive charts 396

  20.5 Machine learning and statistics 396

1 Introduction

1.1 Motivation

Over the last few years I've spent most of my professional life teaching programming and bioinformatics, mostly to researchers working in the field of biological sciences. As you might imagine, my students have been involved in many different areas of research, working with many diverse kinds of biological data. However, across many courses and research institutions, one topic recurs with great predictability: the need to organize, manipulate and visualize large volumes of data.

When we stop and think about it, this is not surprising. All forms of science rely on data to formulate and test hypotheses, so these are fundamental tools for researchers. The recent interest in biology specifically can be put down, I think, to two factors. Firstly, with the advent of next generation sequencing technologies, datasets have grown in size to the point where the need for efficient tools becomes clear to everyone. Second, the increasing use of computation in biology - which includes programming, but also simply using software in our research - has caused many of us to wonder what other tools might be out there to make our lives easier.

This book is my attempt to provide an introduction to what I think is the best set of tools for manipulating and visualizing biological data. The Python programming language is an excellent, popular, general purpose programming language, which probably needs no introduction to people involved in biological and bioinformatics research. However, the real strength of the language lies in the libraries that are available, and it is this collection of libraries (which in Python are called *packages*) that we'll be discussing.

1.1.1 Python's data processing stack

Four packages in particular are of interest to us. On the data manipulation side we have **pandas**, which is for dealing with tabular data, and **numpy**, which is for dealing with numerical data. These two packages are designed to work together - pandas gives us a very concise set of tools for reading, filtering, cleaning and reshaping data, and numpy uses clever programming techniques to make sure that the resulting code runs quickly.

On the data visualization side we have **matplotlib**, which is a low-level general purpose charting library, and **seaborn**, which is a high-level library for drawing statistical charts. Again, these two packages are designed to work well together. Seaborn allows us to create sophisticated charts with minimal code, while matplotlib allows us to work at a low level to adjust specific chart elements when needed.

Taken as a whole, these four packages form an incredibly powerful stack for carrying out data manipulation and visualization.

1.1.2 Structure and what's covered

There's a useful principle when using complex tools, which states that only around 20% of the features are necessary to do 80% of the tasks you need to accomplish. Even if you would pick different percentages, if you think about the computational tools that you already use, hopefully you will agree with the principle. If we're using a word processor, some features - for example making text bold - we use all the time, whereas some - like changing page the bullet symbol in a list - we only need rarely. The same applies to bioinformatics tools, programming languages, and libraries.

Our goal in this book, then, is to cover the features of the pandas/numpy/seaborn/matplotlib stack that will allow us to accomplish the majority of the data analysis we need to do in our research. With a good understanding of the core features, it will be possible to easily look up the more specialized tools when we need them. We will concentrate on the kind of exploratory programming that forms the bulk of the work when dealing with real life datasets. This will involve an emphasis on quickly experimenting with different types of manipulation and visualization to get insights into our data. For the most part, we won't worry too much about tweaking every tiny aspect of each chart.

When exploring real life datasets, the tasks of data manipulation (importing, filtering, cleaning and reshaping data) and data visualization (drawing charts) cannot be easily separated - each informs the other. When exploring a dataset, we tend to cycle between visualizing and processing the data. In this book, we will work in the same way, mixing discussions of data manipulation and visualization in our examples.

The book is divided broadly into four parts. In the first part, we will introduce pandas, see how to get our data into Python, and learn some of its basic syntax. In the second, we will introduce seaborn, take a tour of the various chart types available, and get familiar with the style of mapping data columns to chart aspects. In the third part, we return to pandas to look at some more advanced topics to do with grouping, binning and reshaping data, making use of seaborn to see the results. And in the final section, we tackle more specific issues: how to draw matrix charts, how to deal with large, fragmented datasets, how to write performant code, and how construct custom chart types.

Mixed in with examples of how to use the different libraries will be discussions of best practices for data visualization. This is a large field of research in its own right, so we will only be able to touch on the most important points, but a few observations about effective use of color and grids will go a long way.

You may notice that the chapters in these sections are of very different lengths. This is simply because some topics are more complex than others. Rather than worry about dividing up long chapters, it makes more sense to put related material together. On the topic of length, you may currently be feeling the weight of the book (if you have a physical copy) or looking at the page count (if you have an electronic copy) and worrying that reading it will be a long slog. Have no fear! Although the book is large, that's mostly because it has a lot of figures and a lot of code examples, both of which take up a lot of space on the page.

1.1.3 What's not covered

Perhaps the most important part of writing a technical book is deciding what to leave out. So let's quickly mention a few topics that we don't have room to cover. Firstly, we won't be discussing basic Python programming - this book assumes that you know the basics and can write a loop and call a function. If you're a complete beginner, check out *Python for Biologists*, my introductory programming book.

We also won't be covering any basic biology or bioinformatics. In choosing data files, I've deliberately picked examples that should be easy to follow, so as long as you have a background in biology you should be able to make sense of them. If you know that organisms have a genome and species name, that DNA is made up of four bases, and that genomes are assembled from small fragments, then you probably have enough knowledge to follow along.

Two enormous topics that are often associated with large datasets are statistics and machine learning. Both of these topics are complex enough to require a complete book, or possibly a shelf of them! So although we will carry out some simple statistical tests, and make heavy use of descriptive statistics, we won't dive any deeper - although I have put some links in the final chapter to useful resources.

We also won't be trying to comprehensively cover every slight variation of charts that we can make. As mentioned above, we will concentrate on techniques for rapidly exploring datasets and mining them for insights, which requires us to mostly stick with default styles.

1.2 Your programming environment

One of the nice aspects of the Python programming language is that we have so many choices for environments in which to write our code, ranging from simple text editors to sophisticated integrated development environments (IDEs). For the type of programming that we will be doing, by far the best environment is Jupyter notebook. If you are already familiar with Jupyter notebook then skip the rest of this section. If you haven't used it before, all you need to know is that it's an interactive programming environment that runs in a web browser, and allows us to make documents containing a mixture of text, code and figures. It's rapidly becomming a standard for interactive publications and reproducable science, and is a tool well worth learning to use.

If you don't already have it, the easiest way to install Jupyter notebook along with all of the packages that we'll need for this book is to install the Anaconda distribution:

https://www.anaconda.com/distribution/

Make sure you get the Python 3 version. The Jupyter notebook documentation has a quickstart guide:

1.2.1 Packages and versions

All of the code in this book is written using Python 3.7. Version 3.6 will also work, but anything older than that lacks certain features that we will rely on. The packages that we will be using are under fairly rapid development, so it's important that you have recent versions to avoid conflicts. For this book, the versions are:

- pandas 1.0.3
- seaborn 0.10.0
- matplotlib 3.2

Newer versions will probably work ok, older versions may produce odd results or errors.

1.3 Formatting conventions

This is quite a complicated book in terms of what we see on the page - we have a mixture of text, code, output, figures and tables. So to make it as easy as possible to follow we will use different formatting for each type of content.

Python code will be indented slightly, have a solid border, and a pale blue background. The plain text output from code will be the same, but with a pale pink background. So a code example along with its output will look like this:

```
print("Hello world")
```

```
Hello world
```

Code and output are both in a monospaced font. For larger code examples, we will often split statements - especially function calls - over multiple lines to make them easier to read.

Because we will be working with tabular data, the output from our code will often take the form as a table. To make these easier to read, tables will look like this:

	Species	Kingdom	Number of genes
100	Drosophila yakuba	Animals	16079
101	Tetraodon nigroviridis	Animals	27918
102	[Candida] glabrata	Fungi	5458
103	Yarrowia lipolytica CLIB122	Fungi	7144
104	Kluyveromyces lactis	Fungi	5335

This behaviour - where plain text output from code displays as plain text, but tabular output displays as a table - matches the behaviour that you'll see if you run the examples in a Jupyter notebook.

In the main text, small bits of code - generally things like function or variable names - will be in a monospaced font with a light blue background, `like this`, to match the main code examples. Special terms will be written in italics *like this*, and we will use bold text **like this** for emphasis and for column names.

When we have code that produces a figure, the figure will come directly after the code - hopefully it will be obvious. To prevent the figures from taking up too much space, we will scale them to be no bigger than needed while still being easy to read. Rather than trying to make the figures look beautiful, we will keep the defaults for most of the styling - so you might notice, for example, that marker sizes are different between different figures, or that the fonts don't match those used in the rest of the books. This is deliberate, as it will allow us to keep the code as simple as possible, while making the figures resemble those that you'll get when you run the examples yourself.

Because this book contains many figures and code blocks that can't be split over multiple pages, occasionally it's necessary to have a large blank space on a page. Just ignore the blank spaces, and hoepfully the layout will make sense.

1.3.1 Terminology

I have tried to use American English throughout this book, to match argument and function names. If any British spellings or idioms have slipped through, hopefully they will not be too distracting.

Since in programming and bioinformatics we use the word *graph* to refer to a network, I have used the words *chart* and *plot* to refer to the figures that we will create. We will often discuss the concept of an *index*, for which there are two common plurals: *indexes* and *indices* - I have used the latter.

When writing a practical book, as I hope this book is, it's tricky to know which voice to use. Should it be "I can set the X axis labels", "You can set the X axis labels", or "We can set the X axis labels"? Or even the dreaded passive voice: "The X axis labels can be set"? For this book I've decided to stick with the collaborative tone that I'm used to from teaching in person. So for our purposes, it will be "we can set the X axis labels".

1.3.2 Examples

Most of the examples that we will discuss in this book require quite a bit of code to run, as they involve reading, cleaning and filtering data before carrying out analysis or visualization. This poses a difficulty for writing the example code and accompanying example files. If we put the entire code required to produce a given figure into the text, then most of the book will be made up of repeated code! On the other hand, if we only put the minimal code into each example, then it won't be possible to run them in isolation.

For this book, we will use a compromise. For large examples, we will prepare separate Python files. You can download these from:

https://pythonforbiologists.com/datavis_examples

The examples are organized into folders by chapter. When looking at the text, you'll know which examples have associated Python files because they will have a comment with the filename as the first line, like this:

```
# example.py

print("Hello world")
```

```
Hello world
```

These example files will have the code that you see in the text, plus a standard header section at the start which imports the necessary modules and loads the input files. This will make it possible to concentrate on the interesting bit of each code example without having to repeatedly look at a lot of identical code. In each chapter folder, there's also a special file called *all.py* which contains all of the Python code from that chapter. This might be useful if there's a particular line that you want to copy and use in your own code.

For some examples, we will split the process up into several pieces of code. If you want to run them on your own computer, you may have to execute several different code sections in order. Doing this will be a good test of your understanding - if you can figure out which bits of code to run in which order, then you have probably followed the material well!

Nearly all of the code examples rely on being in an environment that automatically evaluates the statement on the last line. In other words, rather than explicitly printing the output like this:

```
print(2 + 2)
```

```
4
```

We will simply evaluate it:

```
2 + 2
```

```
4
```

This is necessary in order for pandas to display tables, and for seaborn to display figures, in the right format. If you're working in Jupyter notebook, which is highly recommended, then these examples will work as intended.

1.4 Example data files

Since this book has a very practical focus, we will be making extensive use of example datasets. In choosing which datasets to explore, we have to choose examples that are easy to understand, not too large, and that will allow us to illustrate the full range of tools available. So let's introduce them.

1.4.1 `eukaryotes.tsv`

This is going to be our main dataset for most of the book, and is a summary of eukaryote genome sequences compiled by the NCBI. The raw data are available here:

ftp://ftp.ncbi.nlm.nih.gov/genomes/GENOME_REPORTS/eukaryotes.txt

but we will be working with a slightly edited version.

As you might guess from the filename, this is a Tab Separated Values file, where each line in the file holds information for a single genome. Each line has 9 pieces of information about the genome. When we view this file as a table, these will be the columns). They are:

- The name of the species to which the genome belongs
- The kingdom that the species belongs to
- The class that the species belongs to
- The size of the genome in megabases
- The GC% of the genome, i.e what percentage of the bases are either G or C
- The number of predicted genes in the genome
- The number of predicted proteins in the genome
- The year when the genome was published
- The assembly status of the genome

Hopefully most of these fields are easy to understand. The only one that might be unfamiliar is assembly status. In order to understand the assembly status, you need to know that newly sequenced genomes go through a series of steps to turn them from raw DNA reads into a finished genome. First, very short reads are assembled into medium length sequences called *contigs*. Next, contigs are assembled into longer sequences called *scaffolds*. Then scaffolds are assembled into *chromosomes*. Finally, when the genome reaches a certain level of completeness, we declare it a *complete genome*. Readers who are involved with genome assembly will hopefully forgive this greatly abbreviated version of a complex field!

We will explore this dataset in great detail during the course of the book, so there's not too much more to say about it here. We will just mention that it is small (about 8000 lines), contains a mixture of numerical, time and categorical data, and has lots of missing data.

Later in the book we will see a different version of this dataset that has a more complicated format, which we will use to learn about dealing with difficult data files.

1.4.2 `common_names.csv`

This is a very simple file that stores scientific names along with matching common names for species that have them. It has a very simple format: each line has a scientific and common name separated by a comma. There are around 14,000 lines. This file has a very interesting property: there may be multiple common names for each scientific name. We will use this file to investigate how to deal with this fact.

1.4.3 `contigs.csv`

This file is effectively an example of zooming in on one of the very summarized descriptions from the previous file. It contains information for each contig that is the result of the first step of genome assembly. Each line in the file contains information for a single contig, and contains just 5 pieces of information:

- The name of the contig (which is not meaningful)
- The length of the contig in bases
- The GC content of the contig, i.e. what proportion of the bases are G or C
- The mean coverage, i.e. on average how many times has each base been sequenced
- The taxonomic annotation, i.e. what phylum does the contig belong to

As with the previous dataset, these are real data. They are taken from a project that aimed to sequence the genome of a microscopic eukaryote called a tardigrade (later published at https://doi.org/10.1073/pnas.1600338113). The taxonomic annotation was carried out in order to identify bacterial contaminants in the raw DNA sequences.

This file presents different challenges to the eukaryote genome file. It's much longer, with over 20,000 lines, and so will require a different approach to visualization. It also has columns with a very large span of values: the lengths of the contigs range from two thousand bases to one and a half million bases. However, it has no missing data.

1.4.4 `weather.csv`

This file contains long term recordings of weather - specifically, mean daily temperature - from three cities: London, Edinburgh and Berlin. There's one line per day and city, and the columns are:

- The name of the city
- The year
- The month
- The day of the month
- The day of the year
- The mean temperature for that day

This will make a nice example of a file that contains very long term trends, and that has only a single measurement (temperature) but a lot of metadata (city and date). It's fairly large with around 60,000 measurements containing 60 years worth of data. It will also allow us to investigate how to integrate multiple datasets when we combine it with the next set of files.

1.4.5 `Berlin_daily_rain.csv`, `London_daily_rain.csv`, `Edinburgh_daily_rain.csv`

These three files have a similar format to the `weather.csv` file, with two differences: each file stores information for only a single city, and the measurements are not temperature but rainfall. This will be our example of a dataset that's split over multiple files.

1.4.6 `london_rainfall.csv`

This is a summary of total monthly rainfall in London since 1960. Each line contains information for a whole year, with twelve columns, one for each month. This will be our example of a wide format data file.

1.4.7 `fungi_genomes.csv`

This file stores the proportions of different six base sequences in the genomes of 30 different fungal genomes. It's an example of a dataset with a very large number of columns, which is more of a matrix than a table. Each row stores information for a single genome, and has the species and class name followed by 4096 columns, one for each six base sequence (**AAAAAA** to **CCCCCC**). The number in each cell is the proportion of the genome that's made up of that specific six base sequence. Since all possible six base sequences are in the file, the numbers on each row will always add up to 1.

2 Introduction to pandas

pandas is our first choice for dealing with tabular data in Python. By *tabular data*, we simply mean data that has a shape like a table, with rows and columns. This encompasses the vast majority of datasets that we encounter in bioinformatics and biology - the only real exception is graphlike data like phylogenetic trees or networks of protein interactions (and even those can often be stored in a tabular format if we pick the representation carefully).

Many file types that we work with in bioinformatics have a tabular format - formats like SAM (Sequence Alignment Map) and VCF (Variant Call Format) files are just examples of tabular data with specific columns and separators. Many analysis tools also produce output in a tabular form (command-line BLAST is a good example). However, most of the data that we need to work with comes from a spreadsheet or database and will end up in something like CSV (Comma Separated Values) or TSV (Tab Separated Values) format.

Let's start by importing the pandas module. By convention, we use the short alias `pd` for pandas, like this:

```
# you'll see this alias in documentation, examples, etc.
import pandas as pd
```

All this means is that from now on when we want to refer to the pandas module we can just use the short name `pd`, which will save us some typing.

2.0.1 Series and dataframe objects

We will be spending most of our time with pandas working with two different data types. In the real world we will nearly always read our data in from an existing file, but to keep things simple we'll start by just creating some examples of these data types directly.

The first type that we need to know about is a `Series`. We can create one by using the `Series` constructor and passing it a list of values:

```
pd.Series([1, 1, 2, 3, 5, 8, 13])
```

```
0     1
1     1
2     2
3     3
4     5
5     8
6    13
dtype: int64
```

A `Series` is like a Python list in that it's an ordered collection of values. As we can see from the output above, however, it doesn't look particularly like a list. That's because it has two things that a list doesn't have. First, it has an explicit index - the numbers that go from 0 to 6 on the left. Second, it has a type (in pandas this is called a **dtype**, short for **data type**) which is given at the end - in this case `int64` because the numbers are integers. The `64` in the dtype name tells us that Python is storing this number with 64 bits of precision - we won't worry about that for now.

If instead of passing in a list of integers we pass in a list of floating point numbers:

```
pd.Series([3.1415, 2.7182, 1.4142])
```

```
0    3.1415
1    2.7182
2    1.4142
dtype: float64
```

or a list of strings:

```
pd.Series(["apple", "banana", "orange"])
```

```
0    apple
1    banana
2    orange
dtype: object
```

We can see that the index remains the same (simply counting up from zero) but the dtype changes. Notice that in the example with strings, the dtype is `object`, not `str` as we might expect. That's because these data types are actually defined in `numpy` and `object` is the most generic one, which pandas uses by default for strings. In recent versions of pandas, there's a specific string data type, which we can tell pandas to use by setting the `dtypes` argument:

```
pd.Series(["apple", "banana", "orange"], dtype="string")
```

```
0    apple
1    banana
2    orange
dtype: string
```

Notice how the `dtype` bit of the output changes. We won't go into the advantages of storing text as `string` rather than `object` right now; suffice to say that getting into the habit now will prevent problems in the future.

When looking at Python's representation of a series, as in the examples above, it's very tempting to think of it as a small table with two columns. However, that would be misleading - don't think of the index as a column in a table, but as a collection of labels for the values in the series.

If we put several series objects together, then we get a different type of object - a `DataFrame`. There are many ways to make a dataframe in pandas - here we will pass the `DataFrame` constructor a dictionary where the keys are the column names and the values are the series objects:

```
# simple_dataframe.py

s1 = pd.Series(["a", "b", "c", "d"], dtype="string")
s2 = pd.Series([2, 4, 8, 16])
pd.DataFrame({"letter": s1, "number": s2})
```

	letter	number
0	a	2
1	b	4
2	c	8
3	d	16

As we mentioned in the introduction, it's easy - at least when working in a Jupyter notebook environment - to tell the difference between a series and a dataframe. Series objects are displayed as plain text, whereas dataframes are displayed as tables.

Just like when we make a series, when we make a dataframe we get an explicit index running down the left hand side. It's important to remember that this isn't actually a column - again, think of it as a collection of labels for the rows in the dataframe.

When we display a dataframe, pandas doesn't show us the data types, but we can view them explicitly:

```
df = pd.DataFrame({"letter": s1, "number": s2})
df.dtypes
```

```
letter    string
number     int64
dtype: object
```

Notice that **dtypes** is an attribute of the **DataFrame** object, so we don't use parentheses when we type it. As expected, our letter columns has a data type of **string** (because we specified it) and our number column has an integer data type (because pandas guessed it correctly).

For the name of our dataframe we've used the rather generic name **df**. This is another convention which is used throughout the pandas documentation, so it's a good idea to get used to it.

2.0.2 Reading data from files

In the above examples we created series and dataframe objects by directly calling their constructors. However, in the real world, we will nearly always create a dataframe by reading in a file. Let's read the eukaryotic genomes summary file that we saw earlier.

The function that reads plain text files in pandas is **read_csv**. It has many options, but for this particular data file we can leave most of them as default. The only complication we have is that our data file is in tab separated rather than comma separated format. So we will have to pass the **sep** argument (short for separator) to tell pandas that our data are tab separated:

```
# read_file.py

euk = pd.read_csv("eukaryotes.tsv", sep="\t")
euk
```

	Species	Kingdom	Class	Size (Mb)	GC%	Number of genes	Number of proteins	Publication year	Assembly status
0	Emiliania huxleyi CCMP1516	Protists	Other Protists	167.676	64.5	38549	38554	2013	Scaffold
1	Arabidopsis thaliana	Plants	Land Plants	119.669	36.0529	38311	48265	2001	Chromosome
2	Glycine max	Plants	Land Plants	979.046	35.1153	59847	71219	2010	Chromosome
3	Medicago truncatula	Plants	Land Plants	412.924	34.047	37603	41939	2011	Chromosome
4	Solanum lycopersicum	Plants	Land Plants	828.349	35.6991	31200	37660	2010	Chromosome
...	...	...	...	...	...	...	...	...	...
8297	Saccharomyces cerevisiae	Fungi	Ascomycetes	3.99392	38.2	-	-	2017	Scaffold
8298	Saccharomyces cerevisiae	Fungi	Ascomycetes	0.586761	38.5921	155	298	1992	Chromosome
8299	Saccharomyces cerevisiae	Fungi	Ascomycetes	12.0204	38.2971	-	-	2018	Chromosome
8300	Saccharomyces cerevisiae	Fungi	Ascomycetes	11.9609	38.2413	-	-	2018	Chromosome
8301	Saccharomyces cerevisiae	Fungi	Ascomycetes	11.8207	38.2536	-	-	2018	Chromosome

Now that we're working with real data, we'll stop using the generic **df** variable name and pick something more descriptive. We will use the variable name **euk** (short for eukaryotes) for this dataset. Although the ouput from the code above is much bigger than our inital examples, we can see that it has the same structure, just with more rows and columns.

Just as before, we're looking at a table with column names along the top and an index down the left hand side. In this case, the column names came from the file itself - **read_csv** assumes that the first line of the file has the column names - so we didn't have to specify them. Just as before, the index simply counts up from zero. We can think of it as representing the number of each row in the original file.

Because there are so many rows and columns, pandas just displays the start and end of the **DataFrame**. We can see in the middle a row full of dots - this is just a placeholder to represent all the rows that are not being shown. For large dataframes, pandas will tell us at the end of the output how many rows and columns we have.

Because in this dataframe we have quite a few columns, the text ends up being very small when we display them all. To make it easier to read, we'll often display our dataframes in this book with fewer columns, which will look like this:

```
euk
```

	Species	Kingdom	...	Publication year	Assembly status
0	Emiliania huxleyi CCMP1516	Protists	...	2013	Scaffold
1	Arabidopsis thaliana	Plants	...	2001	Chromosome
2	Glycine max	Plants	...	2010	Chromosome
3	Medicago truncatula	Plants	...	2011	Chromosome
4	Solanum lycopersicum	Plants	...	2010	Chromosome
...	...		...	...	...
8297	Saccharomyces cerevisiae	Fungi	...	2017	Scaffold
8298	Saccharomyces cerevisiae	Fungi	...	1992	Chromosome
8299	Saccharomyces cerevisiae	Fungi	...	2018	Chromosome
8300	Saccharomyces cerevisiae	Fungi	...	2018	Chromosome
8301	Saccharomyces cerevisiae	Fungi	...	2018	Chromosome

Just like before we have a row of dots to represent the fact that there are some rows not being shown. We also have a column of dots to represent the columns in the middle that are not being shown.

Notice that in order to view the `DataFrame`, we have just evaluated the variable name `df` by putting it on the last line of the code. If we print it instead:

```
print(euk)
```

```
                        Species   Kingdom ... Publication year  \
0      Emiliania huxleyi CCMP1516  Protists ...             2013
1            Arabidopsis thaliana    Plants ...             2001
2                     Glycine max    Plants ...             2010
3             Medicago truncatula    Plants ...             2011
4           Solanum lycopersicum    Plants ...             2010
...                           ...       ... ...              ...
8297     Saccharomyces cerevisiae     Fungi ...             2017
8298     Saccharomyces cerevisiae     Fungi ...             1992
8299     Saccharomyces cerevisiae     Fungi ...             2018
8300     Saccharomyces cerevisiae     Fungi ...             2018
8301     Saccharomyces cerevisiae     Fungi ...             2018

     Assembly status
0           Scaffold
1         Chromosome
2         Chromosome
3         Chromosome
4         Chromosome
...              ...
8297        Scaffold
8298      Chromosome
8299      Chromosome
8300      Chromosome
8301      Chromosome

[8302 rows x 9 columns]
```

We get slightly different output that, depending on our environment, might be harder to read.

2.0.3 Investigating a dataframe

Now that we have a dataframe stored in the `euk` variable, there are a few useful functions and methods that we can use on it. We've already seen the `dtypes` attribute, which tells us what type of data is in each column:

```
euk.dtypes
```

```
Species              object
Kingdom              object
Class                object
Size (Mb)            float64
GC%                  object
Number of genes      object
Number of proteins   object
Publication year     int64
Assembly status      object
dtype: object
```

Just like when we made our series objects, text data ends up with an `object` data type, so we need to specify that those columns should be stored as strings. The `dtype` argument to `read_csv` will allow us to give a dictionary mapping column names to the types we want. We could supply this directly in the call to `read_csv`, but for this example we'll store it as a variable so that we can reuse it later:

```
my_types = {
    "Species": "string",
    "Kingdom": "string",
    "Class": "string",
    "Assembly status": "string",
}

euk = pd.read_csv("eukaryotes.tsv", sep="\t", dtype=my_types)
```

Now when we look at our data types:

```
euk.dtypes
```

```
Species              string
Kingdom              string
Class                string
Size (Mb)            float64
GC%                  object
Number of genes      object
Number of proteins   object
Publication year     int64
Assembly status      string
dtype: object
```

The columns that hold text data are correctly stored as strings.

The columns that still look wrong are **GC%**, **Number of genes** and **Number of proteins**. We know that these columns contain numbers, so why are they being stored as `object`? Recall from our description of the input file that some of the values in these three columns are missing, and that these missing values are represented in the file by the placeholder `-`. We can actually see some examples by looking at the last few rows in the dataframe, which we can do by calling `tail`:

```
euk.tail()
```

	Species	Kingdom	Class	Size (Mb)	GC%	Number of genes	Number of proteins	Publication year	Assembly status
8297	Saccharomyces cerevisiae	Fungi	Ascomycetes	3.993920	38.2	-	-	2017	Scaffold
8298	Saccharomyces cerevisiae	Fungi	Ascomycetes	0.586761	38.5921	155	298	1992	Chromosome
8299	Saccharomyces cerevisiae	Fungi	Ascomycetes	12.020400	38.2971	-	-	2018	Chromosome
8300	Saccharomyces cerevisiae	Fungi	Ascomycetes	11.960900	38.2413	-	-	2018	Chromosome
8301	Saccharomyces cerevisiae	Fungi	Ascomycetes	11.820700	38.2536	-	-	2018	Chromosome

We see that for the last few genomes in the file, the number of genes and proteins are missing, so we see a `-` instead of a number. The problem is that pandas doesn't know that `-` means missing data.

How to fix this? We could just edit the file and delete all the rows for genomes that have missing data, but that would throw away a lot of useful data as well. We could edit the file to replace all the dashes with zeros (we could easily do this using Python itself), but that seems misleading - it's not the case that these genomes have *no* genes or proteins, but rather that they have an *unknown* number of genes and proteins.

So the best thing to do is to tell pandas that the dash symbol means missing data. Look what happens when we read in the data file again, this time using the `na_values` argument to `read_csv`. To use `na_values` we make a list of the strings that we want to represent missing data in the input file - in this case it's just a list of the string `'-'`:

```
euk = pd.read_csv("eukaryotes.tsv", sep="\t", dtype=my_types, na_values=["-"])
```

Now when we look at the last few rows again:

```
euk.tail()
```

	Species	Kingdom	Class	Size (Mb)	GC%	Number of genes	Number of proteins	Publication year	Assembly status
8297	Saccharomyces cerevisiae	Fungi	Ascomycetes	3.993920	38.2000	NaN	NaN	2017	Scaffold
8298	Saccharomyces cerevisiae	Fungi	Ascomycetes	0.586761	38.5921	155.0	298.0	1992	Chromosome
8299	Saccharomyces cerevisiae	Fungi	Ascomycetes	12.020400	38.2971	NaN	NaN	2018	Chromosome
8300	Saccharomyces cerevisiae	Fungi	Ascomycetes	11.960900	38.2413	NaN	NaN	2018	Chromosome
8301	Saccharomyces cerevisiae	Fungi	Ascomycetes	11.820700	38.2536	NaN	NaN	2018	Chromosome

instead of displaying the dash symbol in the **Number of genes** and **Number of proteins** column, it now displays the special value `NaN`. This is short for Not a Number, and is pandas' way of representing missing data, regardless of how it was represented in the original file. This approach to missing data give us the most flexibility: we don't have to delete the rows or fill in any arbitrary values, and pandas will be able to use the information about missing data in useful ways as we'll see soon.

Looking at the update dataframe above, we notice something else: the values in the **Number of genes** and **Number of proteins** colums are showing up as floating point numbers rather than integers (`155.0` rather than `155`). A look at the output from `dtype` confirms that they have `float64` data type:

```
euk.dtypes
```

```
Species              string
Kingdom              string
Class                string
Size (Mb)            float64
GC%                  float64
Number of genes      float64
Number of proteins   float64
Publication year     int64
Assembly status      string
dtype: object
```

The reason for this is that for historical reasons, pandas assumes that any numerical column with missing data must be floating point. This behaviour might change in future versions of pandas, but for now we will have to give the data types explicitly. To do this we just have to add these columns to our `dtype` dictionary:

```
# read_file_with_types.py

my_types = {
    "Species": "string",
    "Kingdom": "string",
    "Class": "string",
    "Assembly status": "string",
    "Number of genes": "Int64",
    "Number of proteins": "Int64",
}

euk = pd.read_csv("eukaryotes.tsv", sep="\t", dtype=my_types, na_values=["-"])
```

Now we can take a final look at our data types:

```
euk.dtypes
```

```
Species             string
Kingdom             string
Class               string
Size (Mb)           float64
GC%                 float64
Number of genes     Int64
Number of proteins  Int64
Publication year    int64
Assembly status     string
dtype: object
```

and verify that all the columns are being stored as the correct type. This seems like a lot of work just to get our data file into pandas! But all of the analyses we will want to do on this file rely on data having the correct type, so doing this work at the start will make our lives easier later on. If you're lucky enough to be working with a simpler data file with no missing data, your code will be much briefer.

Now that we have our dataframe with the correct types, what can we do with it?

We can get even more information about the columns by calling the **info** method:

```
euk.info()
```

```
<class 'pandas.core.frame.DataFrame'>
RangeIndex: 8302 entries, 0 to 8301
Data columns (total 9 columns):
 #   Column              Non-Null Count  Dtype
---  ------              --------------  -----
 0   Species             8302 non-null   string
 1   Kingdom             8302 non-null   string
 2   Class               8302 non-null   string
 3   Size (Mb)           8302 non-null   float64
 4   GC%                 7895 non-null   float64
 5   Number of genes     2372 non-null   Int64
 6   Number of proteins  2371 non-null   Int64
 7   Publication year    8302 non-null   int64
 8   Assembly status     8302 non-null   string
dtypes: Int64(2), float64(2), int64(1), string(4)
memory usage: 600.1 KB
```

This will tell us a bunch more information. From top to bottom we can see:

- what class the object is (a **DataFrame**)
- what the index looks like (a range from 0 to 8301)
- how many data columns we have
- for each column, how many values and their dtype
- a summary of how many columns have each dtype
- how much memory the object is taking up (more on that in a future chapter)

Notice the slight difference between the data types for **Number of genes** and **Publication year**. **Number of genes** has a data type of **Int64** with a capital **I**, whereas **Publication year** has **int64** with a lowercase **i**. This is because there are no missing values in the **Publication year** column.

To get even more information about the contents of the different columns, we can try the **describe** method:

```
euk.describe()
```

	Size (Mb)	GC%	Number of genes	Number of proteins	Publication year
count	8302.000000	7895.000000	2372.000000	2371.000000	8302.000000
mean	401.918437	43.230469	15098.307336	17137.252636	2015.849313
std	1111.538289	7.998250	11505.437961	14735.085888	2.924305
min	0.011236	3.100000	3.000000	3.000000	1992.000000
25%	19.249775	38.219700	7361.500000	7010.500000	2015.000000
50%	39.559700	42.700000	11998.500000	12051.000000	2017.000000
75%	258.848000	49.000000	18303.500000	21671.000000	2018.000000
max	32396.400000	73.500000	119453.000000	123467.000000	2019.000000

This will give us descriptive statistics for all the numerical columns, including the number of values, the mean and standard deviation, the minimum and maximum, and the quartiles.

Because our dataframe has too many rows to conveniently display, it's useful to be able to see just the first or last rows. We can do this using the `head` and `tail` methods, both of which take an argument specifying how many rows we want to see:

```
# show the first three rows
euk.head(3)
```

	Species	Kingdom	...	Publication year	Assembly status
0	Emiliania huxleyi CCMP1516	Protists	...	2013	Scaffold
1	Arabidopsis thaliana	Plants	...	2001	Chromosome
2	Glycine max	Plants	...	2010	Chromosome

Finally, let's note that some of Python's built in functions work quite happily with a `DataFrame` object. If we want to check what type of object we are working with, we can always use the `type` function:

```
type(euk)
```

```
pandas.core.frame.DataFrame
```

And if we want to know how many rows, we can use the `len` function:

```
len(euk)
```

```
8302
```

2.1 A note about column names

When it comes to naming columns in our dataframes, there are two schools of thought. One is that we should make them as short as possible and remove any spaces or capitalization. We can change the names of our columns easily in pandas, either by setting the `names` argument when we call `read_csv`:

```
# read_file_with_names.py

my_types = {
    "Species": "string", "Kingdom": "string", "Class": "string", "Assembly status": "string",
    "Number of genes": "Int64", "Number of proteins": "Int64",
}

my_names = [
    "species", "kingdom", "class", "size", "gc", "genes",
    "proteins", "year", "status",
]

pd.read_csv(
    "eukaryotes.tsv",
    sep="\t",
    dtype=my_types,
    na_values=["-"],
    names=my_names,
).head()
```

	species	kingdom	class	size	gc	genes	proteins	year	status
0	Species	Kingdom	Class	Size (Mb)	GC%	Number of genes	Number of proteins	Publication year	Assembly status
1	Emiliania huxleyi CCMP1516	Protists	Other Protists	167.676	64.5	38549	38554	2013	Scaffold
2	Arabidopsis thaliana	Plants	Land Plants	119.669	36.0529	38311	48265	2001	Chromosome
3	Glycine max	Plants	Land Plants	979.046	35.1153	59847	71219	2010	Chromosome
4	Medicago truncatula	Plants	Land Plants	412.924	34.047	37603	41939	2011	Chromosome

or by setting the `columns` property of an existing DataFrame:

```
df = pd.read_csv(
    "eukaryotes.tsv",
    sep="\t",
    na_values=["-"],
    dtype={"Number of genes": "Int64", "Number of proteins": "Int64"},
)

df.columns = my_names
df.head()
```

	species	kingdom	class	size	gc	genes	proteins	year	status
0	Emiliania huxleyi CCMP1516	Protists	Other Protists	167.676	64.5000	38549	38554	2013	Scaffold
1	Arabidopsis thaliana	Plants	Land Plants	119.669	36.0529	38311	48265	2001	Chromosome
2	Glycine max	Plants	Land Plants	979.046	35.1153	59847	71219	2010	Chromosome
3	Medicago truncatula	Plants	Land Plants	412.924	34.0470	37603	41939	2011	Chromosome
4	Solanum lycopersicum	Plants	Land Plants	828.349	35.6991	31200	37660	2010	Chromosome

The advantage of naming columns in this style is that they are very quick and easy to type. As we'll see in the rest of this book, most of the code we'll write involves referring to columns, so making it easier to type them is a tempting prospect.

However, this approach comes with a drawback: the column names in the DataFrame will be used whenever we make a summary table or a chart. If we make our column names very concise, then we will end up with charts and tables that only make sense to a reader who is already very familiar with the source data. You can see the problem just by glancing at the table above: is it saying that *Arabidopsis thaliana* has a genome that's around 120 bases, kilobases, megabases, or gigabases? Or is it saying that a single copy of the genome has a molecular weight of around 120 kDa, or that the total length of the unravelled chromosomes would be about 120 milimetres? Is the GC content of the genome around 36%, or are there 36 million G and C nucleotides in total? Does the year column tell us when the genome sequencing started, or when the genome was published, or when it was last updated, or when it evolved?

Some of these may be obvious, depending on your background, but in real world datasets there will often be ambiguity, which tends to be particularly apparent when you want to show a figure or table to someone else.

So for the purposes of this book we will use column names that are descriptive at the expense of taking a little longer to type. This also has the side benefit of making the code more readable in most cases.

2.2 Wrapping up

Now that we know how to get our data into pandas, with the correct data types, and in the right format, we can start to explore it. Rather than repeating the code to read the data file for every example, the code in future chapters will assume that the `euk` dataframe is already stored in memory.

In developing the code in this chapter to read the eukaryote genome dataset, we've used integer data types where possible. For some types of analysis that we'll look at in future chapters, we will occasionally need to convert these back to floating point numbers. We'll explain those situations when we come to them.

To keep things simple for now, we've chosen a data file that's in a fairly straightforward format. In future chapters, we'll see examples of much more complicated data files and how to deal with getting them into pandas.

2.2.1 Encoding errors

The most common obstacles to reading data files that we encounter in the real world are encoding errors. By default, pandas will assume that your data file is in a format called **UTF-8**. Some types of characters might cause this assumption to fail; if you get `UnicodeDecodeError` when reading your data file, try adding `encoding='latin1'` to your `read_csv` function call.

2.2.2 Reading Excel files

One common situation involves reading a file in Excel format. Happily, pandas will cope with this without much trouble - there's a `read_excel` function that behaves much like `read_csv`, and shares many of the same arguments. The main complication when reading Excel files is that they can contain multiple sheets, so we generally need to specify which one we want to import.

3 Working with Series

3.1 Working with columns

In our initial simple examples, we created a dataframe object by joining together several series objects, each of which became a column in the dataframe. Now that we have a dataframe that shows real data, we can go the other way - extracting a single column from the dataframe will give us a series. To extract a single column, we just put the column name as a string inside square brackets:

```
euk["Size (Mb)"]
```

```
0        167.676000
1        119.669000
2        979.046000
3        412.924000
4        828.349000
            ...
8297       3.993920
8298       0.586761
8299      12.020400
8300      11.960900
8301      11.820700
Name: Size (Mb), Length: 8302, dtype: float64
```

Notice the special syntax here. If we saw this line in a normal Python program, we might guess that `euk` is a dict and we are getting the value for the key `size`. But because `euk` is a pandas `DataFrame` object, we know that the output of this expression is going to be a series. Just like the simple series that we made manually before, this series has a dtype and an index, and because it's much longer, we just see the first and last values, with `...` in the middle to represent the values that aren't shown.

If you look at any of the pandas documentation you'll probably notice that for short variable names we can also use a dot syntax to refer to a single column:

```
euk.Kingdom
```

```
0        Protists
1          Plants
2          Plants
3          Plants
4          Plants
           ...
8297        Fungi
8298        Fungi
8299        Fungi
8300        Fungi
8301        Fungi
Name: Kingdom, Length: 8302, dtype: string
```

Although this can be very convenient, we won't use this syntax for this book because:

- it doesn't work for all cases (for example, we can't use it for **Size (Mb)** as it contains a space
- it doesn't work when we want to refer to multiple columns as we will do later
- it doesn't work for functions where we need to pass the name of a column

So we will stick to the more explicit syntax where we give the name of the column as a string.

Once we have extracted a Series in this way, we can make it more convenient to work with by storing it in a variable:

```
sizes = euk["Size (Mb)"]
```

We said before that a series is like a list of values, and we can use it like a list in many ways:

```python
# iterate_over_series.py

sizes = euk["Size (Mb)"]

# use the first ten values of the series in a loop
for s in sizes[:10]:
    print("one size is " + str(s) + " Megabases")
```

```
one size is 167.676 Megabases
one size is 119.669 Megabases
one size is 979.046 Megabases
one size is 412.92400000000004 Megabases
one size is 828.3489999999997 Megabases
one size is 4006.12 Megabases
one size is 374.423 Megabases
one size is 14547.3 Megabases
one size is 12.1571 Megabases
one size is 2135.08 Megabases
```

```python
# what's the biggest value?
max(sizes)
```

```
32396.4
```

However, series objects can do lots of useful things that lists can't do. They have a range of methods for giving us descriptive statistics:

```python
# descriptive_statisics_series.py

sizes = euk["Size (Mb)"]

print("The minimum size is " + str(sizes.min()))
print("The maximum size is " + str(sizes.max()))
print("The mean size is " + str(sizes.mean()))
print("The median size is " + str(sizes.median()))
print("The standard deviation of the sizes is " + str(sizes.std()))
print("The skey of the size is " + str(sizes.skew()))
print("The 90th percentile size is " + str(sizes.quantile(0.9)))
```

```
The minimum size is 0.011236
The maximum size is 32396.4
The mean size is 401.91843726053963
The median size is 39.5597
The standard deviation of the sizes is 1111.5382890873323
The skey of the size is 11.096216999207364
The 90th percentile size is 1204.6580000000001
```

These methods all take a list of values - in our case, all 8302 genome sizes - and produce a single value. Methods that have this signature are all forms of *aggregation* - a concept that will be very useful later on.

There are other methods that do slightly more sophisticated things. For example, the `nlargest` method will give us a series of the largest values:

```python
sizes.nlargest(10)
```

```
210      32396.4
957      27602.7
4670     26936.2
820      24633.1
798      22103.6
5022     15344.7
940      14673.2
7        14547.3
5992     13916.9
5693     13427.4
Name: Size (Mb), dtype: float64
```

Notice that in the output above the genome size values still have the same index. The order is different, of course, because we are now effectively sorting the values from largest to smallest.

A similar thing happens when we use the `sample` method to randomly sample a number of values:

```
sizes.sample(5)
```

```
560      28.7004
3031     28.4899
2082     35.1733
3689     10.3826
6376     53.5754
Name: Size (Mb), dtype: float64
```

And just like with dataframes, we can use `head` to show just the first few values:

```
sizes.head()
```

```
0    167.676
1    119.669
2    979.046
3    412.924
4    828.349
Name: Size (Mb), dtype: float64
```

Let's finish our tour of operations on a single series with `value_counts`:

```
euk["Species"].value_counts()
```

```
Saccharomyces cerevisiae            576
Homo sapiens                        210
Pyricularia oryzae                  199
Venturia inaequalis                  85
Oryza rufipogon                      62
                                    ...
Ogataea zsoltii                       1
Leucoagaricus gongylophorus Ac12      1
Macaca nemestrina                     1
Dioszegia aurantiaca                  1
Beauveria bassiana D1-5               1
Name: Species, Length: 4936, dtype: Int64
```

This method tells us how many times each unique value occurs in the series - in our case, this is the number of genome sequences we have for each species. This is a different type of aggregation than we've seen previously - notice that the values in the species column in the original dataframe have become the index for this new series.

3.2 Broadcasting operations on series

3.2.1 Numerical operations

The real magic of `Series` objects comes into play when we try doing arbitrary calculations on them. Our list of genome sizes is measured in megabases, so if we want to convert them to bases we need to multiply by one million. If we were dealing with a normal Python list then we'd need something like a loop, `map` or list comprehension, but with a series we can just write the expression:

```
sizes * 1_000_000
```

```
0          167676000.0
1          119669000.0
2          979046000.0
3          412924000.0
4          828349000.0
              ...
8297         3993920.0
8298          586761.0
8299        12020400.0
8300        11960900.0
8301        11820700.0
Name: Size (Mb), Length: 8302, dtype: float64
```

and pandas will apply it to each of the elements. This is really a feature of numpy (which pandas uses under the hood) and is called *broadcasting* or *vectorization*.

This broadcasting magic works in many different situations. We can do more complicated mathematical calculations - for example, to convert the GC percentages to AT contents we first divide by 100 to get GC content then subtract that number from one:

```
# calculate AT content
1 - (euk["GC%"] / 100)
```

```
0          0.355000
1          0.639471
2          0.648847
3          0.659530
4          0.643009
            ...
8297       0.618000
8298       0.614079
8299       0.617029
8300       0.617587
8301       0.617464
Name: GC%, Length: 8302, dtype: float64
```

We can also use multiple columns in the expression. For example, to calculate the gene density of each genome in genes per kilobase we have to multiply the size by 1000, then divide the number of genes by the result:

```
# broadcasting_series.py

# calculate number of genes per kilobase
euk["Number of genes"] / (euk["Size (Mb)"] * 1000)
```

```
0       0.229902
1       0.320141
2       0.061128
3       0.091065
4       0.037665
         ...
8297         NaN
8298    0.264162
8299         NaN
8300         NaN
8301         NaN
Length: 8302, dtype: float64
```

Notice something interesting about the output above; the last few values are all **nan**, meaning missing data. That's because the last few rows in the dataframe have missing data for the number of genes, as we saw before. Pandas has *propogated* the missing data to the new calculation - if the number of genes for a particular genome is unknown, then the gene density is unknown as well.

All of the examples above involve operators (**+** , **-** , ***** and **/**) rather than functions. If we try to pass a series into a Python function, it probably won't work. For example, say we want to calculate the log of genome size. If we try to use the **log** function from Python's **math** module:

```
import math

math.log(sizes)
```

We get a **TypeError**. That's because **math.log** only takes a single number as its argument, and can't deal with a list of numbers.

Luckily, numpy has a huge library of mathematical functions which **can** operate on lists (in the numpy world, these are called *ufuncs*, short for *universal functions*). So **np.log** will happily take a list of numbers:

```
import numpy as np

np.log([1, 2, 3, 4])
```

```
array([0.        , 0.69314718, 1.09861229, 1.38629436])
```

and will also work fine on our series:

```
np.log(sizes)
```

```
0       5.122034
1       4.784730
2       6.886579
3       6.023264
4       6.719435
         ...
8297    1.384773
8298   -0.533138
8299    2.486605
8300    2.481643
8301    2.469852
Name: Size (Mb), Length: 8302, dtype: float64
```

We can find a list of the numpy functions that behave this way at

https://docs.scipy.org/doc/numpy/reference/ufuncs.html#available-ufuncs

3.2.2 String operations

If we select columns containing strings, we can concatenate them just like we normally do in Python:

```
# string_series.py

# we can concatenate strings
euk["Species"] + " (" + euk["Class"] + ")"
```

```
0        Emiliania huxleyi CCMP1516 (Other Protists)
1                  Arabidopsis thaliana (Land Plants)
2                           Glycine max (Land Plants)
3                   Medicago truncatula (Land Plants)
4                 Solanum lycopersicum (Land Plants)
                            ...
8297        Saccharomyces cerevisiae (Ascomycetes)
8298        Saccharomyces cerevisiae (Ascomycetes)
8299        Saccharomyces cerevisiae (Ascomycetes)
8300        Saccharomyces cerevisiae (Ascomycetes)
8301        Saccharomyces cerevisiae (Ascomycetes)
Length: 8302, dtype: string
```

However, when we try to use familiar string methods:

```
# get species name in upper case
euk["Species"].upper()
```

we'll run into difficulties: `AttributeError: 'Series' object has no attribute 'upper'`.

Because `upper` is a method of strings, not of `Series` objects, this syntax doesn't work. If we want to do vectorized operations on strings, we need to call the method on the special `str` attribute of the series like this:

```
# string_methods.py

# get species name in upper case
euk["Species"].str.upper()
```

```
0           EMILIANIA HUXLEYI CCMP1516
1                 ARABIDOPSIS THALIANA
2                          GLYCINE MAX
3                  MEDICAGO TRUNCATULA
4                 SOLANUM LYCOPERSICUM
                       ...
8297        SACCHAROMYCES CEREVISIAE
8298        SACCHAROMYCES CEREVISIAE
8299        SACCHAROMYCES CEREVISIAE
8300        SACCHAROMYCES CEREVISIAE
8301        SACCHAROMYCES CEREVISIAE
Name: Species, Length: 8302, dtype: string
```

We can find a list of the pandas string methods here:

https://pandas.pydata.org/pandas-docs/stable/user_guide/text.html#method-summary

They include most of the common Python string methods (like `lower`, `split`, and `count`) along with a bunch of regular expression operations.

All of these expressions we've written take a series as their starting point and produce a new series as their output, so we can often chain them together. For example, let's get the mean of the log genome sizes:

```
np.log(euk["Size (Mb)"]).mean()
```

```
4.201547332780875
```

For mathematical operations, it might be necessary to either use parentheses to contain the series:

```
# get the median gene density
(euk["Number of genes"] / (euk["Size (Mb)"] * 1000)).median()
```

```
0.2883939418821724
```

or to assign the new series to a variable:

```
# get the median gene density
densities = euk["Number of genes"] / (euk["Size (Mb)"] * 1000)
densities.median()
```

```
0.2883939418821724
```

3.2.3 Selecting multiple columns

All of the examples above involve selecting a single column. Even the gene density examples, which require working with two columns, only select one at a time. To select multiple columns, we can just give a list of column names instead of a single one:

```
euk[["Species", "Size (Mb)", "Number of genes"]].head()
```

	Species	Size (Mb)	Number of genes
0	Emiliania huxleyi CCMP1516	167.676	38549
1	Arabidopsis thaliana	119.669	38311
2	Glycine max	979.046	59847
3	Medicago truncatula	412.924	37603
4	Solanum lycopersicum	828.349	31200

The only tricky thing about this is the strange looking syntax of having two sets of square brackets. Just rember that the outer pair of square brackets indicates that we're selecting columns, and the inner set is to define a list of column names. Selecting multiple columns like this is generally useful to hide columns that we don't care about when viewing a dataframe.

3.3 Setting an index

When looking at the output from manipulating a series:

```
np.log(euk["Size (Mb)"]).nlargest(3)
```

```
210     10.385803
957     10.225669
4670    10.201226
Name: Size (Mb), dtype: float64
```

or even when simply looking at a column from the dataframe:

```
euk["GC%"]
```

```
0        64.5000
1        36.0529
2        35.1153
3        34.0470
4        35.6991
           ...
8297     38.2000
8298     38.5921
8299     38.2971
8300     38.2413
8301     38.2536
Name: GC%, Length: 8302, dtype: float64
```

it would be useful to have a more meaningful index. For this dataset, knowing the order that the values occurred in the original file isn't very useful. It would be much more interesting to see the actual species that each value belongs to.

We will look at indexing in much more detail later, but for now, we will use the `set_index` method on the dataframe to say which column we want as the label:

```
euk.set_index("Species").head()
```

Species	Kingdom	Class	Size (Mb)	...	Number of proteins	Publication year	Assembly status
Emiliania huxleyi CCMP1516	Protists	Other Protists	167.676	...	38554	2013	Scaffold
Arabidopsis thaliana	Plants	Land Plants	119.669	...	48265	2001	Chromosome
Glycine max	Plants	Land Plants	979.046	...	71219	2010	Chromosome
Medicago truncatula	Plants	Land Plants	412.924	...	41939	2011	Chromosome
Solanum lycopersicum	Plants	Land Plants	828.349	...	37660	2010	Chromosome

Notice how the **Species** column has disappeared, and instead we have the species name along the left hand side as the index. This index will carry over to any series that we get from the dataframe, including any calculations:

```
# series_index.py

# show 5 species with the most genes
euk.set_index("Species")["Number of genes"].nlargest()
```

```
Species
Brassica napus      119453
Vitis vinifera      112321
Arachis hypogaea    111051
Camelina sativa      97832
Papaver somniferum   91114
Name: Number of genes, dtype: Int64
```

As we mentioned earlier, it's tempting to think of this as a two-column table, but that will be unhelpful - it's actually a collection of values with an index. Think of the values in the series as the thing that is measured (the number of genes) and the index as the labels or metadata.

In the above example we are taking the largest values, but we can also sort the entire series of values:

```
euk.set_index("Species")["Number of genes"].sort_values()
```

```
Species
Trichomalopsis sarcophagae      3
Brachionus plicatilis           4
Enteromyxum leei                5
Kudoa iwatai                    7
Leucoraja erinacea             13
                              ...
Saccharomyces cerevisiae     <NA>
Saccharomyces cerevisiae     <NA>
Saccharomyces cerevisiae     <NA>
Saccharomyces cerevisiae     <NA>
Saccharomyces cerevisiae     <NA>
Name: Number of genes, Length: 8302, dtype: Int64
```

Missing data (represented above by `<NA>`) always appears at the end of a sorted series. We could also sort by the index:

```
euk.set_index("Species")["Number of genes"].sort_index()
```

```
Species
Abeoforma whisleri           <NA>
Abrus precatorius           28735
Absidia glauca              15117
Absidia repens              15151
Acanthamoeba astronyxis      <NA>
                              ...
fungal sp. EF0021            <NA>
fungal sp. Mo6-1             <NA>
fungal sp. No.11243          9730
fungal sp. No.14919         14606
uncultured Bathycoccus       <NA>
Name: Number of genes, Length: 8302, dtype: Int64
```

which will put the species names in alphabetical order.

If we don't want to see the missing data values, we can remove them with `dropna`:

```
# remove_missing_data.py

euk.set_index("Species")["Number of genes"].sort_index().dropna()
```

```
Species
Abrus precatorius                      28735
Absidia glauca                         15117
Absidia repens                         15151
Acanthamoeba castellanii str. Neff     15655
Acanthaster planci                     18187
                                         ...
[Candida] intermedia                    6073
[Candida] pseudohaemulonis              5284
[Nectria] haematococca mpVI 77-13-4    15708
fungal sp. No.11243                     9730
fungal sp. No.14919                    14606
Name: Number of genes, Length: 2372, dtype: Int64
```

That expression is a nice example of the kind of method chaining that we tend to use a lot in pandas. There are four separate operations going on to get the answer we want. Sometimes it's helpful to split these long statements over multiple lines, which we can do by surrounding the whole statemement with a pair of parentheses. This is often done so that we can attach comments to the individual steps:

```
# multiline_method_chains.py

(
    euk # start with the dataframe
    .set_index("Species") # set the index to be the species name
    ["Number of genes"]  # get the number of genes
    .sort_index() # sort the series by the index
    .dropna()  # remove any missing data
)
```

```
Species
Abrus precatorius                   28735
Absidia glauca                      15117
Absidia repens                      15151
Acanthamoeba castellanii str. Neff  15655
Acanthaster planci                  18187
                                     ...
[Candida] intermedia                 6073
[Candida] pseudohaemulonis           5284
[Nectria] haematococca mpVI 77-13-4 15708
fungal sp. No.11243                  9730
fungal sp. No.14919                 14606
Name: Number of genes, Length: 2372, dtype: Int64
```

A quick note before we leave this example. Calling `set_index` on a dataframe as we did in the second step above doesn't change the original dataframe, but makes a copy. If we go back and look at the original dataframe:

```
euk.head()
```

	Species	Kingdom	Class	...	Number of proteins	Publication year	Assembly status
0	Emiliania huxleyi CCMP1516	Protists	Other Protists	...	38554	2013	Scaffold
1	Arabidopsis thaliana	Plants	Land Plants	...	48265	2001	Chromosome
2	Glycine max	Plants	Land Plants	...	71219	2010	Chromosome
3	Medicago truncatula	Plants	Land Plants	...	41939	2011	Chromosome
4	Solanum lycopersicum	Plants	Land Plants	...	37660	2010	Chromosome

it still has the simple numerical index that we started with. This is generally true of many dataframe methods: they don't change the original. This is analogous to Python's string methods:

```
s = "Python"
s.upper()  # this doesn't change the original variable
s
```

```
'Python'
```

Many pandas methods take an `inplace` argument, which we can set to `True` to make them change the original. However, this can make it difficult to follow the logic of a piece of code, so we will avoid it in this book.

We will finish this section with one last example of broadcasting. What happens if we write an expression on a series that involves a condition?

```
# is the size greater than 500 megabases?
euk["Size (Mb)"] > 500
```

```
0        False
1        False
2         True
3        False
4         True
         ...
8297     False
8298     False
8299     False
8300     False
8301     False
Name: Size (Mb), Length: 8302, dtype: bool
```

Just as with our previous examples, we get a series with the same index that we started with. The data type of this series, is something new - `bool`, short for *boolean*, which means a collection of True/False values.

Looking at the output, it doesn't seem very useful. However, it turns out this is exactly what we need to do filtering on dataframes.

4 Filtering and selecting data

4.1 Selecting rows from dataframes

A large proportion of data analysis and visualization problems involve selecting (or filtering) data points - in the case of our example, finding just the genomes that we are interested in - then using those for further processing. Considering it's such a common task, the syntax we're about to look at might seem unnecessarily complicated. However, the way that pandas implements filtering is very powerful, and it's worth getting to grips with the weird syntax so that we can take advantage of that power.

We'll start with a very simple example - here's our toy dataframe from before:

```
s1 = pd.Series(["a", "b", "c", "d"], dtype="string")
s2 = pd.Series([2, 4, 8, 16])
small_df = pd.DataFrame({"letter": s1, "number": s2})
small_df
```

	letter	number
0	a	2
1	b	4
2	c	8
3	d	16

We'll assign the dataframe to the variable `small_df` so that we don't get it confused with our real-world data. To select some rows from this dataframe, we make a list of boolean values which is the same length of the dataframe and contains `True` for the rows we want to select and `False` for the ones we don't want:

```
mask = [False, True, True, False]
```

We'll call this list `mask` because this type of list is sometimes called a *boolean mask*.

Now we put that list in square brackets after the name of the dataframe:

```
small_df[mask]
```

	letter	number
1	b	4
2	c	8

and we get a new dataframe containing just the rows where the mask had `True` - in our case, the middle two rows. Notice that the index is the same as in the original dataframe, so the rows with index `0` and `3` are not present in the output. The result of this expression is a new dataframe that has exactly the same structure as the old one - it has the same columns and data, but only a subset of the rows.

For real life data, we obviously don't want to sit and type out a list when we need to select some rows. So we use pandas to write an expression that will produce a series of boolean values, then use that to select the rows we want.

Here's an example using our genome data. We'll write a comparison on the series of genome sizes, which will give us a new series of True/False values:

```
mask = euk["Size (Mb)"] > 500
mask
```

```
0      False
1      False
2       True
3      False
4       True
         ...
8297   False
8298   False
8299   False
8300   False
8301   False
Name: Size (Mb), Length: 8302, dtype: bool
```

Notice that the length of the series is exactly the same as the length of the original dataframe - exactly what we need for filtering. Now we simply put the name of that series in square brackets:

```
euk[mask]
```

	Species	Kingdom	Class	...	Number of proteins	Publication year	Assembly status
2	Glycine max	Plants	Land Plants	...	71219	2010	Chromosome
4	Solanum lycopersicum	Plants	Land Plants	...	37660	2010	Chromosome
5	Hordeum vulgare	Plants	Land Plants	...	<NA>	2019	Scaffold
7	Triticum aestivum	Plants	Land Plants	...	<NA>	2018	Chromosome
9	Zea mays	Plants	Land Plants	...	58411	2010	Chromosome
...	...	...	...	...	...	...	...
7494	Homo sapiens	Animals	Mammals	...	<NA>	2018	Contig
7495	Homo sapiens	Animals	Mammals	...	<NA>	2018	Contig
7501	Homo sapiens	Animals	Mammals	...	<NA>	2018	Contig
7502	Homo sapiens	Animals	Mammals	...	<NA>	2018	Contig
7507	Homo sapiens	Animals	Mammals	...	<NA>	2018	Contig

And we get a new dataframe which contains just the rows for which the comparison was true - all the genomes larger than 500 megabases. As before, the index stays the same, so it no longer counts up from zero as some of the rows are missing. If we check the length:

```
len(euk[mask])
```

```
1500
```

we can see that this new dataframe contains 1500 genomes out of the 8302 that we started with.

For most filtering tasks, we don't really need to store the boolean mask as it has no purpose once we've done the filter. So we generally put the series expression directly in the square brackets:

```
# simple_filter.py

euk[euk["Size (Mb)"] > 500]
```

	Species	Kingdom	Class	...	Number of proteins	Publication year	Assembly status
2	Glycine max	Plants	Land Plants	...	71219	2010	Chromosome
4	Solanum lycopersicum	Plants	Land Plants	...	37660	2010	Chromosome
5	Hordeum vulgare	Plants	Land Plants	...	<NA>	2019	Scaffold
7	Triticum aestivum	Plants	Land Plants	...	<NA>	2018	Chromosome
9	Zea mays	Plants	Land Plants	...	58411	2010	Chromosome
...	...	...	...	...	...	...	...
7494	Homo sapiens	Animals	Mammals	...	<NA>	2018	Contig
7495	Homo sapiens	Animals	Mammals	...	<NA>	2018	Contig
7501	Homo sapiens	Animals	Mammals	...	<NA>	2018	Contig
7502	Homo sapiens	Animals	Mammals	...	<NA>	2018	Contig
7507	Homo sapiens	Animals	Mammals	...	<NA>	2018	Contig

This syntax takes a bit of getting used to, but once we learn it it's a very powerful tool. We can use all of the normal comparison operators, and we can make our filters very specific:

```
# find genomes belonging to a single species
euk[euk["Species"] == "Penicillium expansum"]
```

	Species	Kingdom	Class	...	Number of proteins	Publication year	Assembly status
834	Penicillium expansum	Fungi	Ascomycetes	...	11060	2014	Contig
4662	Penicillium expansum	Fungi	Ascomycetes	...	<NA>	2016	Scaffold
5568	Penicillium expansum	Fungi	Ascomycetes	...	<NA>	2014	Contig
5789	Penicillium expansum	Fungi	Ascomycetes	...	11023	2014	Contig
5927	Penicillium expansum	Fungi	Ascomycetes	...	10089	2014	Contig
6134	Penicillium expansum	Fungi	Ascomycetes	...	<NA>	2019	Contig

or very flexible:

```
# find all genomes that are not fish
euk[euk["Class"] != "Fishes"]
```

	Species	Kingdom	Class	...	Number of proteins	Publication year	Assembly status
0	Emiliania huxleyi CCMP1516	Protists	Other Protists	...	38554	2013	Scaffold
1	Arabidopsis thaliana	Plants	Land Plants	...	48265	2001	Chromosome
2	Glycine max	Plants	Land Plants	...	71219	2010	Chromosome
3	Medicago truncatula	Plants	Land Plants	...	41939	2011	Chromosome
4	Solanum lycopersicum	Plants	Land Plants	...	37660	2010	Chromosome
...	...	...	...	...	...	...	...
8297	Saccharomyces cerevisiae	Fungi	Ascomycetes	...	<NA>	2017	Scaffold
8298	Saccharomyces cerevisiae	Fungi	Ascomycetes	...	298	1992	Chromosome
8299	Saccharomyces cerevisiae	Fungi	Ascomycetes	...	<NA>	2018	Chromosome
8300	Saccharomyces cerevisiae	Fungi	Ascomycetes	...	<NA>	2018	Chromosome
8301	Saccharomyces cerevisiae	Fungi	Ascomycetes	...	<NA>	2018	Chromosome

Once we're used to the syntax, filtering is pretty straightforward as long as we're only using the normal comparison operators (==, !=, <, <=, > and >=). Here are a few situations where filtering becomes a bit trickier...

4.1.1 Selecting things that are in a list

In normal Python, we can use the keyword `in` to test membership of a list:

```
"apple" in ["apple", "banana", "orange"]
```

```
True
```

So when we start using pandas it's very tempting to use it as well:

```
# find bird and fish genomes
euk["Class"] in ["Birds", "Fish"]
```

but this causes an error: `ValueError: The truth value of a Series is ambiguous....` Pandas thinks that we are trying to check for the whole series rather than each value separately. We have to use the `isin` method on the series like this:

```
# list_filter.py

# find all bird and fish genomes
euk[euk["Class"].isin(["Birds", "Fish"])]
```

	Species	Kingdom	Class	...	Number of proteins	Publication year	Assembly status
85	Gallus gallus	Animals	Birds	...	49681	2004	Chromosome
86	Meleagris gallopavo	Animals	Birds	...	33312	2010	Chromosome
87	Coturnix japonica	Animals	Birds	...	39088	2016	Chromosome
88	Eudromia elegans	Animals	Birds	...	<NA>	2018	Scaffold
89	Apteryx haastii	Animals	Birds	...	<NA>	2018	Scaffold
...	...	...	...	...	...	...	...
5343	Calypte anna	Animals	Birds	...	<NA>	2017	Contig
5422	Spheniscus magellanicus	Animals	Birds	...	<NA>	2018	Scaffold
5499	Calypte anna	Animals	Birds	...	<NA>	2018	Scaffold
5585	Anas platyrhynchos	Animals	Birds	...	<NA>	2017	Scaffold
5629	Taeniopygia guttata	Animals	Birds	...	<NA>	2018	Scaffold

4.1.2 Selecting things based on string properties

Python has a very nice set of conditional methods for working with strings. In regular Python it's easy to test whether a string starts with a particular letter:

```
"banana".startswith("b")
```

```
True
```

Trying to apply this same logic to a series:

```
# find genomes for species starting with the letter Q
euk["Species"].startswith("Q")
```

produces an error: `'Series' object has no attribute 'startswith'`

Again, the problem is that pandas thinks we want to check the whole series rather than each value separately. The fix in this case is to use the `str` attribute that we saw earlier:

```
# string_filter.py

# find genomes for species starting with the letter Q

euk[euk["Species"].str.startswith("Q")]
```

	Species	Kingdom	Class	...	Number of proteins	Publication year	Assembly status
789	Quercus robur	Plants	Land Plants	...	<NA>	2018	Scaffold
2400	Quercus lobata	Plants	Land Plants	...	<NA>	2016	Chromosome
3030	Quercus suber	Plants	Land Plants	...	59614	2018	Scaffold
3431	Quillaja saponaria	Plants	Land Plants	...	<NA>	2018	Contig
3874	Quambalaria eucalypti	Fungi	Basidiomycetes	...	<NA>	2019	Contig
4690	Quercus robur	Plants	Land Plants	...	<NA>	2018	Scaffold

4.1.3 Filtering based on multiple conditions

In regular Python, we can easily combine multiple simple conditions to make a complex condition:

```
number = 42

# is my number between 10 and 100?
number > 10 and number < 100
```

```
True
```

This syntax doesn't quite work for pandas conditions. Instead, we have to suround each condition with its own set of parentheses, and use **&** instead of the word **and**:

```
# find genomes between a hundred and a thousand megabases
(euk["Size (Mb)"] > 100) & (euk["Size (Mb)"] < 1000)
```

```
0       True
1       True
2       True
3       True
4       True
        ...
8297    False
8298    False
8299    False
8300    False
8301    False
Name: Size (Mb), Length: 8302, dtype: bool
```

When we add in the code to actually use this mask to get the rows we want we can end up with quite a complicated expression with lots of brackets:

```
# complex_filter.py

# find genomes between a hundred and a thousand megabases
euk[(euk["Size (Mb)"] > 100) & (euk["Size (Mb)"] < 1000)]
```

	Species	Kingdom	Class	...	Number of proteins	Publication year	Assembly status
0	Emiliania huxleyi CCMP1516	Protists	Other Protists	...	38554	2013	Scaffold
1	Arabidopsis thaliana	Plants	Land Plants	...	48265	2001	Chromosome
2	Glycine max	Plants	Land Plants	...	71219	2010	Chromosome
3	Medicago truncatula	Plants	Land Plants	...	41939	2011	Chromosome
4	Solanum lycopersicum	Plants	Land Plants	...	37660	2010	Chromosome
...	...	...	...	...	...	...	...
7486	Homo sapiens	Animals	Mammals	...	<NA>	2018	Contig
7487	Homo sapiens	Animals	Mammals	...	<NA>	2018	Contig
7494	Homo sapiens	Animals	Mammals	...	<NA>	2018	Contig
7495	Homo sapiens	Animals	Mammals	...	<NA>	2018	Contig
7507	Homo sapiens	Animals	Mammals	...	<NA>	2018	Contig

so it may be helpful to split it over multiple lines.

For this particular case, where we want to find values between two limits, there's a special **between** method that gives the same answer more readably:

```
# find genomes between a hundred and a thousand megabases
euk[euk["Size (Mb)"].between(100, 1000)]
```

	Species	Kingdom	Class	...	Number of proteins	Publication year	Assembly status
0	Emiliania huxleyi CCMP1516	Protists	Other Protists	...	38554	2013	Scaffold
1	Arabidopsis thaliana	Plants	Land Plants	...	48265	2001	Chromosome
2	Glycine max	Plants	Land Plants	...	71219	2010	Chromosome
3	Medicago truncatula	Plants	Land Plants	...	41939	2011	Chromosome
4	Solanum lycopersicum	Plants	Land Plants	...	37660	2010	Chromosome
...	...	...	...	...	...	...	...
7486	Homo sapiens	Animals	Mammals	...	<NA>	2018	Contig
7487	Homo sapiens	Animals	Mammals	...	<NA>	2018	Contig
7494	Homo sapiens	Animals	Mammals	...	<NA>	2018	Contig
7495	Homo sapiens	Animals	Mammals	...	<NA>	2018	Contig
7507	Homo sapiens	Animals	Mammals	...	<NA>	2018	Contig

We can also use | instead of **or** and ~ instead of **not**:

```
# find genomes that are not birds of fishes, or have low GC
euk[~(euk["Class"].isin(["Birds", "Fishes"])) | (euk["GC%"] < 40)]
```

	Species	Kingdom	Class	...	Number of proteins	Publication year	Assembly status
0	Emiliania huxleyi CCMP1516	Protists	Other Protists	...	38554	2013	Scaffold
1	Arabidopsis thaliana	Plants	Land Plants	...	48265	2001	Chromosome
2	Glycine max	Plants	Land Plants	...	71219	2010	Chromosome
3	Medicago truncatula	Plants	Land Plants	...	41939	2011	Chromosome
4	Solanum lycopersicum	Plants	Land Plants	...	37660	2010	Chromosome
...	...	...	...	...	...	...	...
8297	Saccharomyces cerevisiae	Fungi	Ascomycetes	...	<NA>	2017	Scaffold
8298	Saccharomyces cerevisiae	Fungi	Ascomycetes	...	298	1992	Chromosome
8299	Saccharomyces cerevisiae	Fungi	Ascomycetes	...	<NA>	2018	Chromosome
8300	Saccharomyces cerevisiae	Fungi	Ascomycetes	...	<NA>	2018	Chromosome
8301	Saccharomyces cerevisiae	Fungi	Ascomycetes	...	<NA>	2018	Chromosome

4.2 Filtering on columns with missing data

One final complication that we need to deal with is situations where the columns involved in the condition have missing data. For example, say we try to figure out which genomes have more than 10,000 predicted genes:

```
euk["Number of genes"] > 10_000
```

```
0        True
1        True
2        True
3        True
4        True
        ...
8297     <NA>
8298    False
8299     <NA>
8300     <NA>
8301     <NA>
Name: Number of genes, Length: 8302, dtype: boolean
```

If we look at the last few values in this boolean series, we'll see that pandas has decided that if a particular value is missing, then we don't know if it is bigger than 10,000 and so that result is also missing. This is a perfectly reasonable assumption, and in many cases this behaviour is useful. For example, if we call `value_counts` on the condition:

```
(euk["Number of genes"] > 10_000).value_counts()
```

```
True     1495
False     877
Name: Number of genes, dtype: Int64
```

we see that there are 1,495 genomes with more than 10,000 genes, and 877 with fewer or exactly 10,000. However, if we add `dropna=False`:

```
(euk["Number of genes"] > 10_000).value_counts(dropna=False)
```

```
NaN      5930
True     1495
False     877
Name: Number of genes, dtype: Int64
```

we see that there are an additional 5,930 genomes where the answer is unknown.

When we try to select just the rows where the condition is true, using the series as a boolean mask as we saw earlier, the missing data values always count as false. So when we try to find the number of genomes with more than 10,000 genes:

```
len(euk[euk["Number of genes"] > 10_000])
```

```
1495
```

we just get the 1,495. Most of the time this is what we want. If we want to include genomes with an unknown number of genes, then the easiest solution is to use `fillna` to replace missing data with a value that's bigger than our cutoff:

```
len(euk[euk["Number of genes"].fillna(20000) > 10_000])
```

```
7425
```

With this adjustment, our filter now gives us the 1,495 genomes with a known number of genes greater than 10,000 plus the 5,930 genomes with an unknown number of genes.

4.3 Putting it all together

Take a look at the output from the filtering examples above. Hopefully it's not too hard to see that in each case we end up with a dataframe that has the same structure as the one we started with. This means that we can use the output of a filter as the starting point for some of the other tools that we've previously looked at. For example, let's get the sizes of all the human genomes:

```
# what are the sizes of all the human genomes?
euk[euk["Species"] == "Homo sapiens"]["Size (Mb)"]
```

```
44       3257.32000
4993     2863.65000
5059     2844.00000
5673     3251.72000
5721     6503.44000
           ...
7783        4.89807
7784        2.09690
7789        4.78084
7790        4.79943
7793        2.78964
Name: Size (Mb), Length: 210, dtype: float64
```

And once we have a series, we already know a bunch of useful things we can do with it. For example, let's say that we want to know the mean genome size for birds. To calculate this there are three steps:

- filter the dataframe to include only bird genomes
- from the filtered dataframe, select only the **Size (Mb)** column
- call the `mean` method on the resulting series

This seems like a lot of work when we type it out like that, but when we convert it into pandas code we get a very concise expression:

```python
# filter_select_aggregate.py

euk[euk["Class"] == "Birds"]["Size (Mb)"].mean()
```

```
1131.3959991860465
```

If it's difficult to see the three stages as a single line we can split it:

```python
(
    euk[euk["Class"] == "Birds"] # find bird genomes
    ["Size (Mb)"] # get size column
    .mean() # calculate mean
)
```

```
1131.3959991860465
```

This chained style of writing code might look odd if you're used to regular Python, but conceptually it's no different to writing something like:

```python
name = "Gorilla gorilla"
name[:10].upper().count("G")
```

```
2
```

which, incidentally, we could also split over multiple lines:

```python
name = "Gorilla gorilla"
(
    name[:10]  # get the first ten letters of the name
    .upper()  # change it to upper case
    .count("G")  # count the number of Gs
)
```

```
2
```

Although we don't normally do this in everyday Python.

An expression like `euk[ euk['Class'] == 'Birds' ]['Size (Mb)'].mean()` involves *filtering* the dataframe, *selecting* a column, then performing some *aggregation* on the series. Once we've learned this general pattern, we can reuse it to do a huge variety of different calculations:

```
# what's the median number of genes for genomes with low GC?
euk[euk["GC%"] < 50]["Number of genes"].median()
```

```
12640.0
```

```
# how many genomes were sequenced for each kingdom in 2010?
euk[euk["Publication year"] == 2010]["Kingdom"].value_counts()
```

```
Animals     24
Fungi       22
Plants      13
Protists     6
Other        1
Name: Kingdom, dtype: Int64
```

```
# what's the largest number of proteins for fish genomes from 2017
(
    euk[
        (euk["Class"] == "Fishes") & (euk["Publication year"] == 2017)
    ]
    ["Number of proteins"]
    .max()
)
```

```
71224
```

4.3.1 Filtering as a building block

As the last few examples make clear, filtering is most often used as the starting point for other types of analysis. In future chapters, we'll use this pattern extensively. In particular, when we come to chapters on visualization, we will often begin by filtering our data to select a subset to display. In such situations we'll usually carry out the filter once, then store the result as a new dataframe so that we can easily reuse it. Look out for patterns like this:

```
animals = euk[euk["Kingdom"] == "Animals"]

# do something with the animals dataframe
```

and you'll easily be able to follow what's going on.

5 Data exploration examples with pandas

In the last few chapters we've looked at a few of the basic building blocks of pandas - selecting, filtering, sorting and transforming data. The power of pandas comes from putting these basic steps together to do more complicated things (computer scientists call this idea *composability*).

To help get a feel for the way that we can tackle real world questions with pandas, let's look at a few examples to show how we go from a question written in natural language to a piece of code.

These example questions all relate to the eukaryote genome data file that we're already familiar with, and assume that it has already been read into a dataframe called `euk`.

5.0.1 How many fungal species have genomes bigger than 100Mb? What are their names?

This is a filtering problem - we want to find rows that satisfy the two criteria, then get the species name column. We will build up the solution one step at a time. First, let's just find the fungal genomes:

```
euk[euk["Kingdom"] == "Fungi"]
```

	Species	Kingdom	Class	...	Number of proteins	Publication year	Assembly status
8	Saccharomyces cerevisiae S288C	Fungi	Ascomycetes	...	6002	1999	Complete Genome
10	Pneumocystis carinii B80	Fungi	Ascomycetes	...	3646	2015	Contig
11	Schizosaccharomyces pombe	Fungi	Ascomycetes	...	5132	2002	Chromosome
12	Aspergillus nidulans FGSC A4	Fungi	Ascomycetes	...	9556	2003	Scaffold
13	Aspergillus fumigatus Af293	Fungi	Ascomycetes	...	19260	2005	Chromosome
...	...	...	...	...	...	...	...
8297	Saccharomyces cerevisiae	Fungi	Ascomycetes	...	<NA>	2017	Scaffold
8298	Saccharomyces cerevisiae	Fungi	Ascomycetes	...	298	1992	Chromosome
8299	Saccharomyces cerevisiae	Fungi	Ascomycetes	...	<NA>	2018	Chromosome
8300	Saccharomyces cerevisiae	Fungi	Ascomycetes	...	<NA>	2018	Chromosome
8301	Saccharomyces cerevisiae	Fungi	Ascomycetes	...	<NA>	2018	Chromosome

Next, we will add the filter on the size column. Remember that now we have two conditions, we need to surround each one with its own pair of parentheses:

```
euk[(euk["Kingdom"] == "Fungi") & (euk["Size (Mb)"] > 100)]
```

	Species	Kingdom	Class	...	Number of proteins	Publication year	Assembly status
323	Blumeria graminis f. sp. hordei DH14	Fungi	Ascomycetes	...	<NA>	2018	Scaffold
347	Puccinia triticina 1-1 BBBD Race 1	Fungi	Basidiomycetes	...	15685	2009	Scaffold
354	Tuber melanosporum	Fungi	Ascomycetes	...	7496	2010	Scaffold
372	Puccinia striiformis f. sp. tritici	Fungi	Basidiomycetes	...	<NA>	2018	Contig
427	Melampsora larici-populina 98AG31	Fungi	Basidiomycetes	...	16372	2011	Scaffold
...	...	...	...	...	...	...	...
6406	Rhizophagus irregularis	Fungi	Other Fungi	...	24485	2016	Scaffold
6502	Rhizophagus irregularis	Fungi	Other Fungi	...	<NA>	2018	Scaffold
6511	Rhizophagus irregularis	Fungi	Other Fungi	...	<NA>	2018	Scaffold
6520	Puccinia striiformis	Fungi	Basidiomycetes	...	<NA>	2019	Scaffold
6579	Puccinia striiformis f. sp. tritici CY32	Fungi	Basidiomycetes	...	<NA>	2013	Scaffold

Finally, we can get the column that we want:

```
euk[(euk["Kingdom"] == "Fungi") & (euk["Size (Mb)"] > 100)]["Species"]
```

```
323            Blumeria graminis f. sp. hordei DH14
347              Puccinia triticina 1-1 BBBD Race 1
354                           Tuber melanosporum
372               Puccinia striiformis f. sp. tritici
427               Melampsora larici-populina 98AG31
                             ...
6406                        Rhizophagus irregularis
6502                        Rhizophagus irregularis
6511                        Rhizophagus irregularis
6520                           Puccinia striiformis
6579    Puccinia striiformis f. sp. tritici CY32
Name: Species, Length: 76, dtype: string
```

The output for this series answers the first part of the question: there are 76 genomes that fit the description we're looking for. The values in the series are the species names. If we want to turn this into a regular Python list we can use the `to_list` method:

```python
# fungal_species_names.py

species = (
    euk[
        (euk["Kingdom"] == "Fungi") & (euk["Size (Mb)"] > 100)
    ]
    ["Species"]
    .to_list()
)

# get first 10 elements
species[:10]
```

```
['Blumeria graminis f. sp. hordei DH14',
 'Puccinia triticina 1-1 BBBD Race 1',
 'Tuber melanosporum',
 'Puccinia striiformis f. sp. tritici',
 'Melampsora larici-populina 98AG31',
 'Ophiocordyceps sinensis',
 'Gigaspora rosea',
 'Leucoagaricus gongylophorus Ac12',
 'Hemileia vastatrix HvCat',
 'Cenococcum geophilum 1.58']
```

Although that's rarely necessary as we can use a series in most of the places that we would normally use a list.

5.0.2 How many genomes are there for each Kingdom (plants, animals, fungi, protists and other), and how many unique species names?

The first part of this problem is relatively easy to answer: any time we see a question involving the words "how many ... for each ..." the answer is `value_counts`:

```python
euk["Kingdom"].value_counts()
```

```
Fungi      4494
Animals    2181
Plants      870
Protists    727
Other        30
Name: Kingdom, dtype: Int64
```

The second part is a bit trickier. As with all programming problems, a good way to get started is by solving part of the problem, so we'll begin by just counting the unique species names for plants. This involves filtering the dataframe:

5 Data exploration examples with pandas

```
euk[euk["Kingdom"] == "Plants"]
```

	Species	Kingdom	Class	...	Number of proteins	Publication year	Assembly status
1	Arabidopsis thaliana	Plants	Land Plants	...	48265	2001	Chromosome
2	Glycine max	Plants	Land Plants	...	71219	2010	Chromosome
3	Medicago truncatula	Plants	Land Plants	...	41939	2011	Chromosome
4	Solanum lycopersicum	Plants	Land Plants	...	37660	2010	Chromosome
5	Hordeum vulgare	Plants	Land Plants	...	<NA>	2019	Scaffold
...	...	...	...	...	...	...	...
7256	Oryza sativa	Plants	Land Plants	...	<NA>	2019	Contig
7259	Oryza sativa	Plants	Land Plants	...	<NA>	2019	Contig
7262	Oryza rufipogon	Plants	Land Plants	...	<NA>	2016	Contig
7267	Oryza rufipogon	Plants	Land Plants	...	<NA>	2014	Chromosome
7270	Oryza sativa	Plants	Land Plants	...	<NA>	2019	Contig

then getting the number of unique species names with **nunique**:

```
euk[euk["Kingdom"] == "Plants"]["Species"].nunique()
```

```
464
```

OK, now how do we expand this to all kingdoms? Well, we are still using Python, so how about a loop?

```
for kingdom in ["Plants", "Animals", "Fungi", "Protists", "Other"]:
    print(kingdom, euk[euk["Kingdom"] == kingdom]["Species"].nunique())
```

```
Plants 464
Animals 1442
Fungi 2554
Protists 449
Other 27
```

We just replace the string `'Plants'` in our original statement with a variable name that we can change each time round the loop.

This solution works, but feels a bit inflexible, as we have to know in advance what kingdoms we want. A more elegant way would be to get a list of unique kingdom names directly from the dataframe:

```
euk["Kingdom"].unique()
```

```
<StringArray>
['Protists', 'Plants', 'Fungi', 'Animals', 'Other']
Length: 5, dtype: string
```

And then use that list directly in our loop:

```
# kingdom_counts.py

for kingdom in euk["Kingdom"].unique():
    print(kingdom, euk[euk["Kingdom"] == kingdom]["Species"].nunique())
```

```
Protists 449
Plants 464
Fungi 2554
Animals 1442
Other 27
```

5.0.3 Make a new dataframe containing just the rows for the *Aquila* genus.

For this challenge we need a bit of biological knowledge. The **Species** column contains the scientific name, which is made up of a genus name and a species name separated by a space (there are some that don't follow that format, but we'll ignore them for now).

The complexity of this problem lies entirely in the fact that we don't have a **Genus** column to work with. If we did, then the answer would be simple - something like

```
euk[euk["Genus"] == "Aquila"]
```

would do the job. However, the genus name is contained inside the species name, so our filter will have to involve some string processing.

There are a couple of approaches to this. One idea is to take the species name and split it where we see a space, remembering that we need to call **split** on the **str** attribute:

```
euk["Species"].str.split(" ")
```

```
0          [Emiliania, huxleyi, CCMP1516]
1                  [Arabidopsis, thaliana]
2                           [Glycine, max]
3                   [Medicago, truncatula]
4                  [Solanum, lycopersicum]
                        ...
8297        [Saccharomyces, cerevisiae]
8298        [Saccharomyces, cerevisiae]
8299        [Saccharomyces, cerevisiae]
8300        [Saccharomyces, cerevisiae]
8301        [Saccharomyces, cerevisiae]
Name: Species, Length: 8302, dtype: object
```

Now we can take the first element of each of the resulting lists (again remembering to refer to the **str** attribute):

```
euk["Species"].str.split(" ").str[0]
```

```
0          Emiliania
1          Arabidopsis
2          Glycine
3          Medicago
4          Solanum
              ...
8297       Saccharomyces
8298       Saccharomyces
8299       Saccharomyces
8300       Saccharomyces
8301       Saccharomyces
Name: Species, Length: 8302, dtype: object
```

This gives us our series of genus names. Now we can add the condition to get a series of boolean values:

```
euk["Species"].str.split(" ").str[0] == "Aquila"
```

```
0       False
1       False
2       False
3       False
4       False
        ...
8297    False
8298    False
8299    False
8300    False
8301    False
Name: Species, Length: 8302, dtype: bool
```

which we can plug into the original dataframe to just select the rows with `True`:

```
# genus_filter.py

euk[euk["Species"].str.split(" ").str[0] == "Aquila"]
```

	Species	Kingdom	Class	...	Number of proteins	Publication year	Assembly status
1755	Aquila chrysaetos canadensis	Animals	Birds	...	31284	2014	Scaffold
4388	Aquila chrysaetos canadensis	Animals	Birds	...	\<NA\>	2014	Scaffold
5342	Aquila chrysaetos chrysaetos	Animals	Birds	...	\<NA\>	2018	Scaffold

As with regular Python, there are usually several different ways to express a conditional test in pandas. Another way to get the same result would be to use `startswith`:

```
euk[euk["Species"].str.startswith("Aquila")]
```

	Species	Kingdom	Class	...	Number of proteins	Publication year	Assembly status
1745	Aquilaria agallochum	Plants	Land Plants	...	\<NA\>	2014	Scaffold
1755	Aquila chrysaetos canadensis	Animals	Birds	...	31284	2014	Scaffold
4388	Aquila chrysaetos canadensis	Animals	Birds	...	\<NA\>	2014	Scaffold
5342	Aquila chrysaetos chrysaetos	Animals	Birds	...	\<NA\>	2018	Scaffold

But we must be careful! Look what has happened above - we've accidentally included the species *Aquilaria agallochum*, whose genus name does indeed start with *Aquila* but which has additional letters after. To be precise we should have a space after *Aquila* in the argument to `startswith`:

```
euk[euk["Species"].str.startswith("Aquila ")]
```

	Species	Kingdom	Class	...	Number of proteins	Publication year	Assembly status
1755	Aquila chrysaetos canadensis	Animals	Birds	...	31284	2014	Scaffold
4388	Aquila chrysaetos canadensis	Animals	Birds	...	\<NA\>	2014	Scaffold
5342	Aquila chrysaetos chrysaetos	Animals	Birds	...	\<NA\>	2018	Scaffold

which avoids this problem.

Of course, once we have figured out how to calculate the genus name we might add it as a new column so that we can use it again later:

```
euk["Genus"] = euk["Species"].str.split(" ").str[0]
euk[["Species", "Genus", "Class", "Kingdom"]]
```

	Species	Genus	Class	Kingdom
0	Emiliania huxleyi CCMP1516	Emiliania	Other Protists	Protists
1	Arabidopsis thaliana	Arabidopsis	Land Plants	Plants
2	Glycine max	Glycine	Land Plants	Plants
3	Medicago truncatula	Medicago	Land Plants	Plants
4	Solanum lycopersicum	Solanum	Land Plants	Plants
...	...	...	...	...
8297	Saccharomyces cerevisiae	Saccharomyces	Ascomycetes	Fungi
8298	Saccharomyces cerevisiae	Saccharomyces	Ascomycetes	Fungi
8299	Saccharomyces cerevisiae	Saccharomyces	Ascomycetes	Fungi
8300	Saccharomyces cerevisiae	Saccharomyces	Ascomycetes	Fungi
8301	Saccharomyces cerevisiae	Saccharomyces	Ascomycetes	Fungi

5.0.4 In which assembly status are the most insect genomes? How about the most amphibian genomes?

This is another case where `value_counts` will help us, although it might not be obvious why. If we simplify the question to ask in which assembly status are the most genomes of *all* classes, then the answer is just the status that occurs most frequently. So we can answer it by doing `value_counts`, then taking the first element:

```
euk["Assembly status"].value_counts().head(1)
```

```
Scaffold    5437
Name: Assembly status, dtype: Int64
```

Now, to make the transition to only considering insect genomes, we just need to filter the dataframe before we get the **Assembly status** column:

```
(
    euk[euk["Class"] == "Insects"]
    ["Assembly status"]
    .value_counts()
    .head(1)
)
```

```
Scaffold    497
Name: Assembly status, dtype: Int64
```

This is an example of a general rule that often comes in useful: since filtering a dataframe doesn't change its structure, we can take any operation on a dataframe (in this case the `['Assembly status'].value_counts().head(1)` part of the expression) and run it on a filtered version of the dataframe.

Having come up with the expression, it's pretty easy to replace 'Insects' with 'Amphibians':

```
euk[euk["Class"] == "Amphibians"]["Assembly status"].value_counts().head(1)
```

```
Chromosome    3
Name: Assembly status, dtype: Int64
```

We could even re use our loop technique from the previous question and find out which is the most common status for every different class:

```
# class_assembly_summary.py

for class_name in euk["Class"].unique():
    top_status = (
        euk[euk["Class"] == class_name]["Assembly status"]
        .value_counts()
        .index[0]
    )
    print(f"Most {class_name} genomes are assmbled to {top_status} status")
```

```
Most Other Protists genomes are assmbled to Scaffold status
Most Land Plants genomes are assmbled to Scaffold status
Most Ascomycetes genomes are assmbled to Scaffold status
Most Basidiomycetes genomes are assmbled to Scaffold status
Most Kinetoplasts genomes are assmbled to Scaffold status
Most Apicomplexans genomes are assmbled to Scaffold status
Most Other Fungi genomes are assmbled to Scaffold status
Most Roundworms genomes are assmbled to Scaffold status
Most Insects genomes are assmbled to Scaffold status
Most Fishes genomes are assmbled to Scaffold status
Most Other Animals genomes are assmbled to Scaffold status
Most Mammals genomes are assmbled to Scaffold status
Most Other genomes are assmbled to Scaffold status
Most Amphibians genomes are assmbled to Chromosome status
Most Birds genomes are assmbled to Scaffold status
Most Green Algae genomes are assmbled to Scaffold status
Most Flatworms genomes are assmbled to Scaffold status
Most Reptiles genomes are assmbled to Scaffold status
Most Other Plants genomes are assmbled to Scaffold status
```

Notice that there's a bit of ceremony involved to get just the name of the top status - after doing value counts we have to refer to `index` to get a list of the index values (i.e. the status names) then use slice syntax to get the first element. Also notice that we haven't used the obvious variable name `class`, as that clashes with Python's reserved keyword `class`.

5.0.5 Which genomes have at least 10% more proteins than genes?

This is a short question which hides quite a bit of complexity. It's obviously a filtering problem, so let's start by defining exactly what we're looking for. There are a few different ways to interpret "10% more", but for the purposes of this question we'll say that we want to divide the number of proteins by the number of genes, and if the result is greater than or equal to 1.1 then we want to include the genome.

Calculating the ratios is quite straightforward thanks to pandas' broadcasting rules:

```
euk["Number of proteins"] / euk["Number of genes"]
```

```
0       1.000130
1       1.259821
2       1.190018
3       1.115310
4       1.207051
          ...
8297         NaN
8298    1.922581
8299         NaN
8300         NaN
8301         NaN
Length: 8302, dtype: float64
```

As we might expect, any genomes which don't have both a number of genes and a number of proteins will result in missing data.

To get our series of boolean values, we can add the condition. We must remember the parentheses:

```
(euk["Number of proteins"] / euk["Number of genes"]) >= 1.1
```

```
0       False
1        True
2        True
3        True
4        True
         ...
8297    False
8298     True
8299    False
8300    False
8301    False
Length: 8302, dtype: bool
```

Now we can use that series to filter the original dataframe:

```
# more_proteins.py

euk[(euk["Number of proteins"] / euk["Number of genes"]) >= 1.1]
```

	Species	Kingdom	Class	...	Publication year	Assembly status	Genus
1	Arabidopsis thaliana	Plants	Land Plants	...	2001	Chromosome	Arabidopsis
2	Glycine max	Plants	Land Plants	...	2010	Chromosome	Glycine
3	Medicago truncatula	Plants	Land Plants	...	2011	Chromosome	Medicago
4	Solanum lycopersicum	Plants	Land Plants	...	2010	Chromosome	Solanum
6	Oryza sativa Japonica Group	Plants	Land Plants	...	2015	Chromosome	Oryza
...	...	...	...	...	...	...	...
6487	Fusarium oxysporum f. sp. melonis 26406	Fungi	Ascomycetes	...	2012	Scaffold	Fusarium
6523	Fusarium oxysporum Fo47	Fungi	Ascomycetes	...	2012	Scaffold	Fusarium
6626	Arabidopsis thaliana	Plants	Land Plants	...	2000	Chromosome	Arabidopsis
6781	Mus musculus	Animals	Mammals	...	2005	Chromosome	Mus
8298	Saccharomyces cerevisiae	Fungi	Ascomycetes	...	1992	Chromosome	Saccharomyces

to get our answer.

Of course, if we think that this value might be useful again in the future we could add it as an extra column:

```
euk["Proteins per gene"] = euk["Number of proteins"] / euk["Number of genes"]
```

Then we could filter on just the column:

```
euk[euk["Proteins per gene"] >= 1.1][
    [
        "Species",
        "Class",
        "Number of proteins",
        "Number of genes",
        "Proteins per gene",
    ]
]
```

5 Data exploration examples with pandas

	Species	Class	Number of proteins	Number of genes	Proteins per gene
1	Arabidopsis thaliana	Land Plants	48265	38311	1.25982
2	Glycine max	Land Plants	71219	59847	1.19002
3	Medicago truncatula	Land Plants	41939	37603	1.11531
4	Solanum lycopersicum	Land Plants	37660	31200	1.20705
6	Oryza sativa Japonica Group	Land Plants	42580	35219	1.20901
...	...	...	...	...	...
6487	Fusarium oxysporum f. sp. melonis 26406	Ascomycetes	26719	20030	1.33395
6523	Fusarium oxysporum Fo47	Ascomycetes	24818	18553	1.33768
6626	Arabidopsis thaliana	Land Plants	20111	16842	1.1941
6781	Mus musculus	Mammals	45437	31682	1.43416
8298	Saccharomyces cerevisiae	Ascomycetes	298	155	1.92258

As well as allowing us to reuse the column in future work, adding the extra column like this makes the meaning of the calculation clearer by virtue of giving it a name.

6 Introduction to Seaborn

In the previous section we looked at various things that we can do to datasets with pandas. In most of the examples that we looked at, the general pattern was to take a large amount of data and summarize it with a few numbers:

```
# what are the five animal classes with the most sequenced genomes?
euk[euk["Kingdom"] == "Animals"]["Class"].value_counts().head(5)
```

```
Mammals          658
Insects          602
Fishes           282
Other Animals    210
Birds            172
Name: Class, dtype: Int64
```

This is one approach to making sense of large datasets, and works well when the information we're looking for can be summed up in a short table. However, this approach fails when we're looking for larger patterns. Humans are not very good at reading very large tables of data. For example, take a look at this table showing the genome size and number of genes for reptiles:

```
# reptiles_size_genes.py

# filter for class and remove outliers
selected = euk[
    (euk["Class"] == "Reptiles")
    & (euk["Number of genes"] > 1000).fillna(False)
]
selected[["Species", "Size (Mb)", "Number of genes"]]
```

	Species	Size (Mb)	Number of genes
282	Anolis carolinensis	1799.14	22092
565	Pogona vitticeps	1716.68	21445
944	Chrysemys picta bellii	2365.77	25289
1122	Chelonia mydas	2208.41	22336
1136	Alligator mississippiensis	2161.73	25012
1150	Crocodylus porosus	2049.54	19551
1218	Notechis scutatus	1665.53	22413
1248	Pelodiscus sinensis	2202.48	24516
1376	Thamnophis sirtalis	1424.90	20101
1513	Python bivittatus	1435.05	21877
1526	Protobothrops mucrosquamatus	1673.88	21073
1576	Alligator sinensis	2270.57	24320
2142	Gekko japonicus	2490.27	21197
3054	Terrapene mexicana triunguis	2571.27	24657
3487	Pseudonaja textilis	1590.04	22151

And see if you can spot the relationship. Even for this small dataset, it's very time consuming to compare the numbers. But if we view the exact same data as a scatter plot:

```
# reptiles_size_genes_plot.py

sns.relplot(data=selected, x="Size (Mb)", y="Number of genes")

plt.title("Genome size and number of genes for reptiles", pad=20)
```

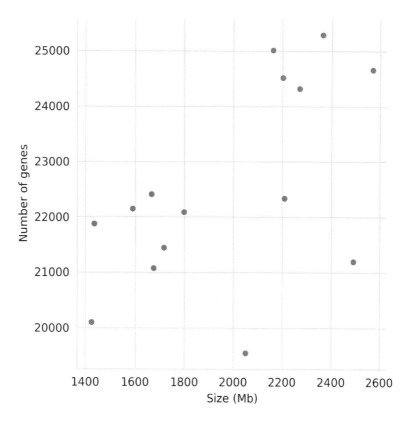

Genome size and number of genes for reptiles

it only takes a glance to see the positive correlation. In this section we will use visualisation, rather than aggregation, to make sense of our data.

For the sake of making distinctions between different datasets, we will sometimes use different colors for our charts in this section. The tools for doing this will be covered in detail in a future chapter; for now, hopefully the arguments will be fairly self-explanatory. And we may occasionally tweak aspects of the chart like label rotations to make the figures easier to read. Again, anything that isn't explained here will be covered when we discuss styles.

6.1 Setting up to draw a chart

Before we can draw our first chart, we have to have a few things in place.

First we will import the libraries that we need. Just as we normally use the alias **pd** for pandas and **np** for numpy:

```
import pandas as pd
import numpy as np
```

we typically use the alias **sns** for seaborn:

```
import seaborn as sns
```

and **plt** for matplotlib:

```
import matplotlib.pyplot as plt
```

In the case of matplotlib, the package is divided into several modules. The functions that we'll need are in the `pyplot` module, so that's the one that we import.

Finally, we need to decide how we want to view our charts once they've been drawn. If we're working inside a Jupyter notebook (which is strongly recommended) then we should run:

```
%matplotlib inline
```

which is a special Jupyter command and means that charts will be shown live in the document.

If we're using matplotlib from inside a regular interactive Python terminal, or we are writing a Python program and executing it, then we have two choices. If we just want to save our figures to a file, then we can call `plt.savefig` with a filename after we draw a chart. If we want to see our figures in an interactive window, we have to set up one of the various *backends*. There are way too many variations of operating system and library to discuss here, so if you're using something other than Jupyter notebook, take a look at the matplotlib FAQ:

https://matplotlib.org/faq/usage_faq.html#what-is-a-backend

and if it seems too complicated, consider switching to Jupyter notebook. For the purposes of this book, we'll put the figures directly underneath the code that produces them.

6.1.1 Plotting distributions

The simplest thing we can do is draw a histogram. The `distplot` function (short for *distribution plot*) takes a list of values, which can be in the form of a pandas series. Unlike the rest of the seaborn functions, `distplot` can't deal with missing data, so we have to call `dropna` to remove it from our series first:

```
# gc_histogram.py

sns.distplot(euk["GC%"].dropna())
```

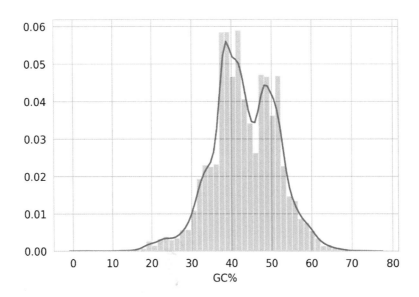

This already looks pretty good. Seaborn picks a sensible number of bins, a pleasing blue color scheme, and an x axis label taken from the name of the series. By default, it draws both a bar chart showing the number of data points in each bin and an estimate of the underlying distribution using kernel density estimation.

Let's look at a few options that we might want to change. We will split the function call over multiple lines to make it easier to comment and read:

```
# gc_histogram_custom.py

# set the shape of the plot
plt.figure(figsize=(8, 4))

sns.distplot(
    euk["GC%"].dropna(),  # this is our series of values
    color="red",  # change the color
    bins=100,  # set the number of bins
    kde=False,  # don't calculate KDE
)

# set the x limit between 0 and 100 for a percentage
plt.xlim((0, 100))

# set a title for the chart
plt.title("Distribution of GC percentage across eukaryote genomes")
```

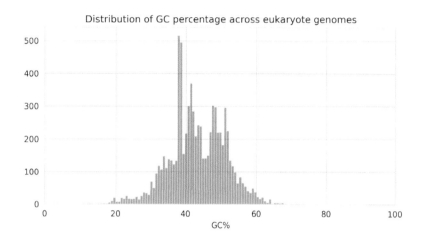

Since all of the seaborn plotting functions have many arguments, and most of the time we want to change only a few, we rely heavily on using keyword arguments.

Notice that to generate this plot we need to use both seaborn and matplotlib. Some aspects of the chart, like the color and the number of bins, are arguments to `distplot`, but others, like the title and x axis limits, have to be set by calling functions in `plt`.

Glancing at the distribution of GC percentage in the chart above, it looks like there might be a few different subpopulations. To see if these correspond to kingdoms, let's plot the genomes belonging to each kingdom separately. We'll use pandas to get a list of the different unique kingdom names, and to select just those genomes from the dataframe. Then we'll call `distplot` once for each group of genomes, attaching a label so that seaborn can draw a legend for us. If we draw a histogram for each group then the chart will be very cluttered, so we'll avoid drawing the bars with `hist=False` and just plot the KDE:

```
# gc_histogram_multiple.py

plt.figure(figsize=(8, 4))

# for each unique kingdom...
for kingdom in euk["Kingdom"].unique():

    # ...select just the rows for that kingdom...
    one_kingdom = euk[euk["Kingdom"] == kingdom]

    # ... and plot the GC values
    sns.distplot(one_kingdom["GC%"].dropna(), hist=False, label=kingdom)

plt.title(
    "Distribution of GC percentage for genomes\nbelonging to different kingdoms"
)
```

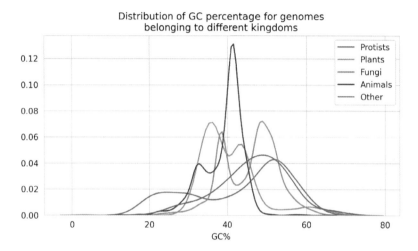

It looks like genomes belonging to different kingdoms do indeed have different distributions of GC percentage. Notice a useful trick for setting the title: if we know that our title is going to be long, we can put in newline characters to split it over multiple lines.

Visualisations like this, which compare distributions of values across several different groups, are usually better handled by categorical plots. We'll see examples of these later.

6.1.2 Visualizing relationships between two variables

The next logical step from looking at the distribution of a single variable (GC percentage in our example above) is look at the joint distribution of two variables. This is the job of the scatter plot, which is handled in seaborn by the `relplot` (short for *relationship plot*) function.

The interface to `relplot` is a bit different to `distplot`. Instead of passing a set of values, we instead pass a dataframe, and the names of the columns that we want on the X and Y axes. Let's look at the relationship between genome size and number of genes:

```
# size_genes_scatter.py

sns.relplot(data=euk, x="Size (Mb)", y="Number of genes")

plt.title("Genome size vs number of genes\n for all genomes")
```

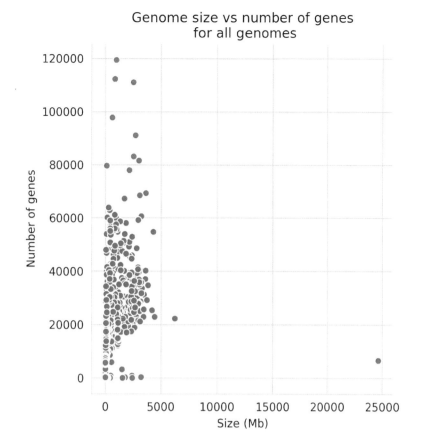

Genome size vs number of genes
for all genomes

With all options left as default, we get an unremarkable scatter plot where each point represents a single genome. Notice that unlike `distplot`, `relplot` has no problem ignoring missing data, so we don't have to filter it.

The chart above shows a problem commonly encountered in real life data: there is a single outlier with a massive genome size, which compresses the rest of the data points over to the left and makes it difficult to see the patterns. We could fix this by manually setting the x axis limits, but it's probably easier to use pandas to filter the dataframe and exclude very large genomes:

```python
# filtered_size_genes_scatter.py

sns.relplot(
    data=euk[euk["Size (Mb)"] < 5000],
    x="Size (Mb)",
    y="Number of genes"
)

plt.title("Genome size vs number of genes\n for genomes < 5000 Mb")
```

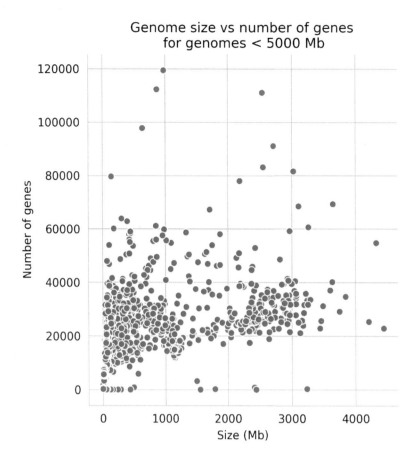

Genome size vs number of genes
for genomes < 5000 Mb

Excluding the outliers makes the relationships in the other data points easier to see.

This style of specifying the data that we want to plot might seem strange at first (though it will be familiar to users of R's **ggplot** package). Rather than giving **relplot** a collection of X and Y values to plot, instead we give it the whole dataframe and then specify which columns we want to determine the X and Y positions of each point.

The benefits of this way of thinking about plots become clear when we start mapping other properties. By setting the **hue** argument we can specify which column we want to determine the color of each point. Here's another plot of size versus number of genes, this time limited to animals and with the GC percentage represented by hue. Due to a quirk in the way that seaborn picks color scales, it's best to remove any rows with missing data before plotting our data:

```
# hue_scatter.py

animals = (
    euk[euk["Kingdom"] == "Animals"].dropna()
)

sns.relplot(
    data=animals,
    x="Size (Mb)",
    y="Number of genes",
    hue="GC%"
)

plt.title("Genome size vs number of genes\n for animal genomes")
```

6 Introduction to Seaborn

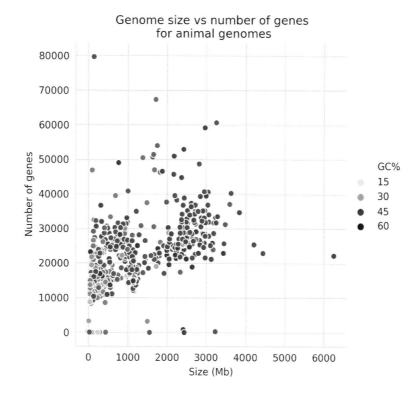

Genome size vs number of genes
for animal genomes

If we pick our mapping carefully, this lets us see multiple relationships between variables in a single plot. Unsurprisingly, larger genomes have more genes, and tend to have more moderate GC percentages - all the extremes of GC percentage (i.e. very light or dark colors) are over to the left of the chart.

Another property that we can map is `size`. Let's plot number of genes versus number of proteins and have the size of each point determined by the size of the genome. We will reuse the filtered `animals` dataframe that we created in the previous example:

```python
# point_size_scatter.py

sns.relplot(
    data=animals,
    x="Number of genes",
    y="Number of proteins",
    size="Size (Mb)",
    sizes=(2, 150),
)
plt.title("Number of genes vs number of proteins\n for animal genomes")
```

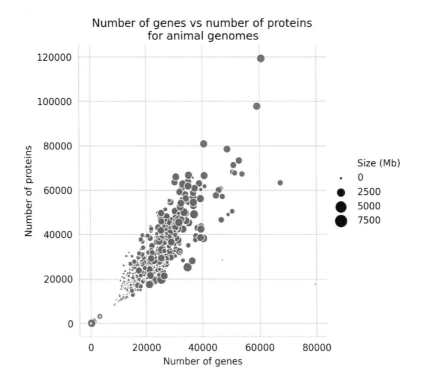

Number of genes vs number of proteins
for animal genomes

Note that when we use `size`, we usually also want to set the `sizes` argument which determines the minimum and maximum sizes that we want for our points. This plot does quite a good job of showing the key relationships - number of genes and number of proteins are very strongly correlated, and genome size tends to increase with them both.

There's nothing to prevent us from using `size` and `hue` together:

```
# complex_scatter.py

sns.relplot(
    data=animals,
    x="Number of genes",
    y="Number of proteins",
    size="Size (Mb)",
    sizes=(2, 150),
    hue="Publication year",
)
plt.title("Number of genes vs number of proteins\n for animal genomes")
```

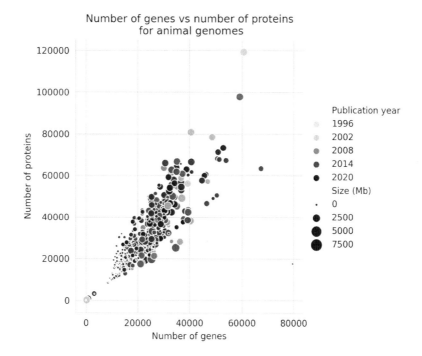

Number of genes vs number of proteins
for animal genomes

But we should show restraint, as the more details we try to fit onto a chart the harder it is to interpret. The relative importance of the different point properties is determined by the way that our vision works. Research has shown that we find it easiest to see patterns in the position of the points (X and Y), followed by the size and finally the hue, so take this into account when deciding which variables to map to which properties.

Remember that the starting point for all of these plots is a pandas dataframe, so we still have access to all the pandas tools that we saw previously. To plot something like gene density, which is not part of the original file, we just need to add it as a new column first:

```
# gene_density_scatter.py

# create gene density column
animals["Genes per Kb"] = animals["Number of genes"] / animals["Size (Mb)"] * 1000

sns.relplot(
    data=animals,
    x="Size (Mb)",
    y="Genes per Kb",
    color="purple",
)

plt.title("Genome size vs gene density\n for animal genomes")
```

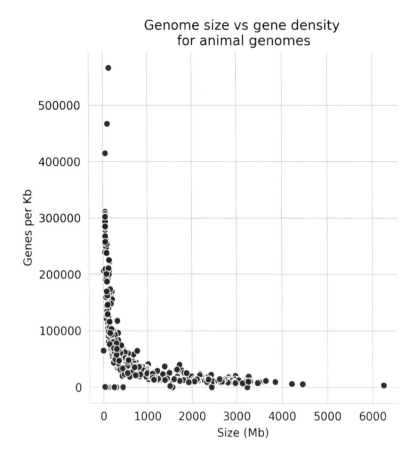

Genome size vs gene density
for animal genomes

We know from our previous plots that there's a strong positive correlation between genome size and number of genes, but this plot tells us that the pattern is reversed for gene density. Large genomes may have more genes, but they also have a lot more intergenic DNA! Although this result isn't particularly surprising, it's reassuring to see it in such a clear figure.

7 Special types of scatter plots

The options outlined in the examples above will take care of most scatter plots, at least until we start dealing with categorical data (which we will do in a later chapter). There are a few situations, however, which require slightly more specialized scatter plots.

7.0.1 Plotting large numbers of points

The first of these arises when we have a datset with a very large number of points. We haven't encountered this problem in our eukaryote genome data, so let's look at our genome assembly contigs dataset. This is a plain CSV file with no missing data, so we can load it using `read_csv` without any extra arguments. We will store it in a variable called `con` so that we don't get it mixed up with our other dataset:

```
con = pd.read_csv("contigs.csv")
con.head()
```

	name	length	GC	coverage	phylum
0	scaffold1_size1534183	1534183	0.4304	0.603315	Bacteroidetes
1	scaffold2_size1255804	1255804	0.4237	1.266944	Bacteroidetes
2	scaffold3_size1208507	1208507	0.5007	0.364660	Armatimonadetes
3	scaffold4_size1204010	1204010	0.4281	0.499764	Bacteroidetes
4	scaffold5_size1189196	1189196	0.4942	0.320681	Proteobacteria

This dataset has many more rows than the eukaryote one:

```
len(con)
```

```
22497
```

Let's try to visualize the relationship between GC content and length (note that for this dataset the GC is measured as a *content*, between 0 and 1, whereas in the previous one it was measured as a *percentage* between 0 and 100):

```
# all_contigs.py

g = sns.relplot(data=con, x="GC", y="length")
plt.title("GC content vs length for all contigs", pad=20)
```

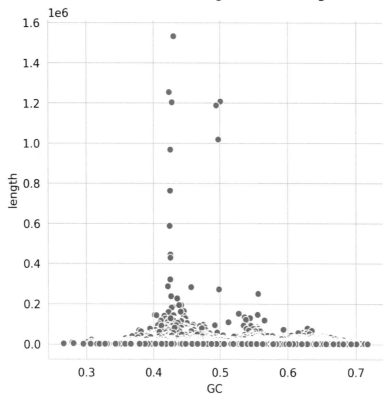

GC content vs length for all contigs

The first thing we notice is the presence of outliers - a small number of very long contigs. Just as we did before, we can use pandas to filter these out in order to better see the distribution of the rest of the data:

```
# filtered_contigs.py

sns.relplot(
    data=con[con["length"] < 100_000],
    x="GC",
    y="length"
)

plt.title("GC content vs length\nfor contigs < 100 Kb", pad=20)
```

7 Special types of scatter plots

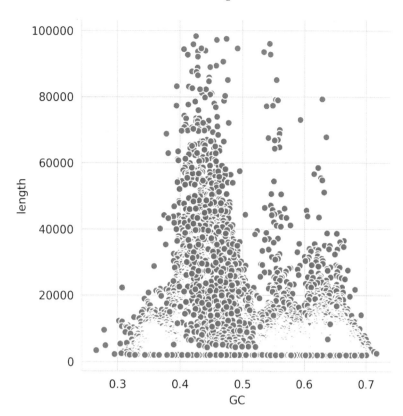

GC content vs length
for contigs < 100 Kb

There is clearly some structure in this plot, but the sheer number of points being plotted make it hard to see. There are simply too many points on top of each other.

There are a few ways to cope with this. One option is to set the points to be transparent using the **alpha** argument:

```
# transparent_contigs.py

sns.relplot(
    data=con[con["length"] < 100_000],
    x="GC",
    y="length",
    alpha=0.01
)

plt.title("GC content vs length\nfor contigs < 100 Kb", pad=20)
```

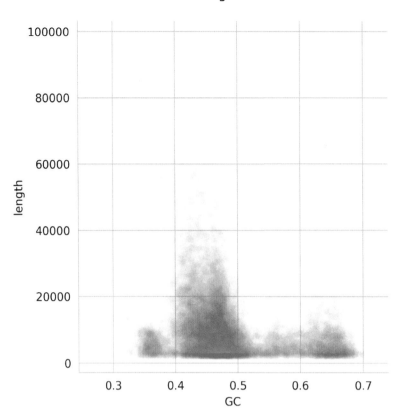

GC content vs length
for contigs < 100 Kb

Setting the points to be 99% transparent turns the circles into a fuzzy cloud, and makes it possible to discern some structure that we couldn't see before. It certainly looks like there are several populations of contigs with different ranges of GC and length.

A similar idea is to shrink the points, which we can do by setting the **s** parameter (**s** is short for *size* - remember from earlier that the `size` parameter is used when we want the size of points to vary). We will also have to remove the border around each point by setting its line width to zero:

```
# small_points_contigs.py

sns.relplot(
    data=con[con["length"] < 100_000],
    x="GC",
    y="length",
    s=1,
    linewidth=0
)
plt.title("GC content vs length\nfor contigs < 100 Kb", pad=20)
```

7 Special types of scatter plots

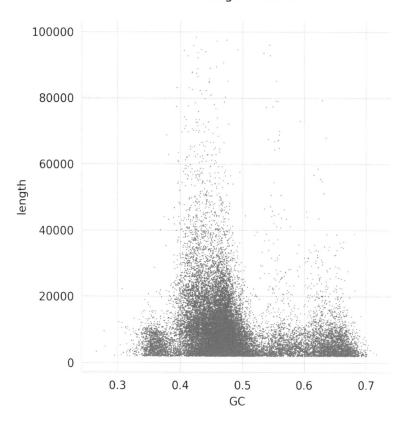

GC content vs length
for contigs < 100 Kb

Another option when we have too many points is to plot just a sample. There's no option to do that in seaborn, but luckily it is easy using pandas:

```
# sampled_contigs.py

sns.relplot(
    data=con[con["length"] < 100_000].sample(1000),
    x="GC",
    y="length"
)

plt.title(
    "GC content vs length for a random sample\n of 1000 contigs < 100 Kb",
    pad=20, # allow a bit more space for a two line title
)
```

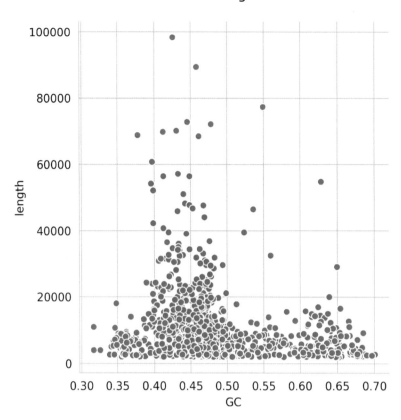

GC content vs length for a random sample
of 1000 contigs < 100 Kb

These first three approaches still use scatter plots, where individual data points are drawn. To get away from this, we could imagine dividing up the area of the chart into different regions and shading them based on the number of points in the area. This gives us a slightly more exotic type of chart - a *hexbin*. We can draw one in seaborn using `jointplot` with the `kind=hex` argument:

```
# just contigs less than 100Kb
g = sns.jointplot(
    data=con[con["length"] < 100_000],
    x="GC",
    y="length",
    kind="hex",
    gridsize=30,  # how many hexes wide and high
)

# set a supertitle for the figure
g.fig.suptitle("GC content vs length for all contigs < 100 Kb", y=1.05)
```

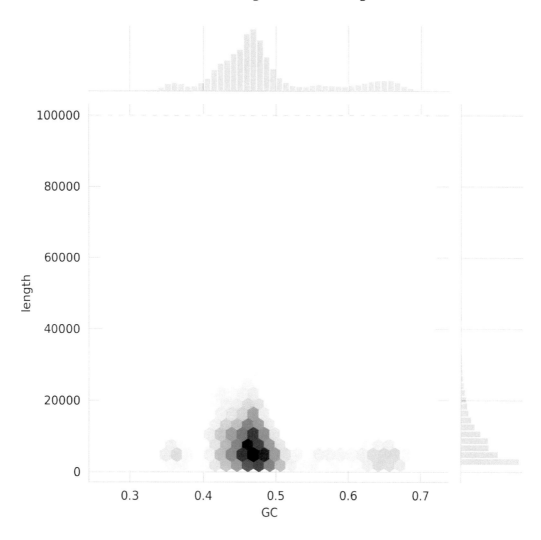

Notice how for this plot, our usual approach of using `plt.title` to set a title doesn't work. For reasons that we'll cover in a later chapter, we have to store the result of the plot, use the `fig` attribute to get a reference to the figure, then call `suptitle` to make a supertitle.

Think of it as the two dimensional equivalent of a histogram. Just as the height of each bar in a histogram tells us how many values fall into that range, the color of each cell above tells us how many points fall into the region. The marginal histograms show us the distribution for each axis separately.

This hexbin plot nicely illustrates one of its weaknesses: the outliers with large size effectively disappear from the chart, as there aren't enough of them in any one hex to raise its density above the background level. This is a fundamental trade off that we see in many types of plots - being able to visualize large datasets generally means that we give up the ability to see individual points.

Given that we can't actually see any data above about 40000 on the y axis, we may as well exclude those contigs by making our pandas filter more stringent:

```
# hexplot.py

# just contigs less than 40Kb
g = sns.jointplot(
    data=con[con["length"] < 40000],
    x="GC",
    y="length",
    kind="hex",
    gridsize=30,  # how many hexes wide and high
)
# set a supertitle for the figure
g.fig.suptitle("GC content vs length for all contigs < 40 Kb", y=1.05)
```

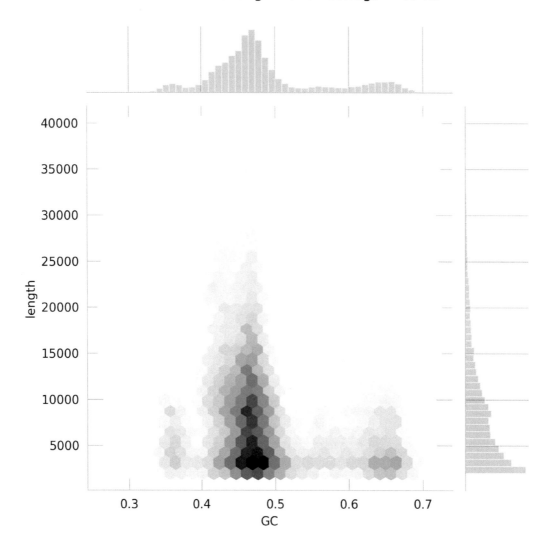

GC content vs length for all contigs < 40 Kb

Which allows us to see the bulk of the data at a higher level of detail.

If a hexbin is the two dimensional equivalent of a histogram, then the KDE is the two dimensional equivalent of the KDE line that we saw earlier in `distplot`. To draw a KDE plot (probably more commonly called a *contour plot*) we call the `jointplot` function with `kind=kde`:

```
# kdeplot.py

# just contigs less than 40Kb
g = sns.jointplot(
    data=con[con["length"] < 40000],
    x="GC",
    y="length",
    kind="kde",
    n_levels=10,
    shade=False,
    color="red",
)
g.fig.suptitle(
    "Contour plot of GC content vs length\n for all contigs < 40 Kb", y=1.05
)
```

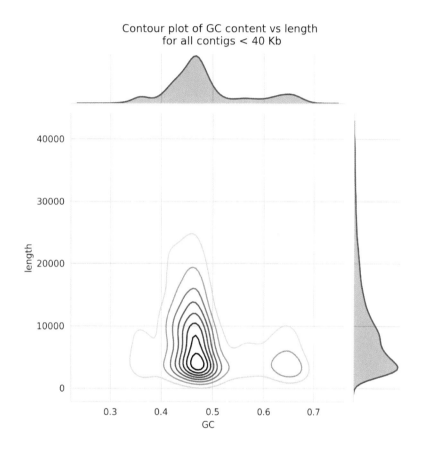

This type of plot can take a long time to draw, as there's a lot of computation going on to estimate the underlying distribution of the data. For styling a contour plot there are two main approaches: with **shade=False** as above we can just draw the contour lines, which tends to work well with a small number of contours (specified by the **n_levels** argument).

Alternatively, with **shade=True** we can specify a color map using **cmap** and draw shaded contours. This usually benefits from a few more levels:

```
# shaded_kdeplot.py

# just contigs less than 40Kb
g = sns.jointplot(
    data=con[con["length"] < 40000],
    x="GC",
    y="length",
    kind="kde",
    n_levels=20,
    shade=True,
    cmap="OrRd",
)
g.fig.suptitle(
    "Contour plot of GC content vs length\n for all contigs < 40 Kb", y=1.05
)
```

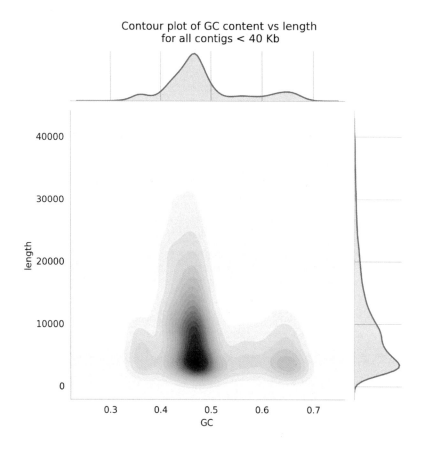

By using the `gist_earth` color map we can make our contig data look like an island, with lush green plains and a snowcapped mountain:

```
# just contigs less than 40Kb
g = sns.jointplot(
    data=con[con["length"] < 40000],
    x="GC",
    y="length",
    kind="kde",
    n_levels=20,
    shade=True,
    cmap="gist_earth",
)
g.fig.suptitle(
    "Island plot of GC content vs length\n for all contigs < 40 Kb", y=1.05
)
```

7 Special types of scatter plots

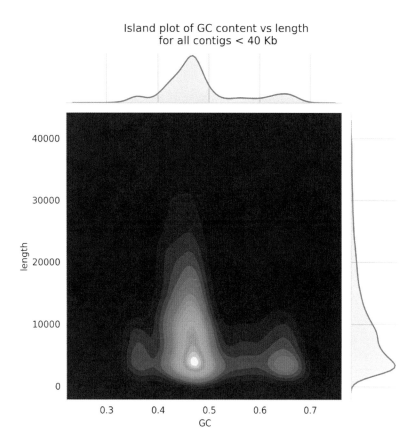

Island plot of GC content vs length
for all contigs < 40 Kb

But this should probably be reserved as a novelty for the lab wall!

7.0.2 Plotting regression lines and confidence intervals

Although seaborn is not a statistics package, it does carry out a few statistical methods for the purposes of visualizion. The various regression functions don't deal well with missing data or integers, so to avoid errors we'll first make a copy of our data with all integer columns converted to floating point, and all missing data removed. We will also filter this copy to remove the very large outlier genomes that were troubling us before:

```
euk_float = euk[euk["Size (Mb)"] < 4_000].dropna()
euk_float["Number of genes"] = euk_float["Number of genes"].astype(float)
euk_float["Number of proteins"] = euk_float["Number of proteins"].astype(float)
euk_float["Publication year"] = euk_float["Publication year"].astype(float)
euk_float.info()
```

```
<class 'pandas.core.frame.DataFrame'>
Int64Index: 2365 entries, 0 to 8298
Data columns (total 9 columns):
 #   Column              Non-Null Count  Dtype
---  ------              --------------  -----
 0   Species             2365 non-null   string
 1   Kingdom             2365 non-null   string
 2   Class               2365 non-null   string
 3   Size (Mb)           2365 non-null   float64
 4   GC%                 2365 non-null   float64
 5   Number of genes     2365 non-null   float64
 6   Number of proteins  2365 non-null   float64
 7   Publication year    2365 non-null   float64
 8   Assembly status     2365 non-null   string
dtypes: float64(5), string(4)
memory usage: 184.8 KB
```

We'll use this floating point version of the dataset for all plots in this section.

The most obvious starting point is linear regression. For this we will use `lmplot` (short for *linear model plot*). The basic interface will be familiar from our discussion of `relplot`:

```
# linear_regression_plot.py

sns.lmplot(
    data=euk_float, x="Size (Mb)", y="Number of genes", height=7,
)

plt.title("Regression of size vs number of genes\nfor genomes < 4Gb")
```

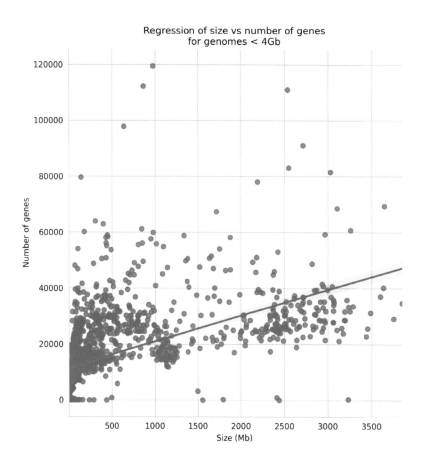

With this we get a regression line with shaded 95% confidence intervals. There are a few options that are commonly useful: setting `ci=None` turns off the confidence intervals (and speeds up plotting large datasets) and setting the `order` argument fits a polynomial regression:

```
# polynomial_regression_plot.py

sns.lmplot(
    data=euk_float,
    x="Size (Mb)",
    y="Number of genes",
    height=7,
    ci=None,
    order=2,
)

plt.title(
    "First order polynomial regression of size vs number of genes\nfor genomes < 4Gb"
)
```

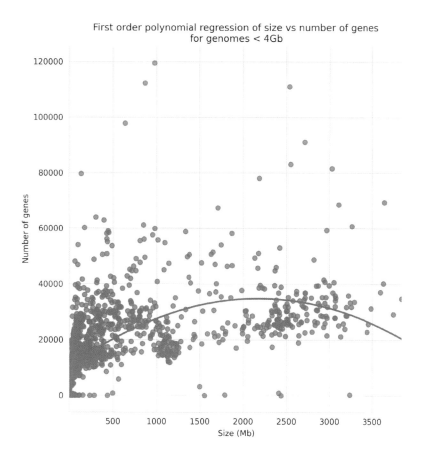

First order polynomial regression of size vs number of genes for genomes < 4Gb

An obvious question is how to get the actual results for the regression. There's no way to obtain these from the plot, but it's not hard to do using `scipy`. We have to make sure to use our floating point version of the data:

```
from scipy import stats

stats.linregress(
    euk_float["Size (Mb)"], euk_float["Number of genes"],
)
```

```
LinregressResult(slope=9.241624440044749, intercept=11703.969342377162, rvalue=0.5834836793744449, pvalue
=7.717426152313987e-216, stderr=0.2646126179180758)
```

From the object that's returned by the `stats.linregress` function we can get the slope, intercept and p-value.

7.0.3 Plotting pairwise relationships

Our final special case is where we need to plot pairwise relationships. This typically happens when starting to look at a new dataset, either to identify variables that might be worth examining in more detail, or as a quick sanity check to look for obvious correlations that shouldn't be there.

The `pairplot` function will take a dataframe and draw scatter plots for all pairs of numerical variables. This typically creates a large figure, so we often want to make the individual charts smaller, and the point size smaller. The arguments that do this (`height` and `plot_kws`) will be discussed properly in a later chapter.

```
# pair_plot.py

g = sns.pairplot(
    data=euk_float,
    plot_kws={"s": 5},  # draw small points
    height=1.5,  # make the individual plots small
)
g.fig.suptitle(
    "Pairwise relationships in the eukaryote genome dataset", y=1.05
)
```

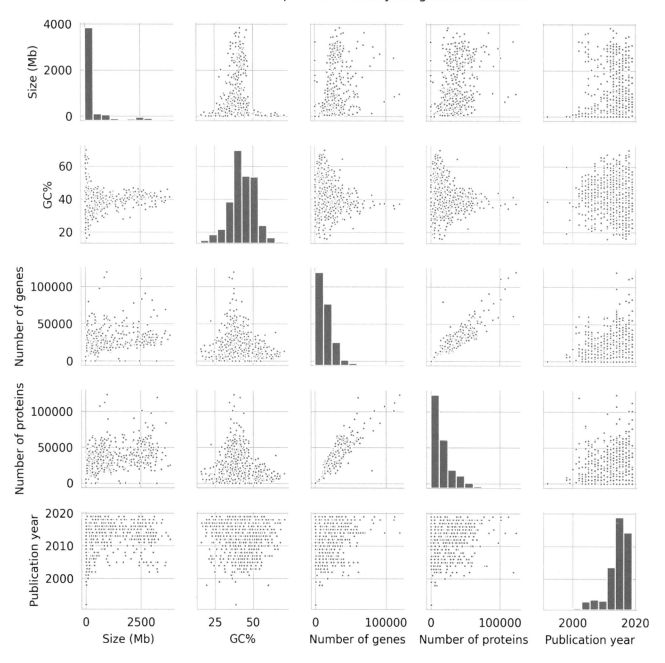

Pairwise relationships in the eukaryote genome dataset

For our eukaryotic genome dataset, this plot shows a number of relationships that we already know about, like the correlation between genome size and number of genes/proteins, and the very strong correlation between number of genes and number of proteins. We can also see that genomes with large sizes/numbers of genes/numbers of proteins tend to have moderate GC percentages, and to have been sequenced more recently (a reasonable pattern, given the rising availability of sequencing technology).

Given the small size of the plots, it's often helpful to draw a regression line to make the patterns clearer. With large numbers of points, it's nice to have the regression line drawn in a different color, to make it easier to see against the background of the points. A neutral, light color gives a good effect, deemphasizing the points to make the regression line stand out. Just like with our individual regression plots, we have to use the floating point version of the data:

```
# styled_pair_plot.py

g = sns.pairplot(
    data=euk_float,
    kind="reg",
    plot_kws={"scatter_kws": {"color": "lightgrey", "s": 5}},
    height=1.5,
)

g.fig.suptitle("Pairwise regressions in the eukaryote genome dataset", y=1.05)
```

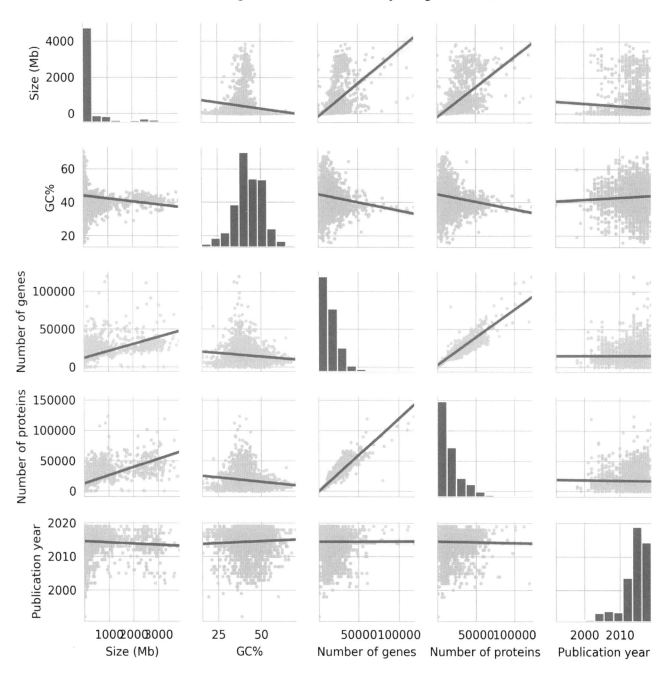

Pairwise regressions in the eukaryote genome dataset

Note one complication when passing the `color` argument - it needs to be in a two level dictionary, as it has to be passed from `pairplot` to `regplot`, and then from `regplot` to the matplotlib `scatter` function. We'll explain these special arguments in the chapter on styling charts.

As well as confirming the patterns we've already noticed, the regression lines make a few others clear. There's a definite negative correlation between GC percentage and genes/proteins/size. And although it's true that the very largest genomes were sequenced recently, there isn't a strong correlation between year and size - if anything the overall correlation is negative, probably due to the fact that modern DNA sequencing technology makes it very cheap to sequence small genomes.

We also have a nice example here of a pattern that simple linear regression fails to identify: the tendency for large genomes to have moderate GC levels. This illustrates the value of having the points and the regression plotted together - glancing just at the slope of the regression line we might conclude that nothing interesting was going on. Switching to a polynomial regression line with `order=2` does a better job of capturing the pattern:

```python
# polynomial_pair_polot.py

g = sns.pairplot(
    data=euk_float,
    kind="reg",
    plot_kws={"scatter_kws": {"color": "lightgrey", "s": 5}, "order": 2},
    height=1.5,
)
g.fig.suptitle(
    "Pairwise polynomial regressions in the eukaryote genome dataset", y=1.05
)
```

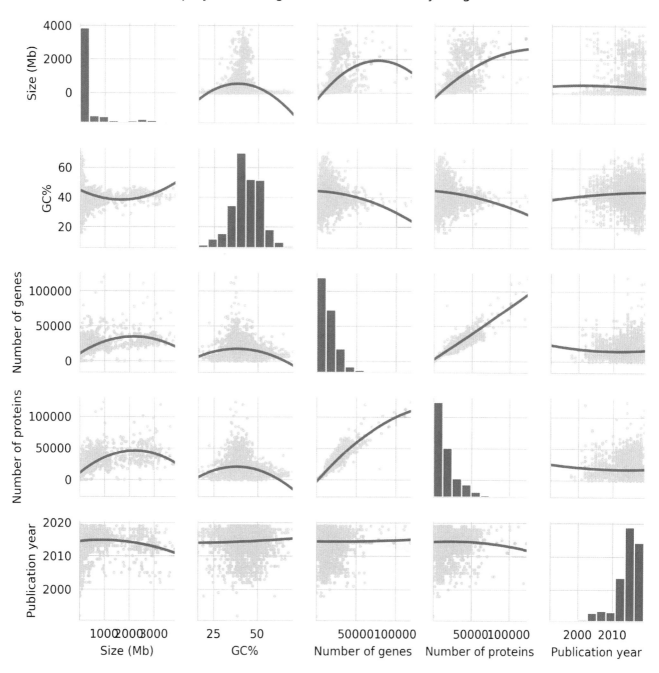

Pairwise polynomial regressions in the eukaryote genome dataset

8 Conditioning charts on categories

In the previous few chapters we have explored the ability of seaborn to draw scatter plots showing various combinations of continuous numerical variables. Here's a recent example which varies both the size and the color of the markers:

```
# select just animals and remove missing data
animals = euk[euk["Kingdom"] == "Animals"].dropna()

sns.relplot(
    data=animals,
    x="Number of genes",
    y="Number of proteins",
    size="Size (Mb)",
    sizes=(2, 150),
    hue="Publication year",
)
plt.title("Number of genes vs number of proteins\n for animal genomes")
```

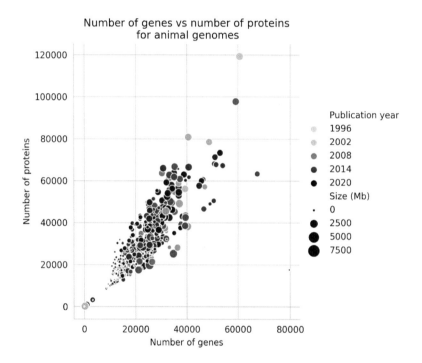

A useful way of thinking about these scatter plots is that each point has four properties - the X position, the Y position, the color and the size - which we can use to represent different properties of the data.

All our examples so far have used continuous numerical columns for these four properties. Let's see what happens if we map `hue` to a categorical variable (leaving size to represent genome size):

```
# category_hue.py
animals = euk[euk["Kingdom"] == "Animals"].dropna()

sns.relplot(
    data=animals,
    x="Number of genes",
    y="Number of proteins",
    size="Size (Mb)",
    sizes=(2, 150),
    hue="Class",
)
plt.title(
    "Number of genes vs number of proteins\n for animal genomes in different classes"
)
```

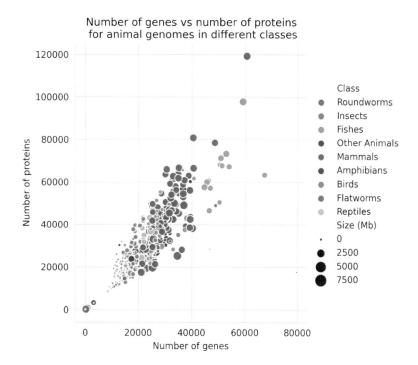

The resulting plot is pretty much what we'd expect: each different value in the **class** column gets assigned a different color. Notice that by default, seaborn picks a categorical palette i.e. one where adjacent classes have very different colors.

So the `hue` argument can be used to represent either a continuous variable or a categorical one. What about our other properties? Well, nothing will stop us using `x` or `y` with categorical variables:

```
# category_axis.py

sns.relplot(
    data=animals,
    y="Class",
    x="Number of genes",
    size="Size (Mb)",
    sizes=(2, 150),
)
plt.title("Number of genes \n for animal genomes in different classes")
```

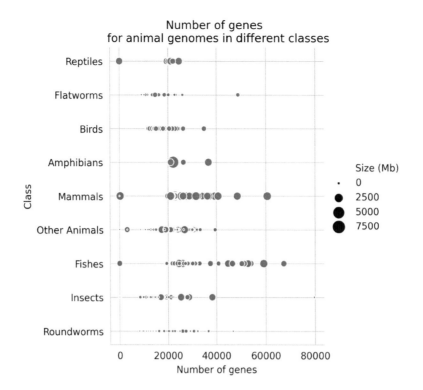

But the results tend not to be very informative unless we have very few points. This type of chart is trying to show a completely different type of relationship: rather than looking at the relationship between number of genes and number of proteins, it's showing differences in number of genes across classes. There are much better choices for displaying these data, which we will look at in detail in a future chapter.

We can also use size to represent categories, but in most cases it's not helpful:

```
# category_size.py

sns.relplot(
    data=animals,
    x="Number of genes",
    y="Number of proteins",
    size="Class",
    sizes=(2, 150),
)
plt.title(
    "Number of genes vs number of proteins\n for animal genomes in different classes"
)
```

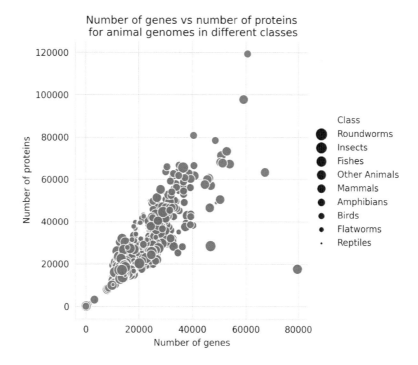

Number of genes vs number of proteins
for animal genomes in different classes

Not only do we find it very difficult to tell the difference on the chart between points of similar size, but the legend is actively misleading. It suggests that, for example, insects and fishes are similar because they have similar sizes, when in fact the order of classes is determined by the order in which they appear in the data. It's way too easy to glance at this legend and get confused into thinking that roundworms have the most genomes, which pandas will easily tell us is wrong:

```
animals["Class"].value_counts()
```

```
Insects          155
Mammals          137
Birds             82
Fishes            72
Other Animals     63
Roundworms        63
Flatworms         21
Reptiles          16
Amphibians         4
Name: Class, dtype: Int64
```

From these examples we see that color is uniquely flexible when it comes to displaying data; depending on the palette it can represent numerical or categorical data equally well.

So if `x`, `y` and `size` are not good for representing categories, what other options do we have besides `hue`? When using `relplot` we can use the marker styles, as long as the number of categories isn't too large. Here we'll use pandas to select just two classes, then assign the **class** column to the `style` argument:

```
# category_style.py

my_genomes = euk[euk["Class"].isin(["Birds", "Fishes"])]

sns.relplot(
    data=my_genomes,
    x="Number of genes",
    y="Number of proteins",
    style="Class",
)
plt.title("Number of genes vs number of proteins\n for bird and fish genomes")
```

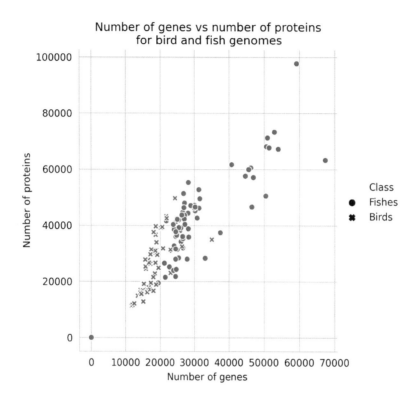

In this plot the two marker styles are sufficient to show the pattern that fish genomes tend to have more genes and proteins than bird genomes, though there's some overlap.

Perhaps the most powerful way to split up our data into categories is simply to draw multiple charts with the same axes. This approach has many names (different tools refer to it as a *trellis*, *lattice* or *grid chart*) but here we will call it *small multiples*. We can draw these in seaborn by assigning column names to the `row` and `col` argument to `relplot`.

Here are the same data as in the previous example, but with different classes side by side:

```
# col_scatter_plot.py

g = sns.relplot(
    data=my_genomes, x="Number of genes", y="Number of proteins", col="Class",
)

g.fig.suptitle("Number of genes vs. number of proteins", y=1.05)
```

8 Conditioning charts on categories

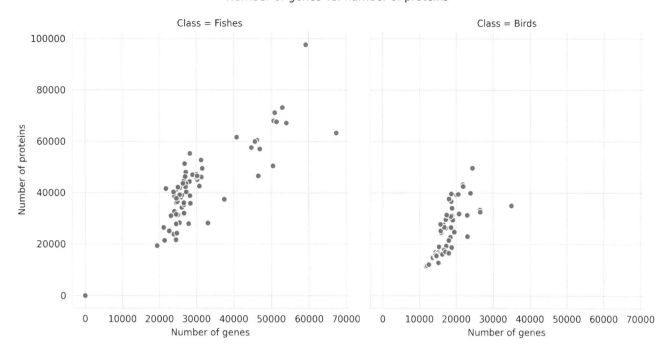

Number of genes vs. number of proteins

Because the two plots share the same axes, it's easy to compare them. Notice that now each plot gets its own title telling us which class it's displaying, so to display an overall title we need to call **suptitle** on the figure. In fact, **relplot** always creates a grid of plots, even when we draw a single plot. This is the reason behind the variable name **g** that we use for the return value. When using a supertitle, we have to tell seaborn how much space we want between the charts and the title by setting the **y** argument. The value of **1.05** which we've used above usually looks good, but we can increase it if we want more spacing.

If we set **col** and **row** separately, we'll get a two dimensional grid. Let's complare animal and plant genomes assembled into chromosomes or scaffolds. The filter is quite complicated now, so we'll do it on a separate line.

```
# grid_plot.py

data = euk[
    (euk["Kingdom"].isin(["Plants", "Animals"]))
    & (euk["Assembly status"].isin(["Chromosome", "Scaffold"]))
    & (euk["Size (Mb)"] < 5000)
    ]

g = sns.relplot(
    data=data,
    x="Size (Mb)",
    y="Number of proteins",
    col="Kingdom",
    row="Assembly status",
    aspect=1.5,
    height=3,
    s=10,
)

g.fig.suptitle("Size vs. number of proteins for plant and animal genomes", y=1.05)
```

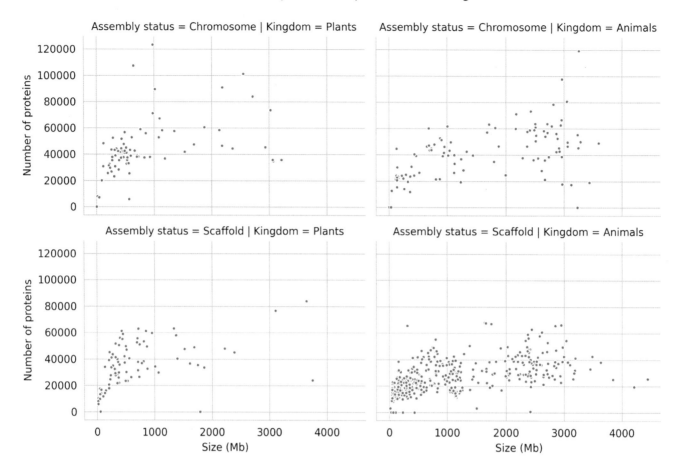

Size vs. number of proteins for plant and animal genomes

Often when drawing small multiples we explicitly set a few style options to get the charts looking acceptable. In the example above we've set the shape and size of each plot, and made the marker size smaller than usual to allow for the smaller area of the plots. Small multiples are good for showing a range of different patterns in a single plot. In the above figure we can see:

- The overall relationship between genome size and number of proteins
- Whether that relationship is affected by either status or kingdom
- The distribution of genome size and number of proteins in the four different categories
- The number of samples that fall into the four different categories

Thus we can point out that there is generally a positive correlation between genome size and number of proteins, that animals in chromosome status (top right) seem to have a higher proportion of large genomes, and that the highest number of genomes belong to animals and are assembled into scaffolds (bottom right).

A useful trick when we want to display small multiples using a single category that has a large number of variables is to wrap columns. This works particularly well when the values have a natural order. For example, the **year** column behaves like a category in that it takes a number of descrete values, but those values have an obvious ordering. Trying to display 20 separate plots - one for each year - on a single row has obvious drawbacks, but if we specify `col_wrap` then we can limit each row to a sensible number of charts:

```
# wrapped_columns.py

g = sns.relplot(
    data=data,
    x="Size (Mb)",
    y="Number of proteins",
    col="Publication year",
    col_wrap=4,
    hue="Assembly status",
    height=2,
    s=20,
)

g.fig.suptitle(
    """Size vs. number of proteins for plant and animal genomes
in different years""",
    y=1.05,
)
```

Size vs. number of proteins for plant and animal genomes
in different years

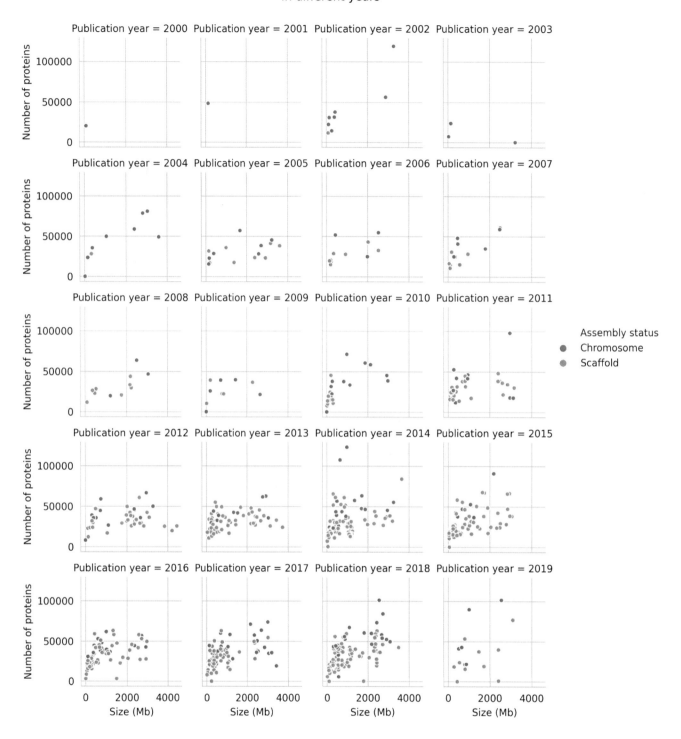

This time using color to represent status we can see that while the overall relationship between genome size and number of genes hasn't changed over the years, genomes sequenced after about 2005 are more likely to be in scaffold status. We can also see the general increase in the numbers of genomes sequenced over time. As I write this, it's halfway through 2019, which explains the apparent drop in sample size in the last chart!

Theoretically, we could use `col`, `row`, `hue`, `style` and `size` on a single chart to display five separate categories, but in practice such dense charts are rarely useful.

We can use the same three conditional variables (`row`, `col` and `hue`) with `lmplot` to draw separate regression lines for each group:

```
# grid_regression_plot.py

g = sns.lmplot(
    data=data,
    x="GC%",
    y="Number of proteins",
    col="Kingdom",
    hue="Assembly status",
)
g.fig.suptitle(
    """Linear regression of GC% vs. number of proteins
for plant and animal genomes""",
    y=1.05,
)
```

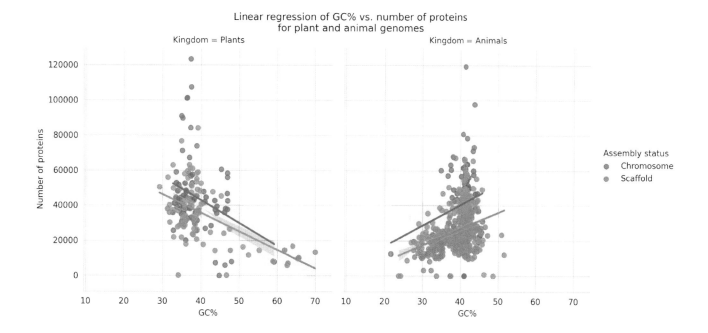

Recall from our earlier examples that when looking at the entire dataset, number of proteins was not particularly strongly correlated with GC percentage. The chart above shows that within animal and plant genomes, the correlation is strong, but goes the opposite way in each group. Further dividing by status and looking at the confidence intervals illustrates that the correlation is more robust for genomes in the scaffold status (though this is likely simply due to the bigger sample size; we must be careful when comparing regressions on unbalanced groups).

The above pair of plots show what might be considered a drawback of using small multiples. Because the x axis is shared between the plots, the range has to accommodate all points. This can often lead to quite a bit of empty space. In our figure, the highest plant GC is around 70%, so that's our X axis maximum. But the highest animal GC is only around 50%, so there's an empty space on the right side of the animals chart.

Although it might seem like wasted space, it's better than the alternative - if we allowed the axes to have independent ranges then it would be very difficult to compare the two plots, which is the whole point of using small multiples in the first place!

9 Categorical axes with seaborn

In the previous few chapters we have looked at several different chart types that seaborn can produce, starting with the basic scatter plot, and moving on to regression plots, contour plots, and hexbin plots. Although these are all distinct plot types, they all belong to the same family - charts that are intended to show how two continuous variables are jointly distributed. These charts fundamentally help us to answer questions about the relationships between two variables, which can be a simple case of correlation or a more complicated pattern. With the mapping of other variables to properties like color and style, and with the use of small multiples to divide the dataset up into groups, we can also tell how the relationships differ between groups.

In this chapter we will discuss the other major family of seaborn chart types: those that primarily allow us to look at how distributions of values differ between groups. Here we find well known chart types like box plots and bar charts, along with less commonly used types like swarm and violin plots. What all of these types have in common is that one axis is a category and the other is a continuous variable.

9.1 Types of categorical plots

Given the relatively large number of different chart types with a categorical axis, it's useful to have some organizing framework. So for this chapter we will follow the lead of the excellent seaborn tutorial, and divide the types up according to what is actually being plotted for each category. For small datasets, it may be possible to plot every data point, giving us either a *strip plot* or a *swarm plot*. Where there are too many points to plot every one, we can resort to plotting a distribution in the form of a *box*, *violin* or *boxen* plot. And for very large datasets, or those with a large number of categories, we can plot just a point estimate of the value for each category along with some measure of the variability, giving us a *bar* or *point* plot.

For the examples in this chapter we will mostly concentrate on exploring the uses of the different chart types, so we'll just concentrate on the most useful and interesting options for each rather than trying to exhaustively list the variants. We will use seaborn's defaults for most aspects of the appearance of each chart, other than occasionally changing color schemes for a bit of variety. We will take a detailed look at chart styles in a future chapter, with a particular emphasis on the role of color.

To enable us to concentrate on the charts themselves, we will limit ourselves to examples that just use the raw data without much processing, except to filter the data. Our main eukaryote genome dataset has only a few categorical variables to look at so many of our examples will be along the same themes. We will be able to explore more variations on categorical plots when we dive into more advanced processing with pandas in future chapters. To avoid repeating filters multiple times, we will first make a couple of filtered dataframes that we can reuse:

```
animals = euk[euk["Kingdom"] == "Animals"].dropna()

animals_and_plants = euk[
    (euk["Kingdom"].isin(["Animals", "Plants"])) & (euk["Size (Mb)"] < 5000)
].dropna()
```

9.2 Categorical scatter plots

The family of categorical charts that plot every point are sometimes known collectively as *categorical scatter plots*. We've actually seen an example of a categorical scatter plot already, when we experimented with passing a categorical column to `relplot`:

```
sns.relplot(
    data=animals, y="Class", x="Number of genes", aspect=2,
)
plt.title("Number of genes for animal genomes in different classes")
```

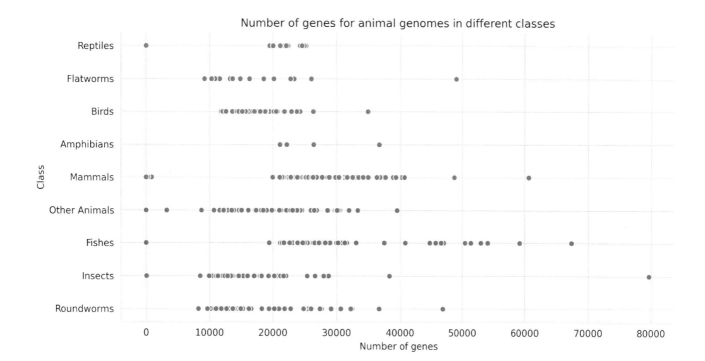

which we did mostly to establish that such charts aren't very useful as the data points tend to lie on top of one another.

9.2.1 Strip plots

To begin, let's try exactly the same function call with the `catplot` function (the name is short for *category plot*):

```
# strip_plot.py

sns.catplot(
    data=animals, y="Class", x="Number of genes", aspect=2,
)
plt.title("Number of genes for animal genomes in different classes")
```

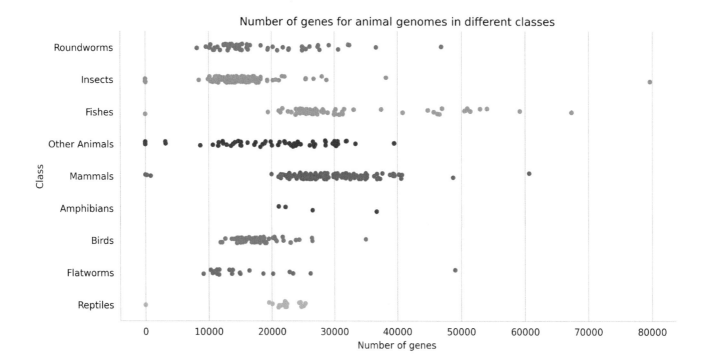

Number of genes for animal genomes in different classes

This is the default kind of categorical chart produced by `catplot` and is called a *strip plot*. It's instructive to see how seaborn attempts to display the same dataset when one of the axes is explicitly assumed to be categorical. The grid lines on the Y axis have disappeared, as the vertical spacing is now meaningless, and different colors have been automatically assigned to the different categories. The most noticable change is that seaborn has added some random noise to the Y position of each point in order to avoid points covering each other.

In the above example, this has not been entirely successful as there are too many points which are too closely grouped to avoid collisions. Despite this, there are still plenty of patterns that we can discern - it's clear from this chart that different classes of animals have different numbers of genes; that animals in the same class have somewhat similar numbers of genes; that most classes have at least some animals with no predicted genes; and that many classes have a small number of outliers with a very large number of predicted genes. This chart also tells us that the number of samples in each class is not equal: there are clearly more mammals than amphibians in our dataset.

For datasets with very small numbers of points, especially if the points are not tightly clustered, a strip plot can do a good job of separating the points, especially if we increase allowable amount of jitter. For example, just taking the animal genomes that have been assembled into chromosomes:

```
# jitter.py

sns.catplot(
    data=animals[animals["Assembly status"] == "Chromosome"],
    y="Class",
    x="Number of genes",
    aspect=2,
    jitter=0.3,
)
plt.title("Number of genes for scaffold animal genomes\n in different classes")
```

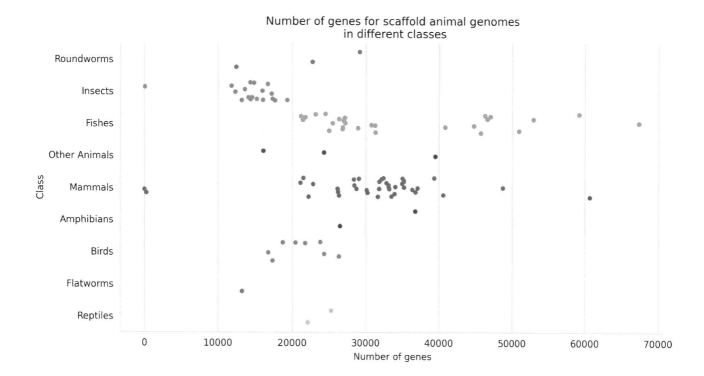

Number of genes for scaffold animal genomes in different classes

gives us a plot where it's just about possible to see every point. In both of these plots the order of the classes is determined simply by the order that they appear in the dataframe.

Just as we saw with `relplot`, `catplot` understands `hue`, `row` and `col` to map different categorical columns, so it's possible to further subdivide the data. Let's look at the sizes of the genomes sequenced in each year for plants and animals, using color to indicate the assembly status. We'll remove any outlier genomes larger than 5000 Mb in order to make the patterns easier to see. Just like when drawing small multiple plots with `relplot`, we need to set a title for the whole figure:

```
# grid_strip_plot.py

g = sns.catplot(
    data=animals_and_plants,
    x="Publication year",
    y="Size (Mb)",
    aspect=2,
    hue="Assembly status",
    row="Kingdom",
)

g.fig.suptitle(
    "Genome size for plants and animals in different assembly status", y=1.05
)
```

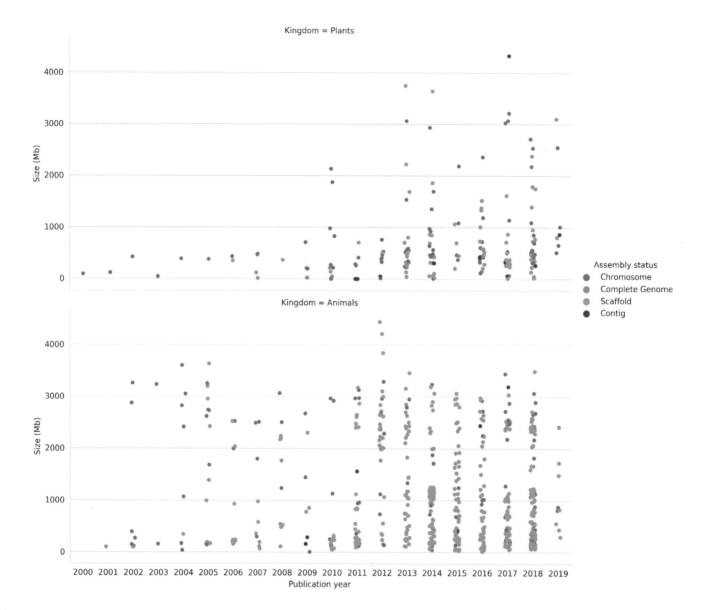

Genome size for plants and animals in different assembly status

Unlike in the previous example, here we've switched our categorical column to the X axis. Notice the difference in how our categorical columns are ordered: because **Publication year** has a numerical data type, seaborn automatically puts it in the correct order. In contrast, the order of the different assembly statuses is determined by the order in which they first appear in the data, and in fact is quite annoying. There's a natural ordering for assembly status from smallest chunks of sequence to biggest chunks (or from worst to best): it goes Contig -> Scaffold -> Chromosome -> Complete Genome. In a later chapter we'll see how to tell pandas about the order; for now we can enforce the order we want by setting the `hue_order` argument:

```
# ordered_grid_strip_plot.py

g = sns.catplot(
    data=animals_and_plants,   # workaround for https://github.com/mwaskom/seaborn/issues/1761
    x="Publication year",
    y="Size (Mb)",
    aspect=2,
    hue="Assembly status",
    hue_order=["Contig", "Scaffold", "Chromosome", "Complete Genome"],
    row="Kingdom",
)

g.fig.suptitle(
    "Genome size for plants and animals in different assembly status", y=1.05
)
```

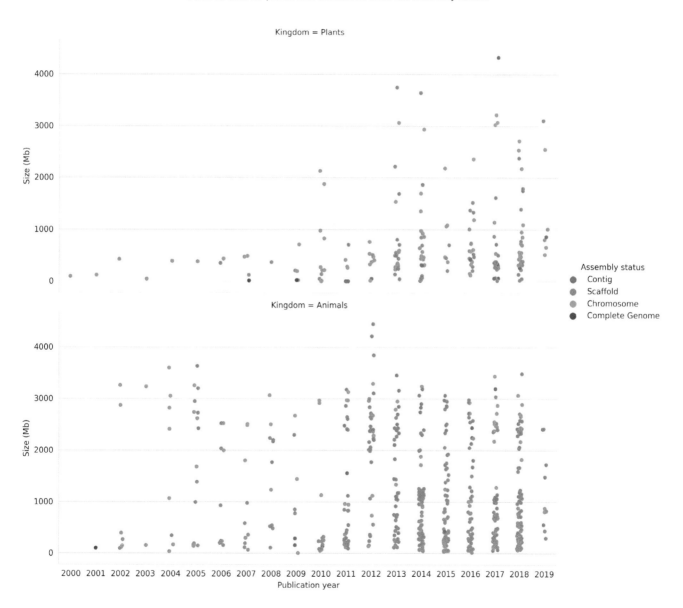

Now that we have fixed the order, this is a nice example of how seaborn's design makes it possible to set up a fairly sophisticated plot using very little code. We can see how the number of genomes has increased over time for both groups, though more dramatically for animals than plants. The average size of sequenced genomes has increased for plants, though not so much for animals. And the colors show us that the vast majority of animal genomes sequenced since about 2010 have been assembled to scaffold status, whereas there's much more variation in the status of plant genomes.

We might even notice that the animal genomes seem to fall into roughly two groups with either relatively high or low size, with a gap around 1000 to 2000 Mb. We might suspect that these two groups correspond to taxonomic groups, which we can easily test by switching color to represent class:

```
# taxonomy_plot.py

g = sns.catplot(
    data=animals_and_plants,
    x="Publication year",
    y="Size (Mb)",
    aspect=2,
    hue="Class",
    row="Kingdom",
    palette="Set2",
)

g.fig.suptitle("Genome size for plants and animals colored by class", y=1.05)
```

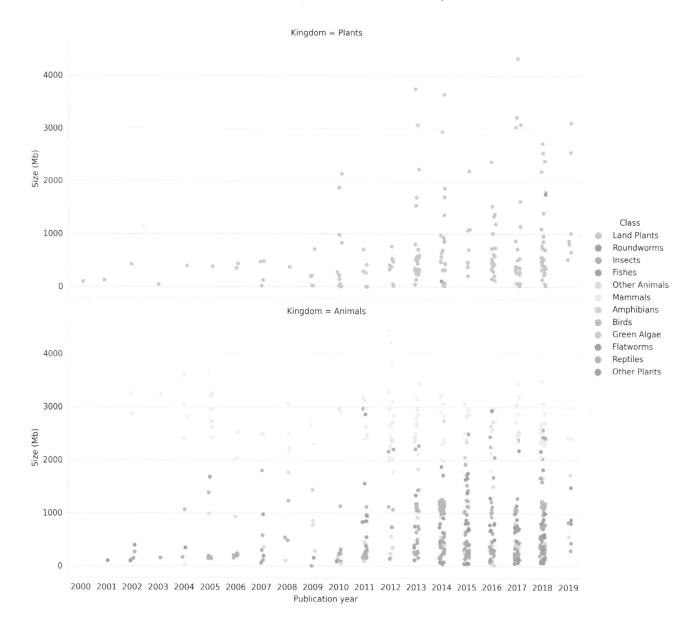

Genome size for plants and animals colored by class

This confirms our suspicion: the group of animal genomes greater than 2000 Mb corresponds mostly to mammals, whereas below 1000 Mb we find the other classes. Notice that seaborn has a bit of trouble finding enough colors to represent all the different classes, so some get recycled. Twelve groups are probably too many to represent with color.

9.2.2 Swarm plots

Our other option for plotting every point is a swarm plot, which we can get by passing `kind='swarm'` to the `catplot` function. Where a strip plot adds random noise to the points, a swarm plot uses a layout algorithm to try and prevent points overlapping. We can see the effect if we plot our animal chromosome genomes again:

```
# swarm_plot.py

sns.catplot(
    data=animals[animals["Assembly status"] == "Chromosome"],
    y="Class",
    x="Number of genes",
    aspect=2,
    kind="swarm",
)
plt.title("Number of genes for scaffold animal genomes in different classes")
```

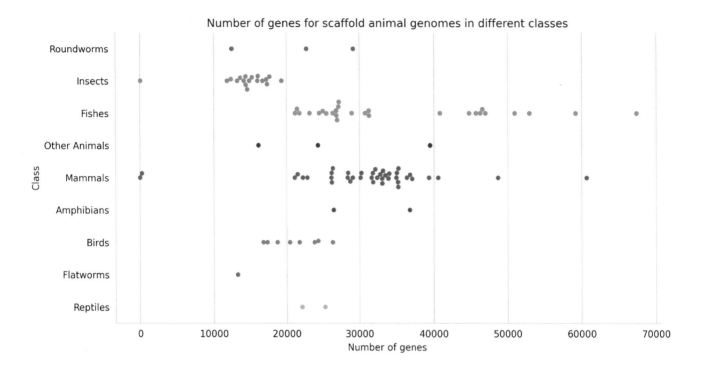

As with strip plots, swarm plots work best with small datasets where the points are not too tightly clustered. The way that the points are laid out gives us some insight into the distribution that might not be apparent in a strip plot. For example, above we can see that for mammals and fishes there are a few small collections of genomes that have very similar numbers of genes, represented by the points arranged in a vertical line. These are likely multiple genomes for the same species that have been annotated similarly.

We can make good use of color in swarm plots by setting `hue`. For example, let's compare the GC% of nematodes (roundworms) and platyhelminths (flatworms):

```
# hue_swarm_plot.py

sns.catplot(
    data=euk[euk["Class"].isin(["Roundworms", "Flatworms"])],
    x="Class",
    y="GC%",
    height=6,
    kind="swarm",
    hue="Assembly status",
    aspect=0.7,
    hue_order=["Contig", "Scaffold", "Chromosome", "Complete Genome"],
)

plt.title("GC% of roundworms and flatworms\nin different assembly status")
```

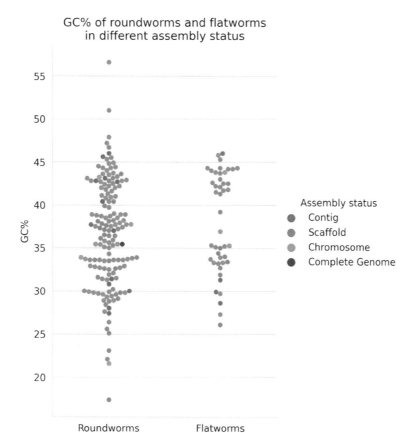

GC% of roundworms and flatworms
in different assembly status

By using hue to represent assembly status (notice that we have reused our `hue_order` list from a previous example) we get a nice overview of the distribution of GC percentages across both class and assembly status.

We can also use `row` and `col` with any of the charts that `catplot` can produce. Here's a small multiple plot comparing the distribution of genome sizes for mammals and birds for each year:

```
# grid_swarm_plot.py

g = sns.catplot(
    data=euk[euk["Class"].isin(["Mammals", "Birds"])],
    x="Class",
    y="Size (Mb)",
    height=2.5,
    kind="swarm",
    col="Publication year",
    col_wrap=5,
)
g.fig.suptitle(
    "Sizes of genomes for mammals and birds published in each year", y=1.05
)
```

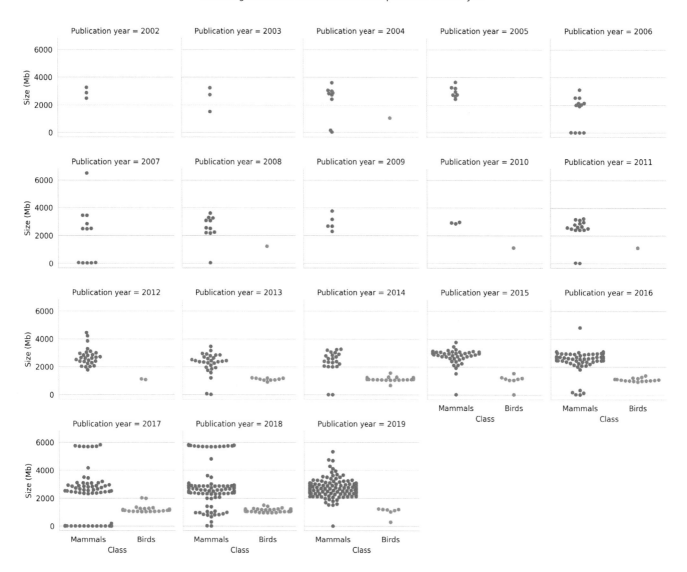

Sizes of genomes for mammals and birds published in each year

This chart illustrates both the benefits and drawbacks of the swarm plot approach. The main benefit is that by plotting every point we can see levels of detail that are absent from more abstract plots. For example, in 2017 and 2018 we can see a big line of mammal genomes with nearly identical sizes. We might guess that these belong to a single genome sequencing project, which we can check by counting the species:

```
(
    euk[
        (euk["Class"] == "Mammals")
        & (euk["Publication year"] == 2018)
    ]
    ["Species"]
    .value_counts()
)
```

```
Homo sapiens                                          51
Bos indicus x Bos taurus                               2
Tursiops truncatus                                     2
Bubalus bubalis                                        2
Phascolarctos cinereus                                 2
                                                      ..
Physeter catodon                                       1
Peromyscus maniculatus bairdii                         1
Neophocaena asiaeorientalis asiaeorientalis            1
Axis porcinus                                          1
Cricetulus griseus                                     1
Name: Species, Length: 48, dtype: Int64
```

Sure enough, in 2017 and 2018 there was a major project looking at structural variants in humans.

The main limitation of the swarm plot approach can be seen by looking at the plots for the final few years. When the number of data points becomes large enough, there isn't enough horizontal space to avoid overlapping the points, so we end up with blobs of points at the extreme left and right positions.

When we have enough data points that it's no longer possible to usefully plot them all, we need to give up on the idea of displaying every point individually, and resort to plots that display a summary of the data in the form of a distribution.

9.3 Distribution plots

9.3.1 Box plots

Probably the most familiar type of plot is the *box plot*. Let's start with a very simple example: looking at the distribution of GC percentage for genomes belonging to each kingdom. If we allow `catplot` to use its default plot type - a strip plot:

```
sns.catplot(data=euk, x="Kingdom", y="GC%")

plt.title("Distribution of GC% across kingdoms")
```

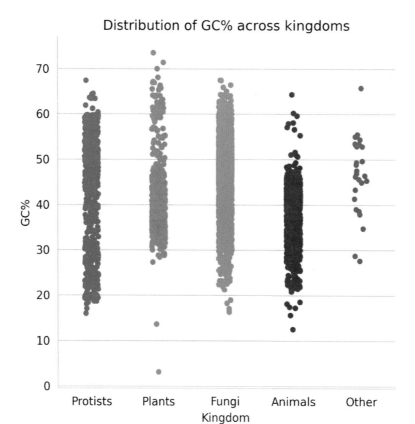

Distribution of GC% across kingdoms

we can easily see that there are way too many points to discern any patterns if we try to plot each one. Adding `kind='box'`:

```
# box_plot.py

sns.catplot(data=euk, x="Kingdom", y="GC%", kind="box")
plt.title("Distribution of GC% across kingdoms")
```

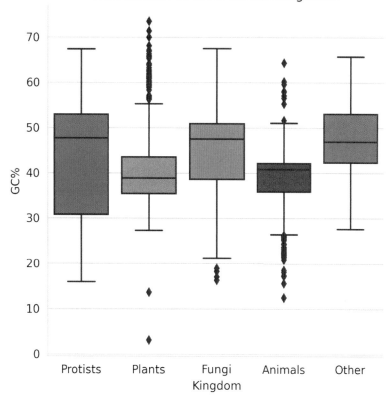

Distribution of GC% across kingdoms

gives us a much more readable plot. For each category the box shows the range that encompasses 75% of the data along with a horizontal line to show us the median value. The whiskers show the range that includes one and a half times the interquartile range beyond the box, and any values outside that are plotted as individual points.

Even this simple plot shows many features of the data. We can see that plants and animals tend to have lower GC percentages than the other kingdoms; that there are some plants with very high GC and some animals with very low GC; and that plants and animals tend to have a more constrained range of GC percentages than the other groups. The position of the horizontal line inside each box also tells us something about the distribution. For example, the line for animals is near the top of the box, which indicates that the median value is high in the interquartile range - in other words, the distribution has a long tail extending down into low GC values.

Because we are still using the `catplot` function to do the charting, we can still use color and small multiples using exactly the same set of arguments that we already know. This allows us to set up a complex plot with relatively little code. By way of an example, let's look at a very specific subset of the data and just find plant and animal genomes from 2017 and 2018. This is a job for pandas:

```
data = euk[
    (euk["Kingdom"].isin(["Plants", "Animals"]))
    & euk["Publication year"].isin([2017, 2018])
]
```

Now we can build a box plot showing GC percentage between the two kingdoms, futher separated by year and assembly status:

```
# col_boxplot.py

data = euk[
    (euk["Kingdom"].isin(["Plants", "Animals"]))
    & euk["Publication year"].isin([2017, 2018])
]

g = sns.catplot(
    data=data,
    x="Kingdom",
    y="GC%",
    kind="box",
    hue="Assembly status",
    col="Publication year",
)

g.fig.suptitle(
    "Distibution of GC% in plant and animal gnomes published in 2017 and 2018",
    y=1.05,
)
```

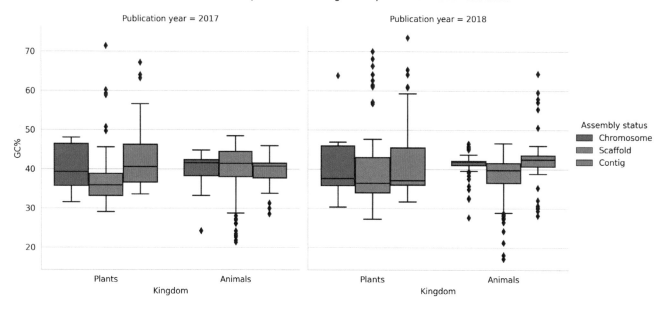

Distibution of GC% in plant and animal gnomes published in 2017 and 2018

Notice a subtlety here in the handling of the various colors. Seaborn is aware that in the dataset we've plotted, there are no genomes with a **Complete Genome** assembly status, so that particular category is missing from the plot. However, we have the same problem with the order of the assembly status that we noticed earlier: they are not in the order that we want. If we try to fix the problem the same way that we did before, by setting the order explicitly:

```
g = sns.catplot(
    data=data,
    x="Kingdom",
    y="GC%",
    kind="box",
    hue="Assembly status",
    col="Publication year",
    hue_order=["Contig", "Scaffold", "Chromosome", "Complete Genome"],
)

g.fig.suptitle(
    "Distibution of GC% in plant and animal gnomes published in 2017 and 2018",
    y=1.05,
)
```

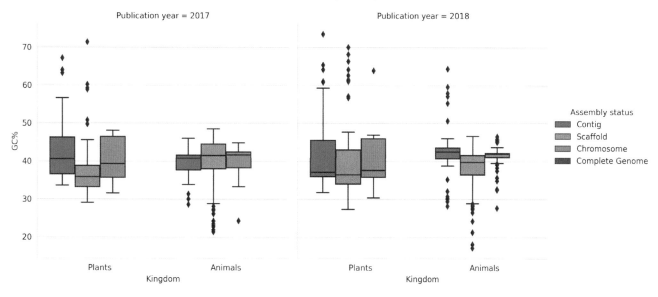

we have a new problem - now the **Complete Genome** assembly status appears in the key even though it doesn't appear in the plot, which is likely to be confusing. There's also a weird gap where there's space for the non-existant **Complete Genome** box. We'll see how to avoid both of these problems in a future chapter.

A noteable feature of boxplots is that they present only a fairly high level summary of the distribution of values. This is both a strength and a weakness. It's a strength in that it allows us to deal with a fairly large number of categories and still have a readable chart:

```
# wide_boxplot.py

sns.catplot(
    data=euk,
    x="Class",
    y="GC%",
    kind="box",
    aspect=3,
    color="orange",
    height=4,
)

plt.xticks(rotation=90)
plt.title("Distribution of GC% across genomes in each class")
```

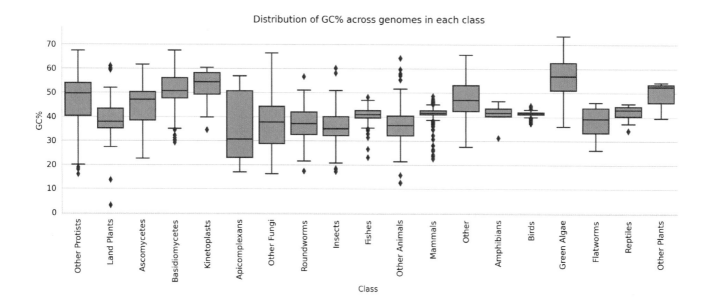

But it's a weakness in that it hides details of the actual distribution of values. We can actually see an example of this limitation in our first boxplot example where we compared the distribution of GC% across kingdoms:

```
sns.catplot(data=euk, x="Kingdom", y="GC%", kind="box")
plt.title("Distribution of GC% across kingdoms")
```

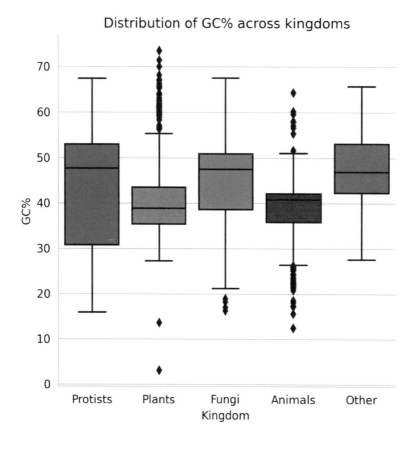

As we discussed earlier, this shows us several interesting patterns, but tells us little about the shape of the distribution within each cateogry.

9 Categorical axes with seaborn

9.3.2 Violin plots

Violin plots attempt to combine the high level view of a box plot with some extra information about the distribution of values. Here's the same plot as above with `kind='violin'`:

```
# violin_plot.py

sns.catplot(data=euk, x="Kingdom", y="GC%", kind="violin")
plt.title("Distribution of GC% across kingdoms")
```

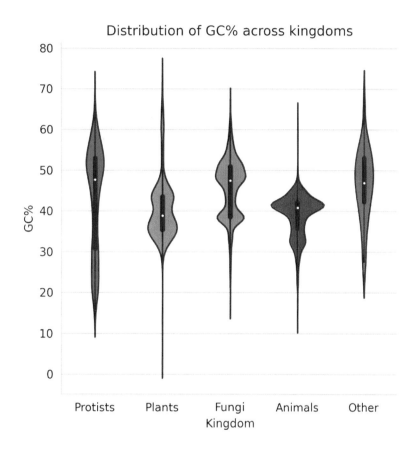

This chart type uses kernel density estimation to draw an estimate of the underlying distribution, revealing that for plants, animals and fungi the distribution of GC values is strongly bimodal, suggesting that it's made up of at least two distinct subpopulations.

Because violin plots show an estimate of the distribution, rather than being directly based on the values themselves, they are sometimes a bit more complicated to design, requiring us to make several decisions.

Firstly, we have to decide whether to extend the distribution beyone the limits of the observed points. Seaborn's default behaviour is to do so, which in the context of a violin plot makes perfect sense. If we assume that our dataset contains only a sample of the data (in this case, of all the genomes belonging to organisms in each kingdom), then it's unlikely that it includes those with the highest and lowest GC percentage. However, this can cause confusion when interpreting the chart. We can see this issue in the chart above, where the tip of the distribution of GC goes below zero for plants. Since the GC is measured as a percentage, this obviously makes no sense! We can get the opposite behaviour - i.e. truncate the distribution at the limits of the observed values - by setting `cut` to zero:

```
sns.catplot(data=euk, x="Kingdom", y="GC%", kind="violin", cut=0)
plt.title("Distribution of GC% across kingdoms")
```

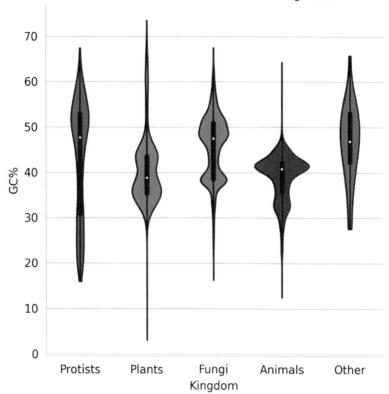

Distribution of GC% across kingdoms

There's also a bandwidth parameter `bw` which effectively controls how smooth the distribution is. Setting this value lower:

```
sns.catplot(data=euk, x="Kingdom", y="GC%", kind="violin", cut=0, bw=0.1)
plt.title("Distribution of GC% across kingdoms")
```

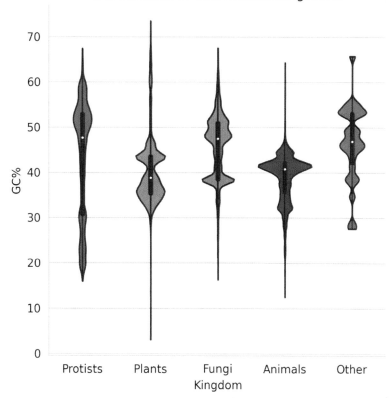

Distribution of GC% across kingdoms

results in a more detailed distribuion, which may show useful patterns, but is also more susceptible to being affected by small numbers of data points.

A further option is how we want to scale each violin. Setting the `scale` argument to `'count'` sets the width of each violin to the number of observations:

```
sns.catplot(
    data=euk, x="Kingdom", y="GC%", kind="violin", cut=0, scale="count"
)
plt.title("Distribution of GC% across kingdoms")
```

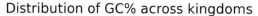

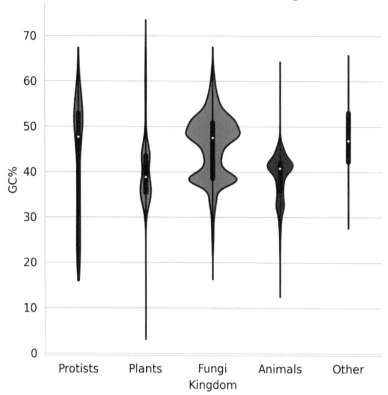

Distribution of GC% across kingdoms

This allows us to see that there are many more genomes for fungi than for other kingdoms, at the expense of making it harder to see the distribution for the other kingdoms.

These extra decisions about how to estimate the distribution are the price that we pay for the ability to show more detail relative to box plots.

We can make good use of color with violin plots just as with box plots. Here we'll use pandas to select just the genomes in either scaffold or chromosome status, and look at the distribution of numbers of genes across kingdoms, using color to represent the status. Because seaborn doesn't, at the time of writing, recognize the `Int64` data type as numeric, we will use the floating point version of our eukaryote genome dataset:

```python
# hue_violin_plot.py

g = sns.catplot(
    data=euk_float[
        euk_float["Assembly status"].isin(["Scaffold", "Chromosome"])
    ],
    x="Kingdom",
    y="Number of genes",
    kind="violin",
    cut=0,
    hue="Assembly status",
    aspect=3,
    height=3,
)

plt.title("Distribution of number of genes across genomes from each kingdom")
```

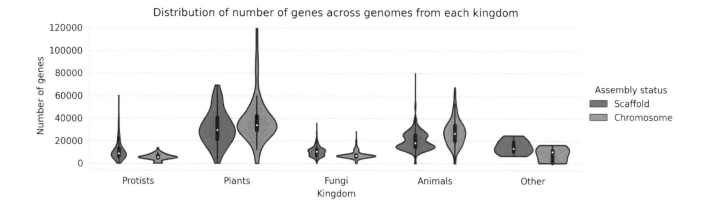

Notice that because we still have `cut = 0`, the distributions are truncated at the limits of the observed data, leading some violins that have a rather blunt-ended, non violin shape.

Because violin plots are symetrical, when we have only two colors we can put one on each side with `split = True`:

```python
# split_violin_plot.py

sns.catplot(
    data=euk_float[
        euk_float["Assembly status"].isin(["Scaffold", "Chromosome"])
    ],
    x="Kingdom",
    y="Number of genes",
    kind="violin",
    cut=0,
    hue="Assembly status",
    aspect=2,
    split=True,
)
plt.title("Distribution of number of genes across genomes from each kingdom")
```

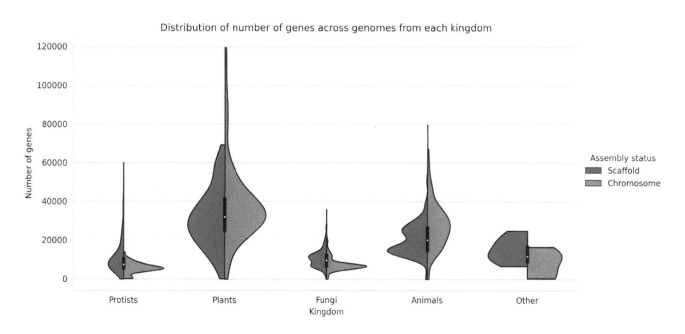

which leads to a more compact chart.

Because violins are more complicated than boxes, the maximum number of categories that we can usefully show tends to be smaller than with a box plot. We can see this if we try to repeat our plot that shows the distribution of GC percentage across classes:

```python
sns.catplot(
    data=euk,
    x="Class",
    y="GC%",
    kind="violin",
    aspect=3,
    color="orange",
    height=4,
)

plt.xticks(rotation=90)
plt.title("Distribution of GC% across genomes from each class")
```

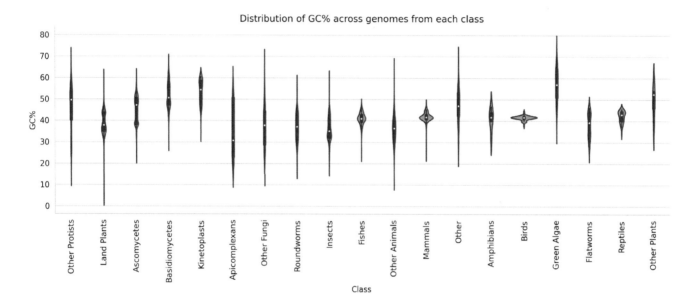

This plot illustrates another problem with violin plots: the continuous scale (here, GC percentage) must encompass the whole range of values. So when we have classes with very different distributions - some narrow, some wide - the scale ends up making it hard to see details

9.3.3 Boxen plots

Closely related to the violin plot is the *boxen plot*. This is like a box plot but rather than just showing a single interquartile range it uses multiple boxes to show multiple quantiles. Let's look at our kingdom plot again:

```python
# boxen_plot.py

sns.catplot(data=euk, x="Kingdom", y="GC%", kind="boxen")
plt.title("Distribution of GC% across genomes from each kingdom")
```

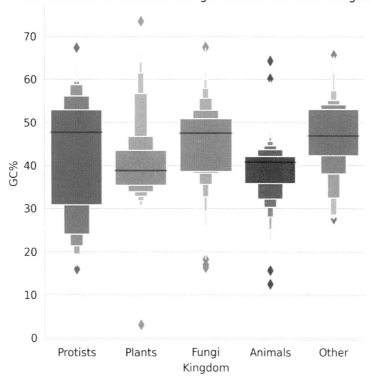

Distribution of GC% across genomes from each kingdom

In terms of the level of detail they present, they lie somewhere between box and violin plots. The above chart gives a better idea of the skew of each category than a simple box plot, but still obscures the fact that some of the distributions are bimodal. Boxen plots might be a good choice when we have a large number of points, a large number of categories, and are reasonably sure that the distributions are somewhat normal, or at least unimodal. Our plot showing GC percentage across classes is a good example:

```
# wide_boxen_plot.py

sns.catplot(
    data=euk, x="Class", y="GC%", kind="boxen", aspect=3, color="orange"
)

plt.xticks(rotation=90)
plt.title("Distribution of GC% across genomes from each class")
```

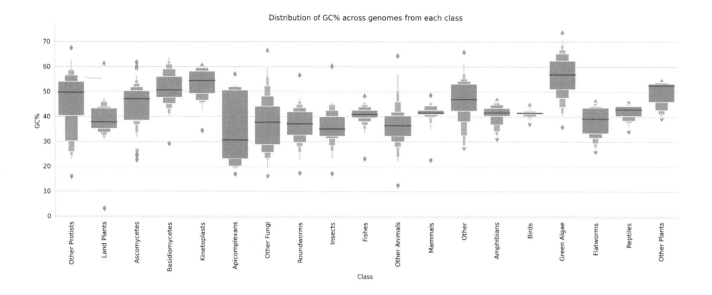

Distribution of GC% across genomes from each class

9.4 Point estimate plots

When we don't particularly care about the distribution of values within a category, or when there are too many categories to show a distribution, we may want to display just a point estimate.

9.4.1 Bar plots

For categories without a natural order, a simple bar plot is usually the answer:

```
# bar_plot.py

sns.catplot(
    data=euk_float,
    y="Class",
    x="Number of genes",
    kind="bar",
    aspect=1,
    color="darkgreen",
)

plt.title(
    "Mean and 95% CI of number of genes\nfor genomes in different classes"
)
plt.xticks(rotation=90)
```

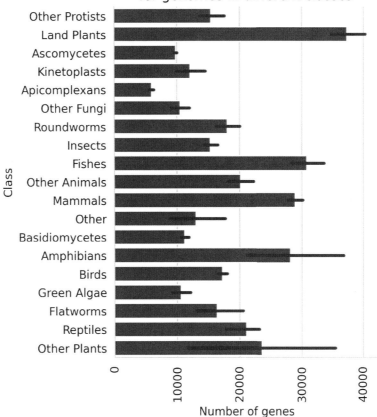

Mean and 95% CI of number of genes for genomes in different classes

By default, `kind = 'bar'` will show us the mean value for each category, plus 95% confidence intervals estimated by bootstrapping. We can pick a different summary statistic or confidence interval range by setting the `estimator` and `ci` arguments respectively. If we want to skip bootstrapping and just show the standard deviation, we can pass `ci = 'sd'`, or omit confidence intervals entirely by passing `ci = None`:

```
sns.catplot(
    data=euk_float,
    y="Class",
    x="Number of genes",
    kind="bar",
    aspect=1,
    color="darkgreen",
    estimator=np.median,
    ci=None,
)

plt.title("Median number of genes\nfor genomes in different classes")
plt.xticks(rotation=90)
```

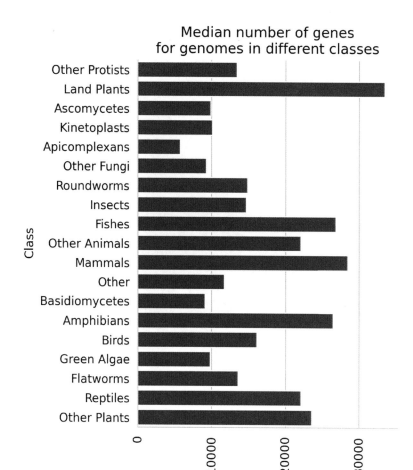

As a general rule, the simpler a chart is to start with, the more additional information we can add without confusing the viewer. Since bar charts are very simple to begin with, we can often get away with adding extra layers of complexity. For example, here's a plot showing the mean number of genes for genomes sequenced in each year for each kingdom:

```
# hue_bar_plot.py

sns.catplot(
    data=euk_float,
    x="Publication year",
    y="Number of genes",
    kind="bar",
    hue="Kingdom",
    ci=None,
    aspect=3,
    height=4,
)

plt.title("Mean number of genes in genomes published in each year")
```

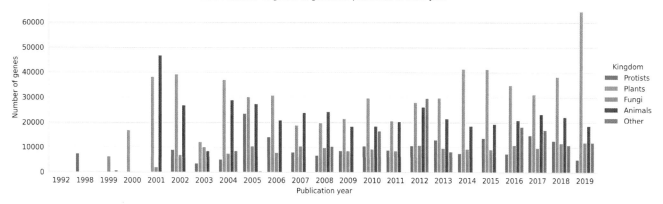

Mean number of genes in genomes published in each year

Trying to show these data by plotting individual points or even distributions would result in an unreadable chart.

A noteable feature of bar charts is that they include zero on the numerical axis. For some plots this makes sense; in the examples above the number of genes is a quantity and some of the values are very small. Having zero on the axis might not make much sense for other datasets. For example, let's look at the distribution of GC percentage instead:

```
sns.catplot(
    data=euk_float,
    y="Class",
    x="GC%",
    kind="bar",
    aspect=1,
    color="lightgreen",
    ci="sd",
    height=6,
)

plt.title(
    "Mean and standard deviation of GC percentage\nfor genomes in different classes"
)
plt.xticks(rotation=90)
```

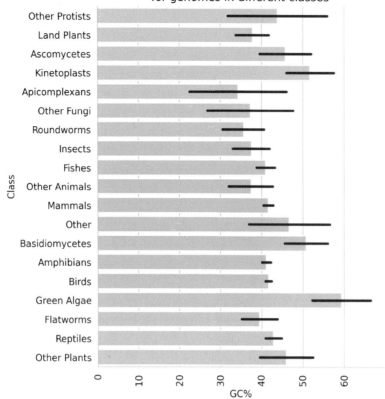

The numerical axis here is fundamentally different from our previous examples. For one, the GC measurement is a percentage, not a quantity, so it's not so important to have zero in the scale. And the range of values is more constrained: the lowest mean GC is around 35%, so the left half of the chart isn't really showing us anything interesting.

9.4.2 Point plots

In a case like this we might turn to the final categorical plot type; the *point plot*:

```
# point_plot.py

sns.catplot(
    data=euk_float,
    y="Class",
    x="GC%",
    kind="point",
    aspect=1,
    color="lightgreen",
    ci="sd",
    join=False,
)

plt.title(
    "Mean and standard deviation of GC percentage\nfor genomes in different classes"
)
plt.xticks(rotation=90)
```

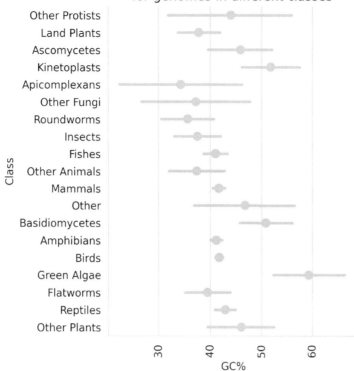

Mean and standard deviation of GC percentage for genomes in different classes

This gives us a single point plus error bars, and allows the numerical scale to take whatever minumum value best shows the data. This allows more of the chart area to be given over to showing the variation between the categories. Notice that for this example we need to pass `join = False` as we don't want the points to be joined together - the categories (classes) have no natural order.

For this dataset we have to be careful when interpreting the error bars, as we know that there are very different numbers of samples in each category.

Let's try our more complicated example, which has year as the category and uses color to represent kingdoms. Unlike bar charts, point plots don't cope well with missing categories - we need all of our kingdoms to have at least one genome in each year so that seaborn can calculate a mean. So rather than plotting the whole dataset we'll use pandas to get just the plant, animal and fungal genomes and only consider years after 2000 before plotting:

```
# hue_point_plot.py

sns.catplot(
    data=euk[
        (euk["Publication year"] > 2000)
        & (euk["Kingdom"].isin(["Plants", "Animals", "Fungi"]))
    ],
    x="Publication year",
    y="Number of genes",
    kind="point",
    hue="Kingdom",
    aspect=3,
    height=4,
    orient="v",
)

plt.title("Mean number of genes in genomes published in each year")
```

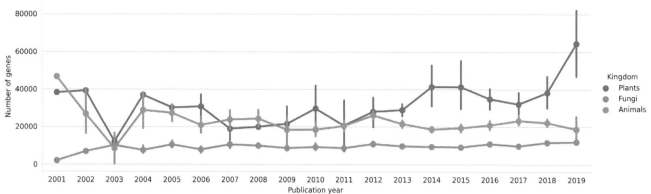

Because in this case the category - year - does have a natural order, we'll use the default `join` argument and allow seaborn to join the points. The above plot shows a very common problem with point plots where the different colored points have similar numerical values: the points and especially the error bars tend to overlap. To get round this problem we can pass `dodge = True` and tell seaborn to separate the points along the categorical axis:

```
sns.catplot(
    data=euk[
        (euk["Publication year"] > 2000)
        & (euk["Kingdom"].isin(["Plants", "Animals", "Fungi"]))
    ],
    x="Publication year",
    y="Number of genes",
    kind="point",
    hue="Kingdom",
    aspect=3,
    height=4,
    dodge=True,
    orient="v",
)

plt.title("Mean number of genes in genomes published in each year")
```

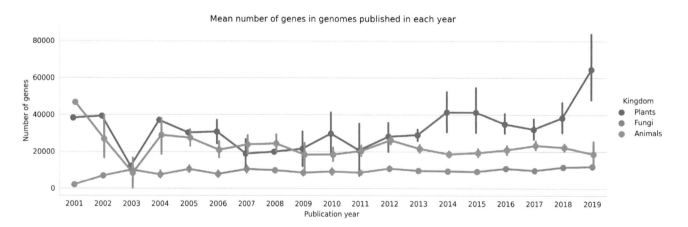

Looking at the data, the obvious outlier is 2003, with very low mean numbers of genes for both plant and animal genomes sequenced that year. To find out why, we'll use pandas to find just those rows:

```
(
    euk[
        (euk["Publication year"] == 2003)
        & (euk["Kingdom"].isin(["Animals", "Plants"]))
    ][["Species", "Kingdom", "Number of genes"]]
)
```

	Species	Kingdom	Number of genes
58	Ciona savignyi	Animals	<NA>
118	Drosophila pseudoobscura pseudoobscura	Animals	16721
4954	Pan troglodytes	Animals	271
4971	Canis lupus familiaris	Animals	<NA>
4996	Apis mellifera	Animals	<NA>
5084	Pan troglodytes	Animals	<NA>
6927	Oryza sativa Japonica Group	Plants	12165

It turns out that, by chance, there are only two animal genomes and one plant genome for that year with an estimated number of genes, and the values are all lower than the means for other years.

When there are exactly two categories, we can use point plots to make *slope charts*, where our focus is on how the values change between the two categories for our different colors. For example, we can look at how the number of proteins differs when we go from contigs to chromosomes, using color to show the different kingdoms:

```
# slope_plot.py

sns.catplot(
    data=euk[
        (euk["Assembly status"].isin(["Contig", "Chromosome"]))
        & (euk["Kingdom"].isin(["Plants", "Animals", "Protists"]))
    ],
    x="Assembly status",
    y="Number of proteins",
    kind="point",
    hue="Kingdom",
    dodge=True,
    palette="Set2",
    order=["Contig", "Chromosome"],
    orient="v",
)

plt.title(
    "Mean and 95% CI of number of proteins \nfor genomes in different assembly states"
)
```

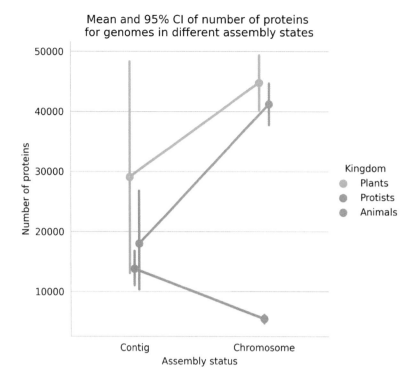

Mean and 95% CI of number of proteins
for genomes in different assembly states

The slope makes it very easy to pick out that the pattern for protists is the opposite of that for plants and animals.

9.5 Comparing means with statistical tests

Consider a very simple bar plot that compares the mean daily temperature of Edinburgh and London:

```
# compare_temp.py

sns.catplot(
    data=weather[weather["City"].isin(["London", "Edinburgh"])],
    x="City",
    y="Mean temperature",
    kind="bar",
    ci="sd",
)
plt.title(
    "Mean and standard deviation\n of daily temperature in London and Edinburgh"
)
```

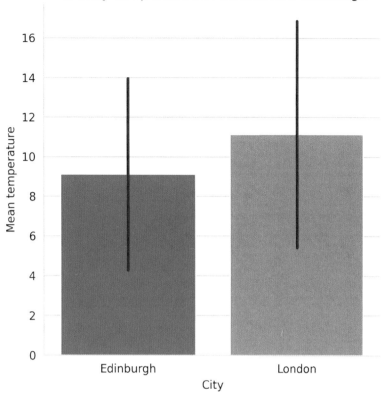

Mean and standard deviation
of daily temperature in London and Edinburgh

As soon as we have two means side by side, we naturally want to know if there's a statistical difference between them. For simple cases like the one above, with large and equal numbers of samples, a t-test is probably the first choice:

```
# ttest_temp.py

from scipy.stats import ttest_ind

edinburgh_temps = weather[weather["City"] == "Edinburgh"]["Mean temperature"]
london_temps = weather[weather["City"] == "London"]["Mean temperature"]

ttest_ind(edinburgh_temps, london_temps)
```

```
Ttest_indResult(statistic=-39.14694915007634, pvalue=0.0)
```

The result is a tuple with the t-statistic and p-value. In our case, the p-value is so low that it gets rounded to zero, so we can be very confident that the mean temperatures are really different. Though we must be careful - the t-test assumes independent samples, but it's likely that temperatures on adjacent days are strongly correlated. A fairer test might be to pick a single day:

```
# ttest_day.py

from scipy.stats import ttest_ind

edinburgh_temps = weather[
    (weather["Day of year"] == 200) & (weather["City"] == "Edinburgh")
]["Mean temperature"]

london_temps = weather[
    (weather["Day of year"] == 200) & (weather["City"] == "London")
]["Mean temperature"]

ttest_ind(edinburgh_temps, london_temps)
```

```
Ttest_indResult(statistic=-8.023971334693872, pvalue=1.0085574332604367e-12)
```

although now we are asking if the two cities have different temperatures at a specific time of year. Such are the perils of statistics!

If we prefer a non-parametric test, we can use a different function from the `scipy.stats` module - most are included. For samples with non-normal distributions and unequal sample sizes, the Mann-Whitney U test might be appropriate:

```
# mwu_test.py

from scipy.stats import mannwhitneyu

# do plant and animals have different genome sizes?
mannwhitneyu(
    euk[euk["Kingdom"] == "Animals"]["Size (Mb)"],
    euk[euk["Kingdom"] == "Plants"]["Size (Mb)"],
)
```

```
MannwhitneyuResult(statistic=711017.0, pvalue=1.36713633671408e-27)
```

9.6 Line charts

When the number of categories gets very large, the point plot approach starts to become difficult to interpret. For an example of this, we'll use the daily mean temperature dataset:

```
weather.head()
```

	City	Year	Month	Day of year	Day of month	Mean temperature
0	Berlin	1960	January	1	1	6.4
1	Berlin	1960	January	2	2	8.1
2	Berlin	1960	January	3	3	5.4
3	Berlin	1960	January	4	4	3.9
4	Berlin	1960	January	5	5	6.0

If we want to show the trend in temperature over the course of a year, then we can use the day of the year as the category and plot the temperature, using color to represent each city. It's clear from the default strip plot that there are way too many points, and too many categories, to plot each day individually:

9 Categorical axes with seaborn

```
sns.catplot(
    data=weather[weather["City"].isin(["Berlin", "Edinburgh"])],
    x="Day of year",
    y="Mean temperature",
    hue="City",
    aspect=3,
    height=4,
)
plt.title(
    "Mean daily temperature for each day of the year\nsince 1960 in Berlin and Edinburgh"
)
```

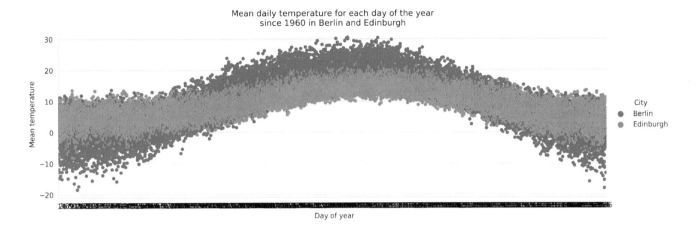

So we might try the obvious thing and just plot the mean temperature for each day of the year averaged over the 60 years that the dataset covers:

```
sns.catplot(
    data=weather[weather["City"].isin(["Berlin", "Edinburgh"])],
    x="Day of year",
    y="Mean temperature",
    hue="City",
    aspect=3,
    height=4,
    kind="point",
    ci="sd",
)
plt.title(
    "Mean daily temperature for each day of the year\nsince 1960 in Berlin and Edinburgh"
)
```

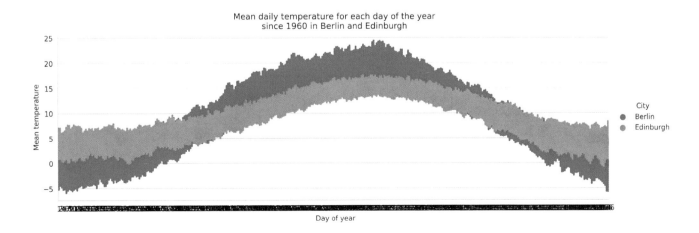

However, this chart doesn't look great either. Because we have 366 categories - one for each day of the year, including leap years - the day of the year behaves more like a numerical variable than a categorical one. The points and error bars of the point plot completely overlap, and because seaborn labels every category, so do the x axis labels.

As an alternative, we can return to `relplot` and pass `kind='line'`:

```
# line_plot.py

sns.relplot(
    data=weather[weather["City"].isin(["Berlin", "Edinburgh"])],
    x="Day of year",
    y="Mean temperature",
    hue="City",
    aspect=3,
    height=4,
    kind="line",
    ci="sd",
)

plt.title(
    "Mean daily temperature for each day of the year\nsince 1960 in Berlin and Edinburgh"
)
```

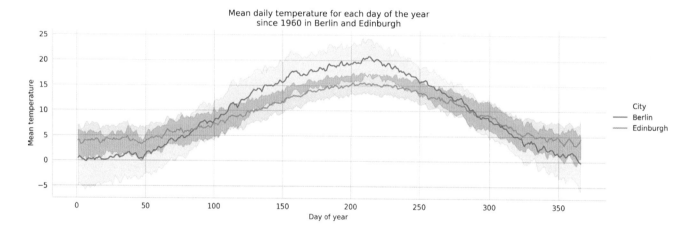

This gives us a plot where the mean is shown by a continuous line, rather than individual points, and instead of error bars we have a continuous shaded area showing us the standard deviation. Treating the day of the year as a continuous variable rather than a category also allows seaborn to avoid drawing every label, and just draw a sensible number of grid lines.

9.7 Count plots

There's one final kind of categorical plot to mention here: one that shows the number of samples in each category rather than an estimate of some numerical value. In a later chapter we'll see how to do this by using pandas' grouping abilities, but we can also do this directly with `catplot` by passing `kind='count'` and ommiting the `x` or `y` variable:

```
# count_plot.py

sns.catplot(
    data=euk,
    x="Publication year",
    kind="count",
    aspect=3,
    height=4,
    hue="Assembly status",
)

plt.title(
    "Total number of genomes sequenced in different assembly status over time"
)
```

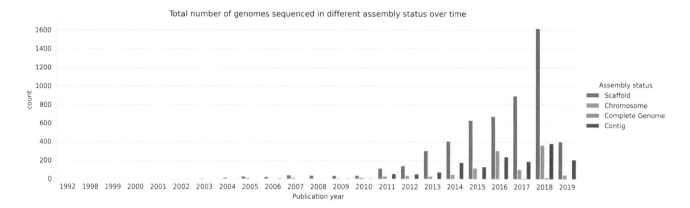

9.7.1 Summary

In this chapter we've been introduced to lots of different category plot types. Despite the wide range of categorical plot types available in seaborn, they are all produced by a single function, `catplot`, by passing different values to the `kind` argument. This is great news for us as programmers, as it means that we only have to learn one interface for setting the color, laying out small multiples, etc., and then use it for diverse plot types.

To avoid confusion between the different values that we can assign to the `kind` argument, remember the three broad catgories that we discussed at the start of the chapter. If we want to plot every individual point, we have `'strip'` and `'swarm'`. If we want to plot a distribution, we have `'box'`, `'violin'` and `'boxen'`. And if we want to plot a point estimate we have `'bar'` and `'point'`, along with the option of a line plot using `relplot`.

10 Styling figures with seaborn

In our examples in the last chapter we've been exploring different ways of presenting the data, and allowed seaborn to make its own decisions about the appearance. For many visualizations, these decisions will be perfectly adequate, allowing us to spend our energy exploring the data rather than worrying about aesthetics. However, eventually we will need to exercise more control over our figures.

There are a few different approaches to changing the look of things when using seaborn. The simplest is to supply arguments to the seaborn functions when we call them. This works well for controlling things like plot size and shape, and color schemes. However, only a limited number of options are implemented at the level of seaborn functions (understandably, since the range of potential customizations is massive).

To control aspects of chart appearance that are not implemented at the seaborn level, we can supply functions to the underlying matplotlib functions. This requires a bit more work than using seaborn directly, and often requires us to dig into the arcane structure of matplotlib in order to figure out the right argument names. The benefit of this approach is that it allows us to control aspects of the chart that are not implemented by seaborn.

As a last resort, if we can't figure out how to get the chart we want by passing arguments to either seaborn or matplotlib, we can allow seaborn to draw charts using its defaults, then call methods on the resulting objects to set their properties. This approach requires the most code, but allows us to do things that would be impossible otherwise.

Probably the most important aspect of styling for the purpose of data visualization is the use of color. Because that's such an important topic, it will get its own chapter later in the book.

For many of the charts in this chapter we'll want to use just the animal genomes, so we'll start by defining a variable here that we can reuse:

```
animals = euk[euk["Kingdom"] == "Animals"].dropna()
```

10.1 Aesthetic arguments to seaborn functions

Unlike with `distplot`, where we had to rely on matplotlib to control the figure size, `relplot` handles size and shape internally. Rather than giving a width and height, instead we give a `height` argument and an `aspect` argument. The `aspect` argument determines the ratio of width to height, so with `aspect=2` we get a figure that is twice as wide as it is high:

```
# aspect.py

sns.relplot(
    data=euk[euk["Size (Mb)"] < 5000],
    x="Size (Mb)",
    y="Number of genes",
    aspect=2,
)

plt.title("Genome size vs number of genes for genomes < 5000 Mb")
plt.xlabel("size (Megabases)")
```

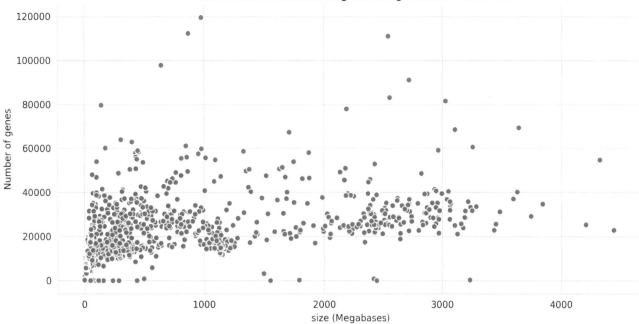

This is very convenient, as it means that we can effectively control the *size* and *shape* of the chart independently.

To set the various labels, the simplest thing is to set descriptive column names as we discussed when we introduced pandas. If we just need to change a few column names, the **rename** method might be helpful:

```
# tweak column names
new_animals = animals.rename(
    columns={
        "Number of genes": "Number of predicted genes",
        "Number of proteins": "Number of predicted proteins",
        "GC%": "GC percentage",
    }
)
new_animals.head()
```

	Species	Kingdom	Class	...	Number of predicted proteins	Publication year	Assembly status
34	Caenorhabditis briggsae	Animals	Roundworms	...	21959	2002	Chromosome
35	Caenorhabditis elegans	Animals	Roundworms	...	28420	2001	Complete Genome
36	Brugia malayi	Animals	Roundworms	...	11472	2002	Scaffold
37	Aedes aegypti	Animals	Insects	...	28317	2017	Chromosome
38	Aedes albopictus	Animals	Insects	...	42912	2016	Contig

Since the seaborn labels are taken directly from the column names, this will fix them in all charts without us having to do anything:

```
sns.relplot(
    data=new_animals,
    x="Number of predicted genes",
    y="Number of predicted proteins",
    size="Size (Mb)",
    sizes=(2, 150),
    hue="GC percentage",
)
plt.title("Number of genes vs number of proteins\n for animal genomes")
```

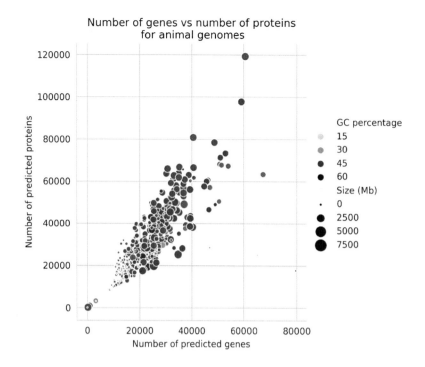

This has a couple of added advantages: it means that we will get nicer labels for any tables that we draw with pandas:

```
new_animals.describe()
```

	Size (Mb)	GC percentage	Number of predicted genes	Number of predicted proteins	Publication year
count	613.000000	613.000000	613.000000	613.000000	613.000000
mean	1126.914765	39.444252	21475.202284	28342.721044	2013.929853
std	1026.477620	4.194044	9662.588264	14840.070530	3.799721
min	1.255350	21.577700	3.000000	3.000000	2001.000000
25%	256.132000	37.200000	14664.000000	17758.000000	2012.000000
50%	807.712000	41.000000	20019.000000	24730.000000	2015.000000
75%	2009.190000	41.900000	26692.000000	37422.000000	2017.000000
max	6250.350000	51.595500	79667.000000	119294.000000	2019.000000

and it improves the readability of the `relplot` function call, since the more descriptive names are used as arguments.

When working in an interactive context such as a jupyter notebook, a useful trick is to have a list of the column names visible somewhere:

```
new_animals.columns
```

```
Index(['Species', 'Kingdom', 'Class', 'Size (Mb)', 'GC percentage',
       'Number of predicted genes', 'Number of predicted proteins',
       'Publication year', 'Assembly status'],
      dtype='object')
```

which allows us to copy and paste the column names whenever we need them.

If we don't want to change the column names, we can manually set the labels after drawing the chart. This isn't too difficult for the axis labels:

```
# set_labels.py

sns.relplot(
    data=animals, x="Number of genes", y="Number of proteins", height=6
)
plt.title("Number of genes vs number of proteins\n for animal genomes")
plt.xlabel("Number of predicted genes")
plt.ylabel("Number of predicted proteins")
```

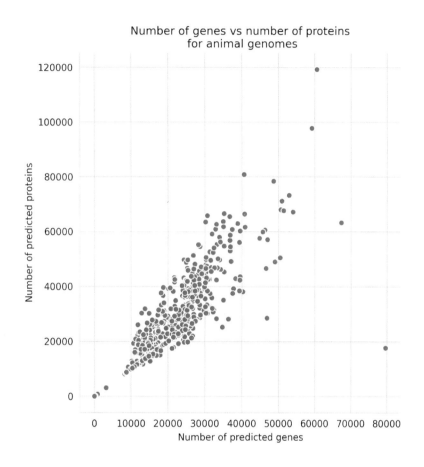

But to manually set the legend labels is positively painful - we have to get the chart object, get the legend object, get a list of the text elements, find the ones we want to change, and call **set_text** on them:

```
# set_legend_labels.py

chart = sns.relplot(
    data=animals,
    x="Number of genes",
    y="Number of proteins",
    size="Size (Mb)",
    sizes=(2, 150),
    hue="Publication year",
)
plt.title("Number of genes vs number of proteins\n for animal genomes")
plt.xlabel("Number of predicted genes")
plt.ylabel("Number of predicted proteins")

chart._legend.get_texts()[0].set_text("Year\nsequenced")
chart._legend.get_texts()[6].set_text("Genome\nsize (Mb)")
```

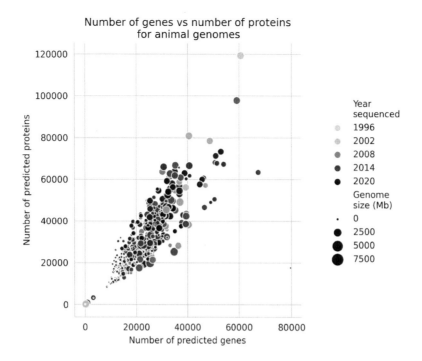

And we have to remember to do this in every plot.

Setting labels is an example of a theme that occurs a lot in data science: when we have something that we want to change, we can either fix it in the data (by changing the column names) or in the figure (by setting the labels after the chart is drawn). As a general rule, it's much easier to fix it in the data.

10.2 Setting styles and contexts

For occasions when we need even more control over our figures, we turn to seaborn's context manager. This is a complex tool to use, but is the best way to control many aspects of our plots.

To use it, we make a dictionary containing the various elements of the chart that we want to set. Here's an example that changes a bunch of settings:

```python
options = {
    "grid.linewidth": 5.0,           # make grid lines thick
    "axes.titlesize": 18.0,          # make title large
    "xtick.major.width": 3,          # make tick lines thick
    "axes.linewidth": 3,             # make axis lines thick
    "axes.facecolor": "lightpink",   # make background pink
    "axes.edgecolor": "green",       # make axis lines green
    "xtick.bottom": True,            # show ticks on the x axis
    "grid.linestyle": "--",          # make grid dotted
}
```

Notice that this is just a normal Python dictionary. Now we pass this dictionary to the `plt.rc_context` context manager. Notice that the plotting code needs to be indented as it's inside the context manager block:

```
# set_styles.py

options = {
    "grid.linewidth": 5.0,          # make grid lines thick
    "axes.titlesize": 18.0,         # make title large
    "xtick.major.width": 3,         # make tick lines thick
    "axes.linewidth": 3,            # make axis lines thick
    "axes.facecolor": "lightpink",  # make background pink
    "axes.edgecolor": "green",      # make axis lines green
    "xtick.bottom": True,           # show ticks on the x axis
    "grid.linestyle": "--",         # make grid dotted
}

with plt.rc_context(options):
    sns.relplot(
        data=animals, x="Number of genes", y="Number of proteins", height=6
    )
    plt.title("Number of genes vs number of proteins\n for animal genomes")
    plt.xlabel("Number of predicted genes")
    plt.ylabel("Number of predicted proteins")
```

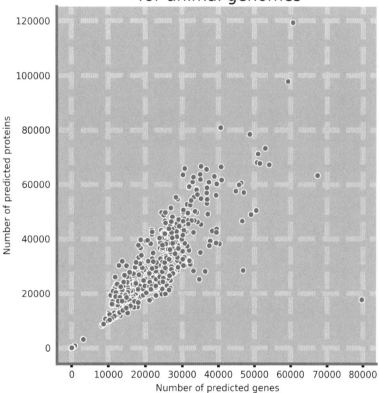

The reason that we use a context manager in this way is to ensure that changes to one chart don't affect another.

As a rule, it's best not to change aspects of the style without good reason. Seaborn's defaults do an excellent job of making the data easy to interpret, and changes are more likely to be distracting than helpful. After all, one of the main benefits of a library like seaborn is that it frees us from the need to worry about stylistic details, allowing us to focus on exploring the data.

10.3 Passing keywords to underlying functions

We mentioned in the introduction to seaborn that it uses matplotlib functions to do the actual plotting. In fact, much of the time it's helpful to think of seaborn as a fairly sophisticated wrapper around matplotlib.

Since seaborn is intended to be a high-level plotting library, its functions generally take only the most important arguments to control the properties of the chart. However, they all have some mechanism to pass arguments along to the underlying matplotlib function. For some seaborn functions, this mechanism is to simply accept arbitrary keyword arguments and pass them along to matplotlib.

For example, `relplot` uses matplotlib's `scatter` function behind the scenes. The `s` argument sets the marker size in matplotlib's `scatter` function. So when calling `relplot`, we can pass the `s` argument - even though that isn't an argument to `relplot` - and `relplot` will take care of passing it along to the matplotlib `scatter` function:

```
# marker_size.py

sns.relplot(
    data=euk[euk["Size (Mb)"] < 5000],
    x="Size (Mb)",
    y="Number of genes",
    s=10,  # specify small marker size
)

plt.title("Genome size vs number of genes\n for genomes < 5000 Mb")
plt.xlabel("size (Megabases)")
```

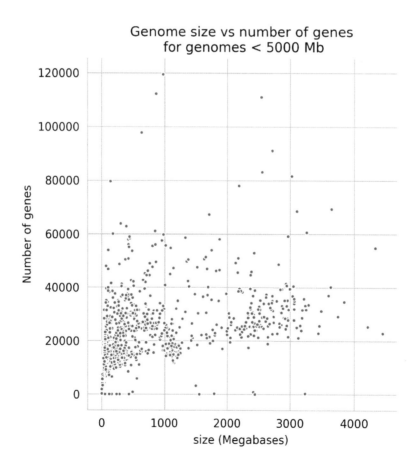

This technique often requires quite a bit of research - we have to figure out the underlying matplotlib function for the seaborn function that we're using, and then go and look up its arguments. This information is easy to obtain from the documentation though, and once we know it this is a very convenient way to put everything in a single function call.

There are a couple of scenarios in which this approach causes trouble. One is when we try to supply an argument to matplotlib that is also part of the seaborn function. For example, the matplotlib `scatter` function takes an argument `c` to specifiy the color. But if we try to change the plot to orange:

```
sns.relplot(
    data=euk[euk["Size (Mb)"] < 5000],
    x="Size (Mb)",
    y="Number of genes",
    c="orange",  # specify orange color
)
```

we get an error: **Supply a 'c' argument or a 'color' kwarg but not both ....**

`relplot` is already using the `color` argument to matplotlib's `scatter`, so our `c` argument conflicts with it. The fix is to pass `color` directly to `relplot` as we saw previously:

```
# passing_color.py

sns.relplot(
    data=euk[euk["Size (Mb)"] < 5000],
    x="Size (Mb)",
    y="Number of genes",
    color="orange",  # specify orange color
)

plt.title("Genome size vs number of genes\n for genomes < 5000 Mb")
plt.xlabel("size (Megabases)")
```

Similarly, seaborn's `distplot` uses the matplotlib `hist` function for drawing the histogram part. The matplotlib `hist` function takes a boolean `cumulative` argument to determine whether to draw a cumulative histogram (this argument is `False` by default). To pass this argument to the `hist` function, we have to use a slightly different mechanism.

Remember that `distplot`, by default, draws both a histogram and an estimate of the underlying distribution:

```
sns.distplot(euk["GC%"].dropna())
plt.title("Distribution of GC% for all genomes")
```

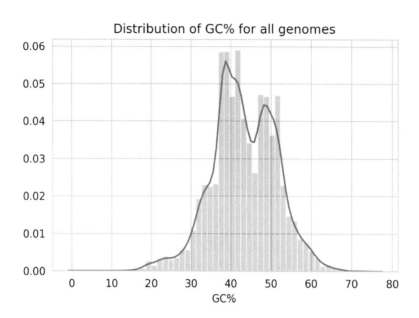

To accomplish this, it actually uses two underlying matplotlib functions: `hist` to draw the bars and `plot` to draw the line. So if we passed `cumulative=True` to `distplot`, how would it know which of the underlying matplotlib functions should get it?

To avoid this ambiguity, rather than taking arbitrary keyword arguments, `distplot` takes a pair of special arguments called `hist_kws` and `kde_kws` which contain the arguments we want to pass to the underlying matplotlib functions `hist` and `plot` respectively. So to draw our cumulative histogram, we package the `cumulative=True` argument into a dict and pass it like this:

```
# cumulative_hist.py

sns.distplot(euk["GC%"].dropna(), hist_kws={"cumulative": True}, kde=False)
plt.title("Cumulative histogram of GC% for all genomes")
```

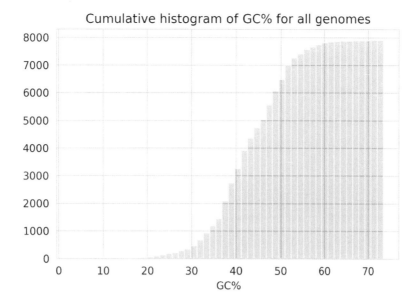

Cumulative histogram of GC% for all genomes

This general pattern will hold true for the other seaborn functions that we'll see in future sections. Functions that only use a single underlying matplotlib function will simply pass on unrecognized keyword arguments, whereas functions that use two or more underlying functions will take dicts of keyword/value pairs.

10.4 Editing charts

An essential tool in our data visualization toolkit is the ability to take a chart and edit it graphically. Being able to do this serves two purposes. Firstly, for one off charts (for example, for a poster or publication) it means that we can make the changes we need without having to trawl through the matplotlib documentation looking for the relevant keyword. But even for charts that we intend to make programatically, it's often much faster to experiment with different styles in a graphical editor, before figuring out the code needed to make those changes.

Being able to edit our charts graphically requires two things. Firstly, we need to save our charts in SVG format (short for Scalable Vector Graphics). This is easy: just call `plt.savefig` with a filename that ends with `.svg`:

```
sns.distplot(euk["GC%"].dropna(), hist_kws={"cumulative": True}, kde=False)
plt.title("Cumulative histogram of GC% for all genomes")
plt.savefig("hist.svg")
```

Secondly, we need an SVG editor program - in other words, one that will allow us to manipulate the chart as a collection of shapes and text rather than as a collection of individual pixels. For Windows and Mac users, Adobe Illustrator is the most popular. For Linux users, Inkscape is a good starting point. And there are many free online SVG editors that will be fine for basic tasks.

11 Working with color in seaborn

11.1 Colors and palettes

Of all the properties that we can set on our charts, color is probably the most complicated. Partly this is due to its flexibility: we can use it to represent both numerical and categorical data, and different color combinations are suitable for different situations. Partly it's due to the many ways that we have of representing colors. And partly it's due to the interaction between individual colors and palettes.

In this chapter we'll look purely at the ways to use color effectively in seaborn. We'll be using a mixture of all the chart types that we've seen over the last few chapters, since they all interact with color in a different way. And we'll also spend a bit of time discussing best practices when using color.

As in the previous chapters, defining a subset of the data will make our code easier to read:

```
animals = euk[euk["Kingdom"] == "Animals"].dropna()
```

11.1.1 Setting a color

For charts where we're not using color to represent anything, we can generally pass an argument to the function to set the color. For the `relplot` function, the argument is simply `color`, and we can set it either with a named color:

```
# named_color.py

sns.relplot(
    data=animals, x="Size (Mb)", y="Number of genes", color="purple",
)
plt.title("Genome size vs number of genes\n for animal genomes")
```

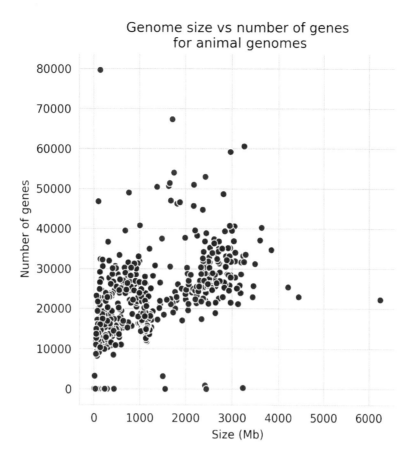

Genome size vs number of genes
for animal genomes

or a hexadecimal color code:

```
# hex_color.py

sns.relplot(
    data=animals, x="Size (Mb)", y="Number of genes", color="#00b3c7",
)
plt.title("Genome size vs number of genes\n for animal genomes")
```

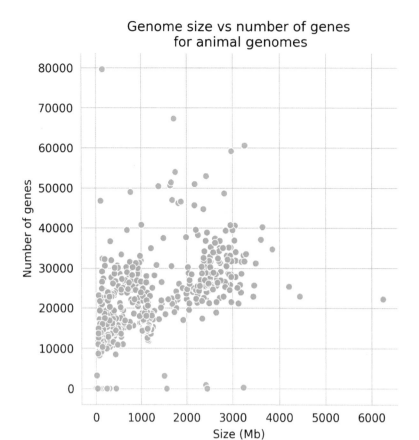

Genome size vs number of genes
for animal genomes

or a tuple of values between 0 and 1 representing red, green and blue components:

```
# rgb_color.py

sns.relplot(
    data=animals, x="Size (Mb)", y="Number of genes", color=(1, 0.5, 0),
)
plt.title("Genome size vs number of genes\n for animal genomes")
```

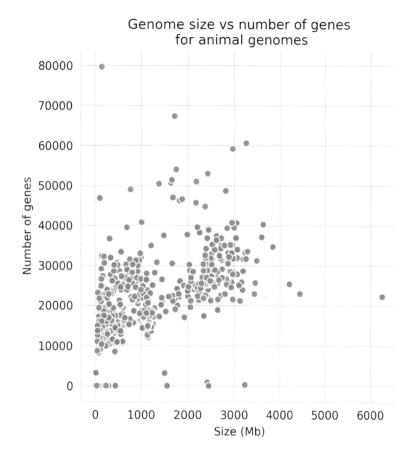

You can easily find online tools to help you pick colors. A useful resource is a list of HTML color names:

https://en.wikipedia.org/wiki/Web_colors#HTML_color_names

11.2 Working with palettes

For single color examples like the ones above, the choice of color doesn't play a huge role in the readability of the chart. As long as we avoid picking colors that are too low contrast to be seen easily:

```
sns.relplot(
    data=animals,
    x="Size (Mb)",
    y="Number of genes",
    color="mintcream",  # too similar to white!
)
plt.title("Genome size vs number of genes\n for animal genomes")
```

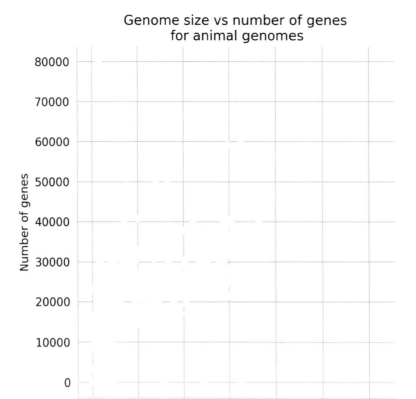

Genome size vs number of genes
for animal genomes

we cannot go far wrong. In fact, many simple charts look great without any use of color at all:

```
# grey_chart.py

sns.catplot(
    data=euk, kind="box", x="Kingdom", y="GC%", color="white", height=4
)
plt.title("Distribution of GC%\n for genomes in different kingdoms", y=1.05)
```

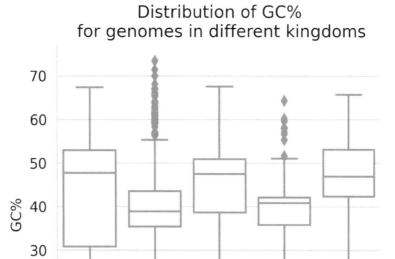

However, most of the time we will be using color to represent something in our charts - either a numerical variable, or a category. Whenever we are working with more than one color, we are dealing with a *palette*.

11.3 Palettes for sequential data

To change the color scheme for most plots, we use the `palette` argument. There are many different ways to use this argument, but for now the easiest is to pass in the name of an existing matplotlib palette. The matplotlib palettes are divided into different types; for numerical data like we have here, we need a *sequential* palette.

For convenience, here's a figure showing the most useful sequential palettes - these are the ones where higher values map to more saturated colors, which tend to be easiest to interpret:

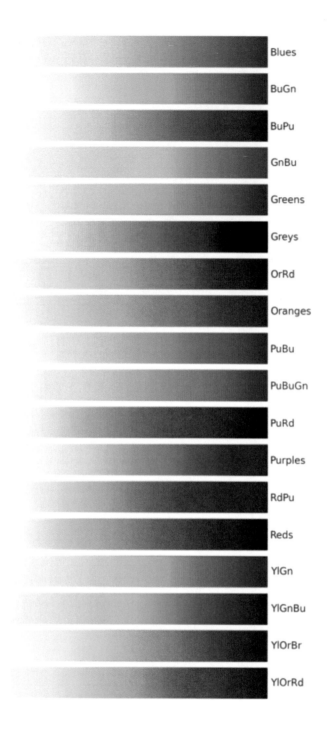

Let's take our plot of genome size versus number of genes, and use color to represent the GC percentage:

```
# sequential_palette.py

sns.relplot(
    data=animals,
    x="Size (Mb)",
    y="Number of genes",
    hue="GC%",
    palette="YlOrBr",
)
plt.title("Genome size vs number of genes\n for animal genomes")
```

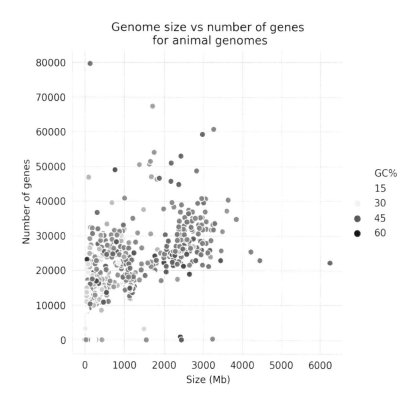

It's often tempting to use one of the various "rainbow" palettes, as they produce very colorful charts:

```
sns.relplot(
    data=animals, x="Size (Mb)", y="Number of genes", hue="GC%", palette="jet",
)
plt.title("Genome size vs number of genes\n for animal genomes")
```

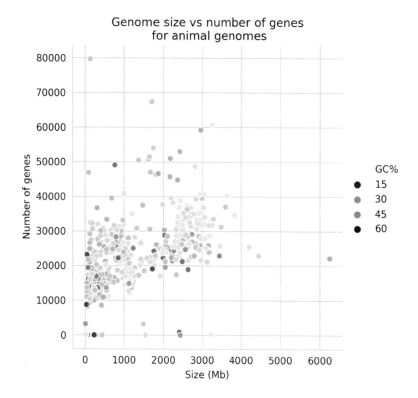

Genome size vs number of genes
for animal genomes

But these tend to make interpretation harder as they represent changes in value with different colors rather than different shades of the same color as in the sequential color maps.

All of the named sequential palettes in the figure above can be reversed by adding `_r` onto the end of the name. So we can map higher values to lighter colors:

```
# reversed_palette.py

sns.relplot(
    data=animals,
    x="Size (Mb)",
    y="Number of genes",
    hue="Publication year",
    palette="OrRd_r",
)
plt.title("Genome size vs number of genes\n for animal genomes")
```

11 Working with color in seaborn

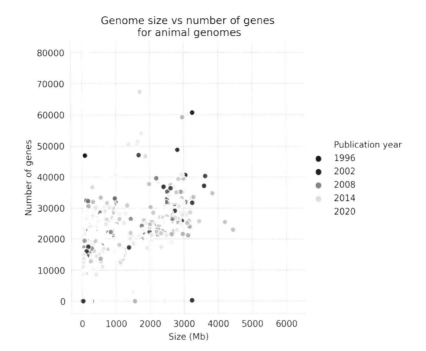

Given the wide range of built in palettes, it's relatively rare that we have to reach for anything else. However, if we want a custom palette we can take a single color and create a palette using the `light_palette` or `dark_palette` functions. Confusingly, we need `light_palette` if we are starting with a dark color, and vice versa. So to build a palette starting with a purple color:

```
# custom_sequential_palette.py

sns.relplot(
    data=animals,
    x="Size (Mb)",
    y="Number of genes",
    hue="Publication year",
    palette=sns.light_palette("purple", as_cmap=True),
)
plt.title("Genome size vs number of genes\n for animal genomes")
```

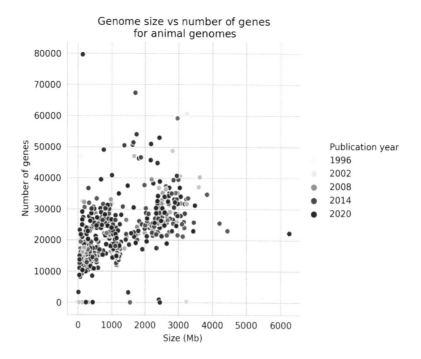

Genome size vs number of genes
for animal genomes

11.4 Palettes for categorical data

All of the palettes in the previous section have been sequential: i.e. similar values get mapped to similar colors. That's exactly what we want for numerical data, as it makes it possible to see patterns and trends. However, this is exactly what we **don't** want for categorical data. Consider our box plot from before:

```
sns.catplot(
    data=euk, kind="box", x="Kingdom", y="GC%", color="white", height=4
)
plt.title("Distribution of GC%\n for genomes in different kingdoms")
```

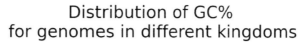

Distribution of GC%
for genomes in different kingdoms

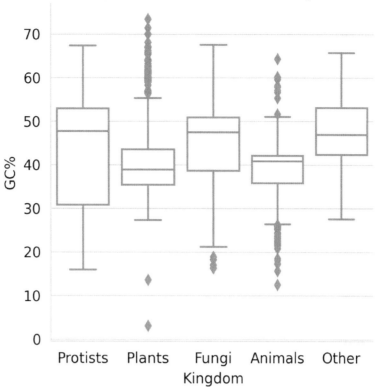

and let's add some color:

```
sns.catplot(
    data=euk, kind="box", x="Kingdom", y="GC%", palette="BuGn", height=4
)
plt.title("Distribution of GC%\n for genomes in different kingdoms")
```

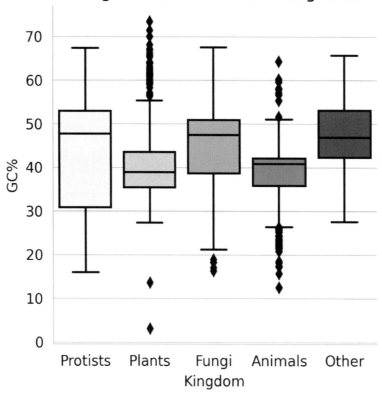

This is certainly prettier to look at, but the problem is that the colors are now actively misleading. The fact that protists and plants are a similar color will trick our brains into thinking that they are similar in some way. In fact, the reason they have similar colors in this plot is that they happened to appear in that order in the dataset.

For categories without a natural order, we want a *qualitative* palette. In seaborn we can choose from `Set1, Set2, Set3, Pastel1, Pastel2, Dark2` and `Accent`. All of these palettes have been designed to avoid having similar colors next to each other:

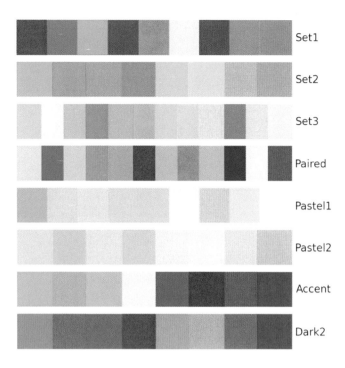

and if we pick one for our box plot, it looks much better:

```
# categorical_palette.py

sns.catplot(
    data=euk, kind="box", x="Kingdom", y="GC%", palette="Set2", height=4
)
plt.title("Distribution of GC%\n for genomes in different kingdoms")
```

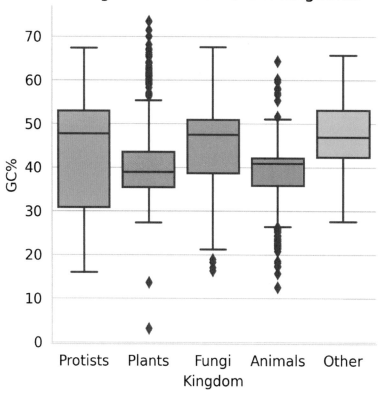

Distribution of GC%
for genomes in different kingdoms

and will help us to avoid misinterpreting color.

In the simple box plot above, the color doens't really add anything except to make the plot more attractive. However, as soon as we have multiple plots, color can play a much more important role. For example, let's turn this plot into a small multiple by drawing a separate chart for each year:

```
# grid_color.py

g = sns.catplot(
    data=euk[euk["Publication year"] > 2013],
    kind="box",
    x="Kingdom",
    y="GC%",
    palette="Dark2",
    height=3.5,
    col="Publication year",
    col_wrap=3,
)
g.fig.suptitle("Distribution of GC% for genomes in different kingdoms", y=1.05)
```

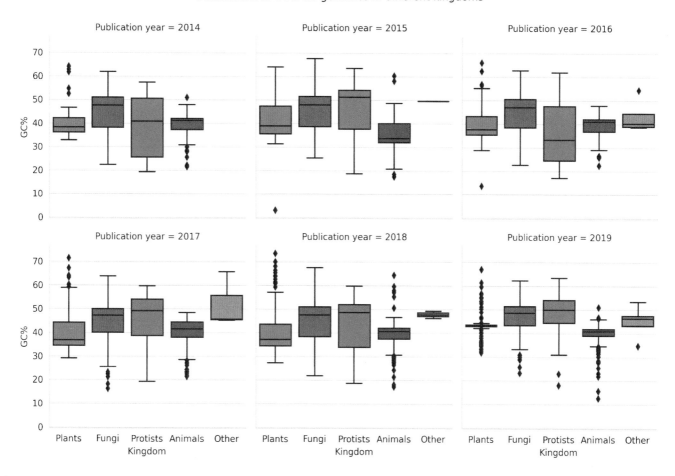

Distribution of GC% for genomes in different kingdoms

Now the color becomes much more useful. Even though it shows us redundant information - it tells us the kingdom, which is also labelled on the x axis - it's much easier to find the matching boxes between different year plots.

Color will also be very useful when we want to use the same categories across multiple plots of different types. Let's draw a matching set of small multiple scatter plots showing size versus number of genes that are also colored by kingdom:

```python
# scatter_grid.py

g = sns.relplot(
    data=euk[euk["Publication year"] > 2013],
    x="Size (Mb)",
    y="Number of genes",
    palette="Dark2",
    height=3.5,
    col="Publication year",
    col_wrap=3,
    hue="Kingdom",
)
g.fig.suptitle(
    "Genome size vs. number of genes for genomes in different kingdoms", y=1.05
)
```

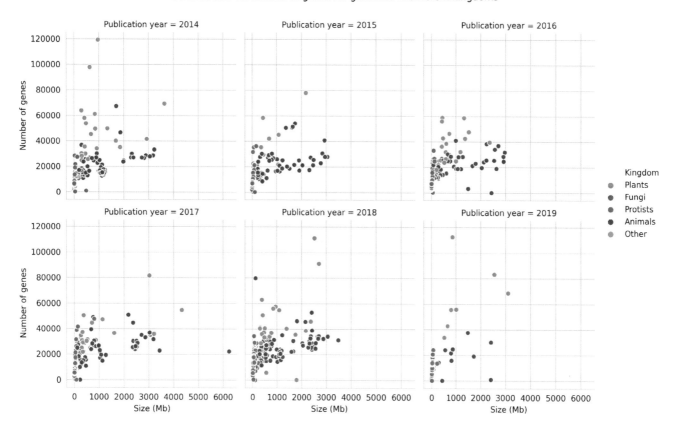

Genome size vs. number of genes for genomes in different kingdoms

Cross referencing this plot with the previous one is a tricky task, but one that is made much easier if we use consistent colors for the categories - in this case, kingdoms. Let's say we notice that a few of the dark green points in the scatter plot for 2014 have more genes than expected for their size, and want to check if there are also outliers in GC% for this group of genomes. Without matching colors in the box plots we'd have to check the legend of the scatter plots to find out which kingdom corresponds to dark green, then go to the relevant box plot and look along the x axis until we found the matching box. As it is, all we have to do is look for the matching color - we don't even necessarily need to know which kingdom we're looking at.

Notice that when using this technique, we have to make sure that the orders of the categories match. In this case they do, but we could always enforce it by using the `order` and `hue_order` arguments.

Making custom qualitative palettes is straightforward; we just make a list of color names, hexes or RGB tuples:

```
# custom_category_colors.py

sns.catplot(
    data=euk,
    kind="box",
    x="Kingdom",
    y="GC%",
    palette=["salmon", "gold", "seagreen", "indigo", "firebrick"],
    height=4,
)
plt.title("Distribution of GC%\n for genomes in different kingdoms")
None
```

Distribution of GC%
for genomes in different kingdoms

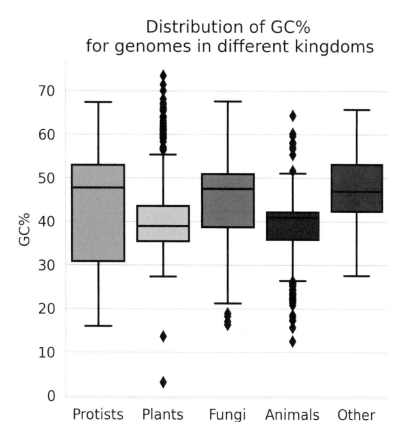

One quirk of seaborn that we have to watch out for is the default behavior when picking palettes for categorical plots. If we make a categorical plot with up to 10 categories it will pick a qualitative palette by default:

```
sns.catplot(data=euk, kind="bar", x="Kingdom", y="Number of genes", orient="v")
plt.title("Distribution of GC%\n for genomes in different kingdoms")
```

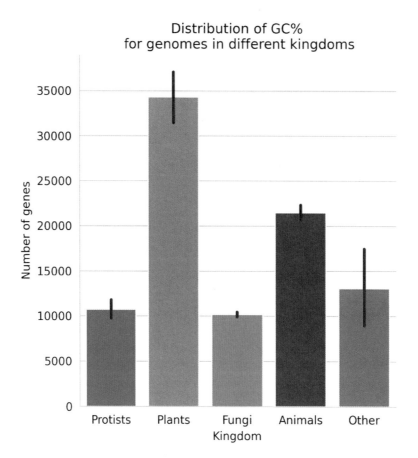

Distribution of GC%
for genomes in different kingdoms

but if we have more than 10 categories it will pick a sequential palette:

```
sns.catplot(
    data=euk, kind="bar", x="Class", y="Number of genes", aspect=3, orient="v"
)
plt.title("Distribution of GC% for genomes in different classes")
plt.xticks(rotation=45, horizontalalignment="right")
```

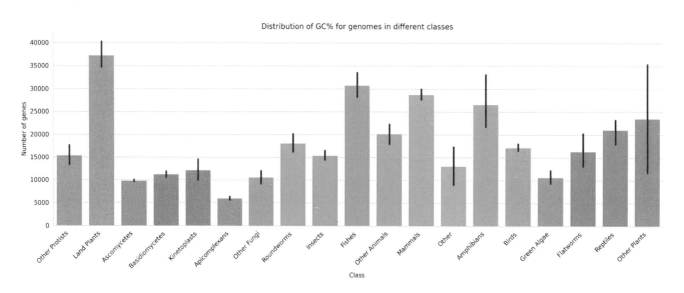

leading to the kind of interpretation problems we saw before. Because of this behaviour it's quite easy, when exploring a dataset, to end up accidentally creating a chart with an inappropriate palette.

11.5 Diverging palettes

The final type of palette that we need to consider requires a bit of explanation. *Diverging* palettes are sequential, in the sense that they are continuous - similar values map to similar colors. But they are intended for cases where we want some value in the middle of the range of values to be perceived as neutral. An example will make this clear.

Given our dataframe of animal genomes, we know that we can easily get the mean of a series - for instance, the GC percentage:

```
animals["GC%"].mean()
```

```
39.44425220228385
```

So we can make a new series to store the difference between each GC percentage and the mean, and store it as a new column:

```
animals["GC difference from mean"] = animals["GC%"] - animals["GC%"].mean()
animals.head()
```

	Species	Kingdom	Class	...	Publication year	Assembly status	GC difference from mean
34	Caenorhabditis briggsae	Animals	Roundworms	...	2002	Chromosome	-1.747652
35	Caenorhabditis elegans	Animals	Roundworms	...	2001	Complete Genome	-4.012552
36	Brugia malayi	Animals	Roundworms	...	2002	Scaffold	-7.945252
37	Aedes aegypti	Animals	Insects	...	2017	Chromosome	-1.277552
38	Aedes albopictus	Animals	Insects	...	2016	Contig	0.955648

This new column tells us, for each genome, whether the GC percentage is above or below the average for animals, and by how much.

Now let's use it in a chart. If we put our new column on an axis it's easy enough to interpret: points to the right of the center line have greater than average GC. The only tweak we might make is to set the x axis limits to make it symmetrical around the zero point:

```
# difference_plot.py

animals["GC difference from mean"] = animals["GC%"] - animals["GC%"].mean()

sns.relplot(data=animals, x="GC difference from mean", y="Number of genes")
plt.xlim(-15, 15)
plt.title("Number of genes vs. GC difference\n from mean for animal genomes")
```

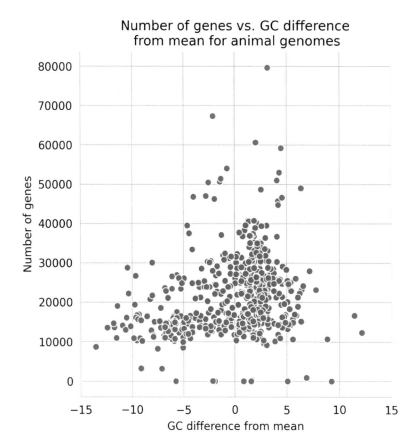

Number of genes vs. GC difference
from mean for animal genomes

When we use this new column as a hue, however, things get a bit trickier:

```
sns.relplot(
    data=animals,
    x="Size (Mb)",
    y="Number of genes",
    hue="GC difference from mean",
)
plt.title("Genome size vs number of genes\n for animal genomes")
```

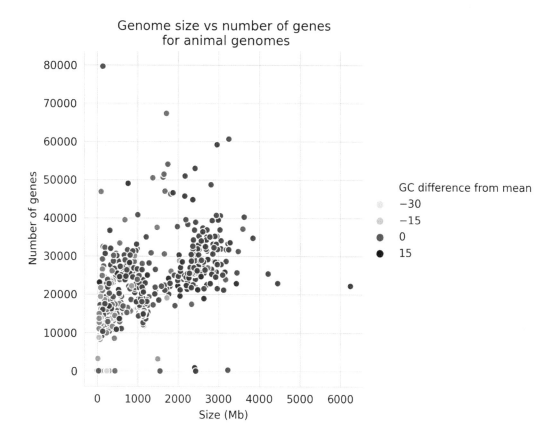

What we are really interested in seeing is, for each point, whether the GC is above or below the average for animals, i.e. whether the difference is positive or negative. But as we can see from the legend, the particular shade of purple that corresponds to zero isn't easy to pick out. We will have the same problem with any of the sequential palettes we have seen.

The solution is to use a diverging palette, which has a neutral color in the middle that we can use to represent zero. For example, the `RdBu` palette goes from red to blue, passing through white in the center. If we use that as our palette then the colors will be much easier to interpret:

```
# diverging_palette.py

animals["GC difference\n from mean"] = animals["GC%"] - animals["GC%"].mean()

sns.relplot(
    data=animals,
    x="Size (Mb)",
    y="Number of genes",
    hue="GC difference\n from mean",
    palette="RdBu",
    hue_norm=(-10, 10),  # make zero the middle of the color scale
)
plt.title("Genome size vs number of genes\n for animal genomes")
```

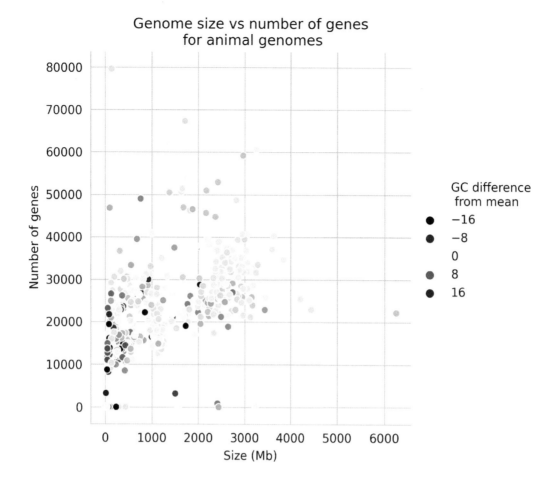

As we can see from the scale, red points are negative and blue points are positive, and the saturation of the color tells us how far away from zero each point is. This makes it easy to see the pattern that big genomes with large numbers of genes tend to have higher GC percentage than the animal average. One little tip: notice how we put a newline character in the name of the new column to make it look nicer on the legend.

Diverging palettes are useful whenever we want to show a value relative to some neutral point. We will make extensive use of diverging palettes when we discuss heatmaps, as it's in that context that they come into play most often. Here are the diverging palettes available:

---

11 Working with color in seaborn

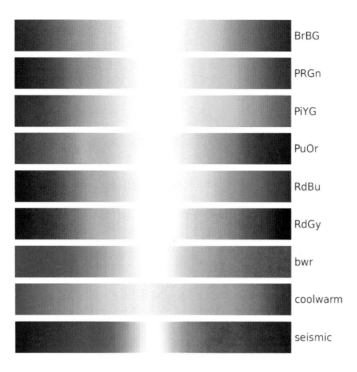

BrBG

PRGn

PiYG

PuOr

RdBu

RdGy

bwr

coolwarm

seismic

11.6 Using color redundantly

One of the best uses of color in data visualization can be to add redundant information. We have already seen an example of this with our small multiple box plots:

```
g = sns.catplot(
    data=euk[euk["Publication year"].isin([2016, 2017, 2018])],
    kind="box",
    x="Kingdom",
    y="GC%",
    palette="Dark2",
    height=3.5,
    col="Publication year",
)
g.fig.suptitle("Distribution of GC% for genomes in different kingdoms", y=1.05)
None
```

Distribution of GC% for genomes in different kingdoms

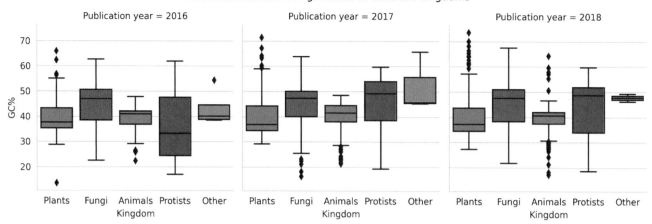

In this chart the color of each bar is redundant in the sense that it tells us the kingdom, which we could also figure out by looking at the x axis labels. However, it's still useful. If we want to compare a given kingdom for different publication years, it's much easier to find the matching color than the matching label on the x axis. Try it: see how long it takes to figure out if there's a difference in the GC% of protist genomes published in 2016 vs 2017, then try to answer the same question using the monochrome version:

```
g = sns.catplot(
    data=euk[euk["Publication year"].isin([2016, 2017, 2018])],
    kind="box",
    x="Kingdom",
    y="GC%",
    color="lightskyblue",
    height=3.5,
    col="Publication year",
)
g.fig.suptitle("Distribution of GC% for genomes in different kingdoms", y=1.05)
None
```

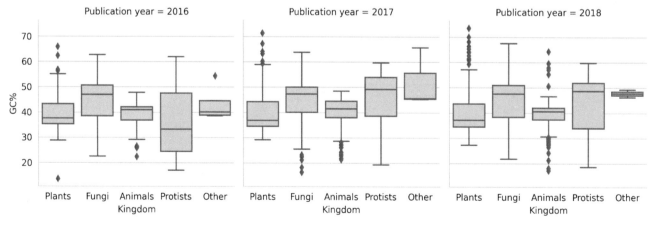

When it comes to interpreting complex charts, redundancy is a good thing. By giving our visual system two aspects of the chart to focus on - in this case, color and X position - we make it easier to make comparisons.

The same is often true for other aspects. For example, we can use color and marker style redundantly in scatter plots:

11 Working with color in seaborn

```
# color_and_marker.py

sns.relplot(
    data=euk[euk["Class"].isin(["Mammals", "Birds"])].dropna(),
    x="Size (Mb)",
    y="Number of genes",
    hue="Class",
    palette="Set1",
    style="Class",
)
plt.title("Genome size vs number of genes\n for mammal and bird genomes")
```

Here we have red circles for mammal genomes and blue crosses for bird genomes. Of course, this means that we can't use color to display a third variable as we've done before.

For numerical columns, it may be useful to use color and size together:

```
# color_and_size.py

sns.relplot(
    data=euk[euk["Class"].isin(["Birds"])].dropna(),
    y="Number of proteins",
    x="Number of genes",
    hue="Size (Mb)",
    palette="YlOrBr",
    size="Size (Mb)",
    sizes=(2, 100),
)
plt.title("Number of genes and number of proteins\n for bird genomes")
```

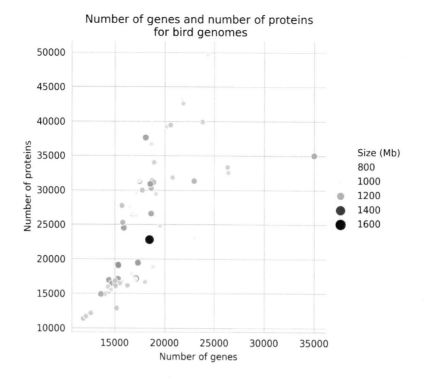

This will doubly emphasize the largest values, which are now represented by points that are both bigger and more saturated.

We can do a similar thing by combining color with style in point plots by setting the `linestyles` argument to a list of strings representing the styles that we want:

```python
# color_and_style.py

sns.catplot(
    data=euk[
        (euk["Publication year"] > 2000)
        & (euk["Kingdom"].isin(["Plants", "Fungi"]))
    ],
    x="Publication year",
    y="Number of genes",
    kind="point",
    hue="Kingdom",
    linestyles=["-", "--"],
    aspect=3,
    height=4,
    dodge=True,
    orient="v",
)

plt.title(
    "Mean number of genes for plant and fungal genomes\nsequenced each year since 2001",
)
```

11 Working with color in seaborn

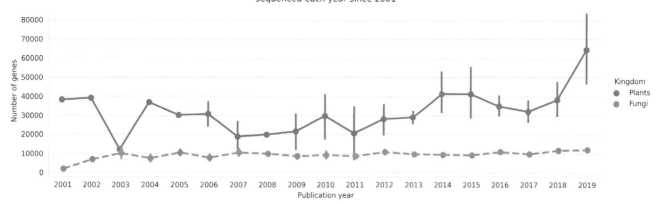

Mean number of genes for plant and fungal genomes
sequenced each year since 2001

or in line plots by setting the `style` argument to the same column as `hue`:

```
# color_and_style_line.py

sns.relplot(
    data=weather[weather["City"].isin(["Berlin", "Edinburgh"])],
    x="Day of year",
    y="Mean temperature",
    hue="City",
    aspect=3,
    height=4,
    kind="line",
    style="City",
    ci="sd",
)

plt.title(
    "Mean daily temperature for each day of the year\nsince 1960 in Berlin and Edinburgh"
)
```

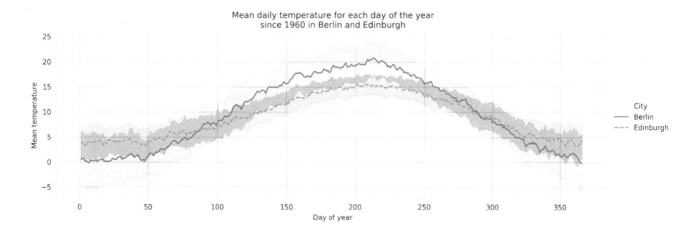

Mean daily temperature for each day of the year
since 1960 in Berlin and Edinburgh

This only works well for small numbers of different styles.

Another way that we can use color redundantly is to use it to display some extra information about a category. Take a chart where the main category is a class:

```
sns.catplot(
    data=euk,
    kind="bar",
    x="Class",
    y="Number of genes",
    aspect=2,
    color="lightblue",
    orient="v",
)
plt.title("Mean number of genes\n for genomes in different classes")
plt.xticks(rotation=45, horizontalalignment="right")
```

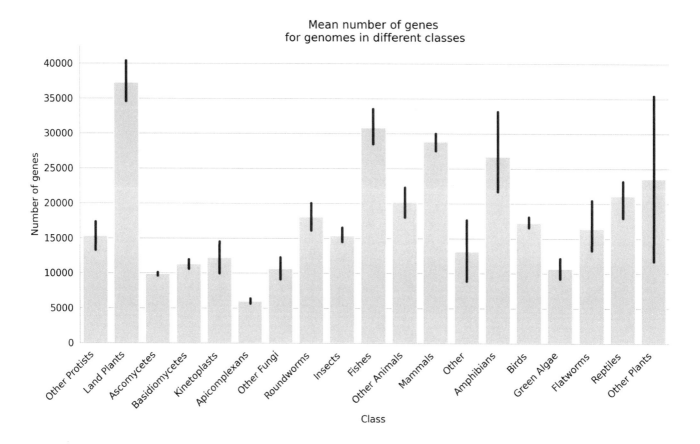

Each class belongs to a kingdom, and so in principle we could figure out which kingdom each bar belongs to by finding its X axis label. It would be much easier, however, if we used color to represent kingdom:

```
sns.catplot(
    data=euk,
    kind="bar",
    x="Class",
    y="Number of genes",
    aspect=2,
    hue="Kingdom",
    orient="v",
)
plt.title("Mean number of genes\n for genomes in different classes")
plt.xticks(rotation=45, horizontalalignment="right")
```

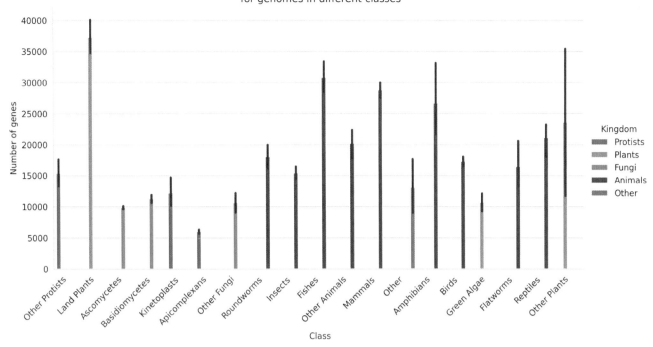

Mean number of genes
for genomes in different classes

Notice the problem with this chart: the bars are very narrow and unevenly spaced. This is because seaborn doesn't "know" that each class belongs to one kingdom, so it is leaving enough space for 5 bars - one per kingdom - at each X axis label. To avoid this, set `dodge` to `False`:

```
# color_as_category.py

sns.catplot(
    data=euk,
    kind="bar",
    x="Class",
    y="Number of genes",
    aspect=2,
    hue="Kingdom",
    dodge=False,
    orient="v",
)
plt.title("Mean number of genes\n for genomes in different classes")
plt.xticks(rotation=45, horizontalalignment="right")
None
```

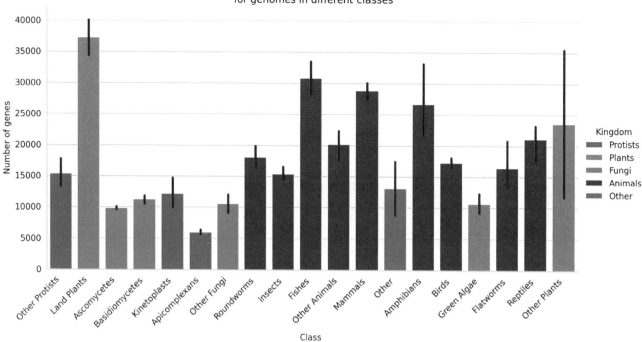

Incidentally, for this chart the default ordering on the X axis make little sense - the classes appear simply in the order that they appear in the data. We can specify an order using `order` - for example, we could group by kingdom:

```python
# ordered_labels.py

labels_order = [
    "Insects", "Other Animals", "Mammals", "Roundworms", "Birds", "Fishes", "Flatworms", "Reptiles",
    "Amphibians", "Basidiomycetes", "Ascomycetes", "Other Fungi", "Other", "Land Plants",
    "Green Algae", "Other Plants", "Apicomplexans", "Kinetoplasts", "Other Protists",
]

sns.catplot(
    data=euk,
    kind="bar",
    x="Class",
    y="Number of genes",
    aspect=2,
    hue="Kingdom",
    dodge=False,
    order=labels_order,
    orient="v",
)
plt.title("Mean number of genes\n for genomes in different classes")
plt.xticks(rotation=45, horizontalalignment="right")
```

11 Working with color in seaborn

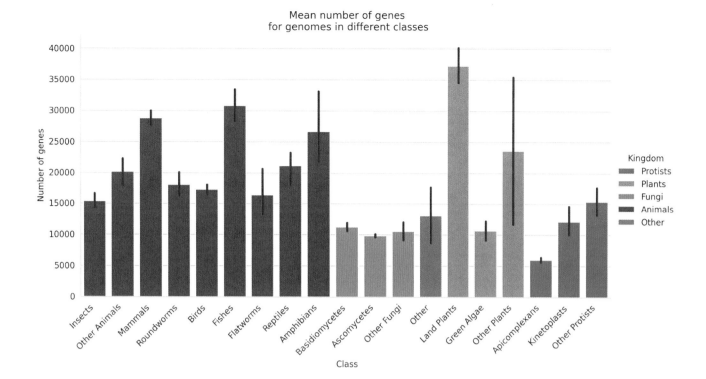

Mean number of genes
for genomes in different classes

or arrange the classes from highest to lowest mean number of genes. We will see how to do this programatically in a future chapter but for now we will just write a literal list:

```python
# sorted_labels.py

labels_order = ["Apicomplexans", "Ascomycetes", "Other Fungi", "Green Algae", "Basidiomycetes",
                "Kinetoplasts", "Other", "Other Protists", "Insects", "Flatworms", "Birds",
                "Roundworms", "Other Animals", "Reptiles","Other Plants", "Amphibians",
                "Mammals", "Fishes", "Land Plants"]

sns.catplot(
    data=euk,
    kind="bar",
    x="Class",
    y="Number of genes",
    aspect=2,
    hue="Kingdom",
    dodge=False,
    order=labels_order,
    orient="v",
)
plt.title("Mean number of genes\n for genomes in different classes")
plt.xticks(rotation=45, horizontalalignment="right")
```

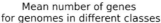

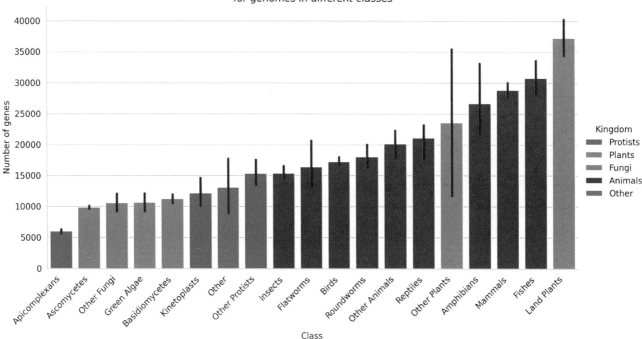

This technique of using color to show extra information about categories can be very flexible when we combine it with pandas processing. We can add arbitrary categories to our data points, then map those to color.

For example, let's take our dataframe of animal genomes and assign each one as belonging to either a warm-blooded or cold-blooded species (these terms are not really used scientifically, but we will use them here for simplicity). The easiest way to do this is to write a function that will take the name of a class and return the answer we want:

```
def warm_or_cold(class_name):
    if class_name == "Mammals" or class_name == "Birds":
        return "Warm-blooded"
    else:
        return "Cold-blooded"
```

and then use `apply` to run it on each of our genomes' class values:

```
animals["Class"].apply(warm_or_cold)
```

```
34      Cold-blooded
35      Cold-blooded
36      Cold-blooded
37      Cold-blooded
38      Cold-blooded
            ...
5642    Cold-blooded
5738    Warm-blooded
5779    Cold-blooded
5797    Cold-blooded
6781    Warm-blooded
Name: Class, Length: 613, dtype: object
```

Once we have our resulting series of classifications, we can add it as a new column:

```
animals["Thermoregulation"] = animals["Class"].apply(warm_or_cold)
animals.head()
```

	Species	Kingdom	Class	...	GC difference from mean	GC difference\n from mean	Thermoregulation
34	Caenorhabditis briggsae	Animals	Roundworms	...	-1.747652	-1.747652	Cold-blooded
35	Caenorhabditis elegans	Animals	Roundworms	...	-4.012552	-4.012552	Cold-blooded
36	Brugia malayi	Animals	Roundworms	...	-7.945252	-7.945252	Cold-blooded
37	Aedes aegypti	Animals	Insects	...	-1.277552	-1.277552	Cold-blooded
38	Aedes albopictus	Animals	Insects	...	0.955648	0.955648	Cold-blooded

And now we can use it as a categorical variable. Because all the genomes belonging to each class will obviously have the same value, we need to use `dodge = False` when using it in conjunction with **Class** as the main variable:

```
# color_as_metadata.py

def warm_or_cold(class_name):
    if class_name == "Mammals" or class_name == "Birds":
        return "Warm-blooded"
    else:
        return "Cold-blooded"

animals["Thermoregulation"] = animals["Class"].apply(warm_or_cold)

sns.catplot(
    data=animals,
    y="Class",
    x="Number of genes",
    kind="bar",
    hue="Thermoregulation",
    dodge=False,
    height=5,
)

plt.title("Mean and 95% CI of number of genes for each class")
```

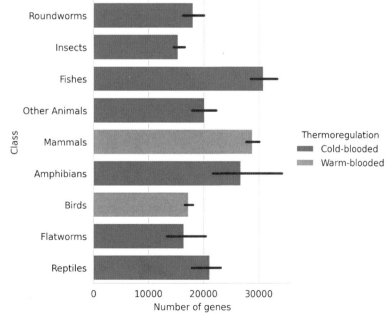

A similar trick is to highlight a single category by giving it a different color to the rest. We can do this by combinig the **order** and **palette** arguments to **catplot**. Returning to our example where we are drawing a boxplot of GC% for each kingdom in different years, here's how we can highlight animals subtly:

```
# highlight_subtle.py

g = sns.catplot(
    data=euk[euk["Publication year"].isin([2016, 2017, 2018])],
    kind="box",
    x="Kingdom",
    y="GC%",
    height=4,
    col="Publication year",
    order=["Plants", "Fungi", "Animals", "Protists", "Other"],
    palette=[
        "goldenrod",
        "goldenrod",
        "saddlebrown",
        "goldenrod",
        "goldenrod",
    ],
)
g.fig.suptitle("Distribution of GC% for genomes in different kingdoms", y=1.05)
```

or more strikingly:

```
# highlight_bold.py

g = sns.catplot(
    data=euk[euk["Publication year"].isin([2016, 2017, 2018])],
    kind="box",
    x="Kingdom",
    y="GC%",
    height=4,
    col="Publication year",
    order=["Plants", "Fungi", "Animals", "Protists", "Other"],
    palette=["white", "white", "crimson", "white", "white"],
)
g.fig.suptitle("Distribution of GC% for genomes in different kingdoms", y=1.05)
```

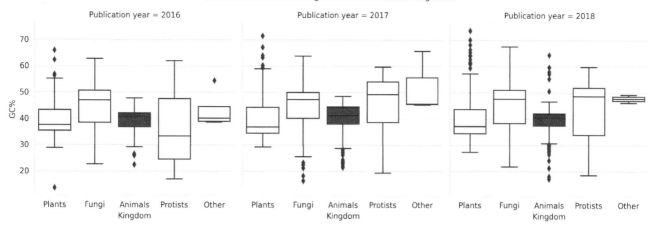

Distribution of GC% for genomes in different kingdoms

11.7 Consistency with colors

As we've seen in earlier examples, using colors consistently between charts can be a great aid to interpretation. Conversely, inconsistent use of color can cause all sorts of problems. One trap that we can fall into is to draw two charts with the same categories and palettes, but different category orders:

```
sns.catplot(
    data=euk[euk["Number of genes"].fillna(0) > 10000],
    x="Kingdom",
    y="GC%",
    palette="Accent",
    kind="boxen",
)
plt.title(
    "Distribution of GC% across kingdoms\nfor genomes with more than 10000 genes"
)
```

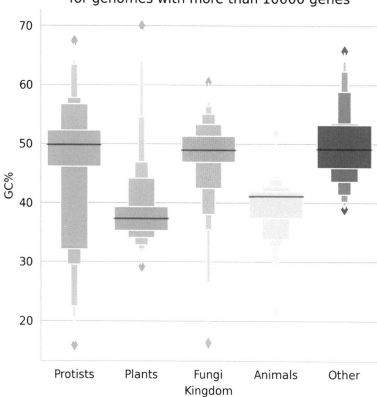

Distribution of GC% across kingdoms
for genomes with more than 10000 genes

```
sns.catplot(
    data=euk[euk["Number of genes"].fillna(0) <= 10000],
    x="Kingdom",
    y="GC%",
    palette="Accent",
    kind="boxen",
)
plt.title(
    "Distribution of GC% across kingdoms\nfor genomes with 10000 genes or fewer"
)
```

11 Working with color in seaborn

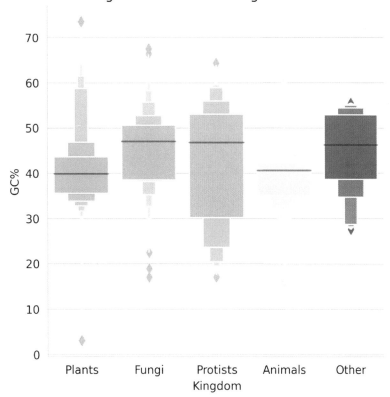

Distribution of GC% across kingdoms
for genomes with 10000 genes or fewer

In the above pair of plots we have divided our dataset into two subsets and plotted them separately. Because the order (and hence the color) of the kingdoms is determined by the order that they appear in the data, it's different for each chart. Either chart in isolation would be fine, but together this is a disaster for interpretation - looking at boxes of the same color and position means that we are comparing two different kingdoms.

One solution is to have an explicit order for the kingdoms, which we define once at the start of the project:

```
kingdom_order = ["Plants", "Animals", "Fungi", "Protists", "Other"]
```

and then reuse each time we draw a chart:

```
sns.catplot(
    data=euk[euk["Number of genes"].fillna(0) > 10000],
    x="Kingdom",
    y="GC%",
    palette="Accent",
    kind="boxen",
    order=kingdom_order,
)
plt.title(
    "Distribution of GC% across kingdoms\nfor genomes with more than 10000 genes"
)
```

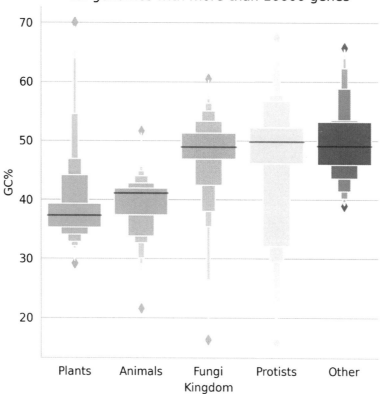

Distribution of GC% across kingdoms
for genomes with more than 10000 genes

```
sns.catplot(
    data=euk[euk["Number of genes"].fillna(0) <= 10000],
    x="Kingdom",
    y="GC%",
    palette="Accent",
    kind="boxen",
    order=kingdom_order,
)
plt.title(
    "Distribution of GC% across kingdoms\nfor genomes with 10000 genes or fewer"
)
```

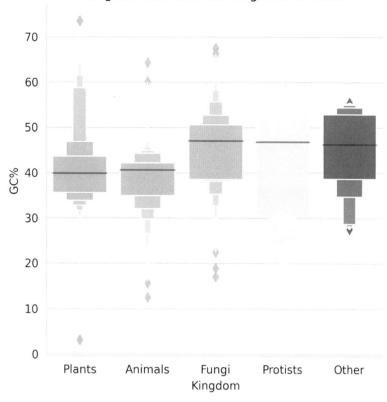

Distribution of GC% across kingdoms
for genomes with 10000 genes or fewer

This forces a consistent order. Another option would be to make a new categorical column containing the property that we want to use to split the data up. This is covered in detail in the chapter on binning, so we'll do it briefly here:

```
euk["Gene count category"] = (
    euk["Number of genes"]
    .fillna(0)
    .apply(lambda x: "More than 10,000" if x > 10000 else "10,000 or fewer")
)
euk.head()
```

	Species	Kingdom	Class	...	Publication year	Assembly status	Gene count category
0	Emiliania huxleyi CCMP1516	Protists	Other Protists	...	2013	Scaffold	More than 10,000
1	Arabidopsis thaliana	Plants	Land Plants	...	2001	Chromosome	More than 10,000
2	Glycine max	Plants	Land Plants	...	2010	Chromosome	More than 10,000
3	Medicago truncatula	Plants	Land Plants	...	2011	Chromosome	More than 10,000
4	Solanum lycopersicum	Plants	Land Plants	...	2010	Chromosome	More than 10,000

Now we can use **catplot** to separate out the two categories in a single chart, and it will take care of enforcing a consistent order between the individual plots:

```
# simple_binning.py

euk["Gene count category"] = (
    euk["Number of genes"]
    .fillna(0)
    .apply(lambda x: "More than 10,000" if x > 10000 else "10,000 or fewer")
)

g = sns.catplot(
    data=euk,
    x="Kingdom",
    y="GC%",
    palette="Accent",
    kind="boxen",
    col="Gene count category",
    col_order=["10,000 or fewer", "More than 10,000"],
)
g.fig.suptitle("Distribution of GC% across kingdoms", y=1.05)
```

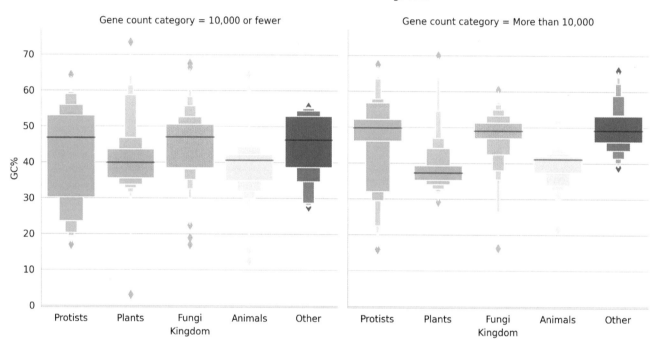

Note that with this approach we have to explicitly specify the order for our small multiple plots to get them in the natural order.

The final approach to ensure consistency between charts would be to make the **Kingdom** column an ordered category. We'll discuss this in a later chapter.

11.7.1 Reusing palettes for different categories

Another problem that's easy to run into is accidentally using the same palettes for different categories. Let's say we start a project by looking at the distribution of GC% across kingdoms, using a similar chart to the examples above:

```
sns.catplot(data=euk, x="Kingdom", y="GC%", kind="boxen")
plt.title("Distribution of GC% across kingdoms")
```

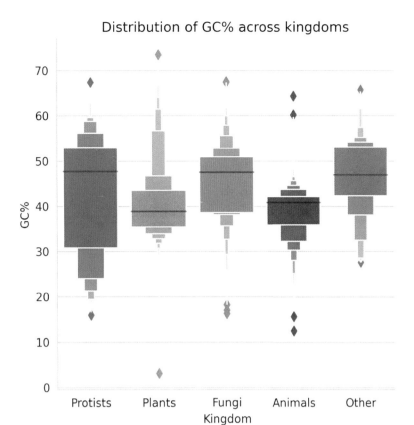

Distribution of GC% across kingdoms

Then later we draw another chart that uses color to represent a different category:

```
sns.relplot(
    data=euk[euk["Size (Mb)"] < 5000],
    x="Size (Mb)",
    y="Number of genes",
    hue="Assembly status",
    aspect=2,
)
plt.title(
    "Genome size vs. number of genes\nfor genomes in different stages of assembly"
)
```

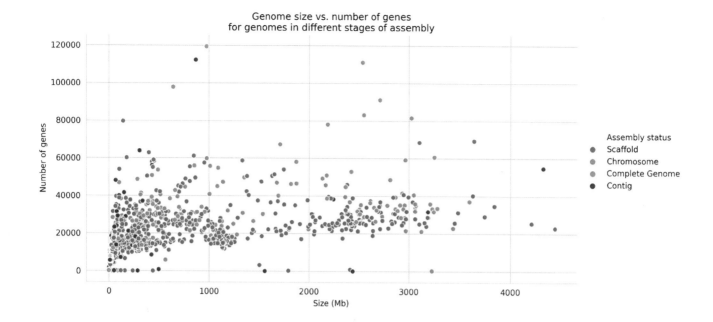

When interpreting these two charts, it's going to be very tempting to assume that the dark blue points in the scatter plot correspond to the dark blue box in the boxen plot. Of course, this is misleading as the two charts are grouping the genomes in completely different ways.

The easiest way to avoid this is to simply use a different palette for one of the charts:

```
sns.relplot(
    data=euk[euk["Size (Mb)"] < 5000],
    x="Size (Mb)",
    y="Number of genes",
    hue="Assembly status",
    aspect=2,
    palette="Set2",
)
plt.title(
    "Genome size vs. number of genes\nfor genomes in different stages of assembly"
)
```

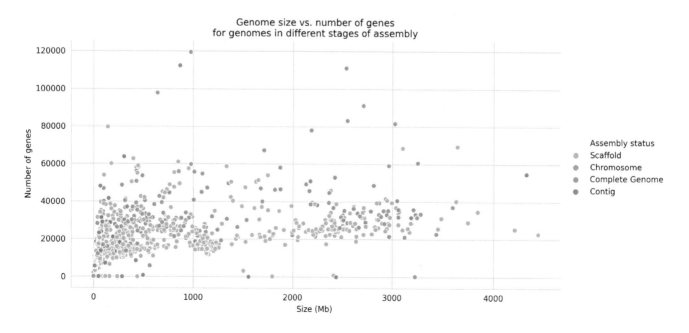

In fact, it's a good idea to get into the habit of always specifying a palette when using `hue`, even if it's just to pick the default (`'Set1'`).

12 Grouping and categories in pandas

In the first few chapters of this book - where we introduced pandas - we concentrated mostly on numerical data and the types of analysis we can do with it. And in subsequent chapters - where we introduced seaborn - we started off looking at numerical data before expanding into looking at categorical data. Now that we have introduced the chart types most suitable for categorical data we can return to pandas and look at some tools for working with categories.

12.1 Types of categories

Although it's often convenient to divide data into categorical and numerical, when we start looking at real data we quickly run into situations where the distinction is a bit more subtle. We've already encountered a few of these in our eukaryote genome dataset.

Is the publication year column a number or a category? Well, it's obviously stored as a number, and has a natural order. But it's also not continuous - it can only take discrete integer values. The values are also measured in a different way: unlike genome size or number of genes, it makes no sense to talk about the mean year, or to say that the year for one genome is 10% larger than the year for another. This is because years are measured from an artibrary point in the past. We might call this a *semi-continuous* column, or possibly an *ordinal* column.

Speaking of genome size and number of genes, let's think about them next. They are both numerical and behave like continuous variables - they both have a base at zero so we can do meaningful statistics on them. However, size is what we might think of as a truly continuous variable, as we can imagine measuring it to any number of decimal places (until we get down to counting single bases!) whereas the number of genes has to be an integer. So in some sense, size is "more continuous" than number of genes.

Finally, let's consider some non-numerical columns. Species, kingdom and class are obviously categorical, but there are some intuitive differences between them. We already know from our previous explorations of this dataset that kingdom and class have a small number of unique values. We can check this using pandas:

```
euk["Kingdom"].nunique(), euk["Class"].nunique()
```

```
(5, 19)
```

Whereas species has a large number of unique values:

```
euk["Species"].nunique()
```

```
4936
```

To put it another way, the vast majority of species are present only once in the dataset. The easiest way to show this is to call **value_counts** twice:

```
euk["Species"].value_counts().value_counts().head()
```

```
1    4051
2     538
3     150
4      62
5      27
Name: Species, dtype: Int64
```

Out of the 4936 unique species names, 4051 are present just once in the dataset.

So if we had to attempt a classification of the different data types we're dealing with in this dataset, we might order them from most to least categorical:

- Columns that have a small number of unique text values (**kingdom**, **class**, **status**)
- Columns that have a large number of unique text values (**species**)
- Columns that have a small number of unique discrete numbers (**year**)
- Columns have have a large number of unqiue discrete numbers (**genes**, **proteins**)
- Columns where nearly every measurement is unique (**size**)

Why are we bothering to go through our columns in this way? Because the type of data in each column greatly affects the ways in which we can analyze and visualize it. For very categorical things like **kingdom**, it might be useful to summarize some property like GC percentage by calculating the median:

```python
for k in euk["Kingdom"].unique():
    my_kingdom = euk[euk["Kingdom"] == k]
    print(k, my_kingdom["GC%"].median())
```

```
Protists 47.7
Plants 38.8437
Fungi 47.5
Animals 40.8
Other 46.905
```

Whereas doing this for each species will be meaningless, since the vast majority of species only have a single genome and we would get nearly as many values in our summary as we had in the original dataset - hardly a summary at all.

Columns with small numbers of unique values also call for different approaches to visualization. Using different colors to represent different kingdoms on a chart works well, as we've seen, but imagine trying to use nearly five thousand different colors to represent the different species!

With this in mind, let's look at some of pandas' tools for dealing with categorical data.

12.2 Grouping

The fundamental tool for working with categories in pandas is the **groupby** method. As with many parts of the pandas universe, this method is concise, powerful, and sometimes a bit tricky to understand, so we'll explore it by way of a few examples.

The best way to think about grouping is as a two stage process. First we tell pandas how to group the rows of our dataframe, and then we tell it what we want to do with the groups. The simplest way to group the rows is by a particular column, and the simplest thing to do is just count how many rows there are.

For the first step, we call **groupby** with the name of the column that determines the groups:

```python
euk.groupby("Kingdom")
```

```
<pandas.core.groupby.generic.DataFrameGroupBy object at 0x7fd604527eb8>
```

The output from this, as we can see, is a **DataFrameGroupBy** object. Just looking at this object is not very exciting - in order to get any useful information from it, we need to tell pandas what to do with the groups. To count the rows in each group, we will use the **size** method:

```python
# count_kingdom.py

# count how many rows for each different kingdom
euk.groupby("Kingdom").size()
```

```
Kingdom
Animals    2181
Fungi      4494
Other        30
Plants      870
Protists    727
dtype: int64
```

The output here is a series where the index is the unique entries from the kingdom column and the values are how many times they occur. We might note that this is very similar to:

```
euk["Kingdom"].value_counts()
```

```
Fungi      4494
Animals    2181
Plants      870
Protists    727
Other        30
Name: Kingdom, dtype: Int64
```

The difference is that when using **groupby** we get the counts ordered alphabetically by the index, whereas with **value_counts** we always get the most common value listed first. For every type of data, pandas has its own idea about how to order them. For strings it's alphabetically; for numbers it's in ascending order:

```
euk.groupby("Publication year").size().tail()
```

```
Publication year
2015     890
2016    1229
2017    1207
2018    2389
2019     670
dtype: int64
```

Later on we'll see how to enforce a specific ordering when we want it.

Let's now try a more complicated grouping - we'll supply a list of two column names to **groupby**:

```
# complex_count.py

euk.groupby(["Kingdom", "Assembly status"]).size()
```

```
Kingdom    Assembly status
Animals    Chromosome          246
           Complete Genome       1
           Contig              203
           Scaffold           1731
Fungi      Chromosome          681
                              ...
Plants     Scaffold            443
Protists   Chromosome          101
           Complete Genome       7
           Contig              160
           Scaffold            459
Length: 20, dtype: int64
```

The output from this statement is something we've not seen before: a series with two indices. Resist the temptation to think of this as a table! Instead, think of it as a list of values (the counts) where each value has two labels. The two indices (kingdom and status) are both ordered alphabetically.

12 Grouping and categories in pandas

12.2.1 Calculating summaries for groups

Now that we know how to specify groups, let's try a few more ambitious calculations. Just like with a normal dataframe, we can extract individual columns from a `GroupBy` object with square bracket syntax:

```
euk.groupby("Kingdom")["GC%"]
```

```
<pandas.core.groupby.generic.SeriesGroupBy object at 0x7fd59a7f1ef0>
```

Hopefully the name of this object makes sense: when we extract a single column from a `DataFrame` we get a `Series`, and when we extract a single column from a `DataFrameGroupBy` we get a `SeriesGroupBy`. To get a useful output here, we need to tell pandas how to summarize the values for each group - in other words, we have to come up with a way to take all the values for a group and come up with a single value. If this sounds familiar, that's because it's the same pattern that we described earlier as *aggregation*. So all of the functions that we used in previous chapters to summarize values can also be used here.

The simplest aggregations to understand are the familiar mean and median:

```
# mean_kingdom_gc.py

# what's the mean GC percentage for each kingdom?
euk.groupby("Kingdom")["GC%"].mean()
```

```
Kingdom
Animals    38.979311
Fungi      45.708512
Other      46.600059
Plants     40.702560
Protists   43.159938
Name: GC%, dtype: float64
```

```
# what's the median size for each status?
euk.groupby("Assembly status")["Size (Mb)"].median()
```

```
Assembly status
Chromosome        13.0771
Complete Genome   15.9383
Contig            35.8714
Scaffold          44.9756
Name: Size (Mb), dtype: float64
```

Many of the questions we need to ask of complex datasets can be answered using the general recipe outlined above: pick a column to group on, pick a column to summarize, and pick a function to summarize it.

12.2.2 Multiple inputs to grouping operations

Now that we've seen the basic recipe for grouping and aggregation, let's experiment with using multiple inputs in each place.

As we saw before, giving multiple column names results in a series with two indices. This works just the same for aggregations as it did for `size` (in fact, we can think of size as just another type of aggregation, which takes a list of values, ignores the values themselves, and gives us the size of the list):

```
# max.py

# what's the maximum GC percentage for each combination
# of kingdom and status?
euk.groupby(["Kingdom", "Assembly status"])["GC%"].max()
```

```
Kingdom     Assembly status
Animals     Chromosome        49.2464
            Complete Genome   35.4317
            Contig            64.3000
            Scaffold          60.2000
Fungi       Chromosome        59.5059
                               ...
Plants      Scaffold          71.4000
Protists    Chromosome        59.7916
            Complete Genome   59.7642
            Contig            63.4000
            Scaffold          67.4000
Name: GC%, Length: 20, dtype: float64
```

What happens if instead of picking multiple columns to group by, we instead pick multiple columns to summarize?

```
# multiple_columns.py

# what's the mean number of genes and proteins for each kingdom?
euk.groupby("Kingdom")[["Number of genes", "Number of proteins"]].mean()
```

Kingdom	Number of genes	Number of proteins
Animals	21475.202284	28342.721044
Fungi	10176.505426	10041.961240
Other	13086.466667	13027.800000
Plants	34303.465608	38652.698413
Protists	10722.800000	10619.056818

This gives us a dataframe with two columns, but a single index. This often lends itself well to visualization. For example let's take the median number of genes and proteins for each class, and plot them on a scatter plot:

```
# class_plot.py

g = sns.relplot(
    data=euk.groupby("Class")[["Number of genes", "Number of proteins"]].median(),
    x="Number of genes",
    y="Number of proteins",
)

g.fig.suptitle("Median numbers of genes and proteins for genomes in each class", y=1.05)
```

Median numbers of genes and proteins for genomes in each class

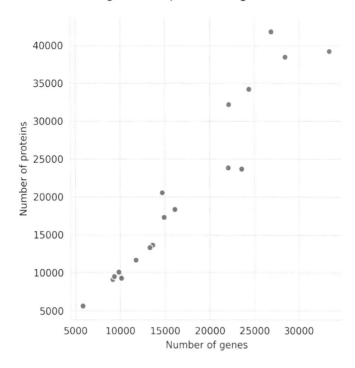

This looks superficially similar to the genes/proteins scatter plots we have drawn previously, but note that here we're displaying the data at a higher level of abstraction. In previous plots, each point represented a single genome; here each point represents an entire class.

So, grouping by multiple columns gives us a series with multiple indices, and summarizing multiple columns gives us a dataframe with multiple rows. What happens when we take a single column but summarize it in multiple ways?

The syntax for this is a little bit tricky: rather than just calling a single aggregation method on a `GroupBy` object, we have to call the `agg` method and give it a list of functions that we want to use for aggregation. Many useful such methods are part of the numpy package:

```
# multiple_stats.py

import numpy as np

euk.groupby("Kingdom")["Size (Mb)"].agg([np.mean, np.median])
```

Kingdom	mean	median
Animals	1128.217706	619.30100
Fungi	31.564293	29.95100
Other	93.289994	68.69715
Plants	800.261036	364.02650
Protists	48.429596	34.15200

By way of a complete example, here's what happens if we use multiple columns for grouping, multiple columns for summarization, and multiple ways to aggregate them:

```
# multiple_everything.py

(
    euk
    .groupby(["Kingdom", "Assembly status"])
    ["Number of genes", "Number of proteins"]
    .agg([np.mean, np.median])
)
```

	Number of genes		Number of proteins	
	mean	median	mean	median
(Animals, Chromosome)	27715.7	26671	41194.9	42019
(Animals, Complete Genome)	46857	46857	28420	28420
(Animals, Contig)	14660.8	15112.5	17969.3	18902.5
(Animals, Scaffold)	20280.4	18253.5	25898.7	23426.5
(Fungi, Chromosome)	7650.4	6848	6739.82	5420
...	...	...	...	...
(Plants, Scaffold)	31339.3	29462	35077.6	34522
(Protists, Chromosome)	5721.68	5482	5475.51	5327
(Protists, Complete Genome)	6804.8	5670	6278.6	5392
(Protists, Contig)	13793.6	14050	13812.3	13643
(Protists, Scaffold)	11750.5	8685.5	11682.3	8625

In the above example, we're using parentheses around the whole expression in order to split it over multiple lines. This is a technique that we'll use heavily in this chapter, as grouping operations often involve several logical steps.

The resulting dataframe is a little tricky to interpret as it has both multiple indices and multiple levels of column labels. To get this summary back into a state we can work with it might be convenient to flatten everything. We can get rid of the indices with `reset_index`:

```
(
    euk
    .groupby(["Kingdom", "Assembly status"])
    ["Number of genes", "Number of proteins"]
    .agg([np.mean, np.median])
    .reset_index()
)
```

	Kingdom	Assembly status	Number of genes		Number of proteins	
	mean	median	mean	median	mean	median
0	Animals	Chromosome	27715.7	26671	41194.9	42019
1	Animals	Complete Genome	46857	46857	28420	28420
2	Animals	Contig	14660.8	15112.5	17969.3	18902.5
3	Animals	Scaffold	20280.4	18253.5	25898.7	23426.5
4	Fungi	Chromosome	7650.4	6848	6739.82	5420
...	...	...	...	...	...	...
15	Plants	Scaffold	31339.3	29462	35077.6	34522
16	Protists	Chromosome	5721.68	5482	5475.51	5327
17	Protists	Complete Genome	6804.8	5670	6278.6	5392
18	Protists	Contig	13793.6	14050	13812.3	13643
19	Protists	Scaffold	11750.5	8685.5	11682.3	8625

And we can fix the column headers by simply renaming them:

```
# summary_table.py

summary = (
    euk
    .groupby(["Kingdom", "Assembly status"])
    ["Number of genes", "Number of proteins"]
    .agg([np.mean, np.median])
    .reset_index()
)

summary.columns = [
    "Kingdom",
    "Assembly status",
    "Mean number of genes",
    "Median number of genes",
    "Mean number of proteins",
    "Median number of proteins",
]

summary.head()
```

	Kingdom	Assembly status	Mean number of genes	Median number of genes	Mean number of proteins	Median number of proteins
0	Animals	Chromosome	27715.653846	26671.0	41194.875000	42019.0
1	Animals	Complete Genome	46857.000000	46857.0	28420.000000	28420.0
2	Animals	Contig	14660.833333	15112.5	17969.333333	18902.5
3	Animals	Scaffold	20280.411290	18253.5	25898.727823	23426.5
4	Fungi	Chromosome	7650.397906	6848.0	6739.816754	5420.0

In all of the above examples, we're using the same aggregation functions to work on all columns. The final complication comes when we want to aggregate different columns in different ways. We do this by passing a dict to the **agg** method, where the keys are the names of the columns and the values are the aggregation functions we want to run.

For example, let's make a summary table showing, for each class, the mean number of genes and proteins along with the number of genomes. Using the techniques we learned above, we can do it pretty easily. To get the number of rows for each group, we can just use Python's built in **len** function:

```
(
    euk
    .groupby("Class")
    [["Number of genes", "Number of proteins"]]
    .agg([np.mean, len])
).head()
```

	Number of genes		Number of proteins	
	mean	len	mean	len
Class				
Amphibians	26670.250000	7	37515.250000	7
Apicomplexans	5993.210084	254	5869.142857	254
Ascomycetes	9846.421053	3570	9687.493548	3570
Basidiomycetes	11231.524000	726	11118.984064	726
Birds	17238.402439	172	23245.365854	172

Notice, however, that the output is a bit awkward to work with. We have calculated the number of genomes twice - once by counting the number of values in the **genes** column, and once by counting the number of values in the **proteins** column. Compare the table above with this version:

```
# aggregate_with_dict.py

(
    euk
    .groupby("Class")
    [["Number of genes", "Number of proteins", "Species"]]
    .agg({
            "Number of genes": np.median,
            "Number of proteins": np.median,
            "Species": len,
        })
).head()
```

Class	Number of genes	Number of proteins	Species
Amphibians	24367.0	34243.0	7
Apicomplexans	5815.0	5653.0	254
Ascomycetes	9925.0	9929.0	3570
Basidiomycetes	9174.5	9133.0	726
Birds	16121.0	18359.0	172

By passing a dictionary to **agg** rather than a list, we explicitly tell pandas that we want to aggregate the **gene** and **protein** columns using **np.median**, and the **species** column using **len**. A very nice way to visualize this table is using a scatter plot with size:

```
# class_scatter_size.py

data = euk.groupby("Class")[
    ["Number of genes", "Number of proteins", "Species"]
].agg(
    {
        "Number of genes": np.median,
        "Number of proteins": np.median,
        "Species": len,
    }
)

g = sns.relplot(
    data=data,
    x="Number of genes",
    y="Number of proteins",
    size="Species",
    sizes=(10, 100),
    color="indigo",
)

g.fig.suptitle(
    "Median numbers of genes and proteins for genomes in each class", y=1.05
)
```

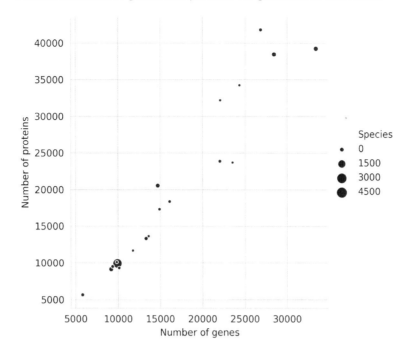

Median numbers of genes and proteins for genomes in each class

Here each circle is a class, and the size represents the number of genomes. This example illustrates very nicely the smooth interaction between pandas and seaborn, where we use pandas to transform the data in the format we want, then pass it to seaborn for plotting.

One drawback of this chart is that it's not possible to tell which point refers to which class. Let's try using color to represent the classes. We have to tweak the data a little bit in order to be able to do this: currently **class** is an index:

```
(
    euk
    .groupby("Class")
    [["Number of genes", "Number of proteins", "Species"]]
    .agg({
            "Number of genes": np.median,
            "Number of proteins": np.median,
            "Species": len,
        })
).head()
```

Class	Number of genes	Number of proteins	Species
Amphibians	24367.0	34243.0	7
Apicomplexans	5815.0	5653.0	254
Ascomycetes	9925.0	9929.0	3570
Basidiomycetes	9174.5	9133.0	726
Birds	16121.0	18359.0	172

and we need it to be a column. We could either call **reset_index** as we saw before, or pass **as_index=False** to **groupby**:

```
(
    euk
    .groupby("Class", as_index=False)
    [["Number of genes", "Number of proteins", "Species"]]
    .agg({
        "Number of genes": np.median,
        "Number of proteins": np.median,
        "Species": len,
    })
).head()
```

	Class	Number of genes	Number of proteins	Species
0	Amphibians	24367.0	34243.0	7
1	Apicomplexans	5815.0	5653.0	254
2	Ascomycetes	9925.0	9929.0	3570
3	Basidiomycetes	9174.5	9133.0	726
4	Birds	16121.0	18359.0	172

Now we can plug this into our seaborn code and use `hue` to represent the class:

```
data = (
    euk
    .groupby("Class", as_index=False)
    [["Number of genes", "Number of proteins", "Species"]]
    .agg({
        "Number of genes": np.median,
        "Number of proteins": np.median,
        "Species": len,
    })
)

g = sns.relplot(
    data=data,
    x="Number of genes",
    y="Number of proteins",
    size="Species",
    sizes=(10, 100),
    hue="Class",
    palette="Set2",
)

# we need a bit more y space to account for the tall legend
g.fig.suptitle(
    "Median numbers of genes and proteins for genomes in each class", y=1.1
)
```

Median numbers of genes and proteins for genomes in each class

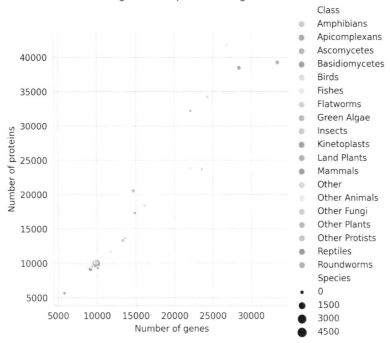

This kind of works, but there are too many different classes to represent with colors. Perhaps we could use color to represent kingdom instead; that way we could at least see the general taxonomic pattern. To get the **kingdom** column into our summary, we can just add it to the `gropuby`:

```
(
    euk.groupby(["Class", "Kingdom"], as_index=False)[
        ["Number of genes", "Number of proteins", "Species"]
    ].agg(
        {
            "Number of genes": np.median,
            "Number of proteins": np.median,
            "Species": len,
        }
    )
).head()
```

	Class	Kingdom	Number of genes	Number of proteins	Species
0	Amphibians	Animals	24367.0	34243.0	7
1	Apicomplexans	Protists	5815.0	5653.0	254
2	Ascomycetes	Fungi	9925.0	9929.0	3570
3	Basidiomycetes	Fungi	9174.5	9133.0	726
4	Birds	Animals	16121.0	18359.0	172

Notice that this particular example of a two-column `groupby` has an interesting property that we haven't seen before: the two columns have a heirarchical relationship. In other words, every class belongs to exactly one kingdom, so grouping on kingdom as well as class doesn't increase the number of groups - we are using it here purely as a convenient way to get a kingdom column in our summary table.

Let's try the plot now:

```
# class_scatter_size_kingdom_color.py

data = (
    euk
    .groupby(["Class", "Kingdom"], as_index=False)
    [["Number of genes", "Number of proteins", "Species"]]
    .agg({
            "Number of genes": np.median,
            "Number of proteins": np.median,
            "Species": len,
        })
)

g = sns.relplot(
    data=data,
    x="Number of genes",
    y="Number of proteins",
    size="Species",
    sizes=(10, 100),
    hue="Kingdom",
    palette="Set2",
)

g.fig.suptitle("Median numbers of genes and proteins for genomes in each kingdomf", y=1.05)
```

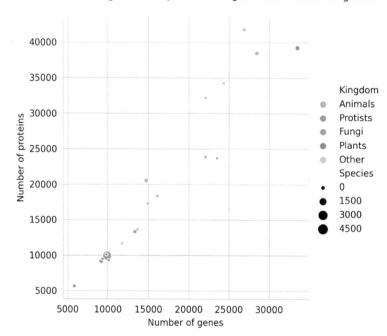

Median numbers of genes and proteins for genomes in each kingdomf

This is a more managable number of colors to deal with, and actually seems to show an interesting pattern: several animal classes seem to have more proteins per gene than the overall average (the pale green points that lie above where a trend line would be). This could be related to a greater incidence of multiple splice variants in animal genomes - or it could be completely artefactual.

Notice that the starting point for our grouping is just a dataframe, so we can easily filter the rows before we start grouping. Let's draw the same summary table but only consider genomes in scaffold status:

```
(
    euk[euk["Assembly status"] == "Scaffold"]
    .groupby(["Class", "Kingdom"], as_index=False)
    [["Number of genes", "Number of proteins", "Species"]]
    .agg({
            "Number of genes": np.median,
            "Number of proteins": np.median,
            "Species": len,
        })
).head()
```

	Class	Kingdom	Number of genes	Number of proteins	Species
0	Amphibians	Animals	21704.5	26764.5	3
1	Apicomplexans	Protists	6297.0	6315.5	138
2	Ascomycetes	Fungi	10550.0	10662.0	2134
3	Basidiomycetes	Fungi	9262.0	9197.5	547
4	Birds	Animals	15630.0	17084.0	150

This is now a very complicated pandas expression, with several different operations. Making liberal use of lines and indentation makes the sequence of operations as clear as possible.

We've seen that expression using **groupby** can range from very complex, like the summary table above, to very simple, like calculating the mean number of genes for each class:

```
euk.groupby("Class")["Number of genes"].mean()
```

```
Class
Amphibians       26670.250000
Apicomplexans     5993.210084
Ascomycetes       9846.421053
Basidiomycetes   11231.524000
Birds            17238.402439
                     ...
Other Fungi      10576.082569
Other Plants     23573.500000
Other Protists   15359.781818
Reptiles         21127.687500
Roundworms       18069.698413
Name: Number of genes, Length: 19, dtype: float64
```

What all of these examples have in common, though, is that they all produce the same kind of output: either a series with one value for group (in simple cases) or a dataframe with one row per group (in more complex cases). We'll conclude our look at **groupby** with a quick look at other things we can do with groups. All of the following examples will use a **groupby** object as their starting point, so the actual grouping will be just as we've seen before.

12.2.3 Filtering based on group properties

We have seen many examples of filtering rows, but the techniques we've seen so far only work when we are filtering based on the properties of each row - for example, the size:

```
euk[euk["Size (Mb)"] < 10]
```

	Species	Kingdom	Class	...	Number of proteins	Publication year	Assembly status
10	Pneumocystis carinii B80	Fungi	Ascomycetes	...	3646	2015	Contig
23	Cryptosporidium parvum Iowa II	Protists	Apicomplexans	...	7610	2004	Chromosome
30	Babesia bovis	Protists	Apicomplexans	...	3706	2007	Chromosome
31	Theileria annulata	Protists	Apicomplexans	...	3795	2005	Chromosome
32	Theileria parva	Protists	Apicomplexans	...	4061	2005	Chromosome
...	...	...	...	...	...	...	...
7793	Homo sapiens	Animals	Mammals	...	<NA>	2017	Scaffold
8244	Saccharomyces cerevisiae	Fungi	Ascomycetes	...	<NA>	2017	Scaffold
8296	Saccharomyces cerevisiae	Fungi	Ascomycetes	...	<NA>	2017	Scaffold
8297	Saccharomyces cerevisiae	Fungi	Ascomycetes	...	<NA>	2017	Scaffold
8298	Saccharomyces cerevisiae	Fungi	Ascomycetes	...	298	1992	Chromosome

If we want instead to filter based on properties of groups, then we need to first use `groupby` then call `filter` on the resulting object. The `filter` method takes as its argument a function that will run on each group and return `True` or `False` to determine whether we want to keep the group or not.

For example, let's select just the rows belonging to classes with at least 1000 genomes. First we write a function that will take the dataframe for a single class and return `True` if it contains more than 1000 rows:

```
def check_df(group_df):
    if len(group_df) > 1000:
        return True
    else:
        return False
```

Then we pass the name of that function as the argument to `filter`:

```
euk.groupby("Class").filter(check_df)
```

	Species	Kingdom	Class	...	Number of proteins	Publication year	Assembly status
8	Saccharomyces cerevisiae S288C	Fungi	Ascomycetes	...	6002	1999	Complete Genome
10	Pneumocystis carinii B80	Fungi	Ascomycetes	...	3646	2015	Contig
11	Schizosaccharomyces pombe	Fungi	Ascomycetes	...	5132	2002	Chromosome
12	Aspergillus nidulans FGSC A4	Fungi	Ascomycetes	...	9556	2003	Scaffold
13	Aspergillus fumigatus Af293	Fungi	Ascomycetes	...	19260	2005	Chromosome
...	...	...	...	...	...	...	...
8297	Saccharomyces cerevisiae	Fungi	Ascomycetes	...	<NA>	2017	Scaffold
8298	Saccharomyces cerevisiae	Fungi	Ascomycetes	...	298	1992	Chromosome
8299	Saccharomyces cerevisiae	Fungi	Ascomycetes	...	<NA>	2018	Chromosome
8300	Saccharomyces cerevisiae	Fungi	Ascomycetes	...	<NA>	2018	Chromosome
8301	Saccharomyces cerevisiae	Fungi	Ascomycetes	...	<NA>	2018	Chromosome

And we get back the rows that we want. Notice how this is different to all the filters we have seen before: we're filtering based on the groups, but we are getting back the original rows.

The more Pythonic way to write our filtering function above would be to return the result of the condition directly:

```
# filter_group.py

def check_df(group_df):
    return len(group_df) > 1000

euk.groupby("Class").filter(check_df)
```

	Species	Kingdom	Class	...	Number of proteins	Publication year	Assembly status
8	Saccharomyces cerevisiae S288C	Fungi	Ascomycetes	...	6002	1999	Complete Genome
10	Pneumocystis carinii B80	Fungi	Ascomycetes	...	3646	2015	Contig
11	Schizosaccharomyces pombe	Fungi	Ascomycetes	...	5132	2002	Chromosome
12	Aspergillus nidulans FGSC A4	Fungi	Ascomycetes	...	9556	2003	Scaffold
13	Aspergillus fumigatus Af293	Fungi	Ascomycetes	...	19260	2005	Chromosome
...	...	...	...	...	...	...	...
8297	Saccharomyces cerevisiae	Fungi	Ascomycetes	...	<NA>	2017	Scaffold
8298	Saccharomyces cerevisiae	Fungi	Ascomycetes	...	298	1992	Chromosome
8299	Saccharomyces cerevisiae	Fungi	Ascomycetes	...	<NA>	2018	Chromosome
8300	Saccharomyces cerevisiae	Fungi	Ascomycetes	...	<NA>	2018	Chromosome
8301	Saccharomyces cerevisiae	Fungi	Ascomycetes	...	<NA>	2018	Chromosome

and since the function is now just one line long, we could even rewrite it as a lambda expression:

```
(euk.groupby("Class").filter(lambda x: len(x) > 1000))
```

	Species	Kingdom	Class	...	Number of proteins	Publication year	Assembly status
8	Saccharomyces cerevisiae S288C	Fungi	Ascomycetes	...	6002	1999	Complete Genome
10	Pneumocystis carinii B80	Fungi	Ascomycetes	...	3646	2015	Contig
11	Schizosaccharomyces pombe	Fungi	Ascomycetes	...	5132	2002	Chromosome
12	Aspergillus nidulans FGSC A4	Fungi	Ascomycetes	...	9556	2003	Scaffold
13	Aspergillus fumigatus Af293	Fungi	Ascomycetes	...	19260	2005	Chromosome
...	...	...	...	...	...	...	...
8297	Saccharomyces cerevisiae	Fungi	Ascomycetes	...	<NA>	2017	Scaffold
8298	Saccharomyces cerevisiae	Fungi	Ascomycetes	...	298	1992	Chromosome
8299	Saccharomyces cerevisiae	Fungi	Ascomycetes	...	<NA>	2018	Chromosome
8300	Saccharomyces cerevisiae	Fungi	Ascomycetes	...	<NA>	2018	Chromosome
8301	Saccharomyces cerevisiae	Fungi	Ascomycetes	...	<NA>	2018	Chromosome

Because we can run arbitrary code on the dataframe for each group, our filters can be as complex as we want. All we have to do is make sure that our filter function takes as its argument a dataframe containing the rows for a given group, and returns a boolean value. For example, let's find all genomes belonging to species where the genome with the most predicted genes has at least twice as many genes as the one with the fewest predicted genes:

```
# complex_group_filter.py

def species_filter(df):
    max_genes = df["Number of genes"].max()
    min_genes = df["Number of genes"].min()
    ratio = max_genes / min_genes
    return ratio > 2

# have to dropna to avoid species where number of genes is all missing
euk.dropna().groupby("Species").filter(species_filter)
```

	Species	Kingdom	Class	...	Number of proteins	Publication year	Assembly status
1	Arabidopsis thaliana	Plants	Land Plants	...	48265	2001	Chromosome
6	Oryza sativa Japonica Group	Plants	Land Plants	...	42580	2015	Chromosome
19	Trypanosoma cruzi	Protists	Kinetoplasts	...	19607	2005	Scaffold
22	Eimeria tenella	Protists	Apicomplexans	...	8609	2013	Scaffold
38	Aedes albopictus	Animals	Insects	...	42912	2016	Contig
...	...	...	...	...	...	...	...
8174	Saccharomyces cerevisiae	Fungi	Ascomycetes	...	5327	2017	Contig
8176	Saccharomyces cerevisiae	Fungi	Ascomycetes	...	5324	2018	Contig
8177	Saccharomyces cerevisiae	Fungi	Ascomycetes	...	5290	2018	Contig
8178	Saccharomyces cerevisiae	Fungi	Ascomycetes	...	5323	2018	Contig
8298	Saccharomyces cerevisiae	Fungi	Ascomycetes	...	298	1992	Chromosome

You can see how in the filtering function we figure out the answer in several steps. We could actually write this as a lambda as well:

```
(
    euk.dropna()
    .groupby("Species")
    .filter(
        lambda x: (x["Number of genes"].max() / x["Number of genes"].min()) > 2
    )
)
```

	Species	Kingdom	Class	...	Number of proteins	Publication year	Assembly status
1	Arabidopsis thaliana	Plants	Land Plants	...	48265	2001	Chromosome
6	Oryza sativa Japonica Group	Plants	Land Plants	...	42580	2015	Chromosome
19	Trypanosoma cruzi	Protists	Kinetoplasts	...	19607	2005	Scaffold
22	Eimeria tenella	Protists	Apicomplexans	...	8609	2013	Scaffold
38	Aedes albopictus	Animals	Insects	...	42912	2016	Contig
...	...	...	...	...	...	...	...
8174	Saccharomyces cerevisiae	Fungi	Ascomycetes	...	5327	2017	Contig
8176	Saccharomyces cerevisiae	Fungi	Ascomycetes	...	5324	2018	Contig
8177	Saccharomyces cerevisiae	Fungi	Ascomycetes	...	5290	2018	Contig
8178	Saccharomyces cerevisiae	Fungi	Ascomycetes	...	5323	2018	Contig
8298	Saccharomyces cerevisiae	Fungi	Ascomycetes	...	298	1992	Chromosome

but it starts to strain the limits of readability.

12.2.4 Normalizing within groups

In the above examples of filtering, we are taking each group and using its properties to decide whether or not to keep it. A similar class of problems involves taking each group and using its properties to make a new series. This will be easier to see with an example.

Let's say that we want to figure out whether genomes belonging to different kingdoms tend to be assembled in different status. To keep things simple, we will just look at contig and scaffold. We will start off by making a summary table showing, for each kingdom, how many genomes are in each assembly status:

```
temp = (
    euk[euk["Assembly status"].isin(["Contig", "Scaffold"])]
    .groupby(["Kingdom", "Assembly status"])
    .size()
    .to_frame(name="Genome count")
    .reset_index()
)
temp
```

	Kingdom	Assembly status	Genome count
0	Animals	Contig	203
1	Animals	Scaffold	1731
2	Fungi	Contig	973
3	Fungi	Scaffold	2790
4	Other	Contig	9
5	Other	Scaffold	14
6	Plants	Contig	238
7	Plants	Scaffold	443
8	Protists	Contig	160
9	Protists	Scaffold	459

We group by the two properties we're interested in, take the size, then turn the resulting series into a dataframe and reset the index so that we end up with three columns.

Now let's try to answer our question: which kingdoms tend to have more of their genomes assembled into scaffolds? Glancing at the table, it's actually quite hard to see, because the number of genomes in each kingdom is not equal.

Look at the numbers for animals and plants. They both have approximately equal numbers of genomes assembled into contigs (plants have slightly more). But it's misleading to conclude that animals and plants are equally likely to have genomes in scaffolds, because we have to take into account the total number for each. The total number of genomes for animals is much higher, so the number in contig status represents a smaller fraction of the whole.

What we would really like to compare is not the **number** of contig genomes in each kingdom, but the **proportion** of contig genomes. This is an example of an incredibly common problem in data analysis, and is solved by the process of *normalization*: we want to normalize each count by dividing it by the total count for the group as a whole. In other words, we want the two numbers for each kingdom to add up to one.

The tool that lets us solve this problem in pandas is the `transform` method. Just like `filter`, we call this method on a `GroupBy` object and, just like `filter`, it takes the name of a function. But unlike `filter`, which just returns a single True/False value, transform runs the function on each group and gives us a series of values. As a first step, let's group our summary by kingdom and transform the **Genome count** column using Python's built in `sum` function:

```
temp.groupby("Kingdom")["Genome count"].transform(sum)
```

```
0    1934
1    1934
2    3763
3    3763
4      23
5      23
6     681
7     681
8     619
9     619
Name: Genome count, dtype: int64
```

Notice that we get a series of 10 values, as we had 10 rows in the starting `temp` dataframe (two numbers for each of five kingdoms). The first two rows correspond to the rows for Animals, and they both have the same value; the total number of genomes for that group (i.e. the `sum` of the values in the **Genome count** column). So to carry out our normalization, we can take those values and add them as a new column:

```
temp["Total for kingdom"] = (
    temp
    .groupby("Kingdom")
    ["Genome count"]
    .transform(sum)
)
temp
```

	Kingdom	Assembly status	Genome count	Total for kingdom
0	Animals	Contig	203	1934
1	Animals	Scaffold	1731	1934
2	Fungi	Contig	973	3763
3	Fungi	Scaffold	2790	3763
4	Other	Contig	9	23
5	Other	Scaffold	14	23
6	Plants	Contig	238	681
7	Plants	Scaffold	443	681
8	Protists	Contig	160	619
9	Protists	Scaffold	459	619

then divide the count by the total:

```
# normalize.py

# make the summary table
temp = (
    euk[euk["Assembly status"].isin(["Contig", "Scaffold"])]
    .groupby(["Kingdom", "Assembly status"])
    .size()
    .to_frame(name="Genome count")
    .reset_index()
)

# calculate the totals
temp["Total for kingdom"] = (
    temp
    .groupby("Kingdom")
    ["Genome count"]
    .transform(sum)
)

# add a new column
temp["Proportion"] = temp["Genome count"] / temp["Total for kingdom"]
temp
```

	Kingdom	Assembly status	Genome count	Total for kingdom	Proportion
0	Animals	Contig	203	1934	0.104964
1	Animals	Scaffold	1731	1934	0.895036
2	Fungi	Contig	973	3763	0.258570
3	Fungi	Scaffold	2790	3763	0.741430
4	Other	Contig	9	23	0.391304
5	Other	Scaffold	14	23	0.608696
6	Plants	Contig	238	681	0.349486
7	Plants	Scaffold	443	681	0.650514
8	Protists	Contig	160	619	0.258481
9	Protists	Scaffold	459	619	0.741519

And it's this new **proportion** column that we will now look at when comparing kingdoms. Going back to our original comparison, it's easy to see that while the absolute numbers of contig genomes are roughly equal for animals and plants, the proportion is much higher for plants: around 35%, compared with 10% for animals.

We can see the difference intuitively by drawing some categorical plots. Here's a bar chart comparing the number of genomes in each status for each kingdom:

```
sns.catplot(
    data=temp, x="Kingdom", y="Genome count", kind="bar", hue="Assembly status"
)
plt.title(
    "Number of genomes in contig and scaffold\n assembly status for each kingdom"
)
```

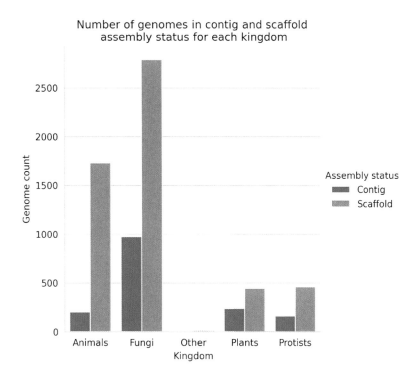

And here's the same chart but looking at the proportion:

```
sns.catplot(
    data=temp, x="Kingdom", y="Proportion", kind="bar", hue="Assembly status"
)
plt.title(
    "Fraction of genomes in contig and scaffold\n assembly status for each kingdom"
)
```

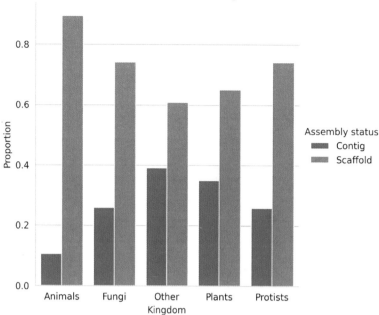

Fraction of genomes in contig and scaffold
assembly status for each kingdom

It's easy to see that in the first chart, the combined bar heights differ wildly between kingdoms, making it very hard to make comparisons. In contrast, in the lower chart, each pair of bars has a combined height of one.

In this example we did the normalization step by step, as it made it easier to follow the logic. However, we normally do this in pandas by doing the normalization directly in the transformation function:

```
def normalize(counts):
    return counts / sum(counts)

temp.groupby("Kingdom")["Genome count"].transform(normalize)
```

```
0    0.104964
1    0.895036
2    0.258570
3    0.741430
4    0.391304
5    0.608696
6    0.349486
7    0.650514
8    0.258481
9    0.741519
Name: Genome count, dtype: float64
```

This gives us the normalized counts directly, which we can then store as a new column if needed.

This kind of normalization crops up a lot in data analysis. Here's one more example; we'll make a summary table showing the total number of megabases sequenced for each kingdom in each year between 2001 and 2018. To get the total we'll need to add up all the values in the **size** column, so our aggregation method will be **sum**. This is another expression with many steps, so we'll split it over multiple lines to make the structure easier to see:

```
# summary_year.py

temp2 = (
    euk[euk["Publication year"].between(2001,2018)]
    .groupby(["Publication year", "Kingdom"])["Size (Mb)"]
    .sum()
    .to_frame("Total Mb sequenced")
    .reset_index()
)
temp2
```

	Publication year	Kingdom	Total Mb sequenced
0	2001	Animals	100.286
1	2001	Fungi	2.49752
2	2001	Plants	119.669
3	2002	Animals	9724.15
4	2002	Fungi	12.7298
...	...	...	...
76	2018	Animals	606867
77	2018	Fungi	51363.7
78	2018	Other	265.241
79	2018	Plants	181508
80	2018	Protists	8459.06

Now we want to compare the amount of sequencing effort applied to different kingdoms over time. Look at the values for plants in 2001 and 2018. The total number is much higher for 2018, but is that because we are devoting more effort to sequencing plant genomes, or simply because sequencing is much cheaper overall? In order to compare the numbers, we have to normalize by year:

```
# normalize_year.py

temp2["Proportion Mb sequenced"] = (
    temp2
    .groupby("Publication year")
    ["Total Mb sequenced"]
    .transform(lambda x: x / sum(x))
)
temp2
```

	Publication year	Kingdom	Total Mb sequenced	Proportion Mb sequenced
0	2001	Animals	100.286	0.45082
1	2001	Fungi	2.49752	0.0112272
2	2001	Plants	119.669	0.537953
3	2002	Animals	9724.15	0.952189
4	2002	Fungi	12.7298	0.0012465
...	...	...	...	...
76	2018	Animals	606867	0.715254
77	2018	Fungi	51363.7	0.0605373
78	2018	Other	265.241	0.000312613
79	2018	Plants	181508	0.213926
80	2018	Protists	8459.06	0.00996986

Now it's easy to see that while just over 100Mb of plant genome was sequenced in 2001, that represented more than half the total sequencing effort for the year, compared to only about 20% of the sequencing effort in 2018.

Again, we can see the effect using visualization. When we plot the total number of megabases sequenced in each kingdom for each year:

```
# plot_year_raw.py

g = sns.catplot(
    data=temp2,
    y="Kingdom",
    x="Total Mb sequenced",
    col="Publication year",
    col_wrap=4,
    kind="bar",
    height=1.5,
    aspect=2,
)

g.fig.suptitle(
    "Total megabases sequenced for each kingdom in each year since 2001", y=1.1
)
```

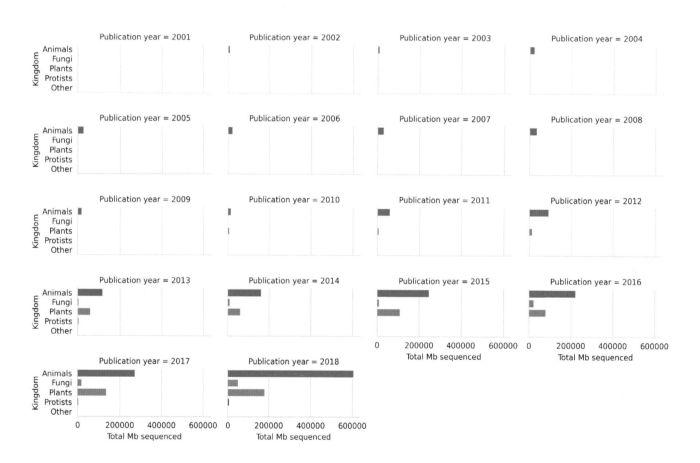

it's impossible to compare years since the total bar lengths are so different. But in the same plot looking at the proportion:

```
# plot_year_normalized.py

g = sns.catplot(
    data=temp2,
    y="Kingdom",
    x="Proportion Mb sequenced",
    col="Publication year",
    col_wrap=4,
    kind="bar",
    height=1.5,
    aspect=2,
)
g.fig.suptitle(
    "Proportion of bases sequenced for each kingdom in each year since 2001",
    y=1.1,
)
```

Proportion of bases sequenced for each kingdom in each year since 2001

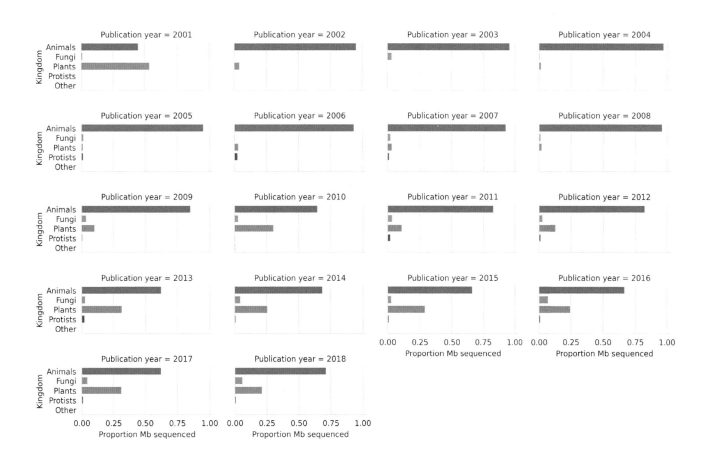

the bars for each year sum to 1, making them easier to compare. To answer our question about plants, all we have to do is note that the green bar for 2001 goes to about halfway along the X axis, whereas in 2018 the green bar goes to about 20%.

An alternative way of looking at these data would be to put all years on a single axis:

```
# plot_year_normalized_line.py

sns.catplot(
    data=temp2,
    x="Publication year",
    y="Proportion Mb sequenced",
    hue="Kingdom",
    aspect=3,
    kind="point",
    height=4,
)

plt.title(
    "Proportion of bases sequenced for each kingdom in each year since 2001"
)
```

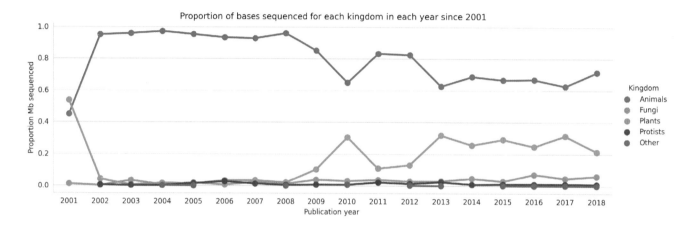

Now the points at each year sum to one, and it's easy to see that as the proportion of sequencing effort devoted to plants goes up, the proportion devoted to animals goes down accordingly. We can answer our question about plants by noting that in 2001 the green and blue lines are about equal, and by 2018 the blue line is about three times higher than the green.

12.2.5 Other types of transformation

The examples we've seen above are by far the most common type of normalization that we require for data analysis. However, we can use `transform` for any situation where we want to calculate a new value for each original row, using a calculation that involves the group. Here's a slightly different way of looking at the change in sequencing over time: for each kingdom, we'll scale all the measurements relative to the amount of bases sequenced in 2001. For this example, we'll have to restrict our analysis to animals, plants and fungi since they are the only kingdoms with a measurement for 2001:

```
temp2[temp2["Kingdom"].isin(["Plants", "Animals", "Fungi"])]
```

	Publication year	Kingdom	Total Mb sequenced	Proportion Mb sequenced
0	2001	Animals	100.286	0.45082
1	2001	Fungi	2.49752	0.0112272
2	2001	Plants	119.669	0.537953
3	2002	Animals	9724.15	0.952189
4	2002	Fungi	12.7298	0.0012465
...	...	...	...	...
72	2017	Fungi	20236	0.0464774
74	2017	Plants	136663	0.313883
76	2018	Animals	606867	0.715254
77	2018	Fungi	51363.7	0.0605373
79	2018	Plants	181508	0.213926

Let's first figure out how to get just the number of bases sequenced in 2001 for each kingdom. The rows in our starting dataframe are already sorted by year, so we just have to take the first row for each group dataframe. To refer to a single value in a series by its position, we use the `iloc` (short for index location) attribute and use square brackets just like a list:

```
(
    temp2[temp2["Kingdom"].isin(["Plants", "Animals", "Fungi"])]
    .groupby("Kingdom")
    ["Total Mb sequenced"]
    .apply(lambda x: x.iloc[0])
)
```

```
Kingdom
Animals    100.28600
Fungi        2.49752
Plants     119.66900
Name: Total Mb sequenced, dtype: float64
```

That gives us a single value for each kingdom: the number of megabases sequenced in 2001. Now to scale all the values relative to this first value, we switch to **transform** and divide the series by the first value:

```
(
    temp2[temp2["Kingdom"].isin(["Plants", "Animals", "Fungi"])]
    .groupby("Kingdom")
    ["Total Mb sequenced"]
    .transform(lambda x: x / x.iloc[0])
)
```

```
0          1.000000
1          1.000000
2          1.000000
3         96.964223
4          5.096984
           ...
72      8102.451892
74      1142.008804
76      6051.361871
77     20565.883825
79      1516.752770
Name: Total Mb sequenced, Length: 54, dtype: float64
```

Now we can add this new series to the original dataframe:

```
# baseline.py

temp2["Increase relative to 2001"] = (
    temp2[temp2["Kingdom"].isin(["Plants", "Animals", "Fungi"])]
    .groupby("Kingdom")
    ["Total Mb sequenced"]
    .transform(lambda x: x / x.iloc[0])
)
```

and use it as the value to plot:

```
# plot_baseline.py

sns.catplot(
    data=temp2[temp2["Kingdom"].isin(["Plants", "Animals", "Fungi"])],
    x="Publication year",
    y="Increase relative to 2001",
    hue="Kingdom",
    aspect=3,
    kind="point",
    height=4,
)

plt.title("Increase in bases sequenced relative to 2001 for each kingdom")
```

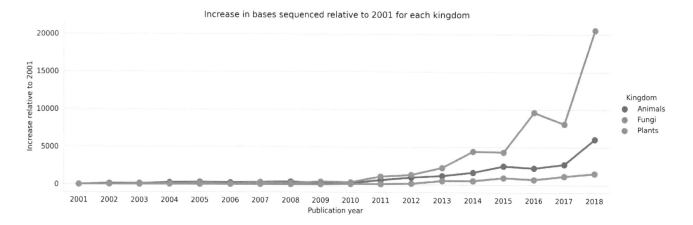

The values are now scaled so that 2001 has the value 1 for each kingdom, and all other values are relative to that.

12.3 Iterating over groups

A very useful trick is to iterate over the groups that we create, which we can do just using Python's normal `for` loop. The only tricky thing is the loop variables: in each iteration we get a tuple where the first element is the label for the group and the second element is a dataframe containing the rows for the group. The best way to iterate is to use two variables in the `for` line like this:

```
for label, group_df in euk.groupby("Kingdom"):
    print(label, len(group_df))
```

```
Animals 2181
Fungi 4494
Other 30
Plants 870
Protists 727
```

This example simply prints the number of rows in each group, but we can write arbitrary code inside the loop. For example, this makes a very convenient way to make new output files based on the groups. The `to_csv` method of dataframes will write an output file, so this code:

```
for label, group_df in euk.groupby("Kingdom"):
    filename = label + ".csv"
    group_df.to_csv(filename, index=False)
```

will create a new CSV file for each kingdom, called *Animals.csv*, *Plants.csv*, etc. We pass in `index=False` to avoid creating a useless column to store the index.

Matters are a bit more complicated when we are grouping on multiple properties. In this case the first element of the tuple is itself a tuple which stores all the group labels:

```
for label, group_df in euk.groupby(["Kingdom", "Assembly status"]):
    print(label)
```

```
('Animals', 'Chromosome')
('Animals', 'Complete Genome')
('Animals', 'Contig')
('Animals', 'Scaffold')
('Fungi', 'Chromosome')
('Fungi', 'Complete Genome')
('Fungi', 'Contig')
('Fungi', 'Scaffold')
('Other', 'Chromosome')
('Other', 'Complete Genome')
('Other', 'Contig')
('Other', 'Scaffold')
('Plants', 'Chromosome')
('Plants', 'Complete Genome')
('Plants', 'Contig')
('Plants', 'Scaffold')
('Protists', 'Chromosome')
('Protists', 'Complete Genome')
('Protists', 'Contig')
('Protists', 'Scaffold')
```

So we generally need to unpack it inside the `for` loop. This loop will write separate output files for each combination of kingdom and status:

```
# iterate_group_labels.py

for label, group_df in euk.groupby(["Kingdom", "Assembly status"]):
    kingdom, status = label
    filename = kingdom + "_" + status + ".csv"
    group_df.to_csv(filename, index=False)
```

Giving us files called *Animals_contig.csv*, etc.

12.4 Sorting groups

Another useful trick we can do with `groupby` is to get lists of group labels sorted according to some property of the group. Recall that when aggregating a single column with `groupby` the result is a series with one value per group:

```
euk.groupby("Class")["Number of genes"].median()
```

```
Class
Amphibians          24367.0
Apicomplexans        5815.0
Ascomycetes          9925.0
Basidiomycetes       9174.5
Birds               16121.0
                      ...
Other Fungi          9344.0
Other Plants        23573.5
Other Protists      13334.5
Reptiles            22121.5
Roundworms          14919.0
Name: Number of genes, Length: 19, dtype: float64
```

If we sort the resulting list of values, then we get the groups in order of median number of genes:

```
euk.groupby("Class")["Number of genes"].median().sort_values()
```

```
Class
Apicomplexans        5815.0
Basidiomycetes       9174.5
Other Fungi          9344.0
Green Algae          9847.5
Ascomycetes          9925.0
                      ...
Other Plants        23573.5
Amphibians          24367.0
Fishes              26863.5
Mammals             28462.0
Land Plants         33462.0
Name: Number of genes, Length: 19, dtype: float64
```

And if we then take the index of that sorted series:

```
# sort_groups.py

euk.groupby("Class")["Number of genes"].median().sort_values().index
```

```
Index(['Apicomplexans', 'Basidiomycetes', 'Other Fungi', 'Green Algae',
       'Ascomycetes', 'Kinetoplasts', 'Other', 'Other Protists', 'Flatworms',
       'Insects', 'Roundworms', 'Birds', 'Other Animals', 'Reptiles',
       'Other Plants', 'Amphibians', 'Fishes', 'Mammals', 'Land Plants'],
      dtype='object', name='Class')
```

we get a list-like object that contains all of the values in the class column, sorted by their median number of genes.

This is extremely useful when drawing categorical charts. If we draw a chart showing the distribution of number of genes for each class:

```
sns.catplot(
    data=euk,
    x="Class",
    y="Number of genes",
    kind="box",
    color="sandybrown",
    aspect=3,
    height=4,
    orient="v",
)
plt.xticks(rotation=45, horizontalalignment="right")
plt.title("Distribution of number of genes for genomes in each class")
```

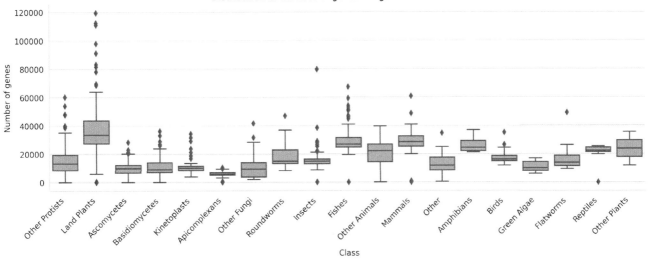

then the order of the categories is whatever order they happen to appear in the data. But if we get a sorted list and pass it as the **order** argument:

```
# plot_sorted_groups.py

sns.catplot(
    data=euk,
    x="Class",
    y="Number of genes",
    kind="box",
    color="sandybrown",
    aspect=3,
    height=4,
    order=euk.groupby("Class")["Number of genes"].median().sort_values().index,
    orient="v",
)
plt.xticks(rotation=45, horizontalalignment="right")
plt.title("Distribution of number of genes for genomes in each class")
```

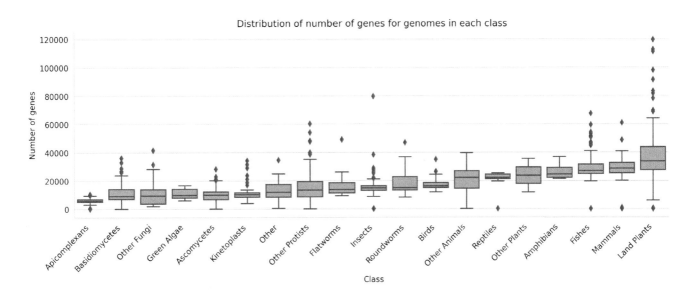

We get the classes sorted by their median Y axis value without having to write the names out explicitly.

---

13 Binning and ordered categories

In previous chapters we've looked at how we can use catgorical data for visualization (using various categorical plots, small multiples, and color) and data analysis (using `groupby`). All of our examples so far have made use of categories that are already present in the data - things like kingdom, status, and publication year.

13.1 Creating a new category

Many of the questions that we want to ask about data, however, require us to make new categories. Imagine that we want to be able to divide our genomes into large and small groups. For the purposes of this example, we'll say that large genomes are ones greater than 500 megabases.

There are a few ways to tackle this. We already know how to calculate a series of boolean values:

```
euk["Size (Mb)"] > 500
```

```
0       False
1       False
2        True
3       False
4        True
      ...
8297    False
8298    False
8299    False
8300    False
8301    False
Name: Size (Mb), Length: 8302, dtype: bool
```

So we could add this as a new column:

```
euk["Is large"] = euk["Size (Mb)"] > 500
euk[["Species", "Kingdom", "Is large"]].head()
```

	Species	Kingdom	Is large
0	Emiliania huxleyi CCMP1516	Protists	False
1	Arabidopsis thaliana	Plants	False
2	Glycine max	Plants	True
3	Medicago truncatula	Plants	False
4	Solanum lycopersicum	Plants	True

We could even use `replace` to make the values a bit more readable:

```
# size_category.py

euk["Is large"] = euk["Size (Mb)"] > 500
euk["Size category"] = euk["Is large"].replace({True: "large", False: "small"})
euk[["Species", "Kingdom", "Is large", "Size category"]].head()
```

	Species	Kingdom	Is large	Size category
0	Emiliania huxleyi CCMP1516	Protists	False	small
1	Arabidopsis thaliana	Plants	False	small
2	Glycine max	Plants	True	large
3	Medicago truncatula	Plants	False	small
4	Solanum lycopersicum	Plants	True	large

and now we have a new categorical column that we can use just like any other. For example, we can use it in a `groupby`:

```
euk.groupby("Size category")["Number of genes"].median()
```

```
Size category
large    26205.0
small    10551.0
Name: Number of genes, dtype: float64
```

Or as a factor in a visualization:

```
# size_category_plot.py

sns.catplot(
    data=euk,
    x="Kingdom",
    y="Number of genes",
    hue="Size category",
    kind="box",
    orient="v",
)
plt.title(
    "Distribution of number of genes\nfor small and large genomes in different kingdoms"
)
```

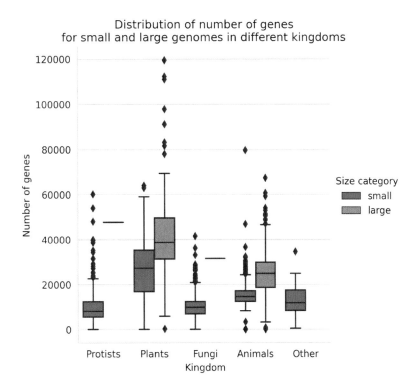

Unsurprisingly, large genomes have more genes than small ones, and the pattern is true across all kingdoms. However, we could also put the boolean series directly into `groupby`:

```
(
    euk
    .groupby(euk["Size (Mb)"] > 500)
    ["Number of genes"]
    .median()
)
```

```
Size (Mb)
False    10551.0
True     26205.0
Name: Number of genes, dtype: float64
```

This is a new way to use **groupby**; as well as passing in the name of the column that we want to use for our groups, we can pass in a series of labels to use. This lets us avoid adding new columns, at the expense of having slightly less readable category names.

Another approach is to use **apply** and write a function that will take a single size value and return the label we want:

```
# apply_bin.py

def large_or_small(size):
    if size > 500:
        return "large"
    else:
        return "small"

euk["Size (Mb)"].apply(large_or_small)
```

```
0       small
1       small
2       large
3       small
4       large
        ...
8297    small
8298    small
8299    small
8300    small
8301    small
Name: Size (Mb), Length: 8302, dtype: object
```

We can plug the result of **apply** directly into **groupby** as well:

```
(
    euk
    .groupby(
        euk["Size (Mb)"].apply(large_or_small)
    )["Number of genes"]
    .median()
)
```

```
Size (Mb)
large    26205.0
small    10551.0
Name: Number of genes, dtype: float64
```

and even mix series and column names when giving a list to **groupby**:

```
(
    euk.groupby([
        euk["Size (Mb)"].apply(large_or_small),
        "Kingdom"
    ])
    ["Number of genes"]
    .median()
)
```

```
Size (Mb)  Kingdom
large      Animals    24986.0
           Fungi      31506.0
           Other          NaN
           Plants     38674.5
           Protists   47715.0
small      Animals    14624.0
           Fungi       9803.0
           Other      11771.0
           Plants     27242.0
           Protists    8142.5
Name: Number of genes, dtype: float64
```

13.1.1 Using our new category for visualization

This division of the genomes into categories based on size doesn't seem like a particularly exciting piece of analysis. However, it's actually an example of an incredibly useful technique for data exploration. By taking a continuous column, and converting it into a category, we open up all sorts of extra possibilities for visualization. Consider the scatter plots that we looked at in a previous chapter. Of the various different properties that we can map, only `x`, `y`, `size` and `hue` are useful for representing numerical variables. And because of the way our visual system works, `size` and `hue` are only really useful for discerning very broad trends.

But `hue` is great for representing categories, and so are `style`, `row` and `col`. In addition, we can put a categorical column on the X or Y axis using categorical plots. We can even make heatmaps and clustermaps with categorical columns on both X and Y. In short, transforming a numerical column to a categorical one gives us far more options in terms of how to display it.

Let's look at a small example using the large versus small genomes that we just created. We will look at a plot that we've seen before, that attempts to show the relationship between GC percentage, number of predicted proteins, and size. Putting **GC%** and **Number of proteins** on the X and Y axes and letting genome size determine the color, we get this plot:

```python
# raw_size_hue.py

sns.relplot(
    data=euk[euk["Size (Mb)"] < 5000].dropna(),
    x="GC%",
    y="Number of proteins",
    hue="Size (Mb)",
    palette="PuRd",
)

plt.title("GC% vs. Number proteins\n for genomes of different sizes")
```

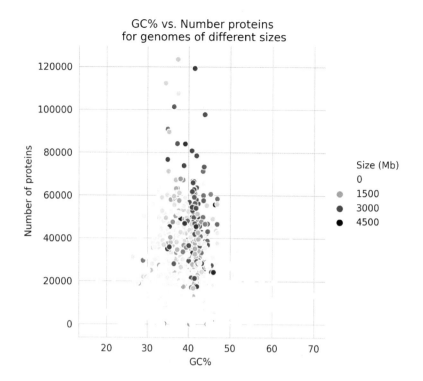

GC% vs. Number proteins
for genomes of different sizes

Which does a reasonably good job of showing the joint distribution of GC and number of proteins. The color also shows a pattern that we noticed before - that genomes with many proteins tend to be in the middle of the distribution of GC. However it's not easy to see exactly where they lie due to the large number of points.

If we abandon the idea of trying to show exact sizes (which our eyes can't really discern anyway) and just work with our size category, we can use two highly contrasting colors, and also use style for redundancy:

```
# binned_size_hue.py

sns.relplot(
    data=euk[euk["Size (Mb)"] < 5000].dropna(),
    x="GC%",
    y="Number of proteins",
    hue="Size category",
    style="Size category",
    palette=["DarkBlue", "Orange"],
)
plt.title("GC% vs. Number proteins\n for genomes of different sizes")
```

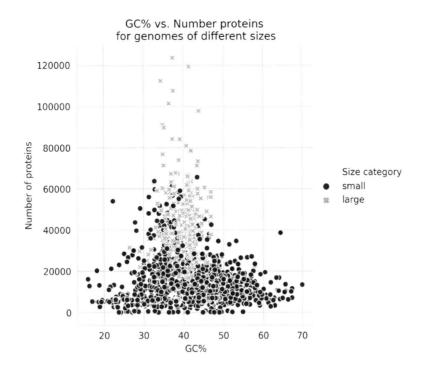

GC% vs. Number proteins
for genomes of different sizes

Or alternatively, we can take a small multiple approach and put small and large genomes in separate subplots:

```python
# binned_col_plot.py

g = sns.relplot(
    data=euk[euk["Size (Mb)"] < 5000].dropna(),
    x="GC%",
    y="Number of proteins",
    col="Size category",
    aspect=0.7,
    color="darkkhaki",
)
g.fig.suptitle(
    "GC% vs. Number of proteins for genomes of different sizes", y=1.1
)
```

GC% vs. Number of proteins for genomes of different sizes

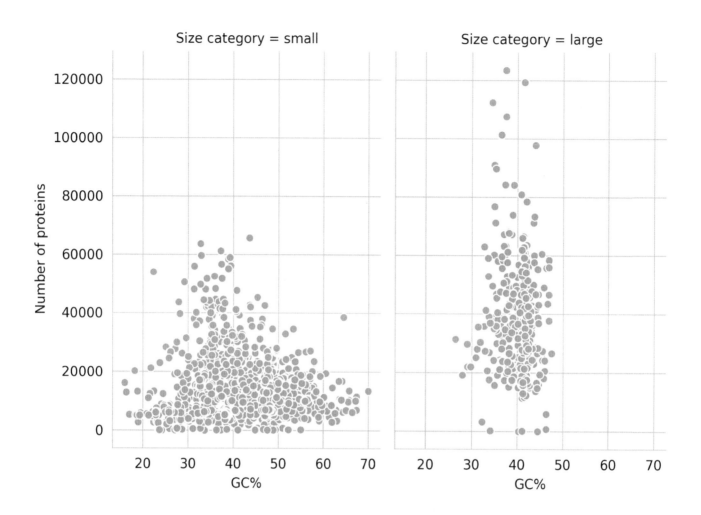

Because the two plots share the same axes, this figure shows very clearly the pattern that large genomes have a narrower range of GC values and tend to have more predicted proteins.

Because we are no longer relying on color to display size, we are free to use it for a different aspect. By taking the same plot and mapping hue to kingdom:

```
# binned_col_plot_with_hue.py

g = sns.relplot(
    data=euk[euk["Size (Mb)"] < 5000].dropna(),
    x="GC%",
    y="Number of proteins",
    col="Size category",
    aspect=0.7,
    hue="Kingdom",
    palette="Set1",
)

g.fig.suptitle(
    "GC% vs. Number of proteins for genomes of different sizes", y=1.1
)
```

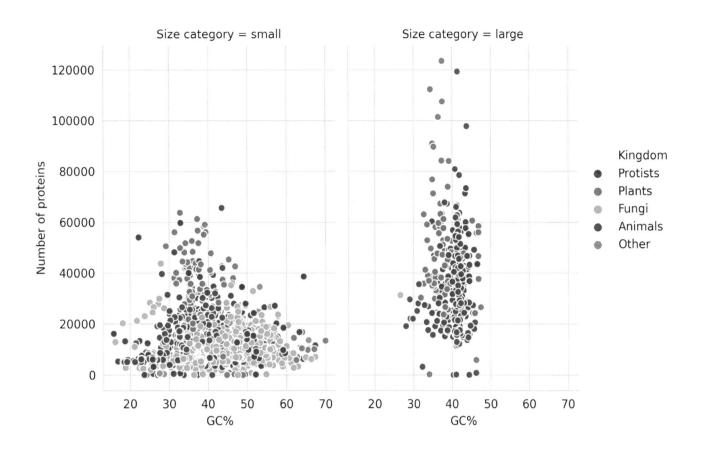

GC% vs. Number of proteins for genomes of different sizes

we get additional information about the taxonomic distribution of our size categories; nearly all of the large genomes belong to plants and animals.

Recall that we can also use categories with `lmplot` for drawing regressions. So we can compare regressions for small and large genomes on a single plot:

```
# binned_regression_plot.py

sns.lmplot(
    data=euk[euk["Size (Mb)"] < 5000].dropna(),
    x="Size (Mb)",
    y="Number of genes",
    hue="Size category",
)
plt.title("GC% vs. Number of proteins\n for genomes of different sizes", y=1.1)
```

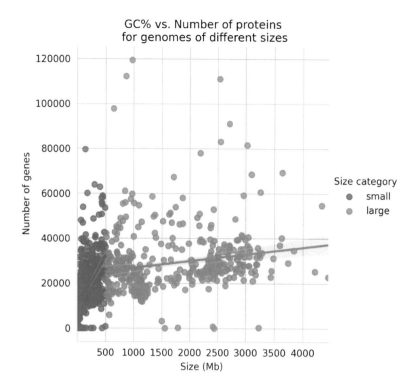

GC% vs. Number of proteins
for genomes of different sizes

or with small multiples:

```
# binned_regression_cols.py

g = sns.lmplot(
    data=euk[euk["Size (Mb)"] < 5000].dropna(),
    x="Size (Mb)",
    y="Number of genes",
    col="Size category",
    scatter_kws={"color": "lightgrey"},
    line_kws={"color": "darkred"},
)

g.fig.suptitle(
    "GC% vs. Number of proteins for genomes of different sizes", y=1.1
)
```

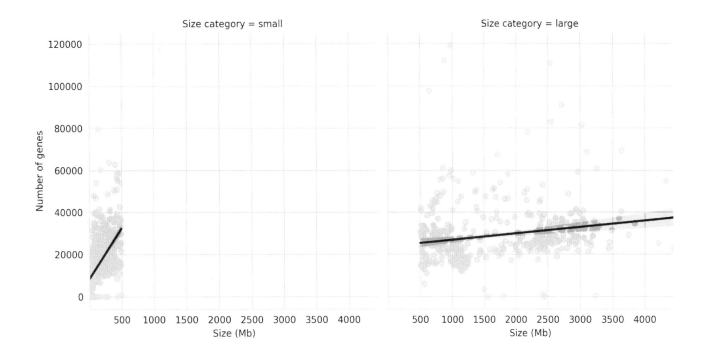

GC% vs. Number of proteins for genomes of different sizes

Either approach illustrates, for this example, that number of genes increases much more rapidly with genome size for small genomes than for large ones. Notice that with these last two plots, we're using both the raw genome size on the x axis, and the size category - another nice use of redundancy.

13.1.2 More on binning

The idea we have just explored - taking a continuous variable and turning it into a categorial one - is often referred to as *binning*. If we think about it, it's actually the first step in drawing a histogram: we (or rather our charting tools) divide our list of values into a number of bins, count how many values are in each bin, and plot the result as a bar chart. Recall from our first examples of seaborn that `distplot` actually has an argument called `bins` which determines the number of bins, and hence the number of bars in the plot.

If we play about with different numbers of bins:

```
sns.distplot(euk["GC%"].dropna(), kde=False, bins=10)
plt.title("Distribution of GC% for all genomes")
```

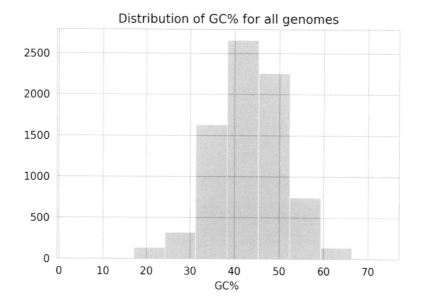

Distribution of GC% for all genomes

```
sns.distplot(euk["GC%"].dropna(), kde=False, bins=100)
plt.title("Distribution of GC% for all genomes")
```

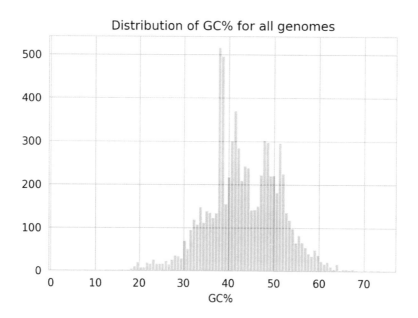

Distribution of GC% for all genomes

we can get an intuitive sense of the trade off; more bins means more detail, but also more noise. We can extend this idea to our size bins as well. Switching from two to three bins:

```
# three_bins.py

def categorize(size):
    if size > 500:
        return "large"
    elif size > 200:
        return "medium"
    else:
        return "small"

euk["Size category"] = euk["Size (Mb)"].apply(categorize)
```

will give us more granularity. We can now divide our genomes into smaller groups:

```
# three_bin_plot.py

g = sns.catplot(
    data=euk,
    x="Size category",
    y="Number of proteins",
    col="Kingdom",
    kind="bar",
    order=["small", "medium", "large"],
    height=2.5,
    orient="v",
)
g.fig.suptitle("Mean number of proteins for genomes of different sizes", y=1.1)
```

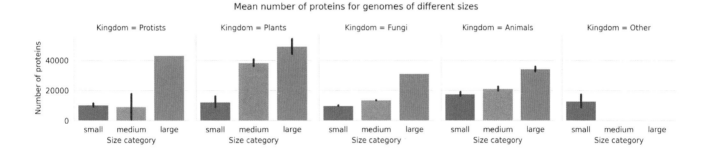

However, as we explore the potential for increasing the number of bins further, we can see a few problems on the horizon.

Firstly, the code for assigning the bins is going to get quite tedious if we have to write a separate condition, and think of a different name, for each bin. When exploring a large dataset it's probable that we will want to experiment with different numbers of bins, so having to explicitly write out the logic each time we want to change something is inelegant and hard to read.

Secondly, and more subtly, when we assign categories in this way pandas doesn't "know" that it's dealing with categorical data. This can lead to some annoying inconsistencies. Notice that in the example above we had to explicitly give the order that we wanted the three bins.

We can see this behaviour in **groupby** as well - if we use our new category as a grouping column, we get the groups in alphabetical order:

```
euk.groupby("Size category")["Number of genes"].median()
```

```
Size category
large     26205.0
medium    19218.5
small      9934.0
Name: Number of genes, dtype: float64
```

which is unlikely to be useful.

13.2 Binning with `pd.cut`

The solution to both of these problems is to let pandas handle the grouping logic using `pd.cut`. The job of `pd.cut` is to take a list of values, and assign each one to a bin. As a minimum we can supply just a list (or Series) of values and a number of bins, and allow pandas to pick the boundaries:

```
pd.cut(euk["GC%"], bins=5).head()
```

```
0    (59.42, 73.5]
1    (31.26, 45.34]
2    (31.26, 45.34]
3    (31.26, 45.34]
4    (31.26, 45.34]
Name: GC%, dtype: category
Categories (5, interval[float64]): [(3.03, 17.18] < (17.18, 31.26] < (31.26, 45.34] < (45.34, 59.42] < (59.42, 73.5]]
```

It's easiest to make sense of the output if we read the last few lines first. Just as normal when displaying a Series, pandas tells us what the data type (`dtype`) is. In previous examples this has been something along the lines of `float`, `int` or `object`. Here we have a new data type - the category. What this means is that pandas "knows" that values in this series have to be one of a fixed number of different options, and that those options have a specific order.

On the last line we can see the bin boundaries that pandas has chosen based on the values that we passed in. The first bin contains all the GC values between 3.03 and 10.14, the second bin between 10.14 and 17.18, etc. The labels for the different bins have been generated automatically. In the bin labels, the square bracket indicates that the upper bound is inclusive; i.e. the bin `(10.14, 17.18]` will include any value that's exactly 17.18. The greater-than symbol in the list of labels shows that they are ordered.

Generally when we make a series of bin labels like this, our next step is to add it as a new column so that we can use it in `groupby`:

```
# cut_bins.py

euk["GC category"] = pd.cut(euk["GC%"], bins=5)
euk.groupby("GC category").size()
```

```
GC category
(3.03, 17.18]      8
(17.18, 31.26]    449
(31.26, 45.34]   4285
(45.34, 59.42]   3003
(59.42, 73.5]    150
dtype: int64
```

or as a category in a plot:

```
# cut_bins_plot.py

g = sns.relplot(
    data=euk[euk["Size (Mb)"] < 5000],
    x="Size (Mb)",
    y="Number of proteins",
    col="GC category",
    height=2.5,
    color="teal",
)

g.fig.suptitle(
    "Genome size vs. number of proteins for genomes with varying GC contents",
    y=1.1,
)
```

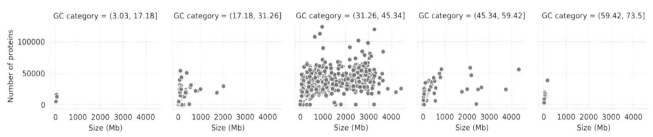

Notice that in both the **groupby** and the chart, the different category labels come out in the correct order - lowest to highest - without us having to specify it.

The logic that pandas uses to pick the bin boundaries is not very sophisticated: it simply divides the span between the lowest and highest values into equally sized chunks and adds a bit at each end. Most of the time we will want to specify the boundaries ourselves, which we can do by passing a list as the **bins** argument. Since GC is measured as a percentage, it makes sense to have bins between zero and 100. We have to remember that because each bin has an upper and lower bound, the number of boundaries we pass in needs to be one greater than the number of bins that we want. For example, to divide the GC into five bins we need to pass a list of six numbers:

```
my_bins = [0, 20, 40, 60, 80, 100]
euk["GC category"] = pd.cut(euk["GC%"], bins=my_bins)
euk.groupby("GC category").size()
```

```
GC category
(0, 20]        49
(20, 40]     2788
(40, 60]     4942
(60, 80]      116
(80, 100]       0
dtype: int64
```

The **range** function often makes a useful shortcut here:

```
# custom_bins.py

my_bins = range(0, 101, 20)
euk["GC category"] = pd.cut(euk["GC%"], bins=my_bins)
euk.groupby("GC category").size()
```

```
GC category
(0, 20]       49
(20, 40]    2788
(40, 60]    4942
(60, 80]     116
(80, 100]      0
dtype: int64
```

Although equally spaced bins are probably the most common, there's nothing that prevents us from using unequal bin boundaries. This can be especially useful when we want narrower bins in the range where most of the points lie:

```
# unqual_bins.py

my_bins = [0, 40, 50, 53, 58, 100]
euk["GC category"] = pd.cut(euk["GC%"], bins=my_bins)
euk.groupby("GC category").size()
```

```
GC category
(0, 40]     2837
(40, 50]    3406
(50, 53]     892
(53, 58]     526
(58, 100]    234
dtype: int64
```

And if we want to have labels other than the pandas default, we can simply supply a list of labels:

```
# custom_labels.py

my_bins = [0, 40, 50, 53, 58, 100]
my_labels = ["very low", "low", "medium", "high", "very high"]
euk["GC category"] = pd.cut(euk["GC%"], bins=my_bins, labels=my_labels)
euk.groupby("GC category").size()
```

```
GC category
very low     2837
low          3406
medium        892
high          526
very high     234
dtype: int64
```

Once we've created our new category, it behaves just like ones that were already in the dataset, with the added bonus of always being in the correct order:

```
# custom_labels_plot.py

sns.catplot(
    data=euk.dropna()[euk.dropna()["Publication year"] == 2018],
    x="GC category",
    y="Number of genes",
    kind="swarm",
    aspect=4,
    height=3,
    orient="v",
)
plt.title(
    "Number of genes for genomes published in 2018 in with varying GC percentages"
)
```

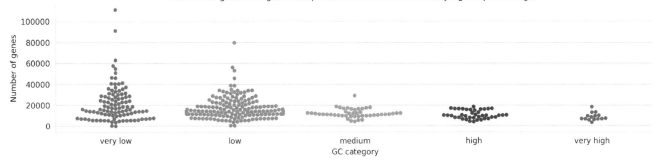
Number of genes for genomes published in 2018 in with varying GC percentages

13.2.1 Unequal bins

In the above example, we have narrower bins in the middle of the distribution, as that's where most of the values lie. But it's a lot of work to manually figure out where the boundaries should be in order to get roughly equal numbers of data points in each bin. Thankfully, pandas can do the work for us. If we use `pd.qcut` instead of `pd.cut`, then we can divide our values into bins with equal numbers of points. In the world of statistics, bins with equal numebrs of points are called *quantiles*, so the argument that determines the number of bins is `q`.

Let's see what happens when we ask pandas to make five quantiles for our GC percentages:

```
pd.qcut(euk["GC%"], q=5)
```

```
0          (50.3, 73.5]
1          (3.099, 37.6]
2          (3.099, 37.6]
3          (3.099, 37.6]
4          (3.099, 37.6]
            ...
8297       (37.6, 41.0]
8298       (37.6, 41.0]
8299       (37.6, 41.0]
8300       (37.6, 41.0]
8301       (37.6, 41.0]
Name: GC%, Length: 8302, dtype: category
Categories (5, interval[float64]): [(3.099, 37.6] < (37.6, 41.0] < (41.0, 45.301] < (45.301, 50.3] < (50.3, 73.5]]
```

Looking at the end of the output, we see that pandas has automatically determined the bin boundaries to ensure nearly equal numbers of points in each bin. If we redraw our chart from above with these new bins:

```
# quantile_bins_plot.py

my_labels = ["very low", "low", "medium", "high", "very high"]
euk["GC category"] = pd.qcut(euk["GC%"], q=5, labels=my_labels)

sns.catplot(
    data=euk.dropna()[euk.dropna()["Publication year"] == 2018],
    x="GC category",
    y="Number of genes",
    kind="swarm",
    aspect=4,
    height=3,
    orient="v",
)
plt.title(
    "Number of genes for genomes published in 2018 in with varying GC percentages"
)
```

---

13 Binning and ordered categories   227

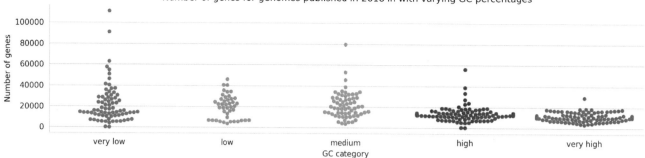
Number of genes for genomes published in 2018 in with varying GC percentages

we can see the more even distribution of points across bins. It's often easier to interpret charts like this than ones where nearly all the points fall into a single bin.

A related problem in binning is when we have a very long-tailed distribution. Look what happens when we try to bin the genomes by size, using 10 bins and allowing pandas to pick the boundaries:

```
pd.cut(euk["Size (Mb)"], bins=10).value_counts().sort_index()
```

```
(-32.385, 3239.65]        8195
(3239.65, 6479.289]         91
(6479.289, 9718.928]         3
(9718.928, 12958.567]        3
(12958.567, 16198.206]       5
(16198.206, 19437.844]       0
(19437.844, 22677.483]       1
(22677.483, 25917.122]       1
(25917.122, 29156.761]       2
(29156.761, 32396.4]         1
Name: Size (Mb), dtype: int64
```

Notice that to get the bins in the correct order, we have to call **sort_index** on the resulting series, otherwise we will get the most common bins first.

Because there are a very large number of small genomes, and a very small number of big ones, we end up with very uneven bins. Of our roughly 8,300 genomes, all but 100 are in the first bin, and all but 16 are in the first two bins. This is likely to be the case in many real-world datasets with long-tailed distributions. Plotting bins like this results in charts that yield little insight into the data:

```
euk["Size category"] = pd.cut(euk["Size (Mb)"], bins=10)

sns.catplot(
    data=euk, y="Size category", kind="count", color="orchid", aspect=2
)
plt.title("Number of genomes in each size category")
```

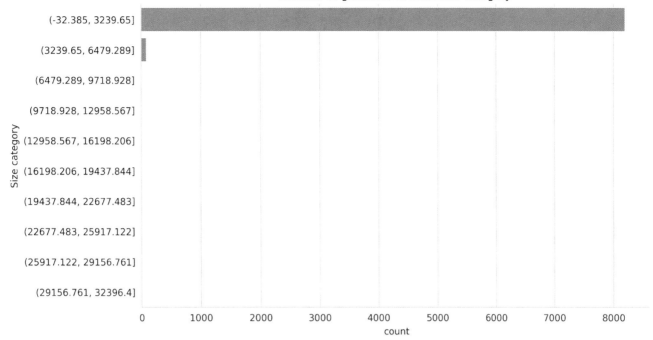

Number of genomes in each size category

We have already seen a few ways to deal with these data. One is to simply use a pandas filter to exclude the largest genomes:

```
no_large = euk[euk["Size (Mb)"] < 5000]
pd.cut(no_large["Size (Mb)"], bins=10).value_counts().sort_index()
```

```
(-4.841, 485.2]        6778
(485.2, 970.389]        501
(970.389, 1455.578]     293
(1455.578, 1940.767]     93
(1940.767, 2425.956]    177
(2425.956, 2911.144]    246
(2911.144, 3396.333]    121
(3396.333, 3881.522]     31
(3881.522, 4366.711]     12
(4366.711, 4851.9]        8
Name: Size (Mb), dtype: int64
```

This gives us very slightly more even bins, at the expense of some genomes not being assigned to a bin.

Another approach would be to take the log of genome size and use that as our value to bin:

```
pd.cut(np.log(euk["Size (Mb)"]), bins=10).value_counts().sort_index()
```

```
(-4.504, -3.001]         4
(-3.001, -1.514]         6
(-1.514, -0.0263]      108
(-0.0263, 1.461]        82
(1.461, 2.949]        1866
(2.949, 4.436]        3465
(4.436, 5.923]        1028
(5.923, 7.411]        1047
(7.411, 8.898]         682
(8.898, 10.386]         14
Name: Size (Mb), dtype: int64
```

This gives us a more normal-looking distribution with most of the data in the middle, but converting the bin labels back to meaningful sizes is hard work for humans.

An alternative is to leave the values as they are, but make the bin boundaries go up expontentially. Let's make a set of bins where each boundary is double that of the previous one:

```
# logarithmic_bins.py

my_bins = [1, 2, 4, 8, 16, 32, 64, 128, 256, 512, 1024, 2048, 4096,
    8192, 16384, 32768, 65536]

pd.cut(euk["Size (Mb)"], bins=my_bins).value_counts().sort_index()
```

```
(1, 2]              24
(2, 4]              51
(4, 8]             159
(8, 16]           1525
(16, 32]          1186
                  ...
(2048, 4096]       556
(4096, 8192]        45
(8192, 16384]        9
(16384, 32768]       5
(32768, 65536]       0
Name: Size (Mb), Length: 16, dtype: int64
```

This gives us a much nicer set of categories to work with. The bins are predicably (though unevenly) spaced; the values are nicely distributed about the middle, and the bin names correspond to real sizes. When we plot this:

```
# log_bins_plot.py

euk["Size category (Mb)"] = pd.cut(euk["Size (Mb)"], bins=my_bins)
sns.catplot(
    data=euk, y="Size category (Mb)", kind="count", color="orchid", aspect=2
)
plt.title("Number of genomes in each size category")
```

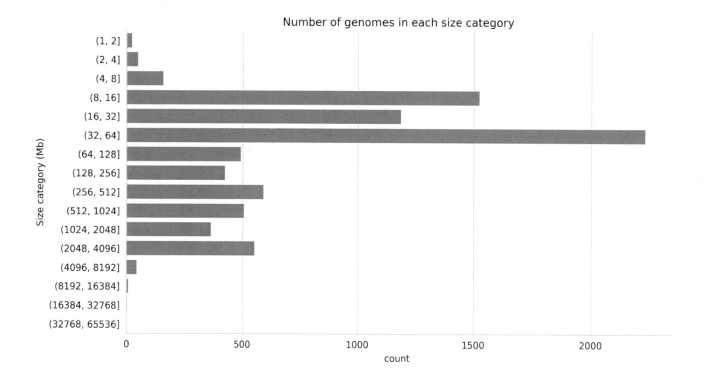

it's not too hard to interpret as long as we pay attention to the X axis labels and remember that the bins are not evenly spaced.

Notice that in the chart above we had to rotate the bin labels to make them fit on the axis. A nice trick to save a bit of space is to use the upper boundary of each bin as the label, which we can do by taking the list of bin boundaries from the second element to the end:

```
# easy_bin_labels.py

euk["Size category (Mb)"] = pd.cut(
    euk["Size (Mb)"], bins=my_bins, labels=my_bins[1:]
)
sns.catplot(
    data=euk, x="Size category (Mb)", kind="count", color="orchid", aspect=2
)
plt.title("Number of genomes in each size category")
```

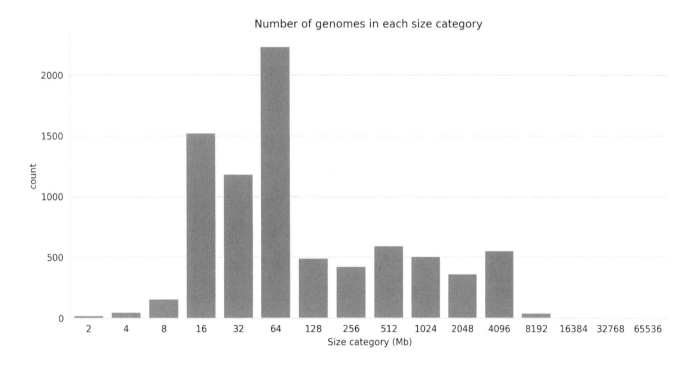

Rather than explicitly writing out a list of bin boundaries, as we did above for clarity, we can usually generate them programatically. List comprehensions can be very useful here. for example, to create our list of doubling bin boundaries that we used above we can just calculate sucesssive powers of two:

```
print([2 ** n for n in range(17)])
```

```
[1, 2, 4, 8, 16, 32, 64, 128, 256, 512, 1024, 2048, 4096, 8192, 16384, 32768, 65536]
```

Once we have our genomes categorized by size bin we have many more options for analysing and visualizing them. For example, we can now use our new category in **groupby** to make a summary table for each kingdom:

```
# bins_summary.py

summary = (
    euk.groupby(["Kingdom", "Size category (Mb)"])
    .size()
    .to_frame("Number of genomes")
    .reset_index()
)
summary.head()
```

	Kingdom	Size category (Mb)	Number of genomes
0	Animals	2	12
1	Animals	4	26
2	Animals	8	93
3	Animals	16	22
4	Animals	32	18

which we can plot:

```
# bins_summary_plot.py

g = sns.catplot(
    data=summary,
    x="Size category (Mb)",
    y="Number of genomes",
    col="Kingdom",
    kind="bar",
    height=2.5,
    color="grey",
)
g.set_xticklabels(rotation=90)
g.fig.suptitle(
    "Number of genomes in each size category for different kingdoms", y=1.1
)
```

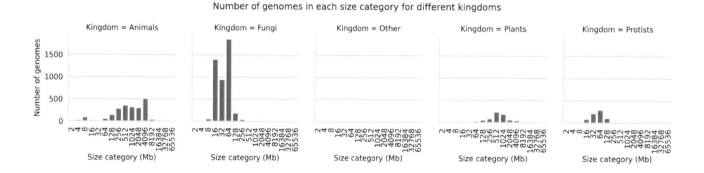

We quickly run into the problem that different kingdoms have very different numbers of genomes, making it hard to compare the distributions. However, we know how to solve this with normalization:

13 Binning and ordered categories

```
# normalized_bins_summary_plot.py

summary["Proportion of genomes"] = (
    summary
    .groupby("Kingdom")
    ["Number of genomes"]
    .transform(lambda x: x / sum(x))
)

g = sns.catplot(
    data=summary,
    x="Size category (Mb)",
    y="Proportion of genomes",
    col="Kingdom",
    kind="bar",
    height=2.5,
    color="grey",
)
g.set_xticklabels(rotation=90)
g.fig.suptitle(
    "Proportion of genomes in each size category for different kingdoms", y=1.1
)
```

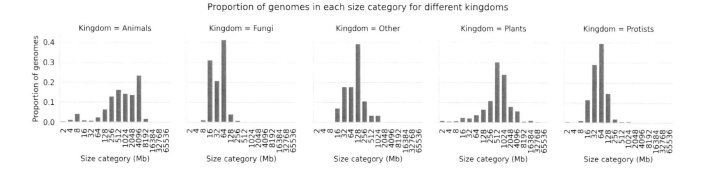

We could also put all of these distributions on a single axis and use color to distinguish the kingdoms:

```
# line_bins_plot.py

sns.catplot(
    data=summary,
    x="Size category (Mb)",
    y="Proportion of genomes",
    hue="Kingdom",
    palette="Accent",
    kind="point",
    aspect=4,
    height=3,
)

plt.title("Proportion of genomes in each size category per kingdom")
```

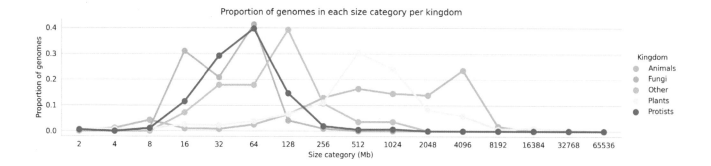

Proportion of genomes in each size category per kingdom

Both of these plots tell the same general story; plants and animals tend to have the largest genomes.

Categories that we create by binning numerical values often work well in heatmaps, which we will discuss in a future chapter.

With small numbers of categories, binning often makes using aspects like size and hue more useful in relational plots. Here's a chart that we've seen before: number of genes vs. number of proteins with the marker size determined by the genome size:

```
sns.relplot(
    data=euk[euk["Class"] == "Birds"].dropna(),
    x="Number of genes",
    y="Number of proteins",
    size="Size (Mb)",
    aspect=2,
)

plt.title("Number of genes vs. number of proteins for bird genomes")
```

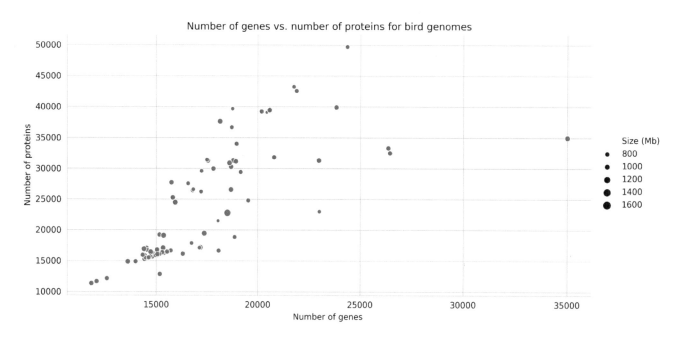

The size of each circle is theoretically unique, since size is a continuous variable. However, we can't realistically distinguish between circles of very similar size, so if we bin the sizes into categories:

```
# bins_for_size.py

my_bins = [0, 800, 1200, 1400, 1600]
my_labels = ["<800", "800-1200", "1200-1400", ">1400"]
my_sizes = {"<800": 10, "800-1200": 30, "1200-1400": 60, ">1400": 120}

euk["Size category (Mb)"] = pd.cut(
    euk["Size (Mb)"], bins=my_bins, labels=my_labels
)

sns.relplot(
    data=euk[euk["Class"] == "Birds"].dropna(),
    x="Number of genes",
    y="Number of proteins",
    size="Size category (Mb)",
    sizes=my_sizes,
    aspect=2,
)

plt.title("Number of genes vs. number of proteins for bird genomes")
```

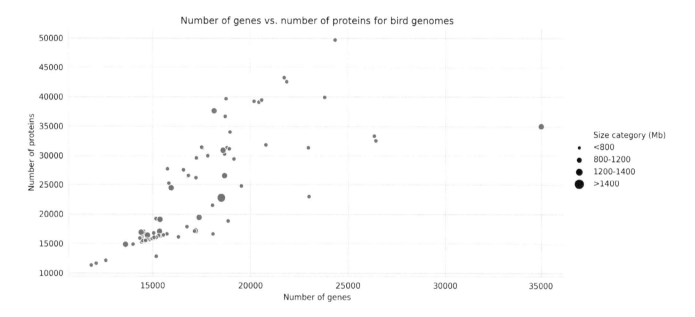

we get a more readable legend and plot with little decrease in perceivable detail. Notice that to set up this plot we have to do quite a bit of preparation. We have to make a list of bin boundaries, a list of bin labels, and a dict mapping the labels to the point sizes we want.

13.3 Custom categories and orders

Let's take a closer look at the data type of the series that results from using `pd.cut`:

```
euk["Size category"].dtype
```

```
CategoricalDtype(categories=[(-32.385, 3239.65], (3239.65, 6479.289], (6479.289, 9718.928], (9718.928, 12958.567],
(12958.567, 16198.206], (16198.206, 19437.844], (19437.844, 22677.483], (22677.483, 25917.122], (25917.122, 29156.761],
(29156.761, 32396.4]],
             ordered=True)
```

As we saw before, the bin lables are not stored as simple strings, but as a set of categories. The categorical data type has two important differences from the string types (recall that in pandas, strings have a data type

---

13 Binning and ordered categories   235

of either `object` or `string`). Firstly, the values are only allowed to take the explicitly enumerated values. If we try to change one of the values to something that's not in the list of categories:

```
df.loc[0, "Size category"] = "banana"
```

we get an error: `Cannot setitem on a Categorical with a new category ...`.

Secondly, because this is an ordered category, pandas (and by extension seaborn) will always list the categories in the correct order. This will be true for plots - as, for example, in our scatter plot above - but also in `groupby` operations:

```
euk.groupby("Size category")["Number of genes"].median()
```

```
Size category
(-32.385, 3239.65]       11973.5
(3239.65, 6479.289]      31682.0
(6479.289, 9718.928]         NaN
(9718.928, 12958.567]        NaN
(12958.567, 16198.206]       NaN
(16198.206, 19437.844]       NaN
(19437.844, 22677.483]       NaN
(22677.483, 25917.122]    6522.0
(25917.122, 29156.761]       NaN
(29156.761, 32396.4]         NaN
Name: Number of genes, dtype: float64
```

These two properties are very useful to have, and being able to apply them to existing categorical columns will resolve a few of the difficulties we have encountered when working with categories. Recall from our discussion of color that the default order for categorical values is the order in which they occur in the data, and hence we can easily get the same categories in different orders when working with different subsets of the data:

```
sns.catplot(
    data=euk[euk["Number of genes"].fillna(0) > 10000],
    x="Kingdom",
    y="GC%",
    kind="boxen",
    color="purple",
    height=4,
)

plt.title(
    "Distribution of GC% across kingdoms\nfor genomes with more than 10000 genes"
)
```

Distribution of GC% across kingdoms for genomes with more than 10000 genes

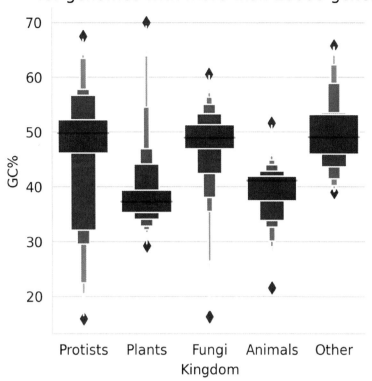

```
sns.catplot(
    data=euk[euk["Number of genes"].fillna(0) <= 10000],
    x="Kingdom",
    y="GC%",
    color="purple",
    kind="boxen",
    height=4,
)
plt.title(
    "Distribution of GC% across kingdoms\nfor genomes with 10000 genes or fewer"
)
```

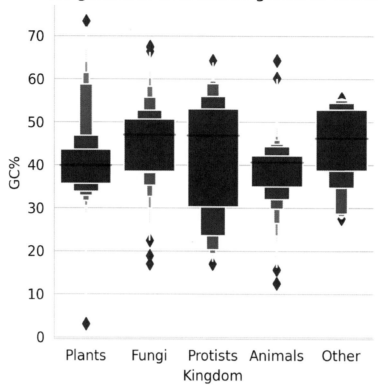

Distribution of GC% across kingdoms
for genomes with 10000 genes or fewer

Compare the X axis labels for the two purple charts. Not only are the order of the kingdoms different between these two charts, they are also both different to the order that we get when using kingdom in a **groupby**:

```
euk.groupby("Kingdom")["GC%"].median()
```

```
Kingdom
Animals    40.8000
Fungi      47.5000
Other      46.9050
Plants     38.8437
Protists   47.7000
Name: GC%, dtype: float64
```

which is alphabetical. In a large project, where we want to cross reference many different charts and tables, this is going to make interpretation difficult.

In the chapter on color, we showed how to get around the first problem by using the **order** argument in **catplot** to force a consistent order, but that doesn't help us with **groupby**. The solution is to make **Kingdom** a category, and give the different categories an explicit order. Note that in order to do this we have to pick an order, which will be somewhat arbitrary - unlike the size bins in our previous example, there's no natural order for the kingdoms. For our purposes, let's say that we want the kingdoms in order of how many genomes they have, largest first. This will allow us to generate our list of values in the order we want using pandas:

```
my_labels = euk["Kingdom"].value_counts().index.to_list()
my_labels
```

```
['Fungi', 'Animals', 'Plants', 'Protists', 'Other']
```

13 Binning and ordered categories

rather than having to type them out.

Having got our list of labels in the correct order, we can now create a new series with the kingdom values as an ordered category:

```
from pandas.api.types import CategoricalDtype

euk["Kingdom"].astype(CategoricalDtype(categories=my_labels, ordered=True))
```

```
0         Protists
1         Plants
2         Plants
3         Plants
4         Plants
           ...
8297      Fungi
8298      Fungi
8299      Fungi
8300      Fungi
8301      Fungi
Name: Kingdom, Length: 8302, dtype: category
Categories (5, object): [Fungi < Animals < Plants < Protists < Other]
```

Notice that the data type description now resembles that of the series that we created earlier using **pd.cut**: the dtype is **category** and the less-than signs indicated that pandas knows the correct order. Normally we will simply overwrite the existing column with this new series:

```
# column_to_category.py

my_labels = euk["Kingdom"].value_counts().index.to_list()

euk["Kingdom"] = euk["Kingdom"].astype(
    CategoricalDtype(categories=my_labels, ordered=True)
)
```

Now pandas will take care of making sure that the kingdoms always appear in the correct order wherever they are used. This includes in grouping operations:

```
euk.groupby("Kingdom")["GC%"].mean()
```

```
Kingdom
Fungi      45.708512
Animals    38.979311
Plants     40.702560
Protists   43.159938
Other      46.600059
Name: GC%, dtype: float64
```

as well as charts:

```
# plot_category.py

sns.catplot(
    data=euk.dropna()[euk.dropna()["Number of genes"] <= 10000],
    x="Kingdom",
    y="GC%",
    color="purple",
    kind="boxen",
    height=4,
)
plt.title(
    "Distribution of GC% across kingdoms\nfor genomes with 10000 genes or fewer"
)
```

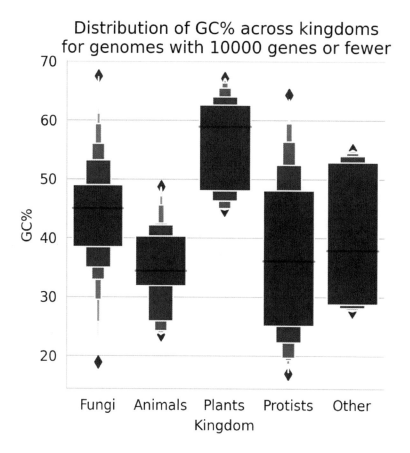

Distribution of GC% across kingdoms for genomes with 10000 genes or fewer

Although creating an ordered category in this way requires a bit of work initially, it will save a great deal of time over the course of a project, as it frees us from the need to explicitly set the order in every chart and table we produce. If we combine this technique with consistent color schemes as described in the chapter on color, we will end up with charts and tables that are easy to cross reference, as categories will always be in the same order.

14 Long form and wide form data

14.1 *Long* or *tidy* form

Whenever we have a data table with more than two columns, we have to make a decision about how to structure the data. Let's consider a very simple example using `groupby`. We will count the number of genomes for each kingdom that are in each status:

```
euk.groupby(["Kingdom", "Assembly status"]).size()
```

```
Kingdom    Assembly status
Animals    Chromosome          246
           Complete Genome       1
           Contig              203
           Scaffold           1731
Fungi      Chromosome          681
                               ...
Plants     Scaffold            443
Protists   Chromosome          101
           Complete Genome       7
           Contig              160
           Scaffold            459
Length: 20, dtype: int64
```

As we saw in the chapter on grouping, when we group on multiple properties of the data then aggregate in a way that produces a single value, we end up with a multi-indexed series. The two columns that we grouped by (**Kingdom** and **Assembly status** in this example) become the two index levels, and the property of the group (the size in this example) becomes the value.

For visualization purposes it's usually easier to have these data as a dataframe rather than a series. Recall from the chapter on `groupby` that to do this we need to call `to_frame`, pick a column name for the values, then call `reset_index`:

```python
# long_summary.py

counts = (
    euk.groupby(["Kingdom", "Assembly status"])
    .size()
    .to_frame("Number of genomes")
    .reset_index()
)
counts
```

	Kingdom	Assembly status	Number of genomes
0	Animals	Chromosome	246
1	Animals	Complete Genome	1
2	Animals	Contig	203
3	Animals	Scaffold	1731
4	Fungi	Chromosome	681
...	...	...	...
15	Plants	Scaffold	443
16	Protists	Chromosome	101
17	Protists	Complete Genome	7
18	Protists	Contig	160
19	Protists	Scaffold	459

This gives us our final table. The data in this table are in what we call *long form*, also known as *tidy form*. This means that there is only one number per row - the number of genomes - and the other columns can be thought of as labels or metadata for the number.

As a rule, long form is the best way to store data that we are going to visualize - in fact, most of the seaborn plotting functions we have looked at require data in long form, since the various properties that we can map have to be column names. Remember that it's this ability to easily map properties of the chart to column names that allows us to quickly iterate on charts. For example, we could visualize these data with a multicolored count plot:

```python
# long_summary_plot.py

sns.catplot(
    data=counts,
    x="Kingdom",
    y="Number of genomes",
    hue="Assembly status",
    kind="bar",
)
plt.title("Number of genomes in different assembly status for each kingdom")
```

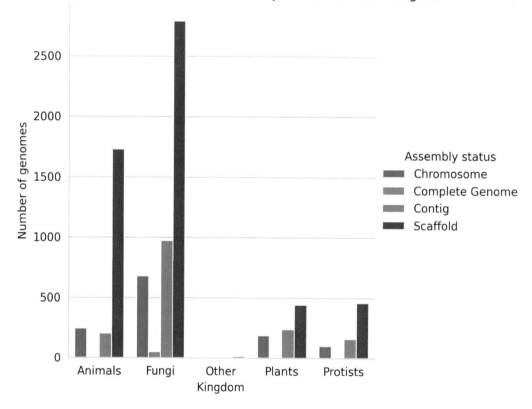

or as a small multiple strip plot:

```
# long_summary_cols.py

g = sns.catplot(
    data=counts,
    y="Kingdom",
    x="Number of genomes",
    col="Assembly status",
    kind="strip",
    height=3,
)
g.set_titles("{col_name}")
g.fig.suptitle(
    "Number of genomes in different assembly status for each kingdom", y=1.1
)
```

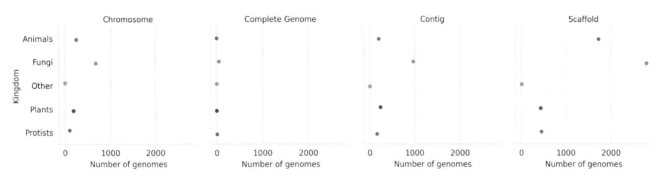

with very minimal changes to the code.

14.2 *Wide* or *summary* form

But this isn't the only way to arrange the data. The alternative is to put it in *wide form*, where there are multiple numbers on each row. Let's go back to the multi-indexed series that we got by grouping:

```
euk.groupby(["Kingdom", "Assembly status"]).size()
```

```
Kingdom    Assembly status
Animals    Chromosome          246
           Complete Genome       1
           Contig              203
           Scaffold           1731
Fungi      Chromosome          681
                               ...
Plants     Scaffold            443
Protists   Chromosome          101
           Complete Genome       7
           Contig              160
           Scaffold            459
Length: 20, dtype: int64
```

and rather than making a dataframe by converting the two indices to columns, we will just take the second index - **Assembly status** - and turn each different value into a column. We do this by calling **unstack**:

```
# wide_summary.py

euk.groupby(["Kingdom", "Assembly status"]).size().unstack()
```

Assembly status Kingdom	Chromosome	Complete Genome	Contig	Scaffold
Animals	246	1	203	1731
Fungi	681	50	973	2790
Other	6	1	9	14
Plants	187	2	238	443
Protists	101	7	160	459

Comparing the two tables hopefully makes the difference clear. Imagine taking the single tall stack of numbers that we have in the series, and unstacking them into four shorter stacks (one for each assembly status) and you will see where the name comes from.

By default, `unstack` takes the rightmost index and turns it into columns, but if we want to take one of the other indices instead we can pass the index number (starting from zero) to `unstack`. So for our example, `unstack(0)` will give us a separate column for each kingdom:

```
euk.groupby(["Kingdom", "Assembly status"]).size().unstack(0)
```

Kingdom Assembly status	Animals	Fungi	Other	Plants	Protists
Chromosome	246	681	6	187	101
Complete Genome	1	50	1	2	7
Contig	203	973	9	238	160
Scaffold	1731	2790	14	443	459

whereas `unstack(1)` (or simply `unstack()` with no argument) will give us a separate column for each status:

```
euk.groupby(["Kingdom", "Assembly status"]).size().unstack(1)
```

Assembly status Kingdom	Chromosome	Complete Genome	Contig	Scaffold
Animals	246	1	203	1731
Fungi	681	50	973	2790
Other	6	1	9	14
Plants	187	2	238	443
Protists	101	7	160	459

Data in wide form, like these last two examples, are often referred to as *summary tables*. The benefit of summary tables is that they tend to be easier for humans to read. In the above example, we can easily compare the numbers within a single kingdom by looking along a single row, or the numbers within a status by looking up and down a column.

In contrast, data in long form are harder for humans to read. In the summary table above it only takes a glance to see that most of the complete genomes are fungi, but try to get the same information from the long form table:

```
(
    euk.groupby(["Kingdom", "Assembly status"])
    .size()
    .to_frame("Number of genomes")
    .reset_index()
)
```

	Kingdom	Assembly status	Number of genomes
0	Animals	Chromosome	246
1	Animals	Complete Genome	1
2	Animals	Contig	203
3	Animals	Scaffold	1731
4	Fungi	Chromosome	681
5	Fungi	Complete Genome	50
6	Fungi	Contig	973
7	Fungi	Scaffold	2790
8	Other	Chromosome	6
9	Other	Complete Genome	1
10	Other	Contig	9
11	Other	Scaffold	14
12	Plants	Chromosome	187
13	Plants	Complete Genome	2
14	Plants	Contig	238
15	Plants	Scaffold	443
16	Protists	Chromosome	101
17	Protists	Complete Genome	7
18	Protists	Contig	160
19	Protists	Scaffold	459

and it's much harder, as we have to look at a bunch of different places in the table to find the numbers we want. At the risk of oversimplifying matters, it's probably fair to say that long form data is easiest for computers to read, whereas wide form data is easiest for humans to read.

And of course, there are some questions that it's easier to answer with the data in wide form. For example, once we've transformed the data:

```
summary = euk.groupby(["Kingdom", "Assembly status"]).size().unstack()
summary
```

Assembly status Kingdom	Chromosome	Complete Genome	Contig	Scaffold
Animals	246	1	203	1731
Fungi	681	50	973	2790
Other	6	1	9	14
Plants	187	2	238	443
Protists	101	7	160	459

it's very easy to calculate the ratio of genomes in contig vs chromosome status for each kingdom:

```
summary["Contig"] / summary["Chromosome"]
```

```
Kingdom
Animals     0.825203
Fungi       1.428781
Other       1.500000
Plants      1.272727
Protists    1.584158
dtype: float64
```

Summary tables are also a necessary step in producing heatmaps, which can be a great way to visualize complex datasets. We'll look at heatmaps in detail in the next chapter.

14.2.1 Chi squared test

When the value in each cell is a count, as in the example above, the summary is in the form of a *crosstab* or *contingency table*, which is a convenient form for carrying out statistical tests. For example, let's test whether plants and animals have significantly different numbers of genomes in contig vs scaffold status. First we'll construct the summary table as before, using a filtered dataframe:

```
# animals_plants.py

animals_vs_plants = (
    euk[
        (euk["Kingdom"].isin(["Animals", "Plants"]))
        & (euk["Assembly status"].isin(["Contig", "Scaffold"]))
    ]
    .groupby(["Kingdom", "Assembly status"])
    .size()
    .unstack()
)
animals_vs_plants
```

Assembly status Kingdom	Contig	Scaffold
Animals	203	1731
Plants	238	443

Then we simply pass the summary table to the `chi2_contingency` functions in the `scipy.stats` module:

```
# chi_square.py

import scipy.stats as stats

stats.chi2_contingency(animals_vs_plants)
```

```
(213.04938955646648,
 2.968914571955448e-48,
 1,
 array([[ 326.15449331, 1607.84550669],
        [ 114.84550669,  566.15449331]]))
```

and it returns a tuple giving us the chi-square statistic, p-value, degrees of freedom, and an array of expected values. The p-value in this case allows us to be very confident that the two categories are not independent.

14.3 Getting data into tidy form

We mentioned above that wide (or summary) form data tends to be easier for humans to read than long (or tidy) form. As a consequence of this, it's quite common to encounter datasets in the real world that are in wide form, simply because they've been designed primarily for humans to read. Any dataset that started off life as a spreadsheet, for example, is almost guaranteed to be in summary form.

This can cause problems when we want to work with such a dataset, especially for visualization. As we've seen in previous chapters, the vast majority of pandas and seaborn functions are designed for long form data. So when we start looking at a dataset that's in wide form, our first job is generally to convert it to long form, in order to take full advantage of our tools.

14.3.1 Using `melt`

The function that handles this task is `melt`. Let's consider a small example using the eukaryote data that we're already familiar with. If we take a subset of the columns:

```
# make_subset.py

subset = euk[
    ["Species", "Kingdom", "Class", "Number of genes", "Number of proteins"]
]
subset.head()
```

	Species	Kingdom	Class	Number of genes	Number of proteins
0	Emiliania huxleyi CCMP1516	Protists	Other Protists	38549	38554
1	Arabidopsis thaliana	Plants	Land Plants	38311	48265
2	Glycine max	Plants	Land Plants	59847	71219
3	Medicago truncatula	Plants	Land Plants	37603	41939
4	Solanum lycopersicum	Plants	Land Plants	31200	37660

we see something that looks a bit like a summary table. We have two measurements on each row: numbers of genes and proteins. To get this into true long form, our goal is to get a single number on each row. This will obviously require us to split each row into two, doubling the number of rows. And to keep track of which rows refer to genes vs. proteins we'll need a new column.

The `melt` function handles all of this for us. To use it, we need to tell `melt`:

- which columns are **not** measurements, i.e. which ones we want to keep as columns. In our case, that is **Species**, **Kingdom** and **Class**. We supply this as a list of column names in the `id_vars` argument.
- what name we want for our new column that contains the names of the old columns. For this example, let's just call it **Measurement type**. This goes in the `var_name` argument.
- what name we want for the column that contains the values from the old columns. For this example, we'll call it **Count**. This goes in the `value_name` argument.

Let's see what happens:

```
# melt.py

long_subset = subset.melt(
    id_vars=["Species", "Kingdom", "Class"],
    var_name="Measurement type",
    value_name="Count",
)
long_subset
```

	Species	Kingdom	Class	Measurement type	Count
0	Emiliania huxleyi CCMP1516	Protists	Other Protists	Number of genes	38549
1	Arabidopsis thaliana	Plants	Land Plants	Number of genes	38311
2	Glycine max	Plants	Land Plants	Number of genes	59847
3	Medicago truncatula	Plants	Land Plants	Number of genes	37603
4	Solanum lycopersicum	Plants	Land Plants	Number of genes	31200
...	...	...	...	...	...
16599	Saccharomyces cerevisiae	Fungi	Ascomycetes	Number of proteins	<NA>
16600	Saccharomyces cerevisiae	Fungi	Ascomycetes	Number of proteins	298
16601	Saccharomyces cerevisiae	Fungi	Ascomycetes	Number of proteins	<NA>
16602	Saccharomyces cerevisiae	Fungi	Ascomycetes	Number of proteins	<NA>
16603	Saccharomyces cerevisiae	Fungi	Ascomycetes	Number of proteins	<NA>

Looking at the output we can see what has happened. The names of the columns that aren't in `id_vars` (**Number of genes** and **Number of proteins**) get put into a new column called **Measurement type**. And the values that were in those two original columns get put in a new column called **Count**.

Hopefully we can see by comparing the original and this transformed version that these are simply two different ways of looking at the same data. We can consider the number of genes and the number of proteins as two completely separate properties of a genome, as in the original dataframe. Or we can think of the count as the measurement, and the things that we're counting (genes or proteins) as another piece of metadata about the count.

Having the data in this long form makes some things easier and some things harder. Recall from the first few chapters that calculating the ratio of genes to proteins was very easy with the data in the original form:

```
euk["Number of proteins"] / euk["Number of genes"]
```

```
0       1.000130
1       1.259821
2       1.190018
3       1.115310
4       1.207051
          ...
8297         NaN
8298    1.922581
8299         NaN
8300         NaN
8301         NaN
Length: 8302, dtype: float64
```

It's much harder now. However, we can now make plots that weren't possible with the original dataframe, where we use the type of count as a category:

```python
# plot_melt.py

sns.catplot(
    data=long_subset.dropna(),
    x="Kingdom",
    y="Count",
    hue="Measurement type",
    kind="box",
)

plt.title(
    "Distributions of numbers of genes and proteins\nfor genomes in different kingdoms"
)
```

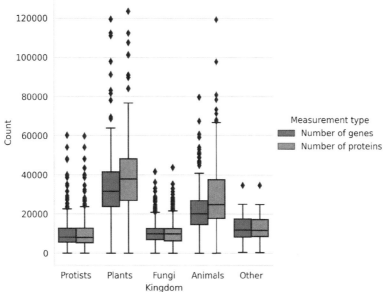

Distributions of numbers of genes and proteins for genomes in different kingdoms

This chart allows us to see a pattern - that plants and animals consistently have more proteins than genes, while other kingdoms don't - that would be harder to see with the data in the original form.

14.3.2 Melting tables with many columns

In real data, we might have a large number of measurements on each line rather than just two. Let's take a look at an example file from the real world: the total amount of rain that fell in London each month:

```
london_rain = pd.read_csv("london_rainfall.csv")
london_rain
```

	Year	January	February	...	October	November	December
0	1960	479	480	...	1555	895	566
1	1961	644	551	...	568	525	886
2	1962	761	126	...	376	419	528
3	1963	129	66	...	347	1190	165
4	1964	178	168	...	292	296	299
...	...	...	...	...	...	...	...
55	2015	634	386	...	398	482	394
56	2016	748	438	...	216	864	104
57	2017	602	382	...	92	342	812
58	2018	574	262	...	600	684	664
59	2019	302	352	...	NaN	NaN	NaN

This data file makes an interesting comparison to our mean daily temperature example. It covers the same years but is at a lower resolution (one measurement per month rather than one per day) and is in a different form. Specifically, the data are in wide form - each row presents a summary of one year, with 12 separate measurements.

This summary form makes it easy to answer some questions about the data. For example, it's pretty straightforward to calculate, for each year, the difference in rainfall between January and June:

```
london_rain["June"] - london_rain["January"]
```

```
0     -51.0
1    -352.0
2    -700.0
3     354.0
4     923.0
        ...
55   -512.0
56    186.0
57   -138.0
58   -570.0
59    520.0
Length: 60, dtype: float64
```

We can even store that as a new column:

```
london_rain["January -> June difference"] = (
    london_rain["June"] - london_rain["January"]
)
```

And then visualize it:

```
# plot_london_rain.py

london_rain["January -> June difference"] = (
    london_rain["June"] - london_rain["January"]
)

sns.distplot(london_rain["January -> June difference"], color="lightblue")
plt.title(
    """Distribution of difference in total rainfall
between January and June in London"""
)
```

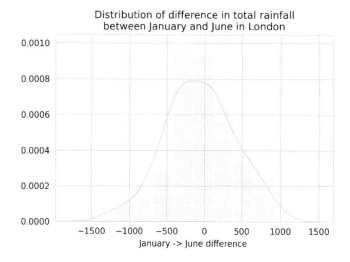

allowing us to draw the conclusion that London is generally drier in June than in January, though with a great deal of year-to-year variation.

We could use a filter to find just the years where June was drier than January:

```
london_rain[london_rain["June"] < london_rain["January"]]
```

	Year	January	February	...	November	December	January -> June difference
0	1960	479	480	...	895	566	-51
1	1961	644	551	...	525	886	-352
2	1962	761	126	...	419	528	-700
8	1968	651	253	...	443	749	-102
9	1969	717	450	...	687	461	-451
...	...	...	...	...	...	...	...
53	2013	501	328	...	500	982	-385
54	2014	1624	898	...	1284	378	-1216
55	2015	634	386	...	482	394	-512
57	2017	602	382	...	342	812	-138
58	2018	574	262	...	684	664	-570

Or count the number of years where it was true or false:

```
(london_rain["June"] < london_rain["January"]).value_counts()
```

```
True     32
False    28
dtype: int64
```

and come to the same conclusion.

However, there are many obvious visualisations that are not easy to draw. With the data in summary form, there's no way to use month as a category, so we can't draw charts that are colored by month, or draw a boxplot with month on the categorical axis.

To make the data easier to work with, let's use `melt` as before to put the data in long form. For this example, the column we want to keep is just **Year**, the names of the other columns should go in a new column called **Month**, and the values from the other columns should go in a new column called **Rainfall (mm)**. Here's the transformation:

```
# tidy_rain.py

london_rain = pd.read_csv("london_rainfall.csv")

tidy_rain = london_rain.melt(
    id_vars=["Year"], var_name="Month", value_name="Rainfall (mm)"
)
tidy_rain
```

	Year	Month	Rainfall (mm)
0	1960	January	479
1	1961	January	644
2	1962	January	761
3	1963	January	129
4	1964	January	178
...	...	...	...
715	2015	December	394
716	2016	December	104
717	2017	December	812
718	2018	December	664
719	2019	December	NaN

Hopefully it's clear enough what we've done. Our tidy dataset has a single measurement per row, and an extra column which tells us the month.

It's now possible to use month as a categry, putting us back into familiar territory and allowing us to use seaborn to make some plots. A point plot does a good job of showing the overall picture:

```
# plot_tidy_rain.py

g = sns.catplot(
    data=tidy_rain,
    x="Month",
    y="Rainfall (mm)",
    kind="point",
    aspect=3,
    height=3.5,
)

g.fig.suptitle("Mean total monthly rainfall in London since 1960")
```

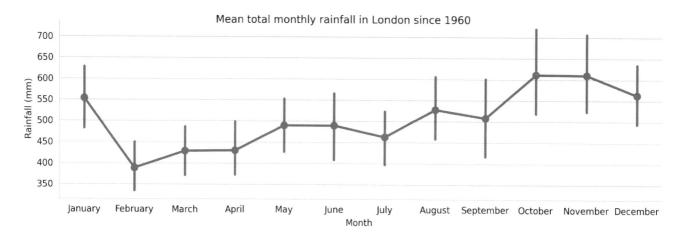

Incidentally, if we try the same chart as a line plot, we notice that something looks wrong:

```
g = sns.relplot(
    data=tidy_rain,
    x="Month",
    y="Rainfall (mm)",
    kind="line",
    aspect=3,
    height=3.5,
)

g.fig.suptitle("Mean total monthly rainfall in London since 1960")
```

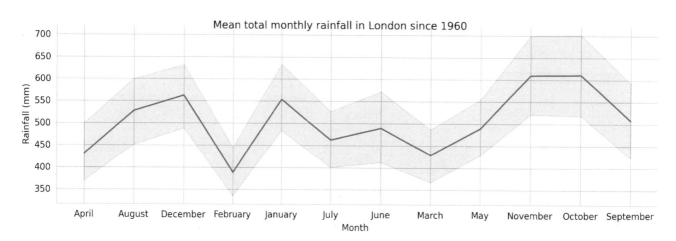

14 Long form and wide form data

The order of the months is wrong in the line plot, even though it was fine in the point plot. This is due to a difference in behaviour between `catplot`, which draws the point plot, and `relplot`, which draws the line plot. Because `catplot` is designed for use with categorical data, it will take the categories in the order which they appear in the data. However, `lineplot` is intended for use with continuous data, so it will attempt to sort the X axis values before plotting them. The default sorting order for strings is alphabetical, so that's the order in which the months appear.

The solution is to set an explicit order for the months. We learned how to do this in the previous chapter: turn the month into an ordered category:

```python
# set_month_category.py

from pandas.api.types import CategoricalDtype

months = ["January", "February", "March", "April", "May", "June", "July", "August",
          "September", "October", "November", "December"]

tidy_rain["Month"] = tidy_rain["Month"].astype(
    CategoricalDtype(categories=months, ordered=True)
)
```

Now the correct order is enforced and we can see the pattern again:

```python
# plot_month_category.py

g = sns.relplot(
    data=tidy_rain,
    x="Month",
    y="Rainfall (mm)",
    kind="line",
    aspect=3,
    height=3.5,
)

g.fig.suptitle("Mean total monthly rainfall in London since 1960")
```

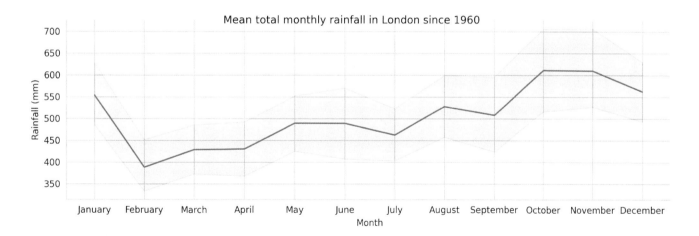

14.3.3 `pivot` and `pivot_table`

If you're used to working with data in a spreadsheet application, or in a relational database, then you may be familiar with using pivot tables to solve the kinds of problems that we've discussed above. Pandas also has these abilities - take a look at the documentation for the `pivot` and `pivot_table` methods:

https://pandas.pydata.org/pandas-docs/stable/user_guide/reshaping.html#pivot-tables

However, we won't discuss them here. Pandas' powerful grouping abilities, and the ability to have heirarchical indices (which we will discuss below) largely replace pivoting. Problems that require pivoting in spreadsheet/database environments are usually better solved in pandas by first getting the data into tidy form, then aggregating and using `unstack` to reshape the data.

14.4 A closer look at indices

So far in this book, we've largely ignored indices, which may seem a strange choice since every series and dataframe has at least one. The reason for our lack of interest is that this book is mainly concerned with visualization of real life datasets, and the seaborn plotting functions can't really take advantage of indices. All of the visualization examples that we've seen work perfectly well using the default numerical index that we get whenever we create a dataframe from a file.

We have seen some examples of useful indices, but these have mainly been generated by pandas itself. For example, if we take a series and call `value_counts`:

```
euk["Species"].value_counts()
```

```
Saccharomyces cerevisiae                576
Homo sapiens                            210
Pyricularia oryzae                      199
Venturia inaequalis                      85
Oryza rufipogon                          62
                                        ...
Ophiocordyceps camponoti-rufipedis        1
Rhizopus delemar Type II NRRL 21477       1
Umbilicaria muehlenbergii                 1
Anaeromyces robustus                      1
Toxoplasma gondii ARI                     1
Name: Species, Length: 4936, dtype: Int64
```

the values in that series become the index for the output. But this happens automatically - we don't need to do anything special to make it happen. The same is true for more complicated indices that arise from grouping operations:

```
euk.groupby(["Kingdom", "Assembly status"])["GC%"].median()
```

```
Kingdom   Assembly status
Animals   Chromosome        41.64775
          Complete Genome   35.43170
          Contig            40.90000
          Scaffold          40.20000
Fungi     Chromosome        38.37770

                              ...
Plants    Scaffold          37.60000
Protists  Chromosome        29.88860
          Complete Genome   41.58030
          Contig            49.40000
          Scaffold          49.60000
Name: GC%, Length: 20, dtype: float64
```

And when we want to do some visualisation on the result, our first step is generally to convert the indices into columns:

```
euk.groupby(["Kingdom", "Assembly status"])["GC%"].median().reset_index()
```

	Kingdom	Assembly status	GC%
0	Animals	Chromosome	41.6478
1	Animals	Complete Genome	35.4317
2	Animals	Contig	40.9
3	Animals	Scaffold	40.2
4	Fungi	Chromosome	38.3777
...	...	...	...
15	Plants	Scaffold	37.6
16	Protists	Chromosome	29.8886
17	Protists	Complete Genome	41.5803
18	Protists	Contig	49.4
19	Protists	Scaffold	49.6

so that we can pass the data to seaborn:

```
# plot_median_gc.py

sns.catplot(
    data=euk.groupby(["Kingdom", "Assembly status"])["GC%"]
    .median()
    .reset_index(),
    x="Kingdom",
    y="GC%",
    hue="Assembly status",
    kind="bar",
)
plt.title("Median GC percentage for each kingdom\ngrouped by assembly status")
```

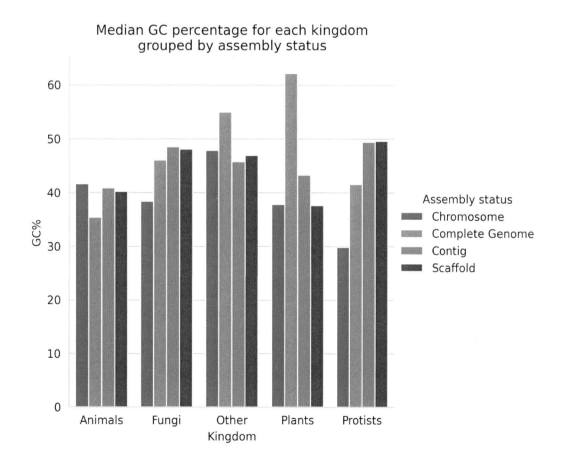

14.4.1 Setting a new index

Sometimes it may be useful to explicitly set an index on a dataframe, if there's a column that makes a natural label for the row. For example, we could make the species column the index for our eukaryote genome dataset:

```
euk2 = euk.set_index("Species")
euk2
```

Species	Kingdom	Class	Size (Mb)	...	Number of proteins	Publication year	Assembly status
Emiliania huxleyi CCMP1516	Protists	Other Protists	167.676	...	38554	2013	Scaffold
Arabidopsis thaliana	Plants	Land Plants	119.669	...	48265	2001	Chromosome
Glycine max	Plants	Land Plants	979.046	...	71219	2010	Chromosome
Medicago truncatula	Plants	Land Plants	412.924	...	41939	2011	Chromosome
Solanum lycopersicum	Plants	Land Plants	828.349	...	37660	2010	Chromosome
...	...	...	...	...	...	...	...
Saccharomyces cerevisiae	Fungi	Ascomycetes	3.99392	...	<NA>	2017	Scaffold
Saccharomyces cerevisiae	Fungi	Ascomycetes	0.586761	...	298	1992	Chromosome
Saccharomyces cerevisiae	Fungi	Ascomycetes	12.0204	...	<NA>	2018	Chromosome
Saccharomyces cerevisiae	Fungi	Ascomycetes	11.9609	...	<NA>	2018	Chromosome
Saccharomyces cerevisiae	Fungi	Ascomycetes	11.8207	...	<NA>	2018	Chromosome

This has a couple of minor benefits. For example, it allows us to use the `loc` attribute to find all the rows that have a particular index value:

```
euk2.loc["Arabidopsis thaliana"]
```

Species	Kingdom	Class	Size (Mb)	...	Number of proteins	Publication year	Assembly status
Arabidopsis thaliana	Plants	Land Plants	119.669	...	48265	2001	Chromosome
Arabidopsis thaliana	Plants	Land Plants	118.891	...	30837	2016	Chromosome
Arabidopsis thaliana	Plants	Land Plants	119.627	...	<NA>	2019	Chromosome
Arabidopsis thaliana	Plants	Land Plants	96.5002	...	<NA>	2011	Scaffold
Arabidopsis thaliana	Plants	Land Plants	98.0662	...	<NA>	2011	Scaffold
...	...	...	...	...	...	...	...
Arabidopsis thaliana	Plants	Land Plants	119.167	...	<NA>	2018	Contig
Arabidopsis thaliana	Plants	Land Plants	119.128	...	<NA>	2018	Contig
Arabidopsis thaliana	Plants	Land Plants	119.75	...	<NA>	2018	Contig
Arabidopsis thaliana	Plants	Land Plants	119.503	...	<NA>	2018	Contig
Arabidopsis thaliana	Plants	Land Plants	93.6545	...	20111	2000	Chromosome

but this is not much less typing than filtering by column:

```
euk[euk["Species"] == "Arabidopsis thaliana"]
```

	Species	Kingdom	Class	...	Number of proteins	Publication year	Assembly status
1	Arabidopsis thaliana	Plants	Land Plants	...	48265	2001	Chromosome
5028	Arabidopsis thaliana	Plants	Land Plants	...	30837	2016	Chromosome
5030	Arabidopsis thaliana	Plants	Land Plants	...	\<NA\>	2019	Chromosome
5699	Arabidopsis thaliana	Plants	Land Plants	...	\<NA\>	2011	Scaffold
5700	Arabidopsis thaliana	Plants	Land Plants	...	\<NA\>	2011	Scaffold
...	...	...	...	...	...	...	...
6455	Arabidopsis thaliana	Plants	Land Plants	...	\<NA\>	2018	Contig
6458	Arabidopsis thaliana	Plants	Land Plants	...	\<NA\>	2018	Contig
6549	Arabidopsis thaliana	Plants	Land Plants	...	\<NA\>	2018	Contig
6554	Arabidopsis thaliana	Plants	Land Plants	...	\<NA\>	2018	Contig
6626	Arabidopsis thaliana	Plants	Land Plants	...	20111	2000	Chromosome

and is arguably less explicit, as we have to know what the index is in order to figure out what we are selecting. And having the species set as the index does absolutely nothing to help us when we need to filter on other columns.

Filtering using an index can give us a performance increase - we'll discuss this in a later chapter.

14.4.2 Making a multi index series

We can create our own multi index by simply passing multiple column names to `set_index`. For example, using our daily temperature data we can turn the date and city columns into indices, and select the temperature column:

```
# weather_index.py

weather = pd.read_csv("weather.csv")

temperatures = (
    weather
    .set_index(["Year", "Month", "Day of month", "City"])
    ["Mean temperature"]
)

temperatures
```

```
Year  Month    Day of month  City
1960  January  1             Berlin   6.4
                2             Berlin   8.1
                3             Berlin   5.4
                4             Berlin   3.9
                5             Berlin   6.0
                                ...
2018  October  27            London   4.9
                28            London   7.4
                29            London   5.8
                30            London   6.6
                31            London   7.0
Name: Mean temperature, Length: 63716, dtype: float64
```

This gives us a series with four indices. When we have multiple indices, we have to give a value for each level to `loc` when referring to a single row. So to find the mean temperature in London on September 7th 1972 we would pass:

```
temperatures.loc[1972, "September", 7, "London"]
```

```
13.8
```

There are a few interesting tricks that we can do with indices like this. If any of the levels are missing from our selection, then we will get all values. So this will give us the mean temperature for that date in all three cities:

```
temperatures.loc[1972, "September", 7]
```

```
City
Berlin       19.2
Edinburgh    12.4
London       13.8
Name: Mean temperature, dtype: float64
```

And this will give us all measurements from 1972:

```
temperatures.loc[1972]
```

```
Month     Day of month  City
January   1             Berlin    1.2
          2             Berlin    0.2
          3             Berlin    1.2
          4             Berlin    2.3
          5             Berlin    0.4
                                  ...
December  27            London    8.6
          28            London    9.4
          29            London    7.7
          30            London    2.2
          31            London    0.1
Name: Mean temperature, Length: 1098, dtype: float64
```

If we just want to get all measurements for Berlin, however, we can't do this:

```
temperatures.loc["Berlin"]
```

becuase city is not the first index. We need to explicitly put in placeholders for the other index levels:

```
temperatures.loc[:, :, :, "Berlin"]
```

```
Year  Month    Day of month
1960  January  1              6.4
               2              8.1
               3              5.4
               4              3.9
               5              6.0
                              ...
2018  October  27             7.9
               28             6.1
               29             4.6
               30             13.3
               31             9.0
Name: Mean temperature, Length: 21489, dtype: float64
```

This weird looking syntax : is Python syntax for a slice that goes from the start of an iterable to the end. You have probably used this slice syntax in regular Python to get a substring:

```
s = "abcdefghijklm"

# just get characters 4 to 8
s[4:8]
```

```
'efgh'
```

If we omit the numbers and just leave the colon, we have a slice that encompasses the whole string:

```
s[:]
```

```
'abcdefghijklm'
```

This is not very useful, but you get the idea - it just means "give me the whole range of whatever values we're looking at". So in our temperature example, we can use it to mean "give me all the years", and combine it with specific values from the other columns:

```
temperatures.loc[:, "July", 18, "Berlin"]
```

```
Year
1960    19.2
1961    14.8
1962    16.3
1963    22.6
1964    24.0
        ...
2014    24.3
2015    23.1
2016    19.1
2017    19.1
2018    23.2
Name: Mean temperature, Length: 59, dtype: float64
```

Just like with a string, we can also use this slice syntax to get values between two limits. We have to sort the dataframe by index first:

```
temperatures.sort_index(inplace=True)
```

And then we can use a slice in `loc`. For example, this will give us the temperature on July 18th in Berlin for all years between 1978 and 1982:

```
temperatures.loc[1978:1982, "July", 18, "Berlin"]
```

```
Year  Month  Day of month  City
1978  July   18            Berlin    17.3
1979  July   18            Berlin    19.4
1980  July   18            Berlin    14.6
1981  July   18            Berlin    14.2
1982  July   18            Berlin    19.6
Name: Mean temperature, dtype: float64
```

Notice a difference between regular Python and pandas: a pandas index slice is inclusive at **both ends**, not just the start. We can even use the extended slices to skip values; here's the same slice but with a step size of 2, skipping odd years:

```
temperatures.loc[1978:1982:2, "July", 18, "Berlin"]
```

```
Year  Month  Day of month  City
1978  July   18            Berlin    17.3
1980  July   18            Berlin    14.6
1982  July   18            Berlin    19.6
Name: Mean temperature, dtype: float64
```

What will happen when we try to slice the months? Let's try to get the mean temperature in Edinburgh on the first day of each month in the summer of 1996. In defiance of the Scottish climate, we'll define the summer as running from May to September:

```
temperatures.loc[1996, "May":"September", 1, "Edinburgh"]
```

```
Year  Month      Day of month  City
1996  May        1             Edinburgh    4.3
      November   1             Edinburgh   11.8
      October    1             Edinburgh    9.6
      September  1             Edinburgh   14.0
Name: Mean temperature, dtype: float64
```

This is one of those troublesome situations where the output looks plausible enough at a glance for us to assume that the expression has worked and move on. However, look closely at the months: what we have actually selected is all the months that are between May and September alphabetically, rather than chronologically. We ran into the same problem earlier in the chapter when we tried to plot monthly rainfall on a line plot: pandas sees these months as strings, so it sorts them alphabetically. The fix is to make month an ordered category:

```
# set_month_order.py

from pandas.api.types import CategoricalDtype

months = ["January", "February", "March", "April", "May", "June", "July", "August",
    "September", "October", "November", "December"]

weather["Month"] = weather["Month"].astype(
    CategoricalDtype(categories=months, ordered=True)
)
```

Then rebuild the multi indexed series:

```
temperatures = weather.set_index(["Year", "Month", "Day of month", "City"])[
    "Mean temperature"
].sort_index()
```

And now the slice works as intended:

```
temperatures.loc[1996, "May":"September", 1, "Edinburgh"]
```

```
Year  Month      Day of month  City
1996  May        1             Edinburgh    4.3
      June       1             Edinburgh   11.2
      July       1             Edinburgh   13.3
      August     1             Edinburgh   14.6
      September  1             Edinburgh   14.0
Name: Mean temperature, dtype: float64
```

Of course, we could have done all of this using regular filters on the original dataframe using a much more verbose syntax. Notice that because we have already made the months an ordered category, we can use **between** to get the months we want:

```
weather[
    (weather["Year"] == 1996)
    & (weather["Month"].between("May", "September"))
    & (weather["Day of month"] == 1)
    & (weather["City"] == "Edinburgh")
]
```

14 Long form and wide form data

	City	Year	Month	Day of year	Day of month	Mean temperature
34742	Edinburgh	1996	May	122	1	4.3
34773	Edinburgh	1996	June	153	1	11.2
34803	Edinburgh	1996	July	183	1	13.3
34834	Edinburgh	1996	August	214	1	14.6
34865	Edinburgh	1996	September	245	1	14.0

In this example dataset we've used separate year, month and day columns to make the examples easier to follow. If we have real-life time series data, then it's probably a good idea to use the `datetime` data type, which would allow us to combine these columns to a single one representing a time point. There's a brief demonstration of this technique in the final chapter of this book.

15 Matrix charts and heatmaps

In this chapter we will take a look at a type of visualization that doens't fit neatly into any of the categories that we've already seen - the heatmap. Heatmaps occupy a unique role in our data visualization universe, as they're the only kind of chart where both axes are categorical. Previously we've seen charts with two numerical axes (histograms and scatter plots) and one numerical axis (the various categorical plots - swarm, box, bar, etc.). With a heatmap, the idea is to put categories on both axes and use the color to represent a numerical variable. Because we are less able to pick out subtle differences in color than subtle differences in position, heatmaps tend to be good for showing very broad, high level patterns. The ability to show two categories on a single axis often allows a more concise summary of the data than other charts would provide.

The reason that we have waited so long to introduce heatmaps is because, more so than other chart types, they require us to understand a number of different techniques to use them effectively. Firstly, the data that we pass to seaborn's `heatmap` function must be in wide or summary form, unlike the other chart types which require long form data. Second, the categories that we display on heatmaps are often created by binning. Finally, heatmaps rely entirely on color to display numerical data. Now that we have dicussed wide form data, binning, and the use of color, we are in a position to explore the use of heatmaps and learn what type of data they are useful for.

15.1 Displaying summary tables

In the previous chapter we saw how by combining `groupby` with aggregation and `unstack` we can create flexible summary tables. For example, let's calculate the mean GC percentage of genomes by kingdom and assembly status:

```
summary = euk.groupby(["Kingdom", "Assembly status"])["GC%"].mean().unstack()
summary
```

Assembly status Kingdom	Chromosome	Complete Genome	Contig	Scaffold
Animals	41.053529	35.431700	40.267332	38.500344
Fungi	39.697680	46.113632	46.895987	46.828819
Other	43.155433	55.017100	46.795575	47.490608
Plants	39.541181	62.132700	42.837814	39.933651
Protists	34.947549	40.290271	44.385549	44.670750

Notice that both the index and the column names now have labels (`Kingdom` and `Assembly status` respectively). Pandas has simply used the column names from the original dataframe that we used in the `groupby`.

At a minimum, all we need to do to draw a heatmap is to pass this summary table to seaborn's `heatmap` function:

```
# heatmap.py

summary = euk.groupby(["Kingdom", "Assembly status"])["GC%"].mean().unstack()

sns.heatmap(summary)
plt.title(
    "Mean GC% for genomes belonging to each kingdom\nin each assembly status"
)
```

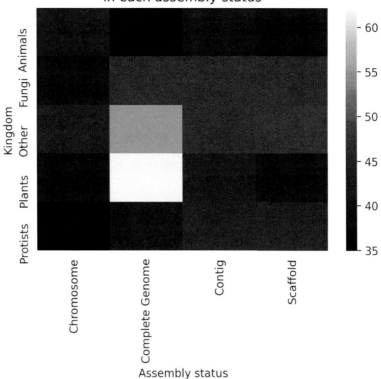

Mean GC% for genomes belonging to each kingdom
in each assembly status

The default styles are not as polished for heatmaps as they are for other chart types, but the figure is easy enough to interpret: plant and "other" genomes in complete status have high GC, while complete animal and chromosome protist genomes have low GC.

Let's look at a few variations. To set the figure size and shape we have to call `plt.figure` with a `figsize` argument giving horizontal and vertical dimensions. We can pick the color map by setting the `cmap` argument - any of the sequential palettes mentioned in the chapter on color will do nicely. We can also set the limits of the color scale using the `vmin` and `vmax` arguments - this is equivalent to setting the axis limits on a scatterplot. Since GC% is a percentage, let's set the color scale between 0 and 100. We will also annotate each cell with the actual value by setting `annot=True`:

```
# styled_heatmap.py

summary = euk.groupby(["Kingdom", "Assembly status"])["GC%"].mean().unstack()

plt.figure(figsize=(3, 3))
sns.heatmap(summary, cmap="Blues", vmin=0, vmax=100, annot=True)
plt.title(
    "Mean GC% for genomes \nbelonging to each kingdom\nin each assembly status"
)
```

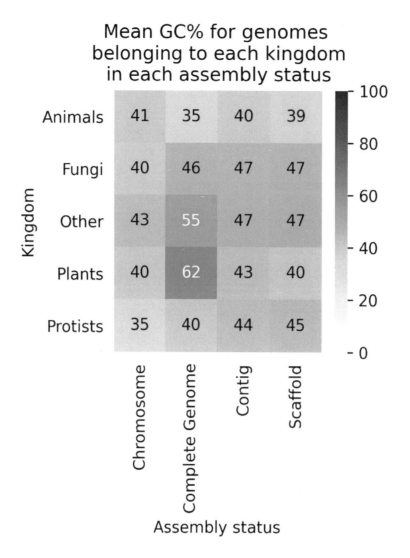

Mean GC% for genomes
belonging to each kingdom
in each assembly status

These changes give us a quite different looking chart. Setting the colur scale to between 0 and 100 nicely illustrates the trade off to be made; it makes it clear that most of the means are somewhere in the middle of the scale, at the expense of making it harder to see differences between cells. Annotating the cells with the actual values counteracts this somewhat.

Notice that the pattern for this new color map is the opposite to the default one: in this version, darker and more saturated colors mean higher values.

15.2 Displaying complex summaries

Let's try a more complicated example. We'll make a summary table that shows the total number of megabases sequenced in each year for each class. This will give us many more cells, and some missing data. For this summary, we'll divide our series by 1000 to convert to gigabases before unstacking:

```
# mb_summary.py

mb_per_year = (
    euk.groupby(["Class", "Publication year"])["Size (Mb)"]
    .sum()
    .apply(lambda x: x / 1000)  # divide each sum by 1000 to get Gb
    .unstack()
)
mb_per_year
```

Publication year Class	1992	1998	1999	...	2017	2018	2019
Amphibians	NaN	NaN	NaN	...	6.25035	34.9482	NaN
Apicomplexans	NaN	0.0233269	NaN	...	0.590813	2.13286	0.618504
Ascomycetes	0.000586761	NaN	0.0121571	...	14.9888	36.8003	7.26618
Basidiomycetes	NaN	NaN	NaN	...	3.68506	11.8585	1.04647
Birds	NaN	NaN	NaN	...	27.9578	62.9177	7.20372
...	...	...	...	...	...	...	...
Other Fungi	NaN	NaN	NaN	...	1.5622	2.70493	0.435296
Other Plants	NaN	NaN	NaN	...	NaN	1.89711	NaN
Other Protists	NaN	NaN	NaN	...	3.93469	4.99576	1.24802
Reptiles	NaN	NaN	NaN	...	NaN	30.4156	6.41208
Roundworms	NaN	NaN	NaN	...	3.7189	8.1105	1.07096

Notice that our aggregator here is not `mean` but `sum` - we want to add up all the sizes, not find their average. Because we have more columns than rows, we'll make a heatmap with a wider shape. We'll also add some space in between cells with the `linewidths` argument, and style the color bar with the `cbar_kws` argument. Just like we saw in the chapter on styles, when we need to pass arguments to underlying matplotlib functions we use a dictionary of key/value pairs - in this case we will shrink the color bar a bit, and give it a label.

```
# mb_summary_heatmap.py

plt.figure(figsize=(15, 5))
sns.heatmap(
    mb_per_year,
    cmap="GnBu",
    cbar_kws={"shrink": 0.5, "label": "Gb sequenced"},
    linewidths=1,
)
plt.title("Gigabases of genome sequence published for each class in each year")
```

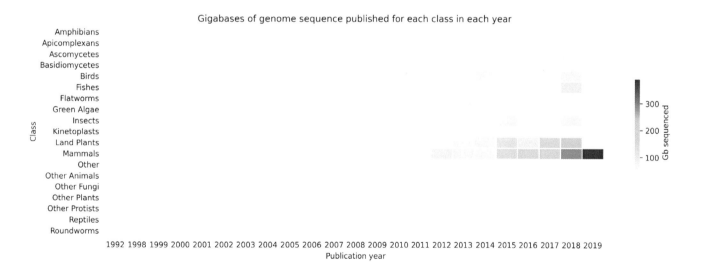

In this plot we have something new: missing data, which by default will not be shaded. This is a useful property, as it makes it possible to distinguish between years in which no genomes were sequenced for a given class, and years in which a very small amount of data were sequenced. This figure nicely illustrates the use case for a heatmap: we can't tell exactly what the value is for mammals in 2019, but we can see that it's the highest on the chart (and that the mammal and plant rows have the highest values overall).

If we want to fill in the missing data, we can do it in the summary table by calling `fillna` with our default value as the argument. For these data, if a particular year/class combination is missing then there were no genomes published so the correct default is zero:

```
# filled_summary.py

mb_per_year = (
    euk.groupby(["Class", "Publication year"])["Size (Mb)"]
    .sum()
    .apply(lambda x: x / 1000)
    .unstack()
    .fillna(0)
)
mb_per_year
```

Publication year Class	1992	1998	1999	...	2017	2018	2019
Amphibians	0	0	0	...	6.25035	34.9482	0
Apicomplexans	0	0.0233269	0	...	0.590813	2.13286	0.618504
Ascomycetes	0.000586761	0	0.0121571	...	14.9888	36.8003	7.26618
Basidiomycetes	0	0	0	...	3.68506	11.8585	1.04647
Birds	0	0	0	...	27.9578	62.9177	7.20372
...	...	...	...	...	...	...	...
Other Fungi	0	0	0	...	1.5622	2.70493	0.435296
Other Plants	0	0	0	...	0	1.89711	0
Other Protists	0	0	0	...	3.93469	4.99576	1.24802
Reptiles	0	0	0	...	0	30.4156	6.41208
Roundworms	0	0	0	...	3.7189	8.1105	1.07096

Which gives us this figure:

```
# filled_summary_heatmap.py

plt.figure(figsize=(15, 5))
sns.heatmap(
    mb_per_year,
    cmap="GnBu",
    cbar_kws={"shrink": 0.5, "label": "Gb sequenced"},
    linewidths=1,
)
plt.title("Gigabases of genome sequence published for each class in each year")
```

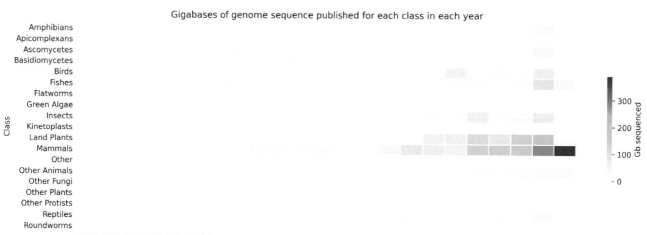

Notice the difference from the previous one: here we get a consistent pale green background color.

15.3 Heatmaps with many categories

Our examples above have a relatively small number of categories on each axis. When we see a particularly bright or dark cell we can, with a bit of effort, look at the axis labels to determine which category it belongs to.

Let's see what happens when we try to display more data. For this we'll turn to our mean daily temperature dataset:

```
weather
```

	City	Year	Month	Day of year	Day of month	Mean temperature
0	Berlin	1960	January	1	1	6.4
1	Berlin	1960	January	2	2	8.1
2	Berlin	1960	January	3	3	5.4
3	Berlin	1960	January	4	4	3.9
4	Berlin	1960	January	5	5	6
...	...	...	...	...	...	...
63711	London	2018	October	300	27	4.9
63712	London	2018	October	301	28	7.4
63713	London	2018	October	302	29	5.8
63714	London	2018	October	303	30	6.6
63715	London	2018	October	304	31	7

We'll begin by trying to visualize the complete weather data for a single city. We'll filter to just find the rows for Berlin, then construct a summary table by putting year as the index and day of the year as the column names:

```python
# berlin_summary.py

berlin_summary = (
    weather[weather["City"] == "Berlin"]
    .groupby(["Year", "Day of year"])["Mean temperature"]
    .first()
    .unstack()
)
berlin_summary
```

Day of year Year	1	2	3	...	364	365	366
1960	6.4	8.1	5.4	...	1.2	0.2	-0.3
1961	1.5	0.4	3.5	...	1.2	2.7	NaN
1962	2.1	-1.6	0	...	-6.1	-7.4	NaN
1963	-12.7	-10.5	-7.4	...	2.7	-0.4	NaN
1964	2.5	4	1	...	-3	-1.4	7
...	...	...	...	...	...	...	...
2014	1.1	3.9	6.5	...	-1.6	3.1	NaN
2015	3.9	5.4	4.8	...	0.7	0.2	NaN
2016	1.6	-3.6	-9.8	...	4.1	0.3	0.8
2017	2.3	1	2.7	...	2.7	9.5	NaN
2018	8.5	4.6	5.1	...	NaN	NaN	NaN

Notice that for the aggregation we can use `first` rather than `mean`, because we know that for each individual day we have only a single measurement, so we can instruct pandas to simply take the first value. An interesting pattern in the data are the leap years - day 366 is missing for non-leap years. And the data for 2018 are missing for the last part of the year, as this dataset ends halfway through that year.

To plot the data we'll pass our summary table to `heatmap` with a generous size and choose a colur palette that fits with the theme of temperature:

```
# temp_heatmap.py

plt.figure(figsize=(15, 5))

sns.heatmap(berlin_summary, cmap="hot")

plt.title(
    "A literal heatmap: mean daily temperature (°C) in Berlin since 1960"
)
```

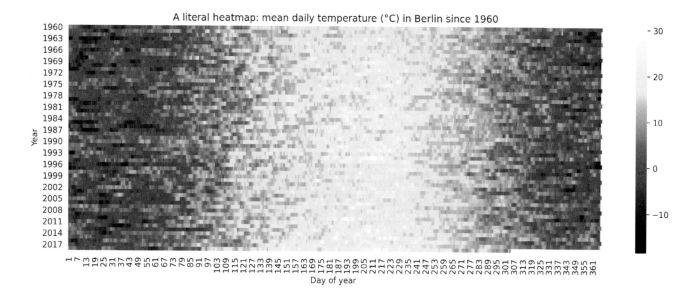

The result is a nice illustration of the power of heatmaps to give overviews. Even though we are plotting over 20,000 individual data points, the patterns of warm summers and cool winters are very apparent. We can also see a level of detail that wouldn't be visible if we plotted these data in any other way. For example, we can pick out short horizontal segments that are either brigher or darker than their surroundings, corresponding to periods of very warm or cold weather.

Importantly, although we can see these outlier regions, we can't easily tell what year or days they belong to. Scanning for the brightest area in the chart we can see a bright white region - a series of very warm days - in the middle of the year around 1993, but there are too many categories to tell exactly which year or days it belongs to. In fact, there are too many categories to draw labels for them all - notice that seaborn has only labelled every seventh day on the horizontal axis, and every third year on the vertical axis.

As we've seen before, this is an example of the fundamental trade off involved in data visualization: the more data we display, the less detail we can see.

15.3.1 Diverging palettes with heatmaps

When there is a natural center point for our data, we can often make good use of a diverging palette to add more context to the data. For temperature, we might pick freezing point - 0 degrees in our dataset, which is measured in Celcius - as the center point. If we pick a diverging palette and set the `center` argument, we get this view of the data:

```
# diverging_heatmap.py

plt.figure(figsize=(15, 5))

sns.heatmap(
    berlin_summary, cmap="RdBu_r", center=0  # reversed so that red is highest
)

plt.title("A literal heatmap: mean daily temperature in Berlin since 1960")
```

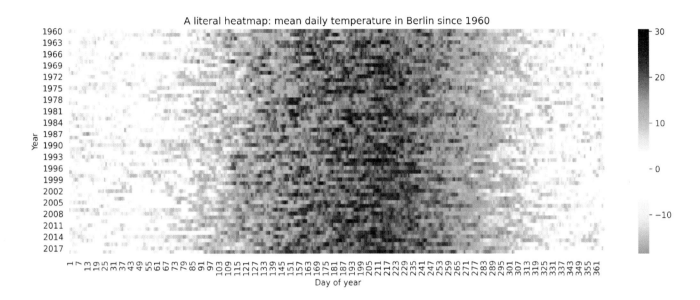

Now we can quickly pick out the regions where the mean daily temperature was below freezing. In this plot, color is doing two jobs: whether a cell is red or blue tells us whether that day's mean was above or below freezing, and the intensity of the color tells us how far away from freezing it was.

Diverging palettes can be useful whenever we are trying to display a difference. For example, let's say we are interested in the difference in daily temperature between Edinburgh and London. The easiest way to calculate this is to make a summary table with each city in a different column:

```
# city_summary.py

city_summary = (
    weather.groupby(["Year", "Day of year", "City"])["Mean temperature"]
    .first()
    .unstack()
)
city_summary
```

City	Berlin	Edinburgh	London
(1960, 1)	6.4	6.4	10.6
(1960, 2)	8.1	1.4	6.1
(1960, 3)	5.4	3.9	8.4
(1960, 4)	3.9	3.6	9.4
(1960, 5)	6	4.2	8.9
...	...	...	...
(2018, 300)	7.9	NaN	4.9
(2018, 301)	6.1	NaN	7.4
(2018, 302)	4.6	NaN	5.8
(2018, 303)	13.3	NaN	6.6
(2018, 304)	9	NaN	7

Now we can calculate the difference by simply subtracting the relevant columns, taking advantage of the ability of series object to broadcast calculations:

```
difference = city_summary["London"] - city_summary["Edinburgh"]
difference
```

```
Year  Day of year
1960  1              4.2
      2              4.7
      3              4.5
      4              5.8
      5              4.7
                     ...
2018  300            NaN
      301            NaN
      302            NaN
      303            NaN
      304            NaN
Length: 21489, dtype: float64
```

Finally we can turn this into the summary table we want by calling **unstack** one more time:

```
difference.unstack()
```

Day of year Year	1	2	3	...	364	365	366
1960	4.2	4.7	4.5	...	1	1.6	0.8
1961	-0.1	-0.8	0	...	6.5	3.8	NaN
1962	-5.9	-4.5	-1.2	...	-0.6	-0.9	NaN
1963	-2.3	-2.1	-2.5	...	-3	-0.8	NaN
1964	-1.4	-3.9	-5.1	...	0.3	0.9	3.6
...	...	...	...	...	...	...	...
2014	2.8	3.1	2.9	...	-3.5	-4	NaN
2015	-4.1	3.5	1.1	...	0.3	5.8	NaN
2016	0.8	1.8	-0.5	...	-5.8	-8.1	-6.6
2017	NaN	NaN	NaN	...	NaN	NaN	NaN
2018	NaN	NaN	NaN	...	NaN	NaN	NaN

We now have a summary table that is the same shape as our earlier one, but where each cell represents a difference in temperature rather than an absolute temperature. Plotting with a normal sequential color palette gives us a figure that is very pretty, but makes it hard to pick out which days were warmer or colder in London than Edinburgh:

15 Matrix charts and heatmaps

```
# difference_heatmap.py

plt.figure(figsize=(15, 5))

sns.heatmap(difference.unstack(), cmap="GnBu", center=0)

plt.title("Difference in daily mean temperature between London and Edinburgh")
```

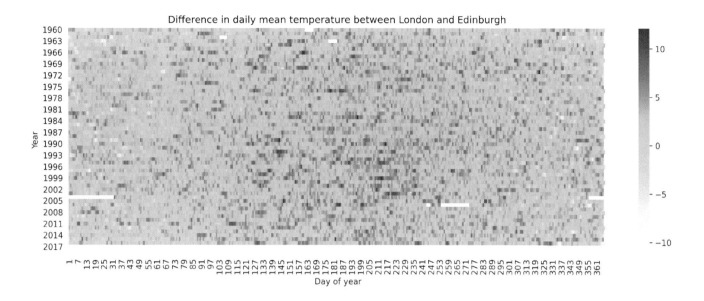

The same chart with a diverging palette, however:

```
# diverging_difference.py

plt.figure(figsize=(15, 5))

sns.heatmap(difference.unstack(), cmap="RdBu_r", center=0)

plt.title("Difference in daily mean temperature between London and Edinburgh")
```

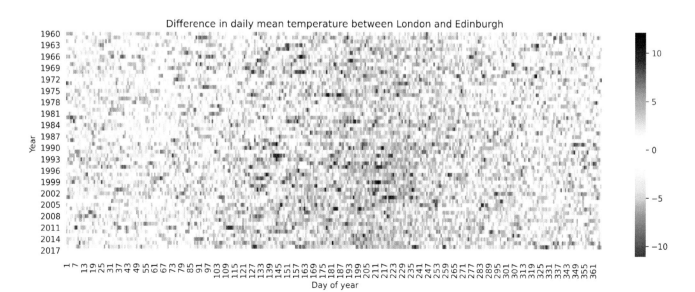

---

makes it much easier to see. There is far more red in the chart than blue, telling us that London is generally warmer than Edinburgh (not surprising, as it's about 300 miles further South). However, we can also see that there are some blue regions (representing days where it's colder in London than Edinburgh) and that they nearly all occur in the winter. Interestingly, we can also see some areas of missing data (for example, look near the start of 2006) representing days when we don't have measurements for one or other city.

For our final look at the temperature data, we'll take a 10-year span and try to visualize the temperature in all three cities. To build our summary table we first have to filter by year, then include city in our grouping:

```
# daily_summary.py

ten_years = (
    weather[weather["Year"].between(1980, 1990)]
    .groupby(["City", "Day of year", "Year"])["Mean temperature"]
    .first()
    .unstack()
    .unstack()
)
ten_years
```

City	(1980, 1)	(1980, 2)	(1980, 3)	...	(1990, 364)	(1990, 365)	(1990, 366)
Berlin	0.8	-0.5	-3.5	...	5.8	3.4	NaN
Edinburgh	-2.0	-2.1	2.0	...	2.2	3.3	NaN
London	-1.8	-1.8	2.6	...	6.3	6.8	NaN

For this summary we need both year and day to be in columns, so we need to call **unstack** twice. This gives us a very wide format table with just three rows, but over four thousand columns! Drawing the heatmap produces a correspondingly wide figure:

```
# daily_summary_plot.py

plt.figure(figsize=(15, 2))

sns.heatmap(ten_years, cmap="hot")

plt.title("Mean daily temperature in three cities between 1980 and 1990")
```

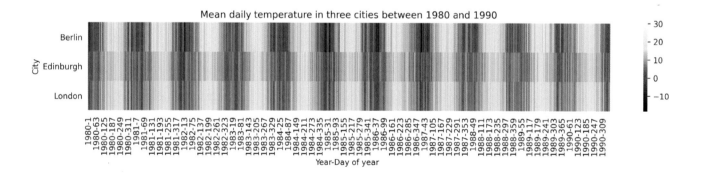

This is an example of a heatmap with very unbalanced axes. With over four thousand days on the horizontal axis it's impossible to see individual daily temperatures. However, we do get a very nice overview of the periodic seasonal pattern, and can pick out some years - 1984, 1985 and 1986 - where Berlin had extremely cold periods in the winter.

Notice that seaborn does a reasonably good job of labeling the horizontal axis given its complexity. It automatically constructs labels consisting of the year and day, and figures out how many will fit on the size of figure that we've asked for.

15.4 Summary tables, binning and heatmaps

In a previous chapter we took a look at the process of binning data - taking continuous values and turning them into a set of categories. One of the motivating reasons for doing this was that we have more options for visualizing categorical data. Nowhere is this more true than when looking at heatmaps.

As an example, let's visualize the distribution of GC% across kingdoms. We've already looked at this particular question in the chapter on plotting distributions:

```
plt.figure(figsize=(8, 4))

# for each unique kingdom...
for kingdom in euk["Kingdom"].unique():

    # ...select just the rows for that kingdom...
    one_kingdom = euk[euk["Kingdom"] == kingdom]

    # ... and plot the GC values
    sns.distplot(one_kingdom["GC%"].dropna(), hist=False, label=kingdom)

plt.title(
    "Distribution of GC percentage for genomes\nbelonging to different kingdoms"
)
```

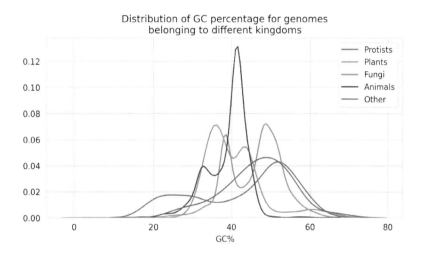

And again in the chapter on categorical plots:

```
sns.catplot(data=euk, x="Kingdom", y="GC%", kind="violin")

plt.title(
    "Distribution of GC percentage for genomes\nbelonging to different kingdoms"
)
```

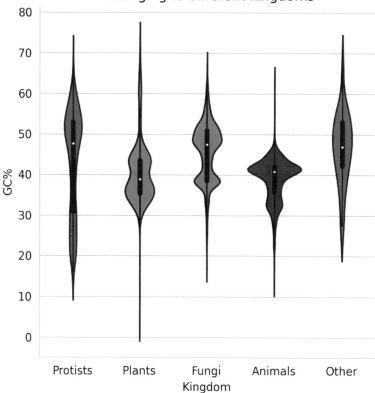

Distribution of GC percentage for genomes belonging to different kingdoms

In each case the GC% axis is continuous. Let's see what happens if we use `pd.cut` to bin the genomes by GC%:

```
pd.cut(euk["GC%"], bins=range(0, 100, 5))
```

```
0        (60, 65]
1        (35, 40]
2        (35, 40]
3        (30, 35]
4        (35, 40]
          ...
8297     (35, 40]
8298     (35, 40]
8299     (35, 40]
8300     (35, 40]
8301     (35, 40]
Name: GC%, Length: 8302, dtype: category
Categories (19, interval[int64]): [(0, 5] < (5, 10] < (10, 15] < (15, 20] ... (75, 80] < (80, 85] < (85, 90] < (90, 95]]
```

The output of `pd.cut` is a series of categories, which we can plug straight into `groupby`, then make a summary table in the usual way.

```
# gc_counts_summary.py

summary = (
    euk.groupby(
        [
            "Kingdom",
            pd.cut(euk["GC%"], bins=range(0, 100, 5), labels=range(5, 100, 5)),
        ]
    )
    .size()
    .unstack()
)
summary
```

GC% Kingdom	5	10	15	...	85	90	95
Animals	0	0	1	...	0	0	0
Fungi	0	0	0	...	0	0	0
Other	0	0	0	...	0	0	0
Plants	1	0	1	...	0	0	0
Protists	0	0	0	...	0	0	0

At this point we have a suitable input for `heatmap`:

```
# gc_counts_heatmap.py

plt.figure(figsize=(15, 5))

sns.heatmap(summary, cmap="PuRd", annot=True)

plt.title("Number of genomes in each GC range per kingdom")
```

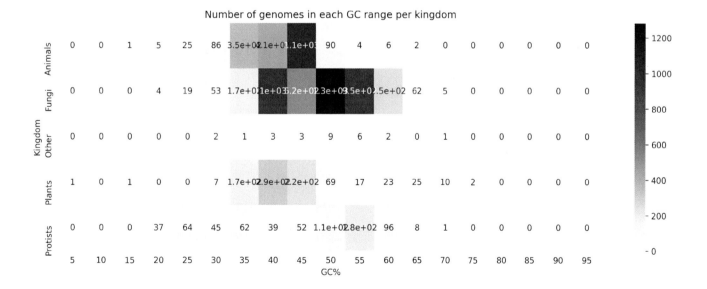

Becuase the absolute number of cells is small, we have space to annotate each one with the actual value. Notice that the default way for seaborn to display the numbers is using exponential notation. This is probably not very convenient to read, so we can force a specific format by giving a formatting string:

```
# annotated_heatmap.py

plt.figure(figsize=(15, 5))

sns.heatmap(summary, cmap="PuRd", annot=True, fmt=".0f")

plt.title("Number of genomes in each GC range per kingdom")
```

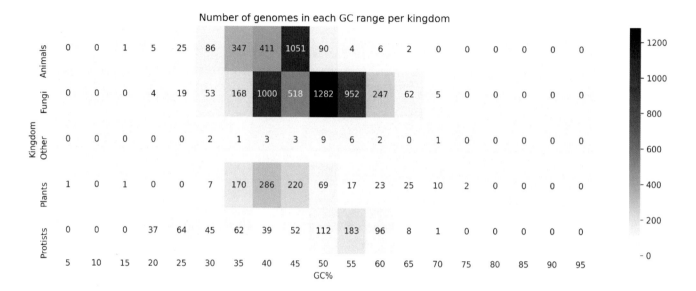

The magic string `".0f"` above means that we want to display each value as a floating point number with zero decimal places.

A nice aspect of binning is that it gives us a very convenient way to control the granularity of our categories. In the above example we've used a range to create a list of 20 bin boundaries, giving us 19 bins. By changing the arguments to `range`, we can quickly adjust both the number of bins, and the highest and lowest values:

```
# more_bins.py

my_bins = range(12, 75, 2)
my_labels = range(14, 75, 2)

summary = (
    euk.groupby(
        ["Kingdom", pd.cut(euk["GC%"], bins=my_bins, labels=my_labels)]
    )
    .size()
    .unstack()
)

plt.figure(figsize=(15, 5))
sns.heatmap(summary, cmap="PuRd", square=True)
plt.title("Number of genomes in each GC range per kingdom")
```

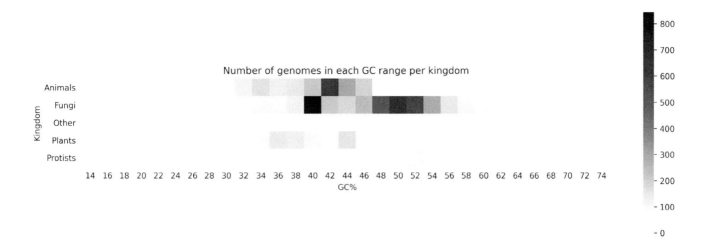
Number of genomes in each GC range per kingdom

A common problem when using heatmaps to look at distributions in unbalanced categories is that it's hard to see difference in the smallest categories because the values are all near the bottom of the color scale. We can see this exact problem above: it's hard to see the distribution of values for protists because there are very few protist genomes compared to other groups.

The solution is usually some kind of normalization. What we need is the same kind of normalization as we saw before in the chapter on groups: if we divide each value by the total for the row, then we will get proportions rather than absolute numbers. The easiest way to do this is to use the `apply` function to run our normalization code on each row. Because we want to do the normalization per row rather than per column, we need to pass `axis=1`. And because we have missing data, we need to call `fillna` first:

```
summary.fillna(0).apply(lambda x: x / sum(x), axis=1)
```

GC% Kingdom	14	16	18	...	70	72	74
Animals	0.000493	0.000493	0.000986	...	0.00000	0.000000	0.000000
Fungi	0.000000	0.000000	0.000464	...	0.00000	0.000000	0.000000
Other	0.000000	0.000000	0.000000	...	0.00000	0.000000	0.000000
Plants	0.001205	0.000000	0.000000	...	0.00241	0.001205	0.001205
Protists	0.000000	0.001431	0.002861	...	0.00000	0.000000	0.000000

Now when we draw the heatmap, the values on each row sum to 1. Another way of looking at it is that each row has the same total amount of color in it, so it's easier to compare distributions:

```
# normalized_heatmap.py

plt.figure(figsize=(20, 5))

sns.heatmap(
    summary.fillna(0).apply(lambda x: x / sum(x), axis=1),
    cmap="PuRd",
    square=True,
)

plt.title("Proprtion of genomes in each GC range per kingdom")
```

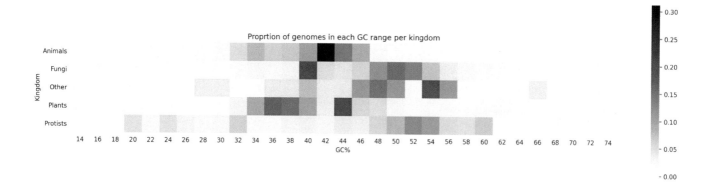

This figure does a good job of showing, for example, the bimodal distribution of GC% in fungal genomes.

We have been looking at a lot of examples that involve size, but remember that we can make summary tables that aggregate any property of a group. For example, with a small change to the code we can make a summary table showing the median number of genes for genomes falling into each bin:

```
# median_summary.py

my_bins = range(12, 75, 2)
my_labels = range(14, 75, 2)

genes_summary = (
    euk.groupby(
        ["Kingdom", pd.cut(euk["GC%"], bins=my_bins, labels=my_labels)]
    )["Number of genes"]
    .median()
    .unstack()
)
genes_summary
```

GC% Kingdom	14	16	18	...	70	72	74
Animals	NaN	NaN	NaN	...	NaN	NaN	NaN
Fungi	NaN	NaN	13083.0	...	NaN	NaN	NaN
Other	NaN	NaN	NaN	...	NaN	NaN	NaN
Plants	NaN	NaN	NaN	...	13428.0	NaN	NaN
Protists	NaN	16426.0	6667.0	...	NaN	NaN	NaN

and draw the corresponding heatmap:

```
# median_heatmap.py

plt.figure(figsize=(15, 5))

sns.heatmap(genes_summary, cmap="YlOrBr", square=True)

plt.title("Median number of genes for genomes in each GC range per genome")
```

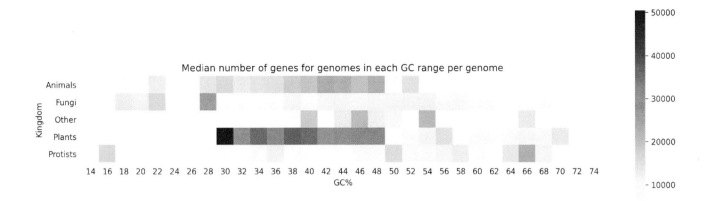

As before, we can run into problems comparing values with very different ranges: fungi have many fewer genes on average than plants. In this case it's probably more meaningful to normalize by dividing each row by its mean rather than its sum. This will give us a set of values where 1 means the same as the average, so it might be helpful to use a diverging color map and set the center at 1:

```
# divergence_from_mean_heatmap.py

plt.figure(figsize=(15, 5))

sns.heatmap(
    genes_summary.apply(lambda x: x / x.mean(), axis=1),
    cmap="PuOr",
    square=True,
    center=1,
)

plt.title("Normalized number of genes for genomes in each GC range per genome")
```

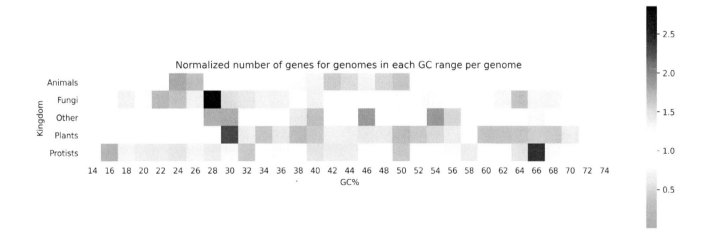

This figure requires quite a bit of interpretation, as we are looking at a highly processed view of the data. A white cell means that the genomes in that bin have around average numbers of genes for the kingdom as a whole. Purple means more genes than average, and orange mean fewer.

With this in mind, we can pick out some interesting patterns quite clearly. For plants, there's a strict division: genomes with GC content higher than 50% have a lower than average number of genes. For animals, the pattern is reversed and higher GC content is associated with higher than average number of genes.

One complication in interpreting a figure like the one above is that we have no way of knowing how many samples each value is based on. If the very high number of genes for fungal genomes around 28% GC is based on a single genome, then we might assign it less importance than if it were the median of a number of genomes.

To indicate this on the figure, we must first make a table which is the same shape as the summary that has the number of genomes in each bin. Conveniently, we alreay have such a table - it's the summary table that our earlier heatmaps were based on:

```
# count_summary.py

my_bins = range(12, 75, 2)
my_labels = range(14, 75, 2)

count_summary = (
    euk
    .groupby([
        "Kingdom",
        pd.cut(euk["GC%"], bins=my_bins, labels=my_labels)
    ])
    .size()
    .unstack()
)
count_summary
```

GC% Kingdom	14	16	18	...	70	72	74
Animals	1	1	2	...	0	0	0
Fungi	0	0	2	...	0	0	0
Other	0	0	0	...	0	0	0
Plants	1	0	0	...	2	1	1
Protists	0	1	2	...	0	0	0

If we pass this table as the value for the **annot** argument, then seaborn will use the values in it to annotate the heatmap:

```
# annotated_with_count.py

plt.figure(figsize=(17, 5))

sns.heatmap(
    genes_summary.apply(lambda x: x / x.mean(), axis=1),
    cmap="PuOr",
    square=True,
    center=1,
    annot=count_summary,
    fmt=".0f",
)

plt.title("Normalized number of genes for genomes in each GC range per genome")
```

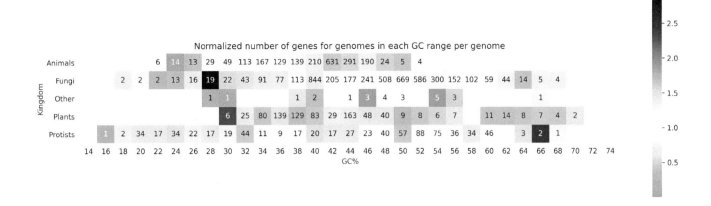

Normalized number of genes for genomes in each GC range per genome

We can see that our fungal outlier is based on 19 genomes, so it's less likely to be due to a single artefact (of course, it could still be several different genomes for a single species).

A figure like the one above requires very careful interpretation, as it's easy to forget that the colors and the numbers are not showing the same thing! A better way to do it might be to highlight just the cells that are based on a small number of genomes. Let's make an annotation table that simply indicates which cells have a value of less than ten. The easiest way to do this is using `applymap` to run a function on each cell of the count summary individually:

```
# classify_cells.py

def classify_cell(value):
    if value < 10:
        return "*"
    else:
        return ""

annotation_table = count_summary.applymap(classify_cell)
annotation_table
```

GC% Kingdom	14	16	18	...	70	72	74
Animals	*	*	*	...	*	*	*
Fungi	*	*	*	...	*	*	*
Other	*	*	*	...	*	*	*
Plants	*	*	*	...	*	*	*
Protists	*	*	*	...	*	*	*

This gives us a dataframe that has the same shape as the one that holds the data, but where each cell is either empty or contains an asterisk if the count was less than ten. When we use this to annotate our heatmap we have to remember to change the format to `'s'` for string:

```
# very_custom_annotation.py

plt.figure(figsize=(15, 5))

sns.heatmap(
    genes_summary.apply(lambda x: x / x.mean(), axis=1),
    cmap="PuOr",
    square=True,
    center=1,
    annot=annotation_table,
    fmt="s",
)

plt.title(
    "Normalized number of genes for genomes in each GC range per genome\n * indicates <10 genomes"
)
```

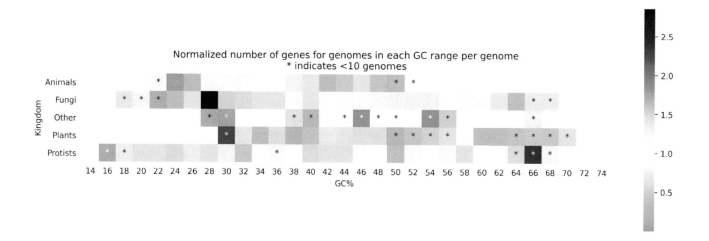

Now we don't have to worry about interpreting a set of numbers - when we see an asterisk in a given cell, we know that it's based on a small number of genomes and so we should be careful about interpreting it.

This technique of using a separate annotation table is actually very powerful for layering another set of information on a heatmap. Consider a summary table that shows the mean temperature for each month in Edinburgh:

```
# edinburgh_summary.py

# first set the month order
from pandas.api.types import CategoricalDtype

months = ["January", "February", "March", "April", "May", "June", "July", "August",
    "September", "October", "November", "December"]

weather["Month"] = weather["Month"].astype(
    CategoricalDtype(categories=months, ordered=True)
)

edinburgh_summary = (
    weather[weather["City"] == "Edinburgh"]
    .groupby(["Year", "Month"])["Mean temperature"]
    .mean()
    .unstack()
)
edinburgh_summary
```

15 Matrix charts and heatmaps

Month Year	January	February	March	...	October	November	December
1960	3.59355	2.73448	5.65484	...	9.93548	5.39667	2.52903
1961	3.06774	6.05357	8.42903	...	10.1484	5.34667	1.55806
1962	3.82581	4.60357	2.63226	...	10.2258	5.09333	2.89032
1963	0.387097	-0.489286	5.63226	...	10.1548	5.93333	4.06129
1964	4.22581	4.34828	4.14516	...	8.31613	6.11	2.94839
...	...	...	...	...	...	...	...
2012	4.88387	5.88621	8.78387	...	7.9	6.17	3.8871
2013	4.37097	3.66786	2.97097	...	11.8226	5.34	6.86452
2014	5.23871	5.91786	7.36774	...	11.4419	8.06	4.62903
2015	4.25806	4.72857	6.40645	...	10.2355	7.91667	7.54194
2016	5.04839	3.92759	6.25806	...	10.0387	4.54	6.95161

And the corresponding heatmap:

```
# edinburgh_summary_heatmap.py

plt.figure(figsize=(10, 10))

sns.heatmap(edinburgh_summary, cmap="hot")

plt.title("Mean monthly temperature (°C) in Edinburgh since 1960")
```

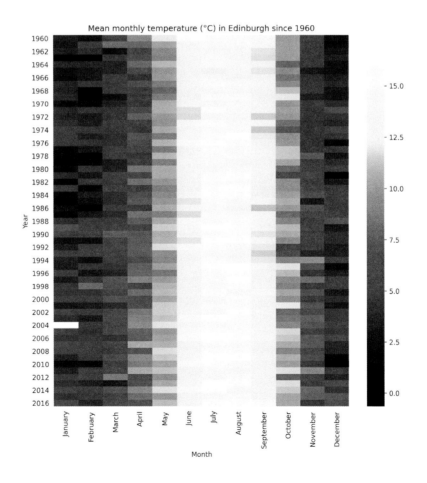

Taking the summary table and using `apply` we can make a new table where each cell contains the difference between the original value and the mean value for the month:

```
# monthly_difference.py

edinburgh_difference = edinburgh_summary.apply(
    lambda month: month - month.mean()
)
edinburgh_difference
```

Month Year	January	February	March	...	October	November	December
1960	-0.382258	-1.42823	-0.184607	...	0.0199208	-0.881228	-1.79134
1961	-0.908065	1.89086	2.58959	...	0.232824	-0.931228	-2.76231
1962	-0.15	0.440863	-3.20719	...	0.310243	-1.18456	-1.43005
1963	-3.58871	-4.65199	-0.207187	...	0.239276	-0.344561	-0.25908
1964	0.25	0.185567	-1.69428	...	-1.59943	-0.167895	-1.37198
...	...	...	...	...	...	...	...
2012	0.908065	1.7235	2.94443	...	-2.01556	-0.107895	-0.433274
2013	0.395161	-0.494851	-2.86848	...	1.90702	-0.937895	2.54415
2014	1.2629	1.75515	1.5283	...	1.52637	1.78211	0.308662
2015	0.282258	0.565863	0.567006	...	0.319921	1.63877	3.22156
2016	1.07258	-0.235122	0.418619	...	0.123147	-1.73789	2.63124

Next we can use `applymap` to classify each cell. If the month was more than 1 degree hotter than average for the month we'll give it a `+`. If it was more than one degree cooler than average for the month we'll give it a `-`, otherwise we'll leave it blank:

```
# classify_months.py

def classify_month(difference):
    if difference > 1:
        return "+"
    elif difference < -1:
        return "-"
    else:
        return ""

edinburgh_annotation = edinburgh_difference.applymap(classify_month)
edinburgh_annotation
```

Month Year	January	February	March	...	October	November	December
1960		-		...			-
1961		+	+	...			-
1962		-		...		-	-
1963	-	-		...			
1964		-		...	-		-
...	...	...	...	...	...	...	...
2012		+	+	...	-		
2013		-		...	+		+
2014	+	+	+	...	+	+	
2015				...		+	+
2016	+			...		-	+

Now let's use this new table to annotate our original heatmap:

```
# custom_edinburgh_annotation.py

plt.figure(figsize=(10, 10))

sns.heatmap(edinburgh_summary, cmap="hot", annot=edinburgh_annotation, fmt="s")

title = """Mean monthly temperature (°C) in Edinburgh since 1960
+/- indicates months that are at least 1° warmer/cooler than average
"""

plt.title(title)
```

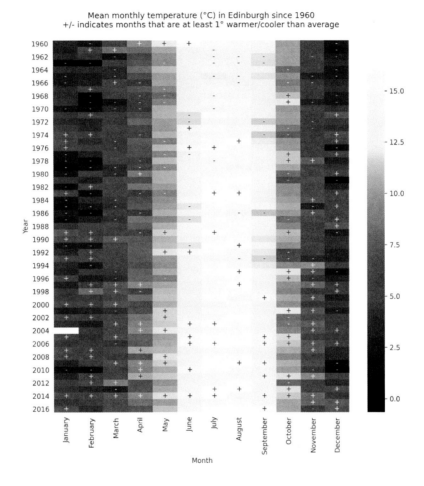

The resulting heatmap has this extra layer of annotation which goes some way to making up for our inability to see subtle changes in color. It would be very difficult for us to look at a cell and decide whether it is higher or lower than the mean for that column, but with pandas we can calculate this easily, then overlay it on the figure.

15.5 Clustermaps

Closely related to the heatmap is the clustermap. To understand how clustermaps work, imagine treating every row as a vector of values and calculating the distance to every other row. This gives us a distance matrix. We can then take this distance matrix and use a clustering algorithm to create a tree (technically a *dendrogram*) showing which groups of rows are most similar.

Let's walk through the process using a simple summary table. We'll construct a table where each row is a city and the columns are the years, with each containing the mean temperature for that entire year:

```
# year_summary.py

city_summary = (
    weather.groupby(["City", "Year"])
    ["Mean temperature"]
    .mean()
    .unstack()
    .dropna(axis=1)  # remove years with missing data
)
city_summary
```

Year / City	1960	1961	1962	...	2014	2015	2016
Berlin	9.366120	9.829041	8.222192	...	11.485205	11.290685	10.832787
Edinburgh	8.916944	9.002192	8.158333	...	10.369041	9.601918	9.541530
London	10.617760	10.989041	9.396712	...	12.660000	12.137260	11.919126

As we can see, this gives us a table with three rows - one per city - and 57 columns.

The next step is to take each pair of rows, and calculate a distance. Essentially this means coming up with a single number that reflects how different the two lists of 57 numbers are for a pair of rows. There are lots of different ways of doing this (called *metrics*) but we still stick with the default, which is the euclidian distance. The function that actually does the work is **pdist**, which is part of the scipy package:

```
from scipy.spatial.distance import pdist

distances = pdist(city_summary)
distances
```

```
array([ 6.66843123, 10.35684149, 15.05727929])
```

Passing our `city_summary` table to the `pdist` function gives us three numbers, corresponding to the three different comparisons (Edinburgh/London, Edinburgh/Berlin, and London/Berlin). With the three numbers in a list like that, it's not very convenient for humans to read, so scipy also has a handy function to convert it into a square table:

```
from scipy.spatial.distance import squareform

distance_matrix = squareform(distances)
distance_matrix
```

```
array([[ 0.        ,  6.66843123, 10.35684149],
       [ 6.66843123,  0.        , 15.05727929],
       [10.35684149, 15.05727929,  0.        ]])
```

That's a little easier to read - we can see that the numbers on the diagonal are zero (becuase each city has a zero distance from itself) and that the numbers are symmetrical (becuase the distance from London to Edinburgh is the same as Edinburgh to London). Even though we're using the word "distance" here, it's important to remember that we're not talking about geographical distance! In this context, "distance" simply means the degree of difference between the set of numbers belonging to each city.

We can make this even more readable by turning the square matrix back into a dataframe and copying the index values from the original summary table:

```
pd.DataFrame(
    distance_matrix, index=city_summary.index, columns=city_summary.index
)
```

15 Matrix charts and heatmaps

City	Berlin	Edinburgh	London
City			
Berlin	0.000000	6.668431	10.356841
Edinburgh	6.668431	0.000000	15.057279
London	10.356841	15.057279	0.000000

This lets us see, for example, that Berlin and London have a distance of around 10 whereas Berlin and Edinburgh have a distance of around 7. In other words, the list of 57 numbers for Berlin is more similar to the list of numbers for Edinburgh than it is to the list of numbers for London.

Reading a distance matrix like this is not too bad for only three cities, but for large numbers of rows it becomes difficult, so to make sense of the numbers we normally cluster the rows into groups based on their distance. There are a number of different ways of carrying out the clustering, but for now we will use the default (single linkage clustering). The function that carries out the clustering is called **linkage** and comes from the **fastcluster** module:

```
import fastcluster

linkage_matrix = fastcluster.linkage(distance_matrix)
linkage_matrix
```

```
array([[ 0.       , 1.       , 10.53708051, 2.       ],
       [ 2.       , 3.       , 16.87901368, 3.       ]])
```

The output from this function is completely impossible for humans to interpret, but if we use scipy again to turn it into a tree representation:

```
from scipy.cluster.hierarchy import dendrogram

dendrogram(linkage_matrix, labels=city_summary.index)
```

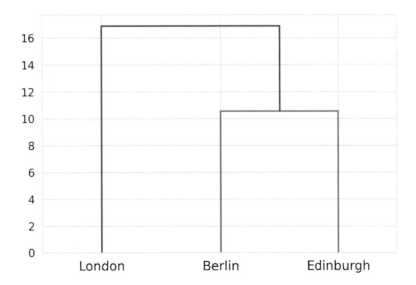

then the interpretation becomes very easy - Berlin and Edinburgh are grouped together, because their numbers are similar, whereas London is connected to the other two by a long branch because its numbers are different to the other two. To put it simply: this figure is telling us that the pattern of mean monthly temperature is most similar in Berlin and Edinburgh.

In the above example, we went through a lot of steps to obtain the dendrogram. But when using seaborn, all we have to do is call `clustermap` and it will take care of all the calculations, then draw the final dendrogram next to the heatmap:

```
# simple_clustermap.py

g = sns.clustermap(
    city_summary, col_cluster=False, cmap="hot", figsize=(10, 4)
)

g.fig.suptitle("Mean yearly temperature for three cities", y=1.05)
```

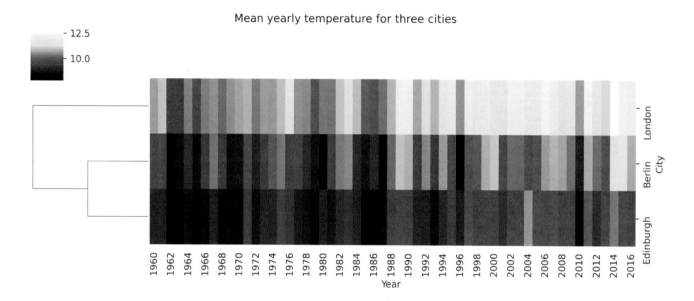

The dendrogram reinforces the pattern that's apparent from the colors in the data: Edinburgh and Berlin are more similar, with London generally warmer. Although `heatmap` and `clustermap` are closely related, their return values are slightly different types. `heatmap` returns a maplotlib `Axes` object, whereas `clustermap` returns a seaborn `ClusterGrid` object. The only real significance of this is that to add a title for a clustermap we need to use the `g.fig.suptitle` just like we did with `relplot`.

Notice that we have to pass `col_cluster=False` because we only want to cluster the rows. If we omit this argument:

```
g = sns.clustermap(city_summary, cmap="hot", figsize=(10, 4))

g.fig.suptitle("Mean yearly temperature for three cities", y=1.05)
```

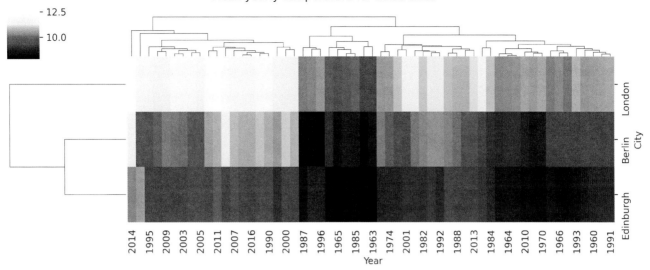

Mean yearly temperature for three cities

then we'll get both rows and column clustered. The dendrogram on top of the heatmap is showing us which years were most similar, which might be interesting for some datasets but is confusing here, as it reorders the years so that they are not in chronological order any more.

15.6 Complex groups with clustermaps

We'll finish our look at heat and clustermaps with a more challenging example. We will pick ten fungal species from each of our three classes - Ascomycetes, Basidiomycetes and Other Fungi and download their genomes. Then we'll take the genomes and count how many times each unique 6-base sequence occurs. In other words, we'll count the number of times we see 'AAAAAA', then 'AAAAAT', etc. When we are discussing short sequences like this we call them *kmers*, where *k* represents the length. So for our experiment here, we are counting 6mers.

How many numbers will we end up with for each genome? Well, there are four different possibilities for the first base, four for the second, and so on. So there are 4^6 different 6mers that we have to count. As Python will tell us:

```
4 ** 6
```

```
4096
```

this gives us 4096 different unique 6mers. Because the genomes are different lengths, we will divide each count by the length of the genome to normalize them. The code to do the 6mer counting is outside the scope of this book, so let's go straight to the final dataset:

```
genomes = pd.read_csv("fungi_genomes.csv")
genomes
```

	species	Class	AAAAAA	...	CCCCCT	CCCCCG	CCCCCC
0	Schizosaccharomyces octosporus	Ascomycetes	0.00244455	...	4.68436e-05	2.68169e-05	2.85359e-05
1	Coniosporium apollinis	Ascomycetes	0.000194447	...	0.000200801	0.000157198	0.000172419
2	Phialophora attae	Ascomycetes	6.05329e-05	...	8.12815e-05	7.29491e-05	4.13982e-05
3	Nannizzia gypsea	Ascomycetes	0.000832512	...	0.000223264	0.000130323	0.00016676
4	Trichoderma asperellum	Ascomycetes	0.00221537	...	0.000209611	0.000125665	0.00027191
...	...	...	...	...	...	...	...
25	Lobosporangium transversale	Other Fungi	0.00959963	...	0.000125465	4.23204e-05	0.000114335
26	Batrachochytrium dendrobatidis	Other Fungi	0.000864155	...	1.63684e-05	1.11453e-05	9.17127e-06
27	Mitosporidium daphniae	Other Fungi	0.00154126	...	0.000110698	7.16699e-05	0.000100054
28	Rhizopus microsporus	Other Fungi	0.00332984	...	9.38304e-05	1.44384e-05	5.502e-05
29	Vittaforma corneae	Other Fungi	0.0010126	...	4.35661e-05	1.92935e-05	1.58705e-05

We have 30 rows, one per species, and 4098 columns. Two of the columns give the species and class, while the remaining 4096 columns are our kmer counts. Notice that these data are already in summary form, so we don't need to reshape the dataset as we did with our earlier examples.

Now, we can try to address our question: do fungal genomes belonging to the same class have the same pattern of kmer counts? Let's start with a heatmap. Becuase this dataframe is already in summary form, we'll need to set the index to the species column explicitly, and we'll also remove the Class column as we're not using it yet:

```python
# kmers_heatmap.py

plt.figure(figsize=(12, 8))
sns.heatmap(genomes.set_index("species").drop(columns=["Class"]), cmap="BuPu")
plt.title("Proportion of kmers in fungal genomes")
```

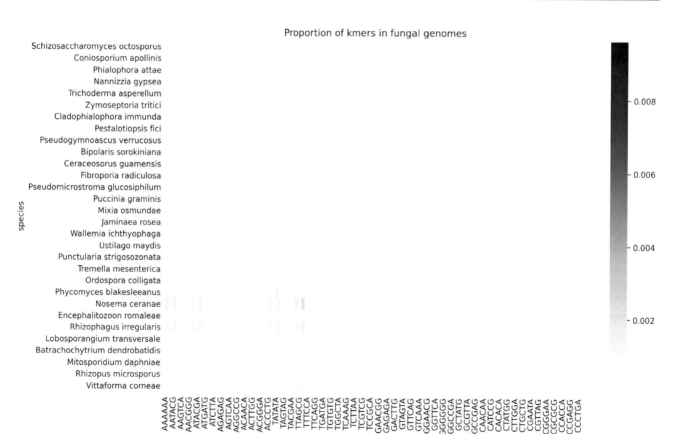

In the figure, we can see a common problem with these kind of data; we have a small number of outliers with very high proportions that are determining the color scale and making it hard to see the patterns. Just like with a scatter plot, where we might manually set the axis limits, we can set the color scale limit with `vmax`:

```
# scaled_kmers_heatmap.py

plt.figure(figsize=(12, 8))
sns.heatmap(
    genomes.set_index("species").drop(columns=["Class"]),
    cmap="BuPu",
    vmax=0.002,
)
plt.title("Proportion of kmers in fungal genomes")
```

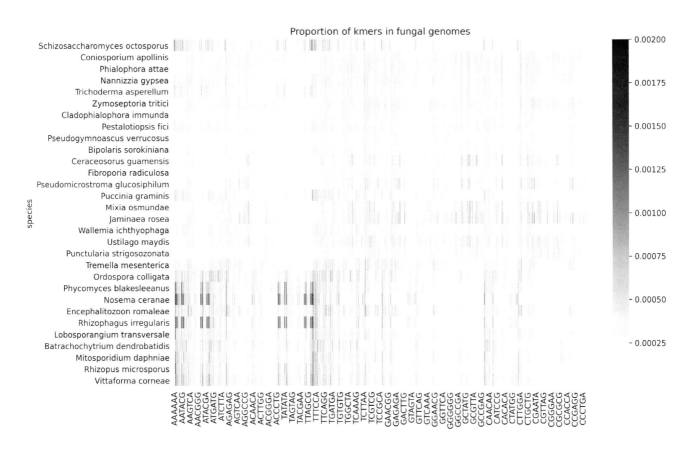

With over four thousand data points on the horizontal axis there are way too many to label them all, but seaborn draws as many labels as will fit in the space available.

This makes things clearer to see. There are definitely patterns in the distribution of 6mer counts, but it's very difficult for us to summarize. Let's get seaborn to do the clustering by switching to `clustermap`:

```
# clustered_kmers_heatmap.py

g = sns.clustermap(
    genomes.set_index("species").drop(columns=["Class"]),
    cmap="BuPu",
    vmax=0.002,
    col_cluster=False,
    figsize=(12, 8),
)
g.fig.suptitle("Proportion of kmers in fungal genomes", y=1.05)
```

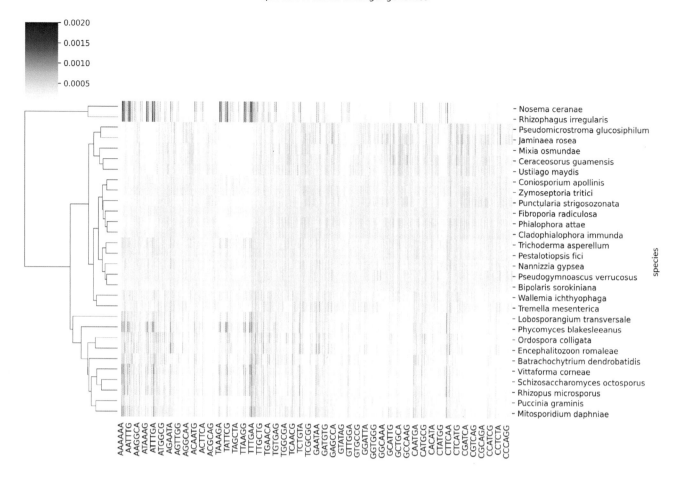

Proportion of kmers in fungal genomes

Notice the slight difference in the way we set the size: `clustermap` has its own `figsize` argument so we don't need to use `plt.figure`.

The dendrogram shows some nicely defined clusters of genomes that have similar patterns. However, it's still difficult to see the answer to our original question. Because the dendrogram is on the opposite side from the species names, it's hard to see which species belong to which clusters. And unless we are very familiar with fungal taxonomy, the species names don't actually tell us what class each one belongs to.

There's one final feature of clustermaps that will help us address both these problems. We can add a column of colors to annotate the dendrogram by passing a `row_colors` argument which contains a series mapping the labels (in our case, species names) to the colors we want. The easiest way to create this list is to start with the list of classes and simply replace the class names with the colors that we want:

```
# make_colors.py

genomes.set_index("species")["Class"].replace(
    {"Ascomycetes": "red", "Basidiomycetes": "green", "Other Fungi": "blue"}
)
```

```
species
Schizosaccharomyces octosporus      red
Coniosporium apollinis              red
Phialophora attae                   red
Nannizzia gypsea                    red
Trichoderma asperellum              red
                                    ...
Lobosporangium transversale         blue
Batrachochytrium dendrobatidis      blue
Mitosporidium daphniae              blue
Rhizopus microsporus                blue
Vittaforma corneae                  blue
Name: Class, Length: 30, dtype: object
```

Notice that for seaborn to know which color belongs to which species name, the species names must be the index.

Now we can add these colors to our clustermap. Adding a legend for these colors is possible, but tricky, so we'll just add a description to the figure title. If we wanted to make a more polished version of this figure we could add a legend by editing the figure in an SVG editor as described in the chapter on styling.

Here's the code:

```
# colored_clustered_heatmap.py

g = sns.clustermap(
    genomes.set_index("species").drop(columns=["Class"]),
    cmap="BuPu",
    vmax=0.002,
    col_cluster=False,
    figsize=(12, 8),
    row_colors=genomes.set_index("species")["Class"].replace(
        {
            "Ascomycetes": "red",
            "Basidiomycetes": "green",
            "Other Fungi": "blue",
        }
    ),
)
g.fig.suptitle(
    """Proportion of kmers in fungal genomes, colored by class
    (red = Ascomycetes, green = Basidiomycetes, blue = Other Fungi)""",
    y=1.05,
)
```

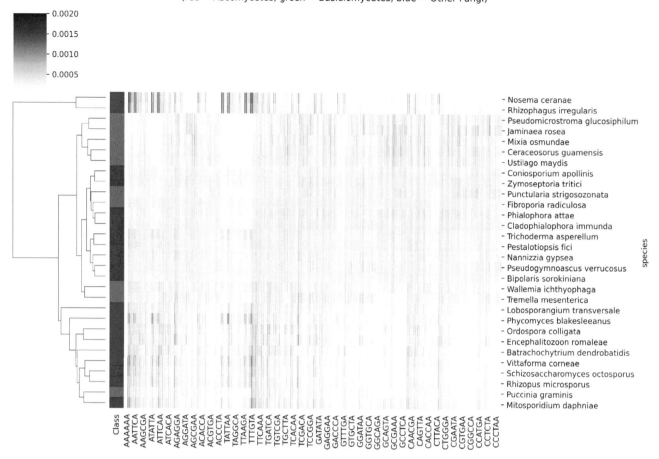

Proportion of kmers in fungal genomes, colored by class
(red = Ascomycetes, green = Basidiomycetes, blue = Other Fungi)

Finally we have a figure that may not be beautiful, but is fairly easy to interpret. The blocks of color to the right of the dendrogram show us which species belong to which classes. So we can see, for instance, that the two species at the top whose genomes have a very different pattern to the others are both blue, so they belong to the Other Fungi class. And there's a nice cluster of green genomes below that, which are Basidiomycetes. But this small cluster is part of a larger cluster which contains both Ascomycete (red) and Basidiomycete (blue) genomes. As with many biological systems, the answer to our original question turns out to be complicated!

15.7 Bubble grid charts

Earlier in this chapter we discussed the unqiue role of heatmaps as the only type of chart that has two categorical axes. If we draw a scatterplot with two categorical axes we can draw a chart with a similar shape, but where marker size represents the quantity that we're trying to display.

Let's say we want to visualize the mean monthly rainfall for our three cities. Using a heatmap, we would first construct a summary table:

```
# monthly_mean_summary.py

weather.groupby(["City", "Month"])["Mean temperature"].mean().unstack()
```

Month City	January	February	March	...	October	November	December
Berlin	0.384746	1.289862	4.609295	...	10.028868	5.084885	1.689043
Edinburgh	3.975806	4.164991	5.839445	...	9.915563	6.277895	4.310194
London	4.864079	5.086563	7.185621	...	11.984910	7.774138	5.468242

then pass it to `heatmap`:

```
# monthly_mean_summary_heatmap.py

sns.heatmap(
    weather.groupby(["City", "Month"])["Mean temperature"].mean().unstack(),
    square=True,
    cmap="BuPu",
    cbar_kws={"shrink": 0.5},
)
plt.title("Mean monthly temperature for three cities")
```

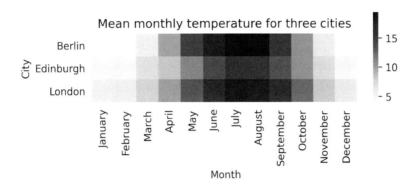

If instead of using `unstack` to make a summary table, we pass `as_index=False`, we'll get the same set of measurements in long form:

```
# long_monthly_mean.py

monthly_mean = weather.groupby(["City", "Month"], as_index=False)[
    "Mean temperature"
].mean()
monthly_mean
```

	City	Month	Mean temperature
0	Berlin	January	0.384746
1	Berlin	February	1.28986
2	Berlin	March	4.60929
3	Berlin	April	9.36486
4	Berlin	May	14.3454
...	...	...	...
31	London	August	17.9781
32	London	September	15.439
33	London	October	11.9849
34	London	November	7.77414
35	London	December	5.46824

Which we can pass to `sns.relplot` and draw as a scatterplot:

```
sns.relplot(
    data=monthly_mean, x="Month", y="City", aspect=4, height=2,
)
plt.xticks(rotation=45, horizontalalignment="right")
```

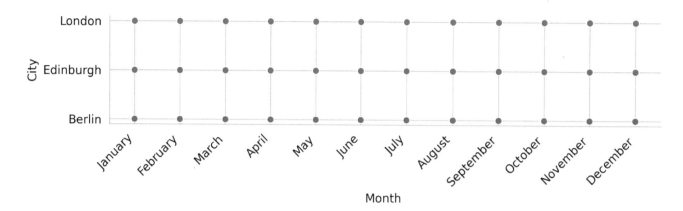

This plot isn't very exciting - it's simply telling us that there is a row in the table for each combination of city and month. By setting the **size** argument to our third column, we get a bubble grid, where the size of each bubble represents the amount of rainfall. With large points, we need a bit more space which we can get by manually setting the y axis limit after drawing the chart:

```
g = sns.relplot(
    data=monthly_mean,
    x="Month",
    y="City",
    size="Mean temperature",
    sizes=(20, 200),
    aspect=4,
    height=2,
)
plt.xticks(rotation=45, horizontalalignment="right")
g.ax.set_ylim(-1, 4)
g.fig.suptitle(
    "Mean monthly temperature for three cities", y=1.1,
)
```

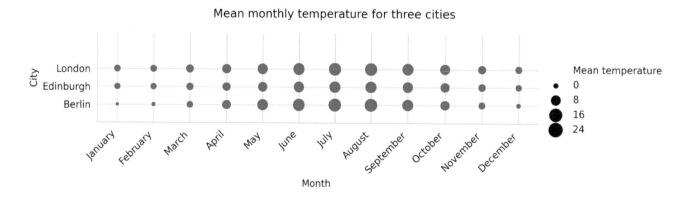

We can even combine this with a **hue** so that larger markers are also darker:

15 Matrix charts and heatmaps

```
g = sns.relplot(
    data=monthly_mean,
    x="Month",
    y="City",
    size="Mean temperature",
    sizes=(20, 200),
    hue="Mean temperature",
    palette="PuBu",
    aspect=4,
    height=2,
)
plt.xticks(rotation=45, horizontalalignment="right")
g.ax.set_ylim(-1, 4)
g.fig.suptitle(
    "Mean monthly temperature for three cities", y=1.1,
)
```

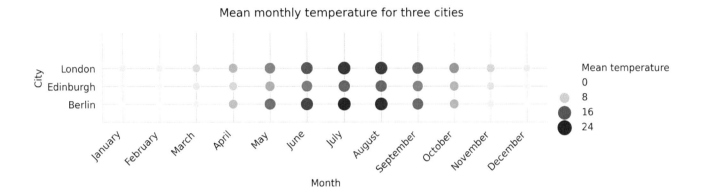

Because the data points always lie directly on the grid lines, we often want to remove them for this type of chart. The `plt.rc_context` context manager that we saw in the chapter on styling will do the job:

```
# monthly_mean_bubble.py

with plt.rc_context({"axes.grid": False}):
    g = sns.relplot(
        data=monthly_mean,
        x="Month",
        y="City",
        size="Mean temperature",
        sizes=(20, 200),
        hue="Mean temperature",
        palette="PuBu",
        aspect=4,
        height=2,
    )
    plt.xticks(rotation=45, horizontalalignment="right")
    g.ax.set_ylim(-1, 4)
    g.fig.suptitle(
        "Mean monthly temperature for three cities", y=1.1,
    )
```

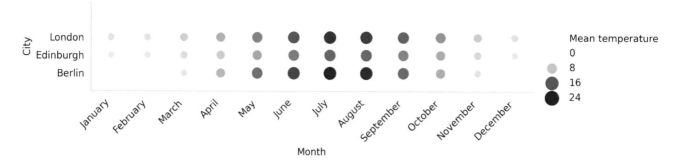

For charts where one of the axes is longer, it may be helpful to use color to indicate which of the groups on the short axis each circle belongs to. In this example, we'll look at the number of genomes in each assembly status for each class.

With large marker sizes we need a bit more space between the data and the X axis line, which we can get by setting the Y axis limits after the chart is drawn. We also need to increase the spacing in the legend by setting the `legend.labelspacing` parameter in our rc dictionary:

```
# class_counts_bubble.py

with plt.rc_context({"legend.labelspacing": 1.2, "axes.grid": False}):

    g = sns.relplot(
        data=euk.groupby(["Class", "Assembly status"], as_index=False)[
            "Species"
        ].count(),
        x="Class",
        y="Assembly status",
        size="Species",
        sizes=(20, 400),
        hue="Assembly status",
        palette="Dark2",
        aspect=4,
        height=3,
    )
    plt.xticks(rotation=45, horizontalalignment="right")
    g.fig.suptitle(
        "Number of genomes in different assembly status for each eukaryote class",
        y=1.1,
    )
    g.ax.set_ylim(-1, 4)
```

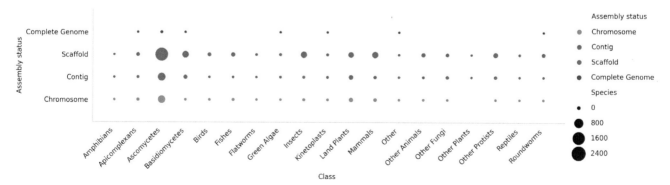

16 Dealing with complicated data files

In order to illustrate the tools that we've been discussing so far in this book, we've relied on a few example files. And to allow us to concentrate on the tools for data manipulation and visualization, we've deliberately picked data files that are easy for pandas to read. In this chapter, we'll look at a few difficulties that often occur when getting our real world data into pandas. These involve dealing with data that are badly formatted; that are spread across multiple files, and that are too big to fit in memory.

16.1 Awkward input files

In the examples that we've been using throughout the book, we've kept our data files relatively well behaved. The only complication that we've encountered was having to specify a tab separator for the eukaryote genome summary file, and explicitly set **na_values**. In the real world, we often don't have much control over the format of our data files, so we have to do a bit more work to get them into pandas.

As an example, let's take a look at the **awkward.csv** file. This has some of the same data as our eukaryote genome summary file, but in a much less convenient format. To keep things simple, it contains only plant and animal genomes. Here are the first few lines:

```
Data file prepared on 4/10/2019
Original data taken from https://www.ncbi.nlm.nih.gov/
From left to right, the columns are:
species name
genome size in megabases
gc percentage
number of genes
publication year
assembly status
whether the genome belongs to an animal
whether the genome belongs to a plant

Arabidopsis thaliana,"119,669",36.0529,38_311,2001.0,Chromosome,False,True,,
Glycine max,"979,046",35.1153,59_847,2010.0,Chromosome,False,True,,
Medicago truncatula,"412,924",34.047,37_603,2011.0,Chromosome,False,True,,
Solanum lycopersicum,"828,349",35.6991,31_200,2010.0,Chromosome,no,yes,,
Hordeum vulgare,"4006,12",44.3,,2019.0,Scaffold,False,True,,
Oryza sativa Japonica Group,"374,423",43.5769,35_219,2015.0,Chromosome,"""f""","""t""",,
Triticum aestivum,"14547,3",46.0544,,2018.0,Chromosome,0,1,,
```

Compared with the original we can see quite a few complications. The file starts with a couple of non-data lines, followed by a description of the columns, and there's no actual header line in the data itself. In order to read it into pandas, we'll have to skip the first section, which we can do with **skiprows**:

```
pd.read_csv("awkward_input.csv", na_values=["-"], skiprows=11)
```

	Arabidopsis thaliana	119,669	36.0529	...	True	Unnamed: 8	Unnamed: 9
0	Glycine max	979,046	35.1153	...	True	NaN	NaN
1	Medicago truncatula	412,924	34.047	...	True	NaN	NaN
2	Solanum lycopersicum	828,349	35.6991	...	yes	NaN	NaN
3	Hordeum vulgare	4006,12	44.3	...	True	NaN	NaN
4	Oryza sativa Japonica Group	374,423	43.5769	...	"t"	NaN	NaN
...	...	...	...	...	...	...	...
3048	Homo sapiens	2,097	45.8	...	0	NaN	NaN
3049	Homo sapiens	4,781	44.6	...	0	NaN	NaN
3050	Homo sapiens	4,799	44.6	...	False	NaN	NaN
3051	Homo sapiens	2,79	34.8	...	False	NaN	NaN
3052	This is version 2.5432 of the file	NaN	NaN	...	NaN	NaN	NaN

Now we have another problem: pandas has assumed that the first line of data is actually the column names. We can fix this by explicitly giving a list of column names that we want in the `names` argument:

```
pd.read_csv(
    "awkward_input.csv",
    skiprows=11,
    na_values=["-"],
    names=["Species", "Genome size", "GC%", "Genes", "Year",
        "Status", "Is animal", "Is plant"]
)
```

	Species	Genome size	GC%	...	Status	Is animal	Is plant
(Arabidopsis thaliana, 119,669)	36.0529	38_311	2001	...	True	NaN	NaN
(Glycine max, 979,046)	35.1153	59_847	2010	...	True	NaN	NaN
(Medicago truncatula, 412,924)	34.047	37_603	2011	...	True	NaN	NaN
(Solanum lycopersicum, 828,349)	35.6991	31_200	2010	...	yes	NaN	NaN
(Hordeum vulgare, 4006,12)	44.3	NaN	2019	...	True	NaN	NaN
...	...	...	...	...	...	...	...
(Homo sapiens, 2,097)	45.8	NaN	2017	...	0	NaN	NaN
(Homo sapiens, 4,781)	44.6	NaN	2017	...	0	NaN	NaN
(Homo sapiens, 4,799)	44.6	missing	2017	...	False	NaN	NaN
(Homo sapiens, 2,79)	34.8	NaN	2017	...	False	NaN	NaN
(This is version 2.5432 of the file, nan)	NaN	NaN	NaN	...	NaN	NaN	NaN

This fixes the column names, but introduces another problem. The first data line in the file looks like this:

```
Arabidopsis thaliana,"119,669",36.0529,38_311,2001.0,Chromosome,False,True,,
```

Notice that it ends with two missing fields, represented by two commas. This is a fairly common occurence, especially in files that have been exported from spreadsheet programs. These two extra commas cause pandas to assume that each row has 10 fields rather than 8, so when we give a list of only 8 column names, it uses the first two as the index. In our case, this means that all of the column names are offset by two places.

The easiest way to fix this is to explicitly tell pandas which columns we want to use with the `usecols` argument. Rather than typing out the list of column names twice, it's more convenient to store it in a variable:

```
my_columns = ["Species", "Genome size", "GC%", "Genes", "Year",
    "Status", "Is animal", "Is plant"]

pd.read_csv(
    "awkward_input.csv",
    skiprows=11,
    na_values=["-"],
    names=my_columns,
    usecols=my_columns,
)
```

	Species	Genome size	GC%	...	Status	Is animal	Is plant
0	Arabidopsis thaliana	119,669	36.0529	...	Chromosome	False	True
1	Glycine max	979,046	35.1153	...	Chromosome	False	True
2	Medicago truncatula	412,924	34.047	...	Chromosome	False	True
3	Solanum lycopersicum	828,349	35.6991	...	Chromosome	no	yes
4	Hordeum vulgare	4006,12	44.3	...	Scaffold	False	True
...	...	...	...	...	...	...	...
3049	Homo sapiens	2,097	45.8	...	Scaffold	1	0
3050	Homo sapiens	4,781	44.6	...	Scaffold	1	0
3051	Homo sapiens	4,799	44.6	...	Scaffold	True	False
3052	Homo sapiens	2,79	34.8	...	Scaffold	True	False
3053	This is version 2.5432 of the file	NaN	NaN	...	NaN	NaN	NaN

With this set of arguments to `read_csv` we are getting closer. Notice the last row in the dataframe - it is obviously not real data as is corresponds to a footer in the original file. The last few lines of the original file look like this:

```
Homo sapiens,"4,781",44.6,,2017.0,Scaffold,1,0,,
Homo sapiens,"4,799",44.6,missing,2017.0,Scaffold,True,False,,
Homo sapiens,"2,79",34.8,,2017.0,Scaffold,True,False,,
This is version 2.5432 of the file
```

Many real life data files include a footer like this. We can tell pandas to skip it by passing **skipfooter** (on some versions, this may cause a **ParserWarning**, but it will still work):

```
df = pd.read_csv(
    "awkward_input.csv",
    skiprows=11,
    names=my_columns,
    na_values=["-"],
    usecols=my_columns,
    skipfooter=1,
)
df
```

	Species	Genome size	GC%	...	Status	Is animal	Is plant
0	Arabidopsis thaliana	119,669	36.0529	...	Chromosome	False	True
1	Glycine max	979,046	35.1153	...	Chromosome	False	True
2	Medicago truncatula	412,924	34.047	...	Chromosome	False	True
3	Solanum lycopersicum	828,349	35.6991	...	Chromosome	no	yes
4	Hordeum vulgare	4006,12	44.3	...	Scaffold	False	True
...	...	...	...	...	...	...	...
3048	Homo sapiens	4,898	44.6	...	Scaffold	yes	no
3049	Homo sapiens	2,097	45.8	...	Scaffold	1	0
3050	Homo sapiens	4,781	44.6	...	Scaffold	1	0
3051	Homo sapiens	4,799	44.6	...	Scaffold	True	False
3052	Homo sapiens	2,79	34.8	...	Scaffold	True	False

Finally, it looks like we have read all our data in sucessfully. Just as we did when first introducing pandas, we'll take a look at the data types that pandas has guessed for our columns:

```
df.info()
```

```
<class 'pandas.core.frame.DataFrame'>
RangeIndex: 3053 entries, 0 to 3052
Data columns (total 8 columns):
 #   Column       Non-Null Count    Dtype
---  ------       --------------    -----
 0   Species      3053 non-null     object
 1   Genome size  3051 non-null     object
 2   GC%          2897 non-null     object
 3   Genes        1296 non-null     object
 4   Year         3051 non-null     float64
 5   Status       3051 non-null     object
 6   Is animal    3051 non-null     object
 7   Is plant     3051 non-null     object
dtypes: float64(1), object(7)
memory usage: 190.9+ KB
```

It looks like we have some work yet to do: these are not correct. The **Genome size**, **GC%** and **Genes** columns should all be numbers, but are being interpreted as strings. Let's take a look at the values to try and figure out what's going wrong. We will start with the genome size:

```
df["Genome size"]
```

```
0         119,669
1         979,046
2         412,924
3         828,349
4         4006,12
          ...
3048        4,898
3049        2,097
3050        4,781
3051        4,799
3052         2,79
Name: Genome size, Length: 3053, dtype: object
```

Looking at the values, we can see that these numbers have been written with a comma rather than a dot as the decimal separator (common practice in many countries). Setting the `decimal` argument will allow these numbers to be parsed correctly and turn our **Genome size** column into a floating point data type:

16 Dealing with complicated data files

```
df = pd.read_csv(
    "awkward_input.csv",
    skiprows=11,
    na_values=["-"],
    names=my_columns,
    usecols=my_columns,
    skipfooter=1,
    decimal=",",
)
df.info()
```

```
<class 'pandas.core.frame.DataFrame'>
RangeIndex: 3053 entries, 0 to 3052
Data columns (total 8 columns):
 #   Column       Non-Null Count  Dtype
---  ------       --------------  -----
 0   Species      3053 non-null   object
 1   Genome size  3051 non-null   float64
 2   GC%          2897 non-null   object
 3   Genes        1296 non-null   object
 4   Year         3051 non-null   float64
 5   Status       3051 non-null   object
 6   Is animal    3051 non-null   object
 7   Is plant     3051 non-null   object
dtypes: float64(2), object(6)
memory usage: 190.9+ KB
```

Next we'll tackle the GC%. As before, looking at the values will hopefully give us a clue as to what's wrong:

```
df["GC%"].head()
```

```
0    36.0529
1    35.1153
2     34.047
3    35.6991
4       44.3
Name: GC%, dtype: object
```

From a quick look at the first few values, it's not clear what the problem is - the formatting looks fine. In this situation, the next step is usually to try `value_counts`:

```
df["GC%"].value_counts().head()
```

```
41.5       45
40.9       45
43.5       40
missing    38
41.8       38
Name: GC%, dtype: int64
```

This reveals the problem. Some of the missing GC% values were represented by a hyphen, as in our original version of this dataset, but some were represented by the string "missing". This scenario, where we have multiple different ways of representing missing data, is very common in datasets that have either been manually annotated or assembled from multiple sources.

Happily, the fix is simple: all we have to do is add **"missing"** to our list of **na_values**:

```
df = pd.read_csv(
    "awkward_input.csv",
    skiprows=11,
    na_values=["-", "missing"],
    names=my_columns,
    usecols=my_columns,
    skipfooter=1,
    decimal=",",
)
df.info()
```

```
<class 'pandas.core.frame.DataFrame'>
RangeIndex: 3053 entries, 0 to 3052
Data columns (total 8 columns):
 #   Column       Non-Null Count  Dtype
---  ------       --------------  -----
 0   Species      3053 non-null   object
 1   Genome size  3051 non-null   float64
 2   GC%          2859 non-null   float64
 3   Genes        802 non-null    object
 4   Year         3051 non-null   float64
 5   Status       3051 non-null   object
 6   Is animal    3051 non-null   object
 7   Is plant     3051 non-null   object
dtypes: float64(3), object(5)
memory usage: 190.9+ KB
```

Next up is the **Genes** column:

```
df["Genes"]
```

```
0        38_311
1        59_847
2        37_603
3        31_200
4           NaN
          ...
3048        NaN
3049        NaN
3050        NaN
3051        NaN
3052        NaN
Name: Genes, Length: 3053, dtype: object
```

The missing data are being handled fine here; the problem is the thousands separator, which is an underscore. Setting the `thousands` argument will allow pandas to parse these numbers properly:

```
df = pd.read_csv(
    "awkward_input.csv",
    skiprows=11,
    na_values=["-", "missing"],
    names=my_columns,
    usecols=my_columns,
    skipfooter=1,
    decimal=",",
    thousands="_",
)
df.info()
```

16 Dealing with complicated data files

```
<class 'pandas.core.frame.DataFrame'>
RangeIndex: 3053 entries, 0 to 3052
Data columns (total 8 columns):
 #   Column       Non-Null Count  Dtype
---  ------       --------------  -----
 0   Species      3053 non-null   object
 1   Genome size  3051 non-null   float64
 2   GC%          2859 non-null   float64
 3   Genes        802 non-null    float64
 4   Year         3051 non-null   float64
 5   Status       3051 non-null   object
 6   Is animal    3051 non-null   object
 7   Is plant     3051 non-null   object
dtypes: float64(4), object(4)
memory usage: 190.9+ KB
```

Now that we have all our columns in the right dtypes, take a look at the numbers of values. We have 3053 rows, but five of the columns that we expect to have no missing data have 3051 values. This is suspicious! Let's find the two rows with a missing size and take a look at the data:

```
df[df["Genome size"].isnull()]
```

	Species	Genome size	GC%	...	Status	Is animal	Is plant
28	# the next two genomes belong to frogs	NaN	NaN	...	None	None	None
86	# three different Caenorhabditis species	NaN	NaN	...	None	None	None

Looking at the species names for these rows gives us a big clue about the problem. There are two lines in the original file that were comments, rather than data. If we look near the start of the file, we'll see this:

```
...
Coffea arabica,"1094,45",36.9585,54_774,2018.0,Chromosome,False,True,,
Felis catus,"2521,86",41.8806,35_234,2006.0,Chromosome,True,False,,
# the next two genomes belong to frogs
Xenopus tropicalis,"1440,4",40.5404,26_496,2009.0,Chromosome,1,0,,
Xenopus laevis,"2718,43",40.2325,36_776,2016.0,Chromosome,True,False,,
...
```

Now we can reconstruct the sequence of events. These comment lines contain no commas, so the entire line has ended up in the **Species** column. The remaining columns for those rows are either missing data (in the case of the numerical columns) or `None` (in the case of the string columns).

To fix this, we just have to tell pandas that lines begining with a hash symbol are comments by setting the `comment` argument:

```
df = pd.read_csv(
    "awkward_input.csv",
    skiprows=11,
    na_values=["-", "missing"],
    names=my_columns,
    usecols=my_columns,
    skipfooter=1,
    decimal=",",
    thousands="_",
    comment="#",
)
df.info()
```

```
<class 'pandas.core.frame.DataFrame'>
RangeIndex: 3051 entries, 0 to 3050
Data columns (total 8 columns):
 #   Column       Non-Null Count   Dtype
---  ------       --------------   -----
 0   Species      3051 non-null    object
 1   Genome size  3051 non-null    float64
 2   GC%          2859 non-null    float64
 3   Genes        802 non-null     float64
 4   Year         3051 non-null    float64
 5   Status       3051 non-null    object
 6   Is animal    3051 non-null    object
 7   Is plant     3051 non-null    object
dtypes: float64(4), object(4)
memory usage: 190.8+ KB
```

This looks better; the two comment lines have disappeared from the dataframe, leaving us with just 3051 values, and all of the columns except **GC%** and **Genes** have exactly that number of values.

Finally, let's take a look at the final two columns: **Is animal** and **Is plant**. These are examples of data types that we've not seen before - *boolean* data, i.e. True/False values. We can specify what data type we want for a given column by passing a `dtype` dict, so let's try making these boolean:

```
df = pd.read_csv(
    "awkward_input.csv",
    skiprows=11,
    na_values=["-", "missing"],
    names=my_columns,
    usecols=my_columns,
    skipfooter=1,
    decimal=",",
    thousands="_",
    comment="#",
    dtype={"Is animal": bool, "Is plant": bool},
)
df.info()
```

```
<class 'pandas.core.frame.DataFrame'>
RangeIndex: 3051 entries, 0 to 3050
Data columns (total 8 columns):
 #   Column       Non-Null Count   Dtype
---  ------       --------------   -----
 0   Species      3051 non-null    object
 1   Genome size  3051 non-null    float64
 2   GC%          2859 non-null    float64
 3   Genes        802 non-null     float64
 4   Year         3051 non-null    float64
 5   Status       3051 non-null    object
 6   Is animal    3051 non-null    bool
 7   Is plant     3051 non-null    bool
dtypes: bool(2), float64(4), object(2)
memory usage: 149.1+ KB
```

At first this seems sucessful - the data type of the **Is animal** column is now listed as `bool`, short for boolean. But when we take a look at the value counts:

```
df["Is animal"].value_counts()
```

```
True    3051
Name: Is animal, dtype: int64
```

we might be suspicious that something has gone wrong: we know for a fact that there are a mixture of plant and animal genomes in our dataset! Let's get rid of the `dtype` argument, let pandas parse the column as a string, and look at the value counts:

16 Dealing with complicated data files

```
df = pd.read_csv(
    "awkward_input.csv",
    skiprows=11,
    na_values=["-", "missing"],
    names=my_columns,
    usecols=my_columns,
    skipfooter=1,
    decimal=",",
    thousands="_",
    comment="#",
)
df["Is animal"].value_counts()
```

```
1        750
True     661
yes      446
"t"      324
0        297
False    254
no       188
"f"      131
Name: Is animal, dtype: int64
```

This reveals a pattern that is distressingly common in real life datasets: we have a variety of different ways in this column of representing true and false. We can safely assume that 0, **False**, **no** and **"f"** are intended to represent False and that 1, **True**, **yes** and **"t"** are intended to represent True.

The reason for the preponderance of **True** values when we tried setting the data type as boolean is because of Python's rule for determining boolean values. The rule for strings is simple: any non-empty string counts as true. So all of the values that are in the file are interpreted as true:

```
for value in df["Is animal"].unique():
    print(repr(value), bool(value))
```

```
'False' True
'no' True
'"f"' True
'0' True
'1' True
'yes' True
'"t"' True
'True' True
```

The only value that counts as false is missing data (represented by **None** in the output above). We will see the reason for the existence of those values later. For now, let's fix the boolean values. Just as with **na_values**, we can pass **true_values** and **false_values** to explicity tell pandas what values we want to interpret as true and false:

---

16 Dealing with complicated data files

307

```
# import_awkward_data_file.py

import numpy as np

df = pd.read_csv(
    "awkward_input.csv",
    skiprows=11,
    na_values=["-", "missing"],
    names=my_columns,
    usecols=my_columns,
    skipfooter=1,
    decimal=",",
    thousands="_",
    comment="#",
    true_values=["True", "1", "yes", '"t"'],
    false_values=["False", "0", "no", '"f"'],
    dtype={"Is animal": np.bool, "Is plant": np.bool},
)
df.info()
```

```
<class 'pandas.core.frame.DataFrame'>
RangeIndex: 3051 entries, 0 to 3050
Data columns (total 8 columns):
 #   Column       Non-Null Count  Dtype
---  ------       --------------  -----
 0   Species      3051 non-null   object
 1   Genome size  3051 non-null   float64
 2   GC%          2859 non-null   float64
 3   Genes        802 non-null    float64
 4   Year         3051 non-null   float64
 5   Status       3051 non-null   object
 6   Is animal    3051 non-null   bool
 7   Is plant     3051 non-null   bool
dtypes: bool(2), float64(4), object(2)
memory usage: 149.1+ KB
```

Once we have explicitly listed the True/False values, and explicitly set the data types, we are left with two boolean columns, and when we check the value counts:

```
df[["Is animal", "Is plant"]].apply(lambda x: x.value_counts())
```

	Is animal	Is plant
False	870	2181
True	2181	870

we can see that they have a mixture of True and False values, and that the numbers are symmetrical as expected.

This particular data file is what we might call a pathological example - a worst case scenario! We have ended up using nearly all of the arguments to `read_csv`; for most real life problems we will only need a few of them.

16.2 Combining multiple files

A very common obstacle to data analysis is when our data are spread out over multiple files. For most of the examples in this book, we've deliberately used single data files to keep things manageable, but in the real world we often have to bring data together from multiple sources before we can start our analysis.

Depending on the situation, combining data from multiple files can require either *concatenation* or *merging*. If we want to simply take two (or more) dataframes and join them together either horiztonally or vertically, then we call that *concatenation*. This is the simpler case, and we use it whenever we have multiple dataframes where either the rows or columns are identical.

16.2.1 Concatenation

Let's look at an example. We have previously looked at the dataframe that contained monthly rainfall data for London. Here's a dataset that has daily rainfall over the same period:

```
london_rain = pd.read_csv("London_daily_rain.csv")
london_rain.head()
```

	Year	Month	Day of month	Day of year	Rainfall (mm)
0	1960	January	1	1	22.0
1	1960	January	2	2	23.0
2	1960	January	3	3	7.0
3	1960	January	4	4	0.0
4	1960	January	5	5	0.0

The columns are the same as our daily temperature data, but with rainfall in mm rather than temperature as the last column.

We also have rainfall data for the other two cities we have been investigating:

```
berlin_rain = pd.read_csv("Berlin_daily_rain.csv")
edinburgh_rain = pd.read_csv("Edinburgh_daily_rain.csv")
```

Once we've got our three dataframes in memory, we can check that they have the same length:

```
all_dataframes = [london_rain, berlin_rain, edinburgh_rain]

for df in all_dataframes:
    print(len(df))
```

```
21762
21762
21762
```

and the same set of columns:

```
for df in all_dataframes:
    print(df.columns)
```

```
Index(['Year', 'Month', 'Day of month', 'Day of year', 'Rainfall (mm)'], dtype='object')
Index(['Year', 'Month', 'Day of month', 'Day of year', 'Rainfall (mm)'], dtype='object')
Index(['Year', 'Month', 'Day of month', 'Day of year', 'Rainfall (mm)'], dtype='object')
```

Once we are satisfied that the columns are all the same, we know that we can combine these dataframes by simply putting them underneath each other to get one long dataframe. The function that does the concatenation is `pd.concat`, and all we have to give it is a list of dataframes to concatenate:

```
big_df = pd.concat(all_dataframes)
big_df
```

	Year	Month	Day of month	Day of year	Rainfall (mm)
0	1960	January	1	1	22
1	1960	January	2	2	23
2	1960	January	3	3	7
3	1960	January	4	4	0
4	1960	January	5	5	0
...	...	...	...	...	...
21757	2019	July	27	208	NaN
21758	2019	July	28	209	NaN
21759	2019	July	29	210	NaN
21760	2019	July	30	211	NaN
21761	2019	July	31	212	NaN

Notice that the dataframe we get out of `pd.concat` has the same 5 columns as all of our original dataframes, but has as many rows as all of them combined:

```
len(big_df)
```

```
65286
```

Although the data look fine from a glance at the big dataframe, in fact we have run into a common problem - we have lost track of which rows belong to which city. In other words, if we take our big dataframe and select a single day:

```
big_df[
    (big_df["Year"] == 1981)
    & (big_df["Month"] == "May")
    & (big_df["Day of month"] == 27)
]
```

	Year	Month	Day of month	Day of year	Rainfall (mm)
7817	1981	May	27	147	49.0
7817	1981	May	27	147	26.0
7817	1981	May	27	147	0.0

We can see that we have three rainfall measurements, but no idea which city they belong to. One way of thinking about this is that the city information was implicitly coded in the name of each input file, rather than being explicitly included in the data.

To fix this, we need to add a city column to each individual dataframe before we concatenate them. This is easy to do:

```
london_rain["City"] = "London"
edinburgh_rain["City"] = "Edinburgh"
berlin_rain["City"] = "Berlin"

big_df = pd.concat(all_dataframes)
big_df
```

	Year	Month	Day of month	Day of year	Rainfall (mm)	City
0	1960	January	1	1	22	London
1	1960	January	2	2	23	London
2	1960	January	3	3	7	London
3	1960	January	4	4	0	London
4	1960	January	5	5	0	London
...	...	...	...	...	...	...
21757	2019	July	27	208	NaN	Edinburgh
21758	2019	July	28	209	NaN	Edinburgh
21759	2019	July	29	210	NaN	Edinburgh
21760	2019	July	30	211	NaN	Edinburgh
21761	2019	July	31	212	NaN	Edinburgh

And now when we repeat out single day filter it's obvious which city each row belongs to:

```
big_df[
    (big_df["Year"] == 1981)
    & (big_df["Month"] == "May")
    & (big_df["Day of month"] == 27)
]
```

	Year	Month	Day of month	Day of year	Rainfall (mm)	City
7817	1981	May	27	147	49.0	London
7817	1981	May	27	147	26.0	Berlin
7817	1981	May	27	147	0.0	Edinburgh

If we wanted to be lazy (always a good property for programmers!) then we could write a loop that loads all files matching a particular pattern, and creates a **City** column based on the file name:

```
# import_all_rain_files.py

import os

# this will hold our dataframes
all_dataframes = []

for filename in os.listdir():

    # only read files matching the pattern
    if filename.endswith("_daily_rain.csv"):
        print(f"reading {filename}...")
        df = pd.read_csv(filename)

        # take the bit of the filename before the underscore
        df["City"] = filename.split("_")[0]

        # add each dataframe to our list
        all_dataframes.append(df)

# now concatenate all the dataframes in the list
big_df = pd.concat(all_dataframes)
big_df
```

```
reading Berlin_daily_rain.csv...
reading Edinburgh_daily_rain.csv...
reading London_daily_rain.csv...
```

	Year	Month	Day of month	Day of year	Rainfall (mm)	City
0	1960	January	1	1	4	Berlin
1	1960	January	2	2	25	Berlin
2	1960	January	3	3	0	Berlin
3	1960	January	4	4	0	Berlin
4	1960	January	5	5	104	Berlin
...	...	...	...	...	...	...
21757	2019	July	27	208	20	London
21758	2019	July	28	209	0	London
21759	2019	July	29	210	0	London
21760	2019	July	30	211	42	London
21761	2019	July	31	212	0	London

Now we have a tidy dataset that we can start analyzing using all of the tools that we've seen in previous chapters. For example, let's set the month order then look at rainfall patterns across the year for each city:

```python
# monthly_rain_plot.py

from pandas.api.types import CategoricalDtype

months = ["January", "February", "March", "April", "May", "June", "July", "August",
    "September", "October", "November", "December"]

big_df["Month"] = big_df["Month"].astype(
    CategoricalDtype(categories=months, ordered=True)
)

sns.relplot(
    data=big_df,
    x="Month",
    y="Rainfall (mm)",
    aspect=3,
    height=4,
    hue="City",
    kind="line",
)

plt.title("Mean daily rainfall in each month since 1960 for three cities")
```

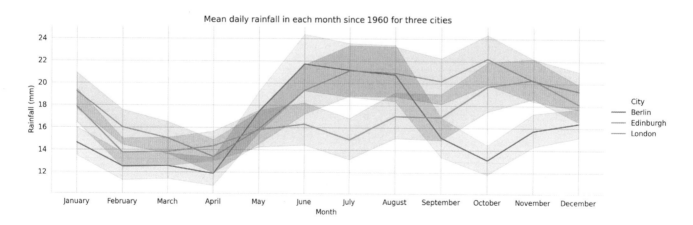

Although much noisier than the temperature data that we looked at in previous chapters, there are clear patterns. Berlin is wettest in the summer, with very dry months at the start of the year, whereas the two cities in the UK have a longer wet period stretching late into the winter.

16.2.2 Adding a single column

To really examine patterns of weather, it would be convenient to have the temperature and rainfall in a single dataframe. Let's read in our temperature data and see how we might proceed:

```
weather
```

	City	Year	Month	Day of year	Day of month	Mean temperature
0	Berlin	1960	January	1	1	6.4
1	Berlin	1960	January	2	2	8.1
2	Berlin	1960	January	3	3	5.4
3	Berlin	1960	January	4	4	3.9
4	Berlin	1960	January	5	5	6
...	...	...	...	...	...	...
63711	London	2018	October	300	27	4.9
63712	London	2018	October	301	28	7.4
63713	London	2018	October	302	29	5.8
63714	London	2018	October	303	30	6.6
63715	London	2018	October	304	31	7

Here we have an example of a problem that commonly occurs in real life: our two datasets have almost - but not exactly - the same number of rows. In this case, it's because the temperature data stops in October 2018, but the rainfall data stops in July 2019. In real world data there can be any number of reasons for slight discrepancies between two datasets.

Because the rows don't match exactly, we can't combine the two datasets using concatenation. But in fact, we don't need to. What we want is to add just a single column from the temperature dataset to our rainfall dataset. The best way to do this is to set the same index on both the big dataframe and the new column that we want to add. By doing this, when we create a new column, pandas will be able to figure out which value should go on each row.

We'll do it step by step to make it easy to follow. First we'll take our temperature dataset, set the index to be a combination of city, year and day, then take just the mean temperature column:

```python
# set_temp_index.py

temperatures = (
    weather
    .set_index(["City", "Year", "Day of year"])
    ["Mean temperature"]
)
temperatures
```

```
City    Year  Day of year
Berlin  1960  1              6.4
              2              8.1
              3              5.4
              4              3.9
              5              6.0
                            ...
London  2018  300            4.9
              301            7.4
              302            5.8
              303            6.6
              304            7.0
Name: Mean temperature, Length: 63716, dtype: float64
```

This gives us a new series with a multiindex consisting of city/year/day. Importantly, the index values are unique - for each combination of city, year and day we have just a single measurement.

Next we will take our big dataframe and set the index to be the same:

```
# set_rain_index.py

big_df = big_df.set_index(["City", "Year", "Day of year"])
big_df
```

	Month	Day of month	Rainfall (mm)
(Berlin, 1960, 1)	January	1	4
(Berlin, 1960, 2)	January	2	25
(Berlin, 1960, 3)	January	3	0
(Berlin, 1960, 4)	January	4	0
(Berlin, 1960, 5)	January	5	104
...	...	...	...
(London, 2019, 208)	July	27	20
(London, 2019, 209)	July	28	0
(London, 2019, 210)	July	29	0
(London, 2019, 211)	July	30	42
(London, 2019, 212)	July	31	0

Now we have done the hard work: we have a series and a dataframe that have the same indices. The indices don't have exactly the same values - we can tell this because the lengths of the series and the dataframe are different (63716 vs 65286 rows), or we can check it:

```
temperatures.index.equals(big_df.index)
```

```
False
```

To add the temperature to our big dataframe, all we have to do is assign a new column like normal:

```
# add_temps.py

big_df["Temperature (°C)"] = temperatures
big_df
```

	Month	Day of month	Rainfall (mm)	Temperature (°C)
(Berlin, 1960, 1)	January	1	4	6.4
(Berlin, 1960, 2)	January	2	25	8.1
(Berlin, 1960, 3)	January	3	0	5.4
(Berlin, 1960, 4)	January	4	0	3.9
(Berlin, 1960, 5)	January	5	104	6
...	...	...	...	...
(London, 2019, 208)	July	27	20	NaN
(London, 2019, 209)	July	28	0	NaN
(London, 2019, 210)	July	29	0	NaN
(London, 2019, 211)	July	30	42	NaN
(London, 2019, 212)	July	31	0	NaN

By glancing at the first and last few lines of the dataframe, we can see what has happened. Pandas has used the matching indices to insert the temperature into the correct rows, and automatically filled in missing data for the rows where there weren't matching temperature values.

Before we can use this dataframe for analysis, we probably want to turn the City/Year/Day indices back into columns:

16 Dealing with complicated data files

```
big_df = big_df.reset_index()
big_df
```

	City	Year	Day of year	Month	Day of month	Rainfall (mm)	Temperature (°C)
0	Berlin	1960	1	January	1	4	6.4
1	Berlin	1960	2	January	2	25	8.1
2	Berlin	1960	3	January	3	0	5.4
3	Berlin	1960	4	January	4	0	3.9
4	Berlin	1960	5	January	5	104	6
...	...	...	...	...	...	...	...
65281	London	2019	208	July	27	20	NaN
65282	London	2019	209	July	28	0	NaN
65283	London	2019	210	July	29	0	NaN
65284	London	2019	211	July	30	42	NaN
65285	London	2019	212	July	31	0	NaN

We can now analyse this dataframe just like any other. For example, is there any correlation between rainfall and temperature?

```python
# temp_and_rain.py

g = sns.lmplot(
    data=big_df,
    col="City",
    x="Rainfall (mm)",
    y="Temperature (°C)",
    scatter_kws={"s": 1, "color": "lightgrey"},
    height=4,
)
g.fig.suptitle(
    "Daily rainfall vs daily temperature since 1960 for three cities", y=1.1
)
```

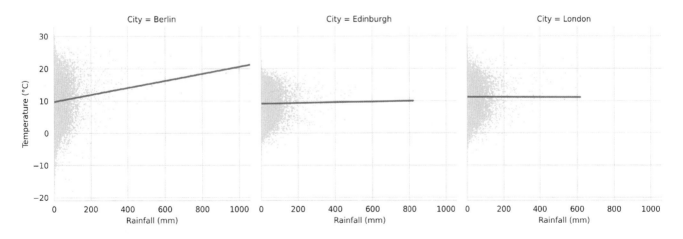

Daily rainfall vs daily temperature since 1960 for three cities

It appears not for the two British cities, but in Berlin, hotter days are definitely wetter.

Generally, the last thing we'll do after concatenating or adding new columns is to save our combined dataframe:

```python
big_df.to_csv("all_weather.csv", index=False)
```

---

16 Dealing with complicated data files 315

16.3 Merging

If we have a situation that's more complicated than either of the two outlined above, then we need a merge. Unlike concatenating or adding single columns, merging allows us to combine two entire dataframes while having much more control over the process. For example, we can specify exactly how to find matching rows, what we want to do when there are missing rows, and what we want to do when there are multiple matching rows.

To illustrate how merging works, let's go back to our eukaryote dataset:

```
euk.head()
```

	Species	Kingdom	Class	...	Number of proteins	Publication year	Assembly status
0	Emiliania huxleyi CCMP1516	Protists	Other Protists	...	38554	2013	Scaffold
1	Arabidopsis thaliana	Plants	Land Plants	...	48265	2001	Chromosome
2	Glycine max	Plants	Land Plants	...	71219	2010	Chromosome
3	Medicago truncatula	Plants	Land Plants	...	41939	2011	Chromosome
4	Solanum lycopersicum	Plants	Land Plants	...	37660	2010	Chromosome

and try to combine it with another dataset. Here's a simple file that contains common names for a bunch of species:

```
names = pd.read_csv("common_names.csv")
names
```

	scientific name	common name
0	Simonsiella muelleri	Scheibenbakterien
1	Simonsiella muelleri	Scheibenbakterien Muller 1911
2	Escherichia coli	E. coli
3	Rickettsia akari	rickettsialpox
4	Anaplasma phagocytophilum	agent of human granulocytic ehrlichiosis
...	...	...
14436	Riboviria	RNA viruses and viroids
14437	Neoheterocotyle quadrispinata	Yotsu-toge-iban-chu
14438	Arthroleptis lameerei	Lameere's squeaker
14439	Erebia albergana	almond-eyed ringlet butterfly
14440	Berardius minimus	Kurotsuchikujira

The structure of our **names** dataframe is pretty straightforward: one column for scientific name, one for common name. Our goal is to add a new column to our eukaryote dataframe that contains the common name.

Why can we not just set the index and then add the new column as we did for our temperature example? The answer is that there are situations that we might encounter in this dataset that we didn't encounter before. With our temperature example, we knew that every value in our temperature series matched exactly one row in the rainfall dataframe, and every row in the rainfall dataframe had a single matching temperature value (with the exception of the missing data). With the species names, we have several extra complications. Not every scientific name will have a matching common name, but some will have multiple common names. And we already know that some species have multiple genomes, so a single common name might match multiple rows in the dataset. Also, most of the species in the names dataframe aren't in the genomes dataframe at all.

To sum up, a single genome from the genomes dataframe can have zero, one, or multiple common names, and a common name from the names dataframe can belong to zero, one or multiple genomes. This is where most of the complication lies in merging: deciding what to do when we have multiple matches and missing data.

Let's get started. The method that we need is `merge`. We will have to tell pandas explicitly which columns we want to match. To do this, we refer to the dataframe on which we called the method (`df`) as the *right* dataframe, and the one that we passed as the argument (`names`) as the *left* dataframe. These are conventional names, simply based on the order in which we write the variables. So, for our dataset, the **Species** column in the left dataframe matches the **scientific name** column from the right dataframe:

```
# simple_merge.py

merged = euk.merge(names, left_on="Species", right_on="scientific name")
merged.head()
```

	Species	Kingdom	Class	...	Assembly status	scientific name	common name
0	Arabidopsis thaliana	Plants	Land Plants	...	Chromosome	Arabidopsis thaliana	mouse-ear cress
1	Arabidopsis thaliana	Plants	Land Plants	...	Chromosome	Arabidopsis thaliana	thale-cress
2	Arabidopsis thaliana	Plants	Land Plants	...	Chromosome	Arabidopsis thaliana	mouse-ear cress
3	Arabidopsis thaliana	Plants	Land Plants	...	Chromosome	Arabidopsis thaliana	thale-cress
4	Arabidopsis thaliana	Plants	Land Plants	...	Chromosome	Arabidopsis thaliana	mouse-ear cress

The columns that we want to match in the left and right dataframe get passed as the `left_on` and `right_on` arguments.

We can see from the output that we have got the desired effect; the two columns from the names dataframe have been added on to the end of the genomes dataframe. We would normally drop the **scientific name** column, as it's just a copy of the **Species** column.

Notice something interesting about the number of rows in the merged dataframe - there are 3342, compared to the 8302 that we started with. The merge has only included the genomes that had a matching common name; the others have been excluded from the result. If we look at the first few rows:

```
merged.head()
```

	Species	Kingdom	Class	...	Assembly status	scientific name	common name
0	Arabidopsis thaliana	Plants	Land Plants	...	Chromosome	Arabidopsis thaliana	mouse-ear cress
1	Arabidopsis thaliana	Plants	Land Plants	...	Chromosome	Arabidopsis thaliana	thale-cress
2	Arabidopsis thaliana	Plants	Land Plants	...	Chromosome	Arabidopsis thaliana	mouse-ear cress
3	Arabidopsis thaliana	Plants	Land Plants	...	Chromosome	Arabidopsis thaliana	thale-cress
4	Arabidopsis thaliana	Plants	Land Plants	...	Chromosome	Arabidopsis thaliana	mouse-ear cress

we can see another interesting phenomenon: where a species has multiple common names, we have ended up with multiple copies of each original row. For example, *Arabidopsis thaliana* has two common names:

```
names[names["scientific name"] == "Arabidopsis thaliana"]
```

	scientific name	common name
249	Arabidopsis thaliana	mouse-ear cress
250	Arabidopsis thaliana	thale-cress

so every *Arabidopsis thaliana* genome in the original dataframe appears twice in the merged dataframe, once with each common name.

Understanding this behavior is very important, so let's summarize:

- genomes that have no matching common name are **missing** from the merged dataframe
- genomes that have multiple common names are **duplicated** in the merged dataframe

If this is the behavior that we want, then our work is done. However, if we wanted a different output, we must investigate `merge` a bit further.

First, let's see how we might avoid duplicated rows in the merged dataframe. The easiest way to avoid this is to make sure that our names dataframe only contains a single common name for each scientific name, which we can do by calling `drop_duplicates` and telling pandas which columns we want to avoid duplicates in:

```
names.drop_duplicates(subset=["scientific name"])
```

	scientific name	common name
0	Simonsiella muelleri	Scheibenbakterien
2	Escherichia coli	E. coli
3	Rickettsia akari	rickettsialpox
4	Anaplasma phagocytophilum	agent of human granulocytic ehrlichiosis
5	Neorickettsia risticii	equine monocytic ehrlichiosis agent
...	...	...
14435	Riboviria	RNA viruses
14437	Neoheterocotyle quadrispinata	Yotsu-toge-iban-chu
14438	Arthroleptis lameerei	Lameere's squeaker
14439	Erebia albergana	almond-eyed ringlet butterfly
14440	Berardius minimus	Kurotsuchikujira

Doing this reduced the size of our names dataset from 14,441 rows to 10,479 rows. If we do the merge using the unique scientific names:

```
# unique_merge.py

euk.merge(
    names.drop_duplicates(subset=["scientific name"]),
    left_on="Species",
    right_on="scientific name",
)
```

	Species	Kingdom	Class	...	Assembly status	scientific name	common name
0	Arabidopsis thaliana	Plants	Land Plants	...	Chromosome	Arabidopsis thaliana	mouse-ear cress
1	Arabidopsis thaliana	Plants	Land Plants	...	Chromosome	Arabidopsis thaliana	mouse-ear cress
2	Arabidopsis thaliana	Plants	Land Plants	...	Chromosome	Arabidopsis thaliana	mouse-ear cress
3	Arabidopsis thaliana	Plants	Land Plants	...	Scaffold	Arabidopsis thaliana	mouse-ear cress
4	Arabidopsis thaliana	Plants	Land Plants	...	Scaffold	Arabidopsis thaliana	mouse-ear cress
...	...	...	...	...	...	...	...
1993	Oryza sativa	Plants	Land Plants	...	Contig	Oryza sativa	red rice
1994	Oryza sativa	Plants	Land Plants	...	Contig	Oryza sativa	red rice
1995	Oryza sativa	Plants	Land Plants	...	Contig	Oryza sativa	red rice
1996	Oryza sativa	Plants	Land Plants	...	Contig	Oryza sativa	red rice
1997	Oryza sativa	Plants	Land Plants	...	Contig	Oryza sativa	red rice

Each genome only appears once in the merged dataframe, and we are down to 1,998 rows - remember, these are only the genomes that have a matching scientific name. By default, calling `drop_duplicates` will keep only the first common name, so that's the one we will end up with ("mouse-ear cress" in the case of *Arabidopsis thaliana*).

If we want something a bit more sophisticated than simply taking the first common name, we can probably do it with pandas. For example, we could make a new common name for each scientific name by joining the common names together with commas:

```
# list_names.py

list_common_names = (
    names.groupby("scientific name")
    .apply(lambda x: ",".join(x["common name"]))
    .to_frame("common name")
    .reset_index()
)
list_common_names
```

	scientific name	common name
0	Abagrotis alternata	mottled gray cutworm
1	Abavorana luctuosa	Malaysian frog,purple frog
2	Abbottina rivularis	Amur false gudgeon
3	Abditibacteriota	phylum FBP
4	Abelia x grandiflora	glossy abelia
...	...	...
10474	triploid Carassius auratus red var. x Culter a...	triploid red crucian carp x topmouth culter
10475	undetermined Cottoidei 'Lake Baikal'	Baikalian cottoid fish
10476	undetermined Sciuridae 'chipmunks'	chipmunks
10477	x Hesperotropsis leylandii	Leyland cypress,Leyland-cypress
10478	x Triticosecale	triticale

Now when we merge:

```
# list_merge.py

euk.merge(list_common_names, left_on="Species", right_on="scientific name")
```

	Species	Kingdom	Class	...	Assembly status	scientific name	common name
0	Arabidopsis thaliana	Plants	Land Plants	...	Chromosome	Arabidopsis thaliana	mouse-ear cress,thale-cress
1	Arabidopsis thaliana	Plants	Land Plants	...	Chromosome	Arabidopsis thaliana	mouse-ear cress,thale-cress
2	Arabidopsis thaliana	Plants	Land Plants	...	Chromosome	Arabidopsis thaliana	mouse-ear cress,thale-cress
3	Arabidopsis thaliana	Plants	Land Plants	...	Scaffold	Arabidopsis thaliana	mouse-ear cress,thale-cress
4	Arabidopsis thaliana	Plants	Land Plants	...	Scaffold	Arabidopsis thaliana	mouse-ear cress,thale-cress
...	...	...	...	...	...	...	...
1993	Oryza sativa	Plants	Land Plants	...	Contig	Oryza sativa	red rice
1994	Oryza sativa	Plants	Land Plants	...	Contig	Oryza sativa	red rice
1995	Oryza sativa	Plants	Land Plants	...	Contig	Oryza sativa	red rice
1996	Oryza sativa	Plants	Land Plants	...	Contig	Oryza sativa	red rice
1997	Oryza sativa	Plants	Land Plants	...	Contig	Oryza sativa	red rice

we get a single output row for each genome that has a common name.

To put back the missing genomes - the ones that don't have matching common names - we need to take a look at the **how** argument to **merge**. The merges that we have been doing so far have been using the default option, which is `'inner'`:

```
euk.merge(
    list_common_names,
    left_on="Species",
    right_on="scientific name",
    how="inner",
)
```

	Species	Kingdom	Class	...	Assembly status	scientific name	common name
0	Arabidopsis thaliana	Plants	Land Plants	...	Chromosome	Arabidopsis thaliana	mouse-ear cress,thale-cress
1	Arabidopsis thaliana	Plants	Land Plants	...	Chromosome	Arabidopsis thaliana	mouse-ear cress,thale-cress
2	Arabidopsis thaliana	Plants	Land Plants	...	Chromosome	Arabidopsis thaliana	mouse-ear cress,thale-cress
3	Arabidopsis thaliana	Plants	Land Plants	...	Scaffold	Arabidopsis thaliana	mouse-ear cress,thale-cress
4	Arabidopsis thaliana	Plants	Land Plants	...	Scaffold	Arabidopsis thaliana	mouse-ear cress,thale-cress
...	...	...	...	...	...	...	...
1993	Oryza sativa	Plants	Land Plants	...	Contig	Oryza sativa	red rice
1994	Oryza sativa	Plants	Land Plants	...	Contig	Oryza sativa	red rice
1995	Oryza sativa	Plants	Land Plants	...	Contig	Oryza sativa	red rice
1996	Oryza sativa	Plants	Land Plants	...	Contig	Oryza sativa	red rice
1997	Oryza sativa	Plants	Land Plants	...	Contig	Oryza sativa	red rice

This means that we want to keep only the rows that are present in both of the input dataframes. Changing this to `'left'` means that we want to include all the rows from the left dataframe, even the ones that have no matching row in the right. In our case, this means keeping all genomes, even the ones that have no common name:

```
euk.merge(
    list_common_names,
    left_on="Species",
    right_on="scientific name",
    how="left",
)
```

	Species	Kingdom	Class	...	Assembly status	scientific name	common name
0	Emiliania huxleyi CCMP1516	Protists	Other Protists	...	Scaffold	NaN	NaN
1	Arabidopsis thaliana	Plants	Land Plants	...	Chromosome	Arabidopsis thaliana	mouse-ear cress,thale-cress
2	Glycine max	Plants	Land Plants	...	Chromosome	Glycine max	soybeans
3	Medicago truncatula	Plants	Land Plants	...	Chromosome	NaN	NaN
4	Solanum lycopersicum	Plants	Land Plants	...	Chromosome	NaN	NaN
...	...	...	...	...	...	...	...
8297	Saccharomyces cerevisiae	Fungi	Ascomycetes	...	Scaffold	Saccharomyces cerevisiae	S. cerevisiae,brewer's yeast
8298	Saccharomyces cerevisiae	Fungi	Ascomycetes	...	Chromosome	Saccharomyces cerevisiae	S. cerevisiae,brewer's yeast
8299	Saccharomyces cerevisiae	Fungi	Ascomycetes	...	Chromosome	Saccharomyces cerevisiae	S. cerevisiae,brewer's yeast
8300	Saccharomyces cerevisiae	Fungi	Ascomycetes	...	Chromosome	Saccharomyces cerevisiae	S. cerevisiae,brewer's yeast
8301	Saccharomyces cerevisiae	Fungi	Ascomycetes	...	Chromosome	Saccharomyces cerevisiae	S. cerevisiae,brewer's yeast

This gives us the same number of rows as we had in the original genomes file. Based on what we've already seen of pandas' handling of missing data, you can probably guess what's going to appear in the **common name** column for genomes that don't have a common name - it will simply be missing.

What will happen if we specify `'right'` rather than `'left'`?

```
euk.merge(
    list_common_names,
    left_on="Species",
    right_on="scientific name",
    how="right",
)
```

	Species	Kingdom	...	scientific name	common name
0	Arabidopsis thaliana	Plants	...	Arabidopsis thaliana	mouse-ear cress,thale-cress
1	Arabidopsis thaliana	Plants	...	Arabidopsis thaliana	mouse-ear cress,thale-cress
2	Arabidopsis thaliana	Plants	...	Arabidopsis thaliana	mouse-ear cress,thale-cress
3	Arabidopsis thaliana	Plants	...	Arabidopsis thaliana	mouse-ear cress,thale-cress
4	Arabidopsis thaliana	Plants	...	Arabidopsis thaliana	mouse-ear cress,thale-cress
...	...	...	...	...	...
11963	NaN	<NA>	...	triploid Carassius auratus red var. x Culter a...	triploid red crucian carp x topmouth culter
11964	NaN	<NA>	...	undetermined Cottoidei 'Lake Baikal'	Baikalian cottoid fish
11965	NaN	<NA>	...	undetermined Sciuridae 'chipmunks'	chipmunks
11966	NaN	<NA>	...	x Hesperotropsis leylandii	Leyland cypress,Leyland-cypress
11967	NaN	<NA>	...	x Triticosecale	triticale

Now we will keep all rows from the right dataframe, even if they don't have a matching row in the left one. In our case, this means including all the common names, including the ones that don't appear in the genome dataframe at all. Notice that the number of rows in the merged dataframe is actually larger than the number of rows in the `list_common_names` dataframe, because some species (like *Arabidopsis thaliana*) appear multiple times.

For common names with no matching genomes (like those in the last few rows), all of the other columns are filled with missing data.

The final option for merging is `'outer'`:

```
euk.merge(
    list_common_names,
    left_on="Species",
    right_on="scientific name",
    how="outer",
)
```

	Species	Kingdom	...	scientific name	common name
0	Emiliania huxleyi CCMP1516	Protists	...	NaN	NaN
1	Arabidopsis thaliana	Plants	...	Arabidopsis thaliana	mouse-ear cress,thale-cress
2	Arabidopsis thaliana	Plants	...	Arabidopsis thaliana	mouse-ear cress,thale-cress
3	Arabidopsis thaliana	Plants	...	Arabidopsis thaliana	mouse-ear cress,thale-cress
4	Arabidopsis thaliana	Plants	...	Arabidopsis thaliana	mouse-ear cress,thale-cress
...	...	...	...	...	...
18267	NaN	<NA>	...	triploid Carassius auratus red var. x Culter a...	triploid red crucian carp x topmouth culter
18268	NaN	<NA>	...	undetermined Cottoidei 'Lake Baikal'	Baikalian cottoid fish
18269	NaN	<NA>	...	undetermined Sciuridae 'chipmunks'	chipmunks
18270	NaN	<NA>	...	x Hesperotropsis leylandii	Leyland cypress,Leyland-cypress
18271	NaN	<NA>	...	x Triticosecale	triticale

As you might guess, this option means that we want to include all rows from both dataframes, and fill in missing data where necessary. So in the merged output we have both genomes without a common name **and** common names that don't match genomes.

For our dataset, `'left'` makes most sense. We will include all genomes, then fill in the missing common names with a placeholder value. A useful trick here is to pass a dict mapping column names to the value we want to fill, to avoid also filling the missing values in the number of genes and proteins columns:

```
final_merge = euk.merge(
    list_common_names,
    left_on="Species",
    right_on="scientific name",
    how="left",
).fillna({"common name": "no common name"})
final_merge
```

	Species	Kingdom	...	scientific name	common name
0	Emiliania huxleyi CCMP1516	Protists	...	NaN	no common name
1	Arabidopsis thaliana	Plants	...	Arabidopsis thaliana	mouse-ear cress,thale-cress
2	Glycine max	Plants	...	Glycine max	soybeans
3	Medicago truncatula	Plants	...	NaN	no common name
4	Solanum lycopersicum	Plants	...	NaN	no common name
...	...	...	...	...	...
8297	Saccharomyces cerevisiae	Fungi	...	Saccharomyces cerevisiae	S. cerevisiae,brewer's yeast
8298	Saccharomyces cerevisiae	Fungi	...	Saccharomyces cerevisiae	S. cerevisiae,brewer's yeast
8299	Saccharomyces cerevisiae	Fungi	...	Saccharomyces cerevisiae	S. cerevisiae,brewer's yeast
8300	Saccharomyces cerevisiae	Fungi	...	Saccharomyces cerevisiae	S. cerevisiae,brewer's yeast
8301	Saccharomyces cerevisiae	Fungi	...	Saccharomyces cerevisiae	S. cerevisiae,brewer's yeast

To make it easier to use the common names in labels, we can make a special display name column by combining the species and common names:

```
display_names = (
    final_merge["Species"] + " (" + final_merge["common name"] + ")"
)
display_names
```

```
0                Emiliania huxleyi CCMP1516 (no common name)
1            Arabidopsis thaliana (mouse-ear cress,thale-cr...
2                                     Glycine max (soybeans)
3                       Medicago truncatula (no common name)
4                     Solanum lycopersicum (no common name)
                              ...
8297    Saccharomyces cerevisiae (S. cerevisiae,brewer...
8298    Saccharomyces cerevisiae (S. cerevisiae,brewer...
8299    Saccharomyces cerevisiae (S. cerevisiae,brewer...
8300    Saccharomyces cerevisiae (S. cerevisiae,brewer...
8301    Saccharomyces cerevisiae (S. cerevisiae,brewer...
Length: 8302, dtype: object
```

Notice that many of these display names are very long! To avoid problems with using them as labels, a useful trick is to use pandas' **wrap** string method to split them over multiple lines:

```
final_merge["display_name"] = display_names.str.wrap(20)
final_merge["display_name"]
```

```
0                Emiliania huxleyi\nCCMP1516 (no common\nname)
1            Arabidopsis thaliana\n(mouse-ear\ncress,thale-...
2                                   Glycine max\n(soybeans)
3                     Medicago truncatula\n(no common name)
4                   Solanum lycopersicum\n(no common name)
                              ...
8297    Saccharomyces\ncerevisiae (S.\ncerevisiae,brew...
8298    Saccharomyces\ncerevisiae (S.\ncerevisiae,brew...
8299    Saccharomyces\ncerevisiae (S.\ncerevisiae,brew...
8300    Saccharomyces\ncerevisiae (S.\ncerevisiae,brew...
8301    Saccharomyces\ncerevisiae (S.\ncerevisiae,brew...
Name: display_name, Length: 8302, dtype: object
```

This method inserts newlines where appropriate to break up long lines. Now let's try using our display names as labels. For example, let's take all the species with more than 30 genome sequences and plot their GC%.

```
# display_name_plot.py

my_data = final_merge.groupby("Species").filter(lambda x: len(x) > 30)

sns.catplot(
    data=my_data,
    x="display_name",
    y="GC%",
    kind="bar",
    aspect=3,
    height=5,
    color="lightblue",
    ci="sd",
)

plt.title(
    "Mean and standard deviation of GC% for species with >30 sequenced genomes"
)
```

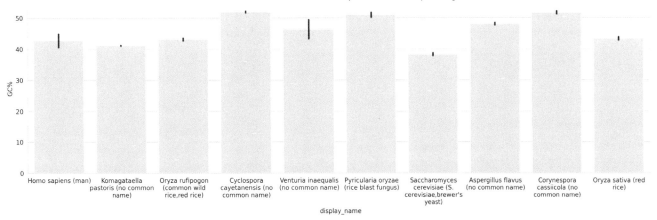

Mean and standard deviation of GC% for species with >30 sequenced genomes

This technique of making a special column to use as a label for visualization is often useful, and of course we can reuse it across multiple charts.

Hopefully these three examples have made it clear that the various tools for combining datasets each have their place. If we just want to add a single column to an existing dataframe, then the easiest way is to create a series with a matching index and simply assign it. If we have a list of dataframes with either the same rows or the same columns, then we can use `pd.concat`. And if we have two dataframes that you need to combine and have control over the output, use `merge`.

16.4 Very large datasets

As mentioned above, most of our example datasets have been well formatted in order to keep the examples as simple as possible. By the same token, our example datasets have been mostly small, to make sure that we can read them without running out of memory. Of course, this will not always be the case in the real world.

To illustrate ways of reducing memory usage in pandas, we could pick a dataset that's too big to fit in memory to use as example. The problem with that approach is that it entirely depends on the environment in which you're running these examples! So instead we will work with the *weather.csv* file that we created earlier in this chapter, and use it to look at memory saving techniques, with the understanding that these techniques will also work on larger files.

We'll start with the usual version that we get by calling `read_csv` with default values:

```
weather = pd.read_csv("all_weather.csv")
weather
```

	City	Year	Day of year	Month	Day of month	Rainfall (mm)	Temperature (°C)
0	Berlin	1960	1	January	1	4	6.4
1	Berlin	1960	2	January	2	25	8.1
2	Berlin	1960	3	January	3	0	5.4
3	Berlin	1960	4	January	4	0	3.9
4	Berlin	1960	5	January	5	104	6
...	...	...	...	...	...	...	...
65281	London	2019	208	July	27	20	NaN
65282	London	2019	209	July	28	0	NaN
65283	London	2019	210	July	29	0	NaN
65284	London	2019	211	July	30	42	NaN
65285	London	2019	212	July	31	0	NaN

Before we can look at techniques for reducing memory, we first need a way to measure how much memory the dataframe is using. There are a few different options here. You many have noticed from previous examples that `info` includes a rough estimate of memory usage for the entire dataframe at the end of the output:

```
weather.info()
```

```
<class 'pandas.core.frame.DataFrame'>
RangeIndex: 65286 entries, 0 to 65285
Data columns (total 7 columns):
 #   Column           Non-Null Count  Dtype
---  ------           --------------  -----
 0   City             65286 non-null  object
 1   Year             65286 non-null  int64
 2   Day of year      65286 non-null  int64
 3   Month            65286 non-null  object
 4   Day of month     65286 non-null  int64
 5   Rainfall (mm)    64343 non-null  float64
 6   Temperature (°C) 63716 non-null  float64
dtypes: float64(2), int64(3), object(2)
memory usage: 3.5+ MB
```

We can get column-by-column information by calling `memory_usage`:

```
# show_mem_usage.py

weather.memory_usage()
```

```
Index               128
City             522288
Year             522288
Day of year      522288
Month            522288
Day of month     522288
Rainfall (mm)    522288
Temperature (°C) 522288
dtype: int64
```

The output is in bytes, which is sometimes awkward for us humans to read. Because the output is itself a Series, we can easily view it in kilobytes:

```
weather.memory_usage() / 1000
```

```
Index               0.128
City              522.288
Year              522.288
Day of year       522.288
Month             522.288
Day of month      522.288
Rainfall (mm)     522.288
Temperature (°C)  522.288
dtype: float64
```

or megabytes:

```
weather.memory_usage() / 1_000_000
```

```
Index               0.000128
City                0.522288
Year                0.522288
Day of year         0.522288
Month               0.522288
Day of month        0.522288
Rainfall (mm)       0.522288
Temperature (°C)    0.522288
dtype: float64
```

We can see from this output that the maths adds up: we have seven columns, each taking up half a megabyte, which gives us our 3.5 megabytes that was estimated by `info`. Because the output from `memory_usage` is a Series, we can even be lazy and get pandas to do the calculation:

```
weather.memory_usage().sum() / 1_000_000
```

```
3.656144
```

When interpreting the output of `memory_usage` it's very important to note that the measurements **don't** include the space to store any values which have a data type of `object` - in our case, the **City** and **Month** columns that contain strings. That's because the process of calculating memory usage for objects can be quite computationally intensive.

To include the amount of memory required to store the strings in those two columns, we need to pass the `deep=True` argument. This will give us a more accurate measurement of the true amount of memory that these data are taking up, at the expense of taking longer to calculate:

```
# show_real_mem_usage.py

weather.memory_usage(deep=True) / 1_000_000
```

```
Index               0.000128
City                4.178304
Year                0.522288
Day of year         0.522288
Month               4.122099
Day of month        0.522288
Rainfall (mm)       0.522288
Temperature (°C)    0.522288
dtype: float64
```

When we include this argument we can see that the **City** and **Month** columns - the two that contain strings - take over 4 megabytes of memory each.

There's also a `memory='deep'` argument to `info` that will tell us roughly the same story:

```
weather.info(memory_usage="deep")
```

```
<class 'pandas.core.frame.DataFrame'>
RangeIndex: 65286 entries, 0 to 65285
Data columns (total 7 columns):
 #   Column          Non-Null Count  Dtype
---  ------          --------------  -----
 0   City            65286 non-null  object
 1   Year            65286 non-null  int64
 2   Day of year     65286 non-null  int64
 3   Month           65286 non-null  object
 4   Day of month    65286 non-null  int64
 5   Rainfall (mm)   64343 non-null  float64
 6   Temperature (°C) 63716 non-null  float64
dtypes: float64(2), int64(3), object(2)
memory usage: 10.4 MB
```

although it won't show us which columns are responsible.

Now we have a reliable way to measure memory usage, we can start to work on reducing it.

16.4.1 Including only the columns we need

The simplest way to reduce the memory footprint of a dataframe is to make it smaller. For example, if we know that we are only going to be looking at patterns of weather across the year, then we may decide that we can work with just the **Year** and **Day of year** columns - we don't need **Month** and **Day of month** at all. We can choose which columns to include by passing the `usecols` argument when we read in the dataset:

```
# just_some_columns.py

weather = pd.read_csv(
    "all_weather.csv",
    usecols=["City", "Year", "Day of year", "Rainfall (mm)", "Temperature (°C)"]
)

print(weather.memory_usage(deep=True))
print(weather.memory_usage(deep=True).sum() / 1_000_000)
```

```
Index                128
City             4178304
Year              522288
Day of year       522288
Rainfall (mm)     522288
Temperature (°C)  522288
dtype: int64
6.267584
```

Here we save a lot of memory by not storing the **Month** column, bringing our total usage down to just over 6 megabytes.

16.4.2 Using categories

The **City** column (and the **Month** column, before we excluded it) both took a lot of memory because they were storing strings. But the number of unique strings in those columns is very small - three for the **City** column, and twelve for **Month**. We can save a lot of memory if we explicity tell pandas to store these as categories, which we can do by passing a dictionary of data types when we read the data file:

16 Dealing with complicated data files

```
# categories.py

weather = pd.read_csv(
    "all_weather.csv",
    usecols=["City", "Year", "Day of year", "Rainfall (mm)", "Temperature (°C)"],
    dtype={"City": "category"},
)

print(weather.memory_usage(deep=True))
print(weather.memory_usage(deep=True).sum() / 1_000_000)
```

```
Index                  128
City                 65478
Year                522288
Day of year         522288
Rainfall (mm)       522288
Temperature (°C)    522288
dtype: int64
2.154758
```

Notice how this shinks the memory usage for the **City** column by a factor of nearly 100. The reason that this saves so much memory is that it allows pandas to only store the city name strings once, then represent the different categorical values as integers.

The **City** column is a best-case scenario for this type of memory saving, as it only stores a small number of unique values. For columns with many unique values, the memory saving will not be as dramatic. For example, let's take the species name column from our eukaryote dataset. We currently have it stored as dtype **string**, as dicussed in the first chapter, and in this form it occupies about 66 kilobytes:

```
euk["Species"].memory_usage(deep=True) / 1000
```

```
66.544
```

Changing the column to a category results in around a ten fold increase in size:

```
euk["Species"].astype("category").memory_usage(deep=True) / 1000
```

```
575.141
```

because the number of unique strings is not that much less than the total number of strings:

```
euk["Species"].count(), euk["Species"].nunique()
```

```
(8302, 4936)
```

so the overhead of creating the categories is much greater than the memory saved.

Incidentally, if we allow pandas to use its default settings when reading in the data file and store the species name as an object:

```
pd.read_csv("eukaryotes.tsv", sep="\t", na_values=["-"]).dtypes
```

```
Species                 object
Kingdom                 object
Class                   object
Size (Mb)              float64
GC%                    float64
Number of genes        float64
Number of proteins     float64
Publication year         int64
Assembly status         object
dtype: object
```

then the memory usage is even greater:

```
pd.read_csv("eukaryotes.tsv", sep="\t", na_values=["-"])[
    "Species"
].memory_usage(deep=True) / 1000
```

```
655.867
```

Assigning a data type of **string** to text columns is likely to become the default in a future version of pandas.

16.4.3 Reducing numerical precision

Let's go back to our weather dataset. The last thing that we can do to reduce memory is to alter the data type of the other columns. If we take another look at the output from **info**:

```
weather.info()
```

```
<class 'pandas.core.frame.DataFrame'>
RangeIndex: 65286 entries, 0 to 65285
Data columns (total 5 columns):
 #   Column          Non-Null Count  Dtype
---  ------          --------------  -----
 0   City            65286 non-null  category
 1   Year            65286 non-null  int64
 2   Day of year     65286 non-null  int64
 3   Rainfall (mm)   64343 non-null  float64
 4   Temperature (°C) 63716 non-null float64
dtypes: category(1), float64(2), int64(2)
memory usage: 2.1 MB
```

We see that **Year** and **Day of year** are both being stored with a data type of **int64**, meaning that they are stored as a 64-bit integer. This allows a massive range of numbers. We can easily check how many different numbers can be stored with 64 bits - it's just 2 to the power of 64:

```
2 ** 64
```

```
18446744073709551616
```

although we have to divide by two to get the largest number because integers can also be negative:

```
2 ** 64 // 2
```

```
9223372036854775808
```

Given that we know our **Year** column only goes up to 2019, we definitely don't need such a wide range of numbers. In fact, a 16-bit integer has plenty of room to store both the year and the day of the year:

```
2 ** 16 / 2
```

```
32768.0
```

so let's try setting that as the data type:

```python
# reduced_precision.py

weather = pd.read_csv(
    "all_weather.csv",
    usecols=["City", "Year", "Day of year", "Rainfall (mm)", "Temperature (°C)"],
    dtype={"City": "category", "Year": "int16", "Day of year": "int16"},
)

print(weather.memory_usage(deep=True))
print(weather.memory_usage(deep=True).sum() / 1_000_000)
```

```
Index                 128
City                65478
Year               130572
Day of year        130572
Rainfall (mm)      522288
Temperature (°C)   522288
dtype: int64
1.371326
```

As we can see, this reduces the memory useage from around 520 kilobytes to around 130 kilobytes.

An easy way to find the most efficient category for a column is to use **astype** to convert it to various data types, then **memory_usage** to show how much space it takes up. See what happens when we read our weather data again using the defaults, then change the **Year** column to various different types:

```python
weather = pd.read_csv("all_weather.csv")
for data_type in ["category", "int64", "int32", "int16", "int8"]:
    usage = weather["Year"].astype(data_type).memory_usage(deep=True) / 1000
    print(data_type, usage)
```

```
category 68.454
int64 522.416
int32 261.272
int16 130.7
int8 65.414
```

Notice from the output a danger with specifying data types: if we specify a data type that's too small to hold our values, they get altered. In this case, if we try to store our year as 8-bit integers, they overflow without warning and are left with negative years:

```python
weather["Year"].astype("int8").head()
```

```
0    -88
1    -88
2    -88
3    -88
4    -88
Name: Year, dtype: int8
```

Because there are a small number of years, storing them as a category is even more memory efficient than storing them as 16-bit integers. For storing the day of the year:

```
weather = pd.read_csv("all_weather.csv")
for data_type in ["category", "int64", "int32", "int16", "int8"]:
    usage = weather["Day of year"].astype(data_type).memory_usage(deep=True) / 1000
    print(data_type, usage)
```

```
category 143.868
int64 522.416
int32 261.272
int16 130.7
int8 65.414
```

there are more unique values, so category has no memory advantage.

The most memory-efficient data type of all is a boolean type (whose name in numpy is `bool`). If we look at our example of awkward input from the start of the chapter:

```
df = pd.read_csv(
    "awkward_input.csv",
    skiprows=11,
    na_values=["-", "missing"],
    names=my_columns,
    usecols=my_columns,
    skipfooter=1,
    decimal=",",
    thousands="_",
    comment="#",
    true_values=["True", "1", "yes", '"t"'],
    false_values=["False", "0", "no", '"f"'],
    dtype={"Is animal": np.bool, "Is plant": np.bool},
)
df.memory_usage(deep=True)
```

```
Index            128
Species       230907
Genome size    24408
GC%            24408
Genes          24408
Year           24408
Status        198320
Is animal       3051
Is plant        3051
dtype: int64
```

we can see that the memory usage for the last two columns is much lower than for the others.

One slight complication when picking types involves missing data. Notice that the default type for the **Rainfall (mm)** column is `float64` rather than `int64`:

```
weather.dtypes
```

```
City              object
Year               int64
Day of year        int64
Month             object
Day of month       int64
Rainfall (mm)    float64
Temperature (°C) float64
dtype: object
```

even though the values are all integers:

```
weather["Rainfall (mm)"].head()
```

```
0      4.0
1     25.0
2      0.0
3      0.0
4    104.0
Name: Rainfall (mm), dtype: float64
```

The reason that pandas has chosen a floating point data type for this column is that, unlike the **Year** column, the **Rainfall (mm)** column contains missing data. So if we want to store it as an integer, we have to explicitly pick the `Int64` data type. If we do this, the memory usage actually goes up:

```
print(weather["Rainfall (mm)"].memory_usage(deep=True) / 1_000)
print(weather["Rainfall (mm)"].astype("Int64").memory_usage(deep=True) / 1_000)
```

```
522.416
587.702
```

But if we use a lower precision integer data type:

```
print(weather["Rainfall (mm)"].astype("Int16").memory_usage(deep=True) / 1_000)
```

```
195.986
```

we get an improvement. A convenient way to check that we are still storing the same values is to take the series, remove missing data, then compare the elements with the new data type and check that they are all the same using Python's built in `all` function:

```
all(
    weather["Rainfall (mm)"].dropna().astype("Int16")
    == weather["Rainfall (mm)"].dropna()
)
```

```
True
```

If the output from that expression is `True`, we know that converting to the new data type hasn't affected the values.

16.4.4 Precision with floating point numbers

Finally, we can use the same approach with floating point numbers. The temperature column in our weather dataframe is stored as a `float64`:

```
weather["Temperature (°C)"].dtype
```

```
dtype('float64')
```

with a high level of precision. However, if we look at the actual values:

```
weather["Temperature (°C)"].head()
```

```
0      6.4
1      8.1
2      5.4
3      3.9
4      6.0
Name: Temperature (°C), dtype: float64
```

we see that they only have one decimal place. Let's see if we can get away with converting to a lower precision, and test for equality using the same approach as before:

```
all(
    weather["Temperature (°C)"].dropna().astype("float32")
    == weather["Temperature (°C)"].dropna()
)
```

```
False
```

The `False` output shows us that converting to `float32` will alter the values. But by how much? We can check by taking the difference of the two data types, using `np.abs` to convert these to absolute values, then taking the maximum:

```
max(
    np.abs(
        weather["Temperature (°C)"]
        - weather["Temperature (°C)"].astype("float32")
    )
)
```

```
7.629394538355427e-07
```

This tells us that by converting the temperatures from `float64` to `float32`, we will at most change them by 0.0000007 degrees. Given the level of precision in the original measurements, this is probably a good trade off! Even converting the temperatures to the lowest floating point precision level:

```
max(
    np.abs(
        weather["Temperature (°C)"]
        - weather["Temperature (°C)"].astype("float16")
    )
)
```

```
0.006250000000001421
```

gives a maximum inaccuracy of 0.006 degrees, which is probably acceptable. The memory saving is significant:

```
print(weather["Temperature (°C)"].memory_usage(deep=True) / 1_000)
print(
    weather["Temperature (°C)"].astype("float16").memory_usage(deep=True)
    / 1_000
)
```

```
522.416
130.7
```

When we've finished figuring out the appropriate columns and their data types, we can plug these values into our final version of `read_csv`:

---

16 Dealing with complicated data files

```
# final_memory_save.py

weather = pd.read_csv(
    "all_weather.csv",
    usecols=[
        "City",
        "Year",
        "Day of year",
        "Rainfall (mm)",
        "Temperature (°C)",
    ],
    dtype={
        "City": "category",
        "Year": "int16",
        "Day of year": "int16",
        "Rainfall (mm)": "Int16",
        "Temperature (°C)": "float16",
    },
)

weather.info(memory_usage="deep")
```

```
<class 'pandas.core.frame.DataFrame'>
RangeIndex: 65286 entries, 0 to 65285
Data columns (total 5 columns):
 #   Column            Non-Null Count  Dtype
---  ------            --------------  -----
 0   City              65286 non-null  category
 1   Year              65286 non-null  int16
 2   Day of year       65286 non-null  int16
 3   Rainfall (mm)     64343 non-null  Int16
 4   Temperature (°C)  63716 non-null  float16
dtypes: Int16(1), category(1), float16(1), int16(2)
memory usage: 637.9 KB
```

and the total amount of memory taken up by the dataset has gone from around ten megabytes to just over 600 kilobytes.

16.4.5 Final memory vs peak memory

One factor that we must bear in mind when talking about memory usage is that the peak memory requirement might be much larger than the final size of the dataframe in memory. Exact measurements are difficult, but regardless of the size of the final dataframe it's not unusual for pandas to use between five and ten times as much memory as the size of the data file. So don't fall into the trap of thinking that because you have enough memory to store your complete dataframe you have enough memory to read it in the first place! Peak memory issues are best dealt with by chunking our input file.

16.4.6 Chunking input data

The final option for dealing with a file that's too large to fit in memory is to read it in chunks rather than all in one go. This approach won't work for all problems, but if we can structure our code in such a way that it deals with each section of the input file independently, then we can effectively read arbitrarily large input files.

A classic example is filtering. Let's imagine that we want to find all the very rainy days in our dataset - the rows where the rainfall is greater than 100mm. With the whole dataset in memory, the problem is easy:

```
weather = pd.read_csv("all_weather.csv")
rainy_days = weather[weather["Rainfall (mm)"] > 100]
```

and unsurprisingly, the amount of memory required to hold just the rainy days:

```
rainy_days.info(memory_usage="deep", verbose=False)
```

```
<class 'pandas.core.frame.DataFrame'>
Int64Index: 2413 entries, 4 to 65280
Columns: 7 entries, City to Temperature (°C)
dtypes: float64(2), int64(3), object(2)
memory usage: 412.7 KB
```

is much less than that required to hold the entire dataset (400 KB versus 10 MB):

```
weather.info(memory_usage="deep", verbose=False)
```

```
<class 'pandas.core.frame.DataFrame'>
RangeIndex: 65286 entries, 0 to 65285
Columns: 7 entries, City to Temperature (°C)
dtypes: float64(2), int64(3), object(2)
memory usage: 10.4 MB
```

Suppose we are working on a machine that has enough memory to hold the rainy days, but not the complete dataset (imagine the dataset is a thousand times larger, and we have a laptop with 8 gigabytes of RAM). We need a way to find the filtered rows without having to hold the entire dataset in memory. The solution is to use the **chunksize** argument to read_csv, which will give us an iterator that will read that many rows at a time.

Let's try it with a chunksize of 10,000 rows. We will print just the number of rows in each chunk, and the total memory usage in megabytes:

```
# chunk_mem.py

for chunk in pd.read_csv("all_weather.csv", chunksize=10000):
    print(len(chunk), chunk.memory_usage(deep=True).sum() / 1_000_000)
```

```
10000 1.661572
10000 1.661536
10000 1.686056
10000 1.691777
10000 1.671863
10000 1.661825
5286 0.878134
```

We see that each chunk is 10,000 rows and occupies about 1.6 megabytes. The exception is the last chunk; because the total number of rows in the file isn't exactly divisible by 10,000 we get a small, partial chunk at the end. If we made both the dataset and the chunk size a thousand times larger, then this process would require only about 1.7 gigabytes of RAM - easily managable by our theoretical 8 gigabyte laptop.

Now we can do the actual processing. Inside the loop, we are dealing with a dataframe that has the exact same structure as the full dataset, so we can simply repeat our filter:

```
# chunk_filter.py

for chunk in pd.read_csv("all_weather.csv", chunksize=10000):
    chunk_rainy_days = chunk[chunk["Rainfall (mm)"] > 100]
    print(f"found {len(chunk_rainy_days)} rainy days")
```

```
found 330 rainy days
found 346 rainy days
found 343 rainy days
found 450 rainy days
found 372 rainy days
found 367 rainy days
found 205 rainy days
```

To end up with the complete collection of rainy days, all we have to do is append all of the filtered chunks to a list, then use `pd.concat` at the end to join them together:

```
# chunk_concat.py

chunk_rainy_days_list = []

for chunk in pd.read_csv("all_weather.csv", chunksize=10000):
    chunk_rainy_days = chunk[chunk["Rainfall (mm)"] > 100]
    chunk_rainy_days_list.append(chunk_rainy_days)

all_chunk_rainy_days = pd.concat(chunk_rainy_days_list)
all_chunk_rainy_days.head()
```

	City	Year	Day of year	Month	Day of month	Rainfall (mm)	Temperature (°C)
4	Berlin	1960	5	January	5	104.0	6.0
164	Berlin	1960	165	June	13	164.0	19.2
169	Berlin	1960	170	June	18	144.0	20.2
184	Berlin	1960	185	July	3	159.0	11.5
189	Berlin	1960	190	July	8	164.0	18.4

Finally, we can check that the dataframe we get using this approach is exactly the same as the one that results from filtering the entire dataset:

```
rainy_days.equals(all_chunk_rainy_days)
```

```
True
```

For some chunk processing operations we need a bit more complex code. Say we want to count how many rainy days occur in each month. We can use `value_counts` on the **Month** column for our rainy days, then turn the results into a dictionary:

```
# chunk_months.py

for chunk in pd.read_csv("all_weather.csv", chunksize=10000):
    chunk_rainy_days = chunk[chunk["Rainfall (mm)"] > 100]
    print(chunk_rainy_days["Month"].value_counts().to_dict())
```

```
{'August': 52, 'June': 51, 'May': 39, 'July': 32, 'September': 29, 'November': 26, 'April': 23, 'December': 20, 'March':
17, 'October': 15, 'February': 14, 'January': 12}
{'July': 58, 'August': 45, 'June': 44, 'May': 43, 'September': 28, 'December': 22, 'November': 22, 'October': 22, 'January
': 20, 'March': 18, 'February': 14, 'April': 10}
{'August': 44, 'July': 44, 'October': 37, 'September': 33, 'June': 33, 'November': 32, 'May': 24, 'January': 22, 'December
': 21, 'March': 19, 'February': 19, 'April': 15}
{'August': 53, 'October': 51, 'July': 49, 'September': 46, 'January': 42, 'December': 41, 'November': 37, 'June': 35, 'May
': 27, 'March': 25, 'February': 24, 'April': 20}
{'July': 45, 'November': 43, 'June': 42, 'September': 38, 'August': 36, 'December': 34, 'October': 34, 'March': 24, 'May':
 21, 'February': 20, 'April': 19, 'January': 16}
{'October': 50, 'May': 36, 'August': 35, 'September': 35, 'January': 34, 'June': 31, 'November': 31, 'December': 30, 'July
': 28, 'April': 27, 'March': 17, 'February': 13}
{'November': 30, 'August': 21, 'May': 20, 'January': 20, 'June': 18, 'December': 16, 'October': 16, 'July': 16, 'September
': 15, 'April': 12, 'February': 11, 'March': 10}
```

But to store the total count across all chunks we need a data structure that exists outside the loop, which we can use to sum the counts. The easiest way to do this for our example is to make an empty dictionary, then use it to store a running total of all counts:

```python
# chunk_dict.py

month_counts = {}

for chunk in pd.read_csv("all_weather.csv", chunksize=10000):
    chunk_rainy_days = chunk[chunk["Rainfall (mm)"] > 100]
    for month, count in (
        chunk_rainy_days["Month"].value_counts().to_dict().items()
    ):

        # look up the current count for the month, with default
        # of zero in case it's the first time we've seen this month
        current_month_count = month_counts.get(month, 0)

        # store the updated count, which is the current count
        # plus the count for this chunk
        month_counts[month] = current_month_count + count
month_counts
```

```
{'August': 286,
 'June': 254,
 'May': 210,
 'July': 272,
 'September': 224,
 'November': 221,
 'April': 126,
 'December': 184,
 'March': 130,
 'October': 225,
 'February': 115,
 'January': 166}
```

In general, code that relies on chunking will always have some kind of data structure outside the loop to accumulate the result we are looking for. In our previous example of filtering, it was the list that held the filtered rows; here it is a dictionary. For other problems, it may be anything from an output file to a single integer.

16.4.7 Other options

If you commonly work with data files that are much too large to fit in memory, then it might be time to look at another tool. A proper discussion is beyond the scope of this book, but two such tools are worth mentioning. **Dask** is a parallel computing library that provides the same interface as pandas, but for datasets that are held on disk rather than in memory, and are generally processed in parallel. This is a good option if you're already familiar with pandas, as you don't have to learn a new set of methods. This is an active area of research in data science, so expect rapid developments.

A more drastic option is to go outside the Python ecosystem entirely and switch to using a database (for example, **postgresql**). Database systems are designed to cope with truly massive datasets, and an approach that often works well is to store our data in a relational database, then write Python code which queries the database to find the information we require.

17 Using `FacetGrid` to lay out small multiples

In the second section of this book, we took a reasonably complete tour of seaborn and saw the various different chart types that were available. In this chapter, we'll look at a few specific situations for which the techniques we've seen before won't quite work.

17.1 Small multiples with arbitrary chart types

In the chapters covering seaborn we saw two functions that were capable of creating multiple charts by using the `row`, `col` and `hue` arguments to represent different columns in our dataframe. For the purposes of this discussion we'll think of `hue` as another example of plotting multiple datasets that happen to share the same axis. To recap: `relplot` can draw multiple scatter and line plots:

```
g = sns.relplot(
    data=euk[euk["Class"].isin(["Birds", "Fishes"])].dropna(),
    x="Number of genes",
    y="Number of proteins",
    col="Class",
    hue="Assembly status",
)
g.fig.suptitle(
    "Number of genes vs. Number of proteins for bird and fish genomes\nin different assembly status",
    y=1.1,
)
```

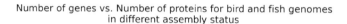
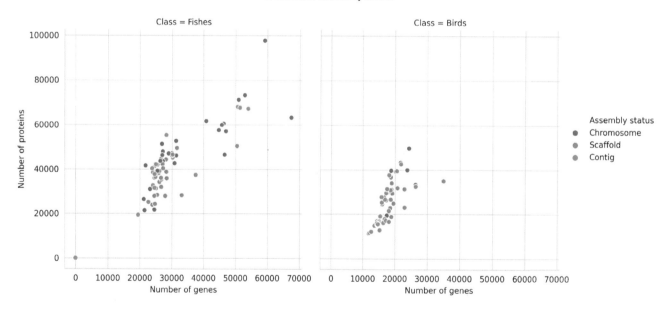

and `catplot` can draw multiple strip, swarm, box, violin, boxen, bar and point plots (all the plots that show distributions between categories):

```
g = sns.catplot(
    data=euk[euk["Class"].isin(["Birds", "Fishes"])].dropna(),
    x="Assembly status",
    y="Number of genes",
    kind="box",
    col="Class",
)
g.fig.suptitle(
    "Distribution of number of genes in bird and fish genomes\nin different assembly status",
    y=1.1,
)
```

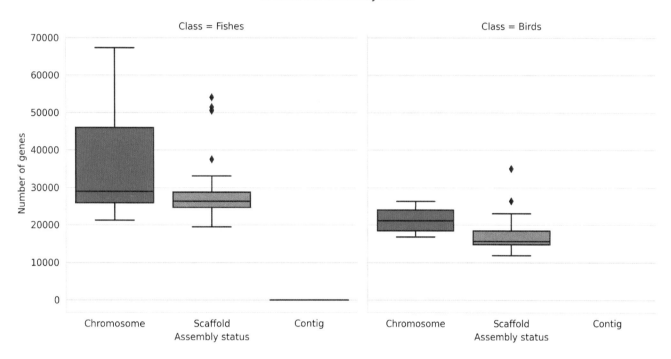

17.1.1 Using `FacetGrid` directly

What happens if we want to make a small multiple plot using a plotting function that doesn't understand `row`, `col` and `hue`? For example, let's take the first function we discussed, `distplot`, and try to draw a separate histogram of GC for each animal class. Attempting to pass the `col` and `col_wrap` arguments, as we did for `relplot`:

```
sns.distplot(
    euk[euk["Class"].isin(["Roundworms", "Flatworms", "Insects"])]["GC%"],
    col="Class",
    col_wrap=3,
)
```

doesn't work. We get an error: `distplot() got an unexpected keyword argument 'col'`.

Instead we need to make use of seaborn's `FacetGrid` object. This is a superb bit of API design that allows us to separate the two processes involved in making a small multiple plot: **splitting up the data into groups**, and **plotting each group**.

Drawing a small multiple plot using `FacetGrid` is a two step process. First we call `FacetGrid` with our `row`, `col` and `hue` arguments. The `FacetGrid` function is also where we set various aspects of the chart

---

that are not restricted to a single chart type - we set the size and shape with `height` and `aspect`, set the `palette` argument, and decide what order we want the rows, columns and colors. This effectively produces an empty grid without any actual plots:

```python
# make_grid.py

sns.FacetGrid(
    data=euk[euk["Class"].isin(["Roundworms", "Flatworms", "Insects"])],
    col="Class",
    col_wrap=3,
    aspect=1,
    height=4,
)
```

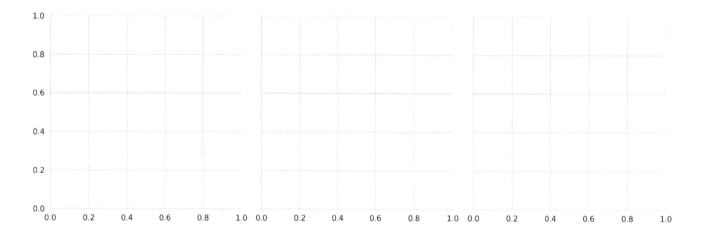

Next, we call the `map` function on the resulting object. The first argument to `map` is the name of the function that we want to use to draw each plot. The next arguments are the columns whose values we want to use, and any keyword arguments get passed to the plotting function.

Let's see what happens when we ask our grid to run `distplot` for each group, with values from the **gc** column and a style argument:

```python
# grid_histogram.py

# first lay out the grid
g = sns.FacetGrid(
    data=euk[euk["Class"].isin(["Roundworms", "Flatworms", "Insects"])],
    col="Class",
    aspect=1,
    height=4,
)

# then plot the charts
g.map(
    sns.distplot,  # this is the function that will draw each chart
    "GC%",  # this is the column that we want to plot
    color="purple",  # this is an extra argument to distplot
)
g.fig.suptitle("Distribution of GC% for each animal class", y=1.05)
```

17 Using `FacetGrid` to lay out small multiples

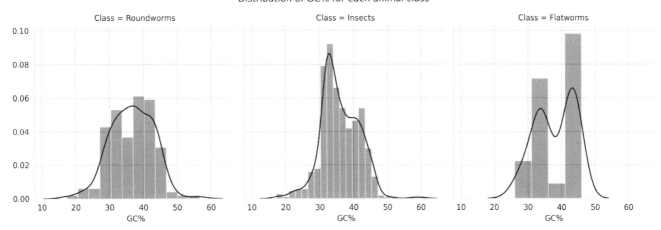

Distribution of GC% for each animal class

Although this two step process may seem a bit clumsy at first, it's actually extremely flexible, because it means that our grid layout logic is completely reusable. If we now want to draw a KDE plot for each animal class showing GC vs number of genes, we can leave the `FacetGrid` call exactly as it is, and just change the call to `map`:

```
# grid_kdeplot.py

# first lay out the grid
g = sns.FacetGrid(
    data=euk[euk["Class"].isin(["Roundworms", "Flatworms", "Insects"])],
    col="Class",
    aspect=1,
    height=4,
)

# then plot the charts
g.map(
    sns.kdeplot,
    "GC%",
    "Number of genes",
    cmap="OrRd",
    shade=True,
    shade_lowest=False,
)

g.fig.suptitle(
    "Density plot of GC% versus number of predicted genes for different animal classes",
    y=1.05,
)
```

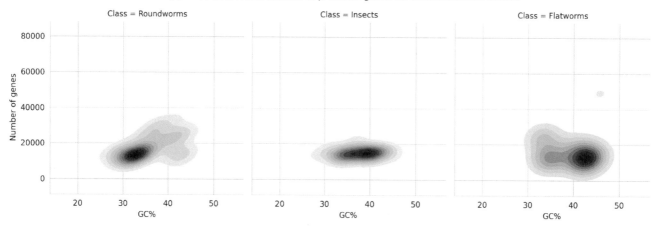

Density plot of GC% versus number of predicted genes for different animal classes

To actually draw the KDE plots we're using `kdeplot` directly rather than `jointplot` as we did before, since we don't want to draw marginal histograms. Notice that in the above code we need to pass both an X and Y column name, along with a few aesthetic arguments.

17.1.2 Mapping with a custom function

For very simple cases it's fine to use `map` as we're doing above, and pass the arguments required by the charting function directly to `map`. But as you can see in the above example it gets a bit awkward when we want to have more control over the chart.

For anything other than very simple examples, it's generally better to write a function that will take the data for a single chart and actually do the plotting. The dataframe will always be passed in a keyword argument called `data`, and the color in a keyword argument called `color`. If we've used the `hue` argument to `FacetGrid` then our function will also have to take a keyword argument called `label`.

Let's see how this will work. First we will write a function that takes a dataframe and a color, and plots a single chart:

```
# plot_single.py

def plot_gc_genes_contourmap(data, color):
    sns.kdeplot(
        data.dropna()["GC%"],
        data.dropna()["Number of genes"],
        cmap="OrRd",
        shade=True,
        shade_lowest=False,
    )
```

Notice that although our function takes a `color` argument, it doesn't actually use it when drawing the plot.

Now we can try calling our function on the entire dataset. Since we know that the `color` argument won't ever be used, we can just pass `None`:

```
plot_gc_genes_contourmap(euk, None)
```

17 Using `FacetGrid` *to lay out small multiples*

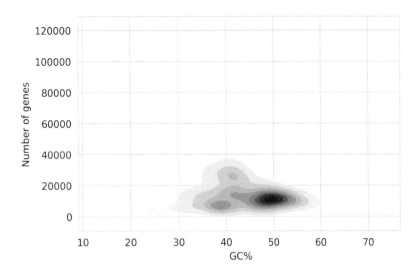

Once we're happy with the way that the chart looks, we can set up our `FacetGrid` as before, but rather than calling `map` we can call `map_dataframe` and give our function name:

```
# grid_function.py

# first lay out the grid
g = sns.FacetGrid(
    data=euk[euk["Class"].isin(["Roundworms", "Flatworms", "Insects"])],
    col="Class",
    aspect=1,
    height=4,
)

g.map_dataframe(plot_gc_genes_contourmap)
g.set_axis_labels("GC%", "Number of genes")

g.fig.suptitle(
    "Density plot of GC% versus number of predicted genes for different animal classes",
    y=1.05,
)
```

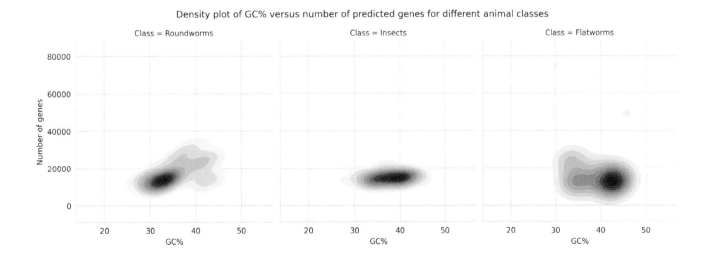

Notice that `map_dataframe` removes the axis labels from the individual plots, since we only need them at the edges, so we have to set them explicitly using `set_axis_labels`.

This seems like a lot of extra work to get the same plot that we saw before! but now that we have everything controlled with a single function, we can do things that would be very difficult to do just using `map`. We can effectively run arbitrary code for each individual plot.

For example, let's say that we want to overlay a regression line on each of our contour plots. We can go back to our function definition, add a call to `regplot` to draw the regression line, and test it on a single chart:

```
# custom_regression.py

def plot_gc_genes_contourmap(data, color):

    # first draw the contour plot
    sns.kdeplot(
        data.dropna()["GC%"],
        data.dropna()["Number of genes"],
        cmap="OrRd",
        shade=True,
        shade_lowest=False,
    )

    # then draw the regression line only
    # no confidence intervals
    sns.regplot(
        data=data,
        x="GC%",
        y="Number of genes",
        scatter=None,
        ci=None,
        color="lightblue",
    )

plot_gc_genes_contourmap(euk, None)
```

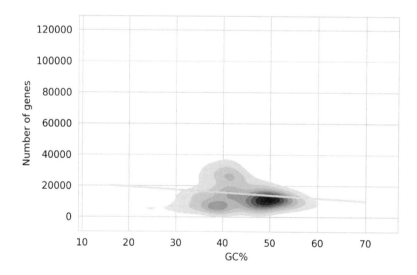

Even though the two plotting functions - `kdeplot` and `regplot` - have completely different arguments and options, this all works because we can call them separately inside our function. Now when we map our function onto the FacetGrid:

```
# grid_custom_regression.py

# first lay out the grid
g = sns.FacetGrid(
    data=euk[euk["Class"].isin(["Roundworms", "Flatworms", "Insects"])],
    col="Class",
    aspect=1,
    height=4,
)

g.map_dataframe(plot_gc_genes_contourmap)
g.set_axis_labels("GC%", "Number of genes")

g.fig.suptitle(
    "Density plot and linear regression of GC% versus number of predicted genes\n for different animal classes",
    y=1.1,
)
None
```

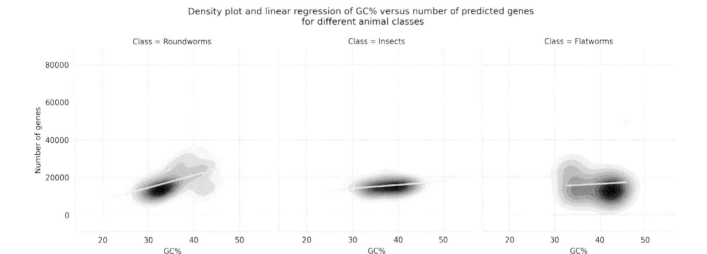

we get our custom contour-plus-regression plot repeated across each subset of the data.

One more example, just to stress the point. Because in our function we have access to the entire dataframe, not just the the values we are plotting, we can use all the pandas tools that we already know about. Let's add some code to our function that will find the 5 largest genomes by sorting on size, then draw a scatter plot of just those 5:

```
# custom_overlay.py

def plot_gc_genes_contourmap(data, color):
    sns.kdeplot(
        data.dropna()["GC%"],
        data.dropna()["Number of genes"],
        cmap="OrRd",
        shade=True,
        shade_lowest=False,
    )

    biggest = data.dropna().sort_values("Size (Mb)").tail(5)

    sns.scatterplot(
        data=biggest, x="GC%", y="Number of genes", color="darkgreen"
    )

plot_gc_genes_contourmap(euk, None)
```

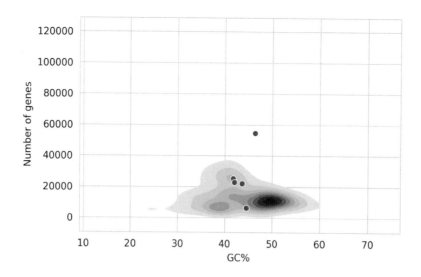

Once again we have designed a kind of custom contour-plus-largest-genomes plot, and using a `FacetGrid` allows us to easily draw small multiples of it:

```
# grid_custom_overlay.py

# first lay out the grid
g = sns.FacetGrid(
    data=euk[euk["Class"].isin(["Roundworms", "Flatworms", "Insects"])],
    col="Class",
    aspect=1,
    height=4,
)

g.map_dataframe(plot_gc_genes_contourmap)
g.set_axis_labels("GC%", "Number of genes")

g.fig.suptitle(
    "Density plot of GC% versus number of predicted genes plus 5 largest genomes\n for different animal classes",
    y=1.1,
)
None
```

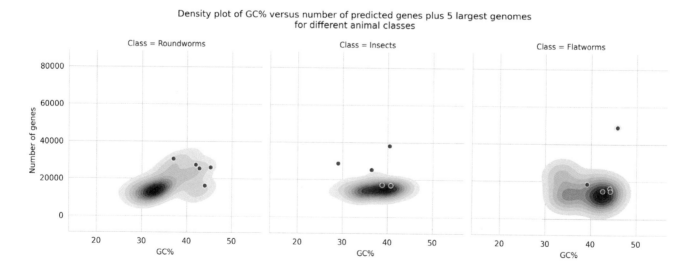

The beauty of this API design is the separation of responsibilities in the code. The `FacetGrid` is responsible for splitting up the dataset into groups, determining the layout of the charts and their size and aspect, and setting the palette. The charting function is responsible for taking a single subset of the data and drawing the appropriate chart. This approach lends itself very well to code reuse. For example, by changing the `FacetGrid` we can easily apply the same custom chart type to a different subset of the data:

```python
# large_grid_overlay.py

# first lay out the grid
g = sns.FacetGrid(
    data=euk[
        (euk["Class"].isin(["Ascomycetes", "Basidiomycetes"]))
        & (euk["Publication year"].between(2010, 2013))
    ].dropna(),
    row="Class",
    col="Publication year",
    aspect=1,
    height=3,
)

g.map_dataframe(plot_gc_genes_contourmap)
g.set_axis_labels("GC%", "Number of genes")

# we need titles with a newline otherwise they are too long
g.set_titles("{row_name}\n{col_name}")

g.fig.suptitle(
    """Density plot of GC%
versus number of predicted genes plus 5 largest genomes
for fungal classes published between 2010 and 2015""",
    y=1.15,
)
```

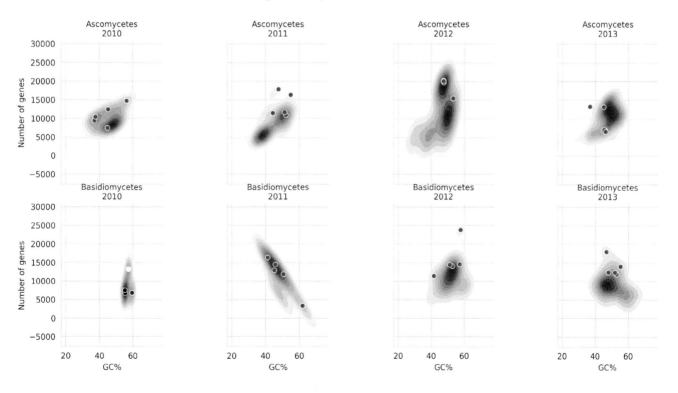

17.1.3 Mapping using hue

In the above example, our plotting function never actually made use of the `color` argument, even though it had to accept it. Let's now look at an example that does use color. Recall one of the very first complex plots that we made with seaborn - a KDE plot showing the distribution of GC% in genomes belonging to each kingdom. To draw the plot, we had to call the plotting function `distplot` inside a loop, and also do some filtering using pandas:

```
plt.figure(figsize=(8, 4))

for kingdom in euk["Kingdom"].unique():

    one_kingdom = euk[euk["Kingdom"] == kingdom]

    sns.distplot(one_kingdom["GC%"].dropna(), hist=False, label=kingdom)

plt.title(
    "Distribution of GC percentage for genomes\nbelonging to different kingdoms"
)
```

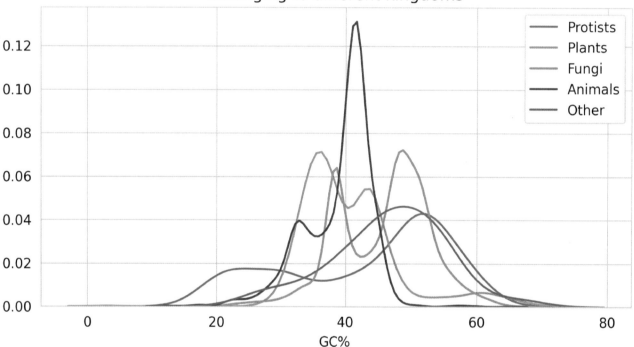

Now that we know about `FacetGrid`, we are in a position to make this plot much more easily. Just as in our earlier example, we'll first write a function that will take a dataframe, a color and a label and generate a single plot, then test it:

```
# draw_one_distribution.py

def draw_distribution(data, color, label):
    sns.distplot(data["GC%"].dropna(), hist=False, label=label, color=color)

draw_distribution(euk, "red", "all genomes")
```

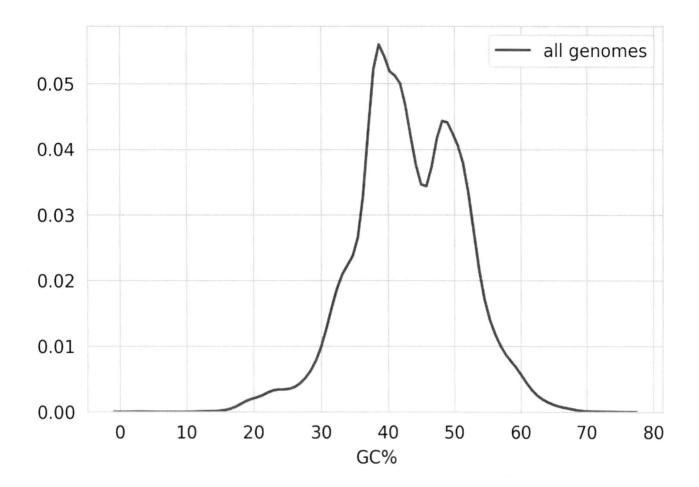

The code here is fairly simple: all we need to do is extract the column we want to plot and pass it to `distplot`, passing on the `color` and `label` arguments and adding `hist=False` to suppress the bars.

Now to create our plot from before, we set up our `FacetGrid` using only `hue`, and use `map_dataframe` to call our function:

```
# grid_distribution.py

g = sns.FacetGrid(data=euk, hue="Kingdom", aspect=2, height=4)

g.map_dataframe(draw_distribution)
g.set_axis_labels("GC%")
g.add_legend()
g.fig.suptitle(
    "Distribution of GC percentage for genomes\nbelonging to different kingdoms",
    y=1.1,
)
```

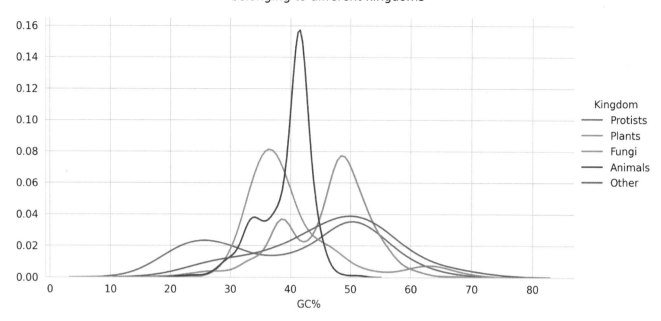

Distribution of GC percentage for genomes
belonging to different kingdoms

Because we haven't used `row` or `col`, we get a single chart, so it might seem odd to think of this as a grid. But it's still plotting multiple datasets - they just happen to be separated by color rather than by row or column. Notice that we have to manually add a legend to the plot with `add_legend`, since color is now significant.

Once we have our plotting function set up, we can use it for many different kinds of plots just by altering the call to `FacetGrid`. For example, we can filter the data just to look at fungal genomes, make a separate plot for each year, and change the palette:

```
# complex_grid_distribution.py

data = euk[
    (euk["Kingdom"] == "Fungi") & (euk["Publication year"].between(2010, 2017))
]

g = sns.FacetGrid(
    data=data,
    hue="Class",
    col="Publication year",
    col_wrap=4,
    aspect=1,
    height=3,
    palette="Set2",
)

g.map_dataframe(draw_distribution)
g.set_axis_labels("GC%")
g.add_legend()
g.fig.suptitle(
    "Distribution of GC percentage for fungal genomes in different classes\nfor years between 2010 and 2017",
    y=1.1,
)
```

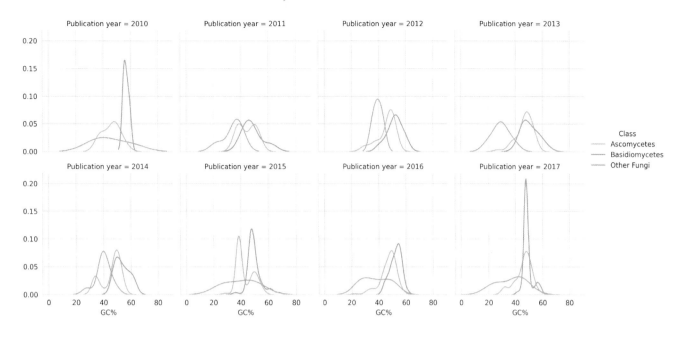

Distribution of GC percentage for fungal genomes in different classes
for years between 2010 and 2017

and end up with a very different figure. But notice that it uses the exact same `draw_distribution` function to do the actual plotting.

17.1.4 Mapping with heatmaps

The trickiest kind of chart to use in a `FacetGrid` is a heatmap or clustermap. As an example, let's take the weather data that we assembled in the previous chapter and set the categorical months:

```
# set_up_weather.py

weather = pd.read_csv("all_weather.csv")

from pandas.api.types import CategoricalDtype

months = ["January", "February", "March", "April", "May", "June", "July",
    "August", "September", "October", "November", "December"]

weather["Month"] = weather["Month"].astype(
    CategoricalDtype(categories=months, ordered=True)
)
weather.head()
```

	City	Year	Day of year	Month	Day of month	Rainfall (mm)	Temperature (°C)
0	Berlin	1960	1	January	1	4.0	6.4
1	Berlin	1960	2	January	2	25.0	8.1
2	Berlin	1960	3	January	3	0.0	5.4
3	Berlin	1960	4	January	4	0.0	3.9
4	Berlin	1960	5	January	5	104.0	6.0

Imagine we want to produce a grid of heatmaps, one for each month. Each individual heatmap will show the mean temperature for each year in each city. We will tackle this in three steps. First, we have to figure out how to get the data into the correct wide format for plotting:

```
(weather.groupby(["City", "Year"])["Temperature (°C)"].mean().unstack(1))
```

Year City	1960	1961	1962	...	2017	2018	2019
Berlin	9.366120	9.829041	8.222192	...	10.712055	13.064474	NaN
Edinburgh	8.916944	9.002192	8.158333	...	NaN	NaN	NaN
London	10.617760	10.989041	9.396712	...	12.343562	13.392434	NaN

Next, we write a function that will take a dataframe, transform it into wide format, then plot a single heatmap. As usual, we can test the function by plotting the entire dataframe, even though the resulting plot doesn't make sense as it mixes up the measurements for all twelve months:

```
# plot_single_heatmap.py

def plot_temperature(data, color):
    sns.heatmap(
        data.groupby(["City", "Year"])["Temperature (°C)"]
        .mean()
        .unstack(1)
        .sort_index(ascending=False),
        cmap="hot",
    )

plot_temperature(weather, None)
```

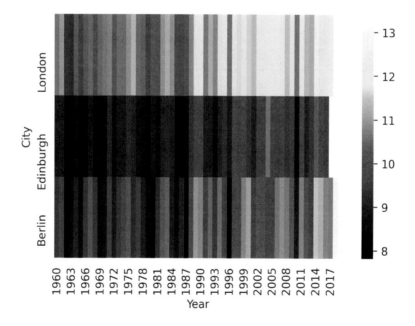

Notice that the data transformation has to happen inside the function, since `FacetGrid` can only work on the data in long form. We will not worry about the size or shape of the heatmap in our function - that will eventually all be controlled by the `FacetGrid`.

Now let's see what happens when we make a `FacetGrid` using month as the column, and map our function:

*17 Using **FacetGrid** to lay out small multiples*

```
# grid_heatmap.py

g = sns.FacetGrid(weather, col="Month", col_wrap=4, aspect=2, height=2)

g.map_dataframe(plot_temperature)

g.fig.suptitle("Mean monthly temperature for three cities by year", y=1.05)
```

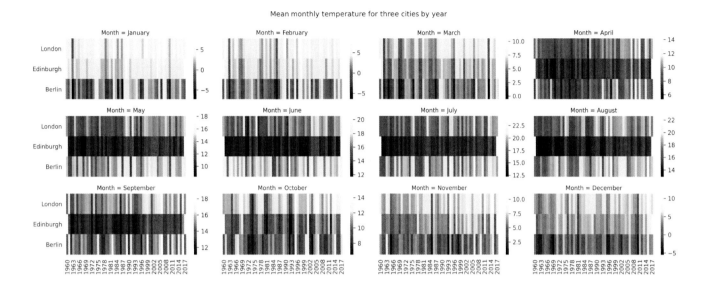

Just as we wanted, we have a grid of heatmaps. One problem that occurs here is that because the temperature scale is set using a colorbar rather than an axis, seaborn has no way to synchronize them across plots. In our figure, each heatmap has a different color scale, making it very difficult to compare months. The solution is to explicitly set the min and max in the function:

```
# grid_heatmap_scale.py

def plot_temperature(data, color):
    sns.heatmap(
        data.groupby(["City", "Year"])["Temperature (°C)"]
        .mean()
        .unstack(1)
        .sort_index(ascending=False),
        vmin=-10,
        vmax=30,
        cmap="hot",
    )

g = sns.FacetGrid(weather, col="Month", col_wrap=4, aspect=2, height=1.5)

g.map_dataframe(plot_temperature)

g.fig.suptitle("Mean monthly temperature for three cities by year", y=1.05)
```

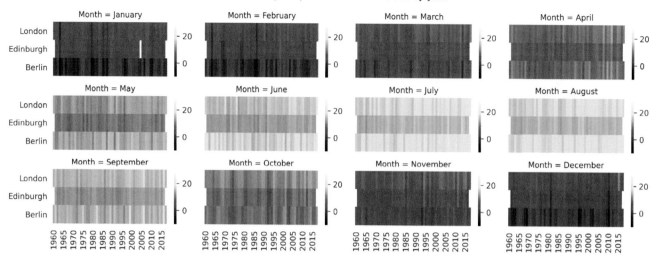

Mean monthly temperature for three cities by year

Readers with a bit of prior programming experience might dislike having the minimum and maximum temperature values hard coded in the function. With the code above, if we want to try different values for the minimum and maximum temperature we have to edit the function. It would be more elegant to have the min and max as arguments to the function:

```
# plot_with_args.py

def plot_temperature(data, color, vmin, vmax):
    sns.heatmap(
        data.groupby(["City", "Year"])["Temperature (°C)"]
        .mean()
        .unstack(1)
        .sort_index(ascending=False),
        vmin=vmin,
        vmax=vmax,
        cmap="hot",
    )
```

which we can pass by adding them as keyword arguments to `map_dataframe`. This allows us to, for instance, determine the min and max by taking them directly from the data:

```
# grid_with_args.py

g = sns.FacetGrid(weather, col="Month", col_wrap=4, aspect=2, height=1.5)

g.map_dataframe(
    plot_temperature,
    vmin=weather["Temperature (°C)"].min(),
    vmax=weather["Temperature (°C)"].max(),
)

g.fig.suptitle("Mean monthly temperature for three cities by year", y=1.05)
```

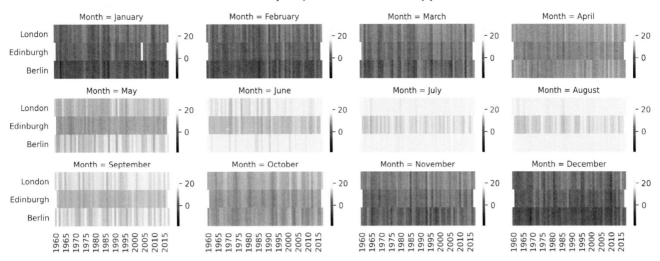

Mean monthly temperature for three cities by year

Finally, we might want to avoid repeating the color scale for each plot and just display it once. This requires a little bit of work. We have to add a colorbar axis argument to our function, which it will pass to `heatmap` to determine where the colorbar gets drawn:

```python
# plot_with_cbar.py

def plot_temperature(data, color, vmin, vmax, cbar_axis):
    sns.heatmap(
        data.groupby(["City", "Year"])["Temperature (°C)"]
        .mean()
        .unstack(1)
        .sort_index(ascending=False),
        vmin=vmin,
        vmax=vmax,
        cmap="hot",
        cbar_ax=cbar_axis,
    )
```

Then in the part of the code which sets up the grid, we have to explicitly make a new axis for the colorbar. The argument for `add_axes` is a list of coordinates which set the distance from the left, the distance from the bottom, the width and the height of the axis, all measured in fractions of the whole figure size.

We will place our colorbar to the right of the heatmaps by putting it 1.05 units from the left, and make it 0.02 of the width of the whole figure. We'll make the height 0.6 of the height of the whole figure, and center it vertically by putting it 0.2 units from the bottom.

```
# grid_with_cbar.py

g = sns.FacetGrid(weather, col="Month", col_wrap=4, aspect=2, height=1.5)

cbar_ax = g.fig.add_axes(
    [
        1.05,  # distance from the left of the figure
        0.2,   # distance from the bottom of the figure
        0.02,  # width of the axis
        0.6,
    ]  # height of the axis
)

g.map_dataframe(
    plot_temperature,
    vmin=weather["Temperature (°C)"].min(),
    vmax=weather["Temperature (°C)"].max(),
    cbar_axis=cbar_ax,
)

g.fig.suptitle(
    "Mean daily temperature in three cities between 1960 and 2017", y=1.1
)
g.fig.suptitle("Mean monthly temperature for three cities by year", y=1.05)
```

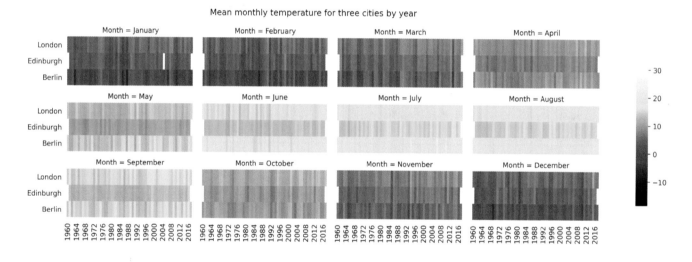

The code required to produce this figure is certainly one of the most complicated we have seen, but it is not too hard to follow, as each part has a well defined job.

17 Using **FacetGrid** *to lay out small multiples*

18 Unexpected behaviors

In this book we have relied on packages like pandas, seaborn, numpy and matplotlib to do the work of manipulating data and drawing charts. Because these packages are large, complex pieces of code, and are under constant development, there are quite a few situations in which they don't do what we expect. Rather than refer to these as "bugs" - which is really a decision for the package maintainers to make - we will instead call them "unexpected behavior".

In this chapter, we'll look at the unexpected behaviors we are most likely to run into when using the packages in our work. We'll consider each package in turn, and for each example will investigate the cause and try to find a workaround. All of the packages that we'll be considering have publicly available issue trackers, so where possible we will find a link to an issue that describes the problem so that we can monitor any progress in fixing it.

If you find that these issues affect your code, it might be useful to subscribe to notifications about them. At the time of writing, all four of the packages we will discuss have issue trackers hosted on Github, so subscribing is simply a question of clicking the "Subscribe" button on the right of the issue page.

18.1 Missing groups in `groupby`

This is the issue that we run into most commonly when working with categorical data, and is also one of the most subtle to explain. Let's start by reminding ourselves of how **groupby** works. If we group on a column name, then **groupby** figures out the group labels by taking the unique values in that column. So if we group by kingdom, we will get a group for each unique value in the kingdom column:

```
euk.groupby("Kingdom").size()
```

```
Kingdom
Animals    2181
Fungi      4494
Other        30
Plants      870
Protists    727
dtype: int64
```

If we filter the dataframe so that some kingdom values don't appear, they also disappear from the list of groups:

```
# missing_groups.py

# the only genomes bigger than 2Gb are plants and animals
euk[euk["Size (Mb)"] > 2000].groupby("Kingdom").size()
```

```
Kingdom
Animals    560
Plants      66
dtype: int64
```

This is a natural consequence of the fact that the groups are determined directly from the data.

However, when the column we are grouping by has a categorical data type, pandas uses the category labels to figure out the groups, so even when some of the counts are zero, the groups still show up:

```
# make a categorical version of the kingdom column
euk["Kingdom category"] = euk["Kingdom"].astype("category")

# repeat the filter and count
euk[euk["Size (Mb)"] > 2000].groupby("Kingdom category").size()
```

```
Kingdom category
Animals     560
Fungi         0
Other         0
Plants       66
Protists      0
dtype: int64
```

In most cases this is exactly the behavior we want (and if we don't want it, we can override it with the `observed=True` argument). To see why this is useful, imagine taking our weather data, picking a single city and decade:

```
# filter_berlin.py

# read in weather data and convert months to categories

weather = pd.read_csv("all_weather.csv")

from pandas.api.types import CategoricalDtype

months = ["January", "February", "March", "April", "May", "June", "July", "August",
    "September", "October", "November", "December"]

weather["Month"] = weather["Month"].astype(
    CategoricalDtype(categories=months, ordered=True)
)

# get just weather in Berlin during the 1960s
berlin = weather[
    (weather["City"] == "Berlin") & (weather["Year"].between(1960, 1969))
]
```

then finding just the very hot days. For this discussion, we'll say that very hot days are the days where the mean temperature is greater than 24 degrees:

```
# filter_warm_days

warm_days = berlin[berlin["Temperature (°C)"] > 24]
warm_days.head()
```

	City	Year	Day of year	Month	Day of month	Rainfall (mm)	Temperature (°C)
212	Berlin	1960	213	July	31	0.0	25.0
238	Berlin	1960	239	August	26	0.0	24.8
239	Berlin	1960	240	August	27	5.0	24.2
542	Berlin	1961	177	June	26	0.0	25.1
547	Berlin	1961	182	July	1	0.0	24.8

Once we have our very hot days, we can count how many of them there were in each year:

```
# count_warm_days.py

year_count = warm_days.groupby("Year").size()
year_count
```

18 Unexpected behaviors

```
Year
1960     3
1961     3
1963     8
1964    10
1966     5
1967     5
1968     4
1969    14
dtype: int64
```

This is easy to interpret, and allows us to see that 1964 and 1969 were much warmer than other years in the decade. But if we look closely at the index, we see that some years are missing. 1962 and 1965 don't appear in the output, because there were no very hot days in those years, so they don't appear in the filtered data.

These missing zero-count groups can lead us to incorrect conclusions if we don't notice them. For example, we may try to count the number of years that had fewer than four warm days:

```
len(year_count[year_count < 4])
```

```
2
```

The correct answer is actually 4 (1960, 1961, 1962 and 1965), but we get only 2 because 1962 and 1965 are missing from the counts. This behavior isn't unique to **size** - we will get the same for any type of aggregation

The same problem can arise when we try to visualize our data. Rather than using **groupby**, we may decide to use seaborn to do a count plot of the years for our warm days:

```
# plot_warm_days.py

g = sns.catplot(data=warm_days, x="Year", kind="count", color="red", aspect=2)

g.fig.suptitle(
    "Number of warm days in Berlin for each year beteween 1960 and 1969", y=1.1
)
```

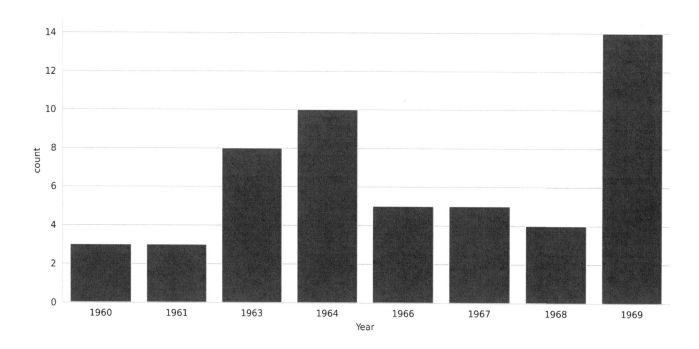
Number of warm days in Berlin for each year beteween 1960 and 1969

As with the tabular output, this clearly shows the warm years, but looking at the X axis labels we see that 1962 and 1965 are missing. The cause is exactly as we saw above: `catplot` uses `groupby` internally to figure out which bars to plot.

This isn't too tricky to spot with a small dataset, but becomes progressively harder as our dataset size increases. For example, if we repeat the analysis for all years:

```
# plot_all_warm_days.py

all_years_warm_days = weather[
    (weather["City"] == "Berlin") & (weather["Temperature (°C)"] > 24)
]

g = sns.catplot(
    data=all_years_warm_days, x="Year", kind="count", color="red", aspect=3
)

plt.xticks(rotation=45)

g.fig.suptitle(
    "Number of warm days in Berlin for each year beteween 1960 and 2018", y=1.1
)
```

18 Unexpected behaviors

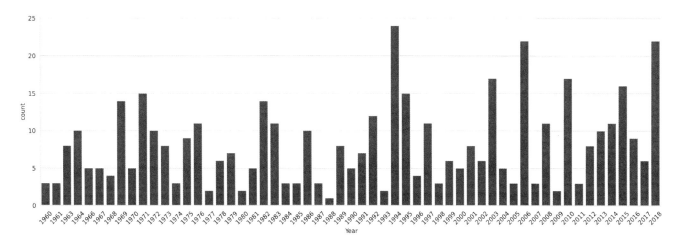
Number of warm days in Berlin for each year beteween 1960 and 2018

it's not easy to see from a glance that some of the years are missing - it looks like there are at least some warm days in every year.

18.1.1 Fixing the problem

There are a couple of ways to avoid this problem once we know about it. For a single series, we can force a specific set of index values using **reindex**. In this case we know the range of years that we want, so we can just use a **range**:

```
warm_days.groupby("Year").size().reindex(range(1960, 1970))
```

```
Year
1960    3.0
1961    3.0
1962    NaN
1963    8.0
1964    10.0
1965    NaN
1966    5.0
1967    5.0
1968    4.0
1969    14.0
dtype: float64
```

This adds back the missing years with missing data as the value, which we can easily fill:

```
warm_days.groupby("Year").size().reindex(range(1960, 1970)).fillna(0)
```

```
Year
1960    3.0
1961    3.0
1962    0.0
1963    8.0
1964    10.0
1965    0.0
1966    5.0
1967    5.0
1968    4.0
1969    14.0
dtype: float64
```

Notice an annoying side effect here: because of the missing data, pandas has converted the counts to floating point numbers, which we have to fix explicitly:

```
(
    warm_days.groupby("Year")
    .size()
    .reindex(range(1960, 1970))
    .fillna(0)
    .astype("Int64")
)
```

```
Year
1960     3
1961     3
1962     0
1963     8
1964    10
1965     0
1966     5
1967     5
1968     4
1969    14
dtype: Int64
```

A better fix would be to make year a category:

```
# year_to_category.py

berlin["Year"] = berlin["Year"].astype("category")
berlin["Year"]
```

```
0       1960
1       1960
2       1960
3       1960
4       1960
        ...
3648    1969
3649    1969
3650    1969
3651    1969
3652    1969
Name: Year, Length: 3653, dtype: category
Categories (10, int64): [1960, 1961, 1962, 1963, ..., 1966, 1967, 1968, 1969]
```

Notice that, unlike the months, pandas can figure out the correct order for the years, so we don't need to specify it.

Now when we do our warm day year counting code again:

```
# filter_with_category.py

warm_days = berlin[berlin["Temperature (°C)"] > 24]

warm_days.groupby("Year").size()
```

```
Year
1960     3
1961     3
1962     0
1963     8
1964    10
1965     0
1966     5
1967     5
1968     4
1969    14
dtype: int64
```

1962 and 1965 are included in the count. Unlike the solution involving **reindex**, we don't need to explicitly fill in the zeros.

This also fixes the behaviour of **catplot**:

```
# plot_with_category.py

g = sns.catplot(data=warm_days, x="Year", kind="count", color="red", aspect=2)

g.fig.suptitle(
    "Number of warm days in Berlin for each year beteween 1960 and 1970", y=1.1
)
```

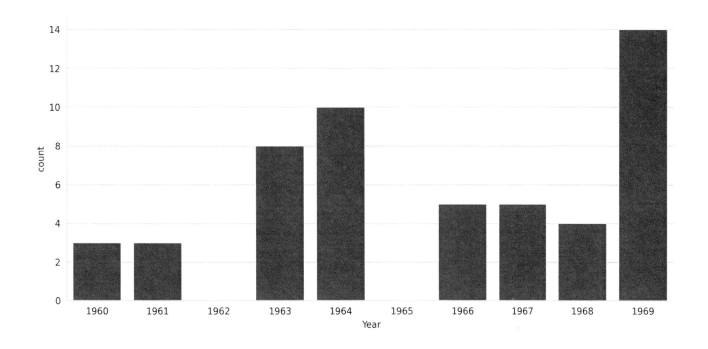

Number of warm days in Berlin for each year beteween 1960 and 1970

18.2 Summing a series returns 0 by default if all the values are missing

If we take a series of numbers and ask for the sum, the answer is usually just as we expect:

```
pd.Series([1, 2, 3, 4]).sum()
```

```
10
```

However, what should the correct answer be when all of the values in the series are unknown?

```
# make_missing.py

#  a series of four missing values
missing = pd.Series([pd.NA] * 4)
missing
```

```
0    <NA>
1    <NA>
2    <NA>
3    <NA>
dtype: object
```

Given the way that pandas generally propagates missing data, it seems natural to assume that any aggregation where all of the input values are unknown will result in a missing data value, and indeed nearly all aggregation methods work that way:

```
missing.mean(), missing.max(), missing.min(), missing.std()
```

```
(nan, nan, nan, nan)
```

The exception is **sum()**, which returns zero for a series of unknown values:

```
missing.sum(min)
```

This can lead to some subtle errors in data analysis. To explore them, we'll use our eukaryote genome dataset and select just the mammal species that have at least three sequenced genomes:

```
# select_genomes.py

mammals = (
    euk[euk["Class"] == "Mammals"]
    .groupby("Species")
    .filter(lambda x: len(x) >= 3)
)
mammals
```

	Species	Kingdom	Class	...	Publication year	Assembly status	Kingdom category
44	Homo sapiens	Animals	Mammals	...	2002	Chromosome	Animals
45	Mus musculus	Animals	Mammals	...	2004	Chromosome	Animals
65	Rattus norvegicus	Animals	Mammals	...	2002	Chromosome	Animals
74	Bos taurus	Animals	Mammals	...	2017	Chromosome	Animals
75	Ovis aries	Animals	Mammals	...	2017	Chromosome	Animals
...	...	...	...	...	...	...	...
7783	Homo sapiens	Animals	Mammals	...	2017	Scaffold	Animals
7784	Homo sapiens	Animals	Mammals	...	2017	Scaffold	Animals
7789	Homo sapiens	Animals	Mammals	...	2017	Scaffold	Animals
7790	Homo sapiens	Animals	Mammals	...	2017	Scaffold	Animals
7793	Homo sapiens	Animals	Mammals	...	2017	Scaffold	Animals

Now let's calculate the total number of predicted genes across all genomes for each species:

```
# sum_predicted_genes.py

mammals.groupby("Species")["Number of genes"].sum()
```

18 Unexpected behaviors

```
Species
Bos taurus                        61343
Bubalus bubalis                   33931
Callithrix jacchus                35188
Camelus dromedarius               24470
Canis lupus familiaris            36809
                                    ...
Pongo abelii                      34030
Rattus norvegicus                 75738
Rhinolophus ferrumequinum             0
Sus scrofa                        30173
Tursiops truncatus                23994
Name: Number of genes, Length: 27, dtype: Int64
```

One of these values obviously stands out: it appears that *Rhinolophus ferrumequinum* has a total of zero predicted genes. If we look at the rows for this species in the dataframe:

```
mammals[mammals["Species"] == "Rhinolophus ferrumequinum"][
    ["Species", "Size (Mb)", "Number of genes"]
]
```

	Species	Size (Mb)	Number of genes
768	Rhinolophus ferrumequinum	1514.62	<NA>
4696	Rhinolophus ferrumequinum	2075.77	<NA>
5214	Rhinolophus ferrumequinum	1926.44	<NA>

we see that there are three genomes, all of which have an unknown number of predicted genes. Rather than zero, it would be more accurate to say that the total number of predicted genes is unknown.

In this case, the problem's easy to spot. But once we start using **sum** in a way that doesn't show us the exact result, it can be harder. For example, let's take all the mammals with at least three genomes and figure out which ones have fewer than 30,000 total predicted genes:

```
(
    mammals.groupby("Species")
    .filter(lambda x: x["Number of genes"].sum() < 30000)["Species"]
    .unique()
)
```

```
<StringArray>
[ 'Ornithorhynchus anatinus',  'Ictidomys tridecemlineatus',
        'Tursiops truncatus',        'Eschrichtius robustus',
          'Castor canadensis',                  'Capra hircus',
       'Camelus dromedarius',   'Rhinolophus ferrumequinum',
               'Lycaon pictus']
Length: 9, dtype: string
```

Because in this expression we never see the results of the **sum** directly, it's hard to spot that for three of the species, the total is zero:

```
(
    mammals.groupby("Species")
    .filter(lambda x: x["Number of genes"].sum() < 30000)
    .groupby("Species")["Number of genes"]
    .sum()
)
```

```
Species
Camelus dromedarius        24470
Capra hircus               28404
Castor canadensis          27186
Eschrichtius robustus          0
Ictidomys tridecemlineatus 25998
Lycaon pictus                  0
Ornithorhynchus anatinus   22225
Rhinolophus ferrumequinum      0
Tursiops truncatus         23994
Name: Number of genes, dtype: Int64
```

and the reason why it's zero is that those species havee all missing data for their numbers of predicted genes:

```
(
    mammals.groupby("Species")
    .filter(lambda x: x["Number of genes"].sum() < 30000)
    .groupby("Species")["Number of genes"]
    .count()  # count returns the number of non-missing values in a series
)
```

```
Species
Camelus dromedarius        1
Capra hircus               1
Castor canadensis          1
Eschrichtius robustus      0
Ictidomys tridecemlineatus 1
Lycaon pictus              0
Ornithorhynchus anatinus   1
Rhinolophus ferrumequinum  0
Tursiops truncatus         1
Name: Number of genes, dtype: int64
```

18.2.1 Fixing the problem

The easiest fix for this behavior is simply to drop any rows with missing numbers of genes before we do any type of aggregation. Rather than just using **dropna**, which would remove rows with missing data in any column, we will be a bit more precise and use **subset** to make sure that we only remove rows with missing data in the column that we are interested in:

```
(
    mammals.dropna(subset=["Number of genes"])
    .groupby("Species")
    .filter(lambda x: x["Number of genes"].sum() < 30000)
    .groupby("Species")["Number of genes"]
    .sum()
)
```

```
Species
Camelus dromedarius        24470
Capra hircus               28404
Castor canadensis          27186
Ictidomys tridecemlineatus 25998
Ornithorhynchus anatinus   22225
Tursiops truncatus         23994
Name: Number of genes, dtype: Int64
```

Now when we take all the mammals with at least three genomes and figure out which ones have fewer than 30,000 total predicted genes:

```
(
    mammals.dropna(subset=["Number of genes"])
    .groupby("Species")
    .filter(lambda x: x["Number of genes"].fillna(0).sum(min_count=1) < 30000)[
        "Species"
    ]
    .unique()
)
```

```
<StringArray>
[  'Ornithorhynchus anatinus', 'Ictidomys tridecemlineatus',
        'Tursiops truncatus',        'Castor canadensis',
            'Capra hircus',        'Camelus dromedarius']
Length: 6, dtype: string
```

we just see the species which have at least one measured number of predicted genes.

18.3 Missing points can affect size and hue with seaborn

This odd behavior affects scatter plots in seaborn where some of the data are missing. To explain it, let's look at a small dataset - just the amphibian genomes:

```
# get_amphibians.py

amphibians = euk[euk["Class"] == "Amphibians"][
    ["Species", "Size (Mb)", "GC%", "Number of genes"]
]
amphibians
```

	Species	Size (Mb)	GC%	Number of genes
72	Xenopus tropicalis	1440.400	40.5404	26496
73	Xenopus laevis	2718.430	40.2325	36776
210	Ambystoma mexicanum	32396.400	46.5211	<NA>
1089	Rhinella marina	2551.760	NaN	<NA>
1599	Rana catesbeiana	6250.350	43.6998	22238
1947	Nanorana parkeri	2053.870	42.7000	21171
4903	Ambystoma mexicanum	353.835	31.3000	<NA>

As we might expect from our previous investigations of this dataset, some of the values are missing. In particular, note that the first genome listed for *Ambystoma mexicanum* is very large, and doesn't have a number of predicted genes.

Now, what do we expect to happen when we draw a scatter plot of these seven genomes to show the relationship between GC% and number of genes? The three genomes where the number of genes is missing are simply left off the chart, and only the four remaining genomes are plotted:

```
g = sns.relplot(data=amphibians, x="Number of genes", y="GC%", height=7)

g.fig.suptitle("GC% vs number of genes for amphibians", y=1.1)
```

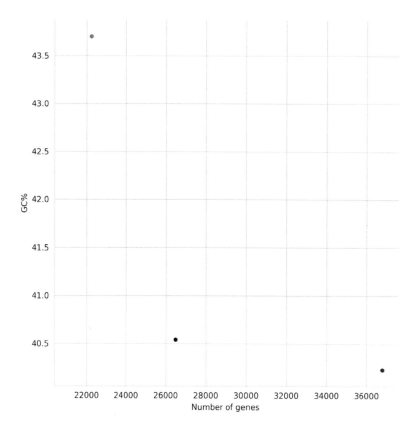

Now look what happens when we add in the genome size as a factor. We'll map the size column to the size of the points:

```
# amphibian_scale.py

g = sns.relplot(
    data=amphibians, x="Number of genes", y="GC%", size="Size (Mb)", height=7
)

g.fig.suptitle("GC% vs number of genes for amphibians", y=1.1)
```

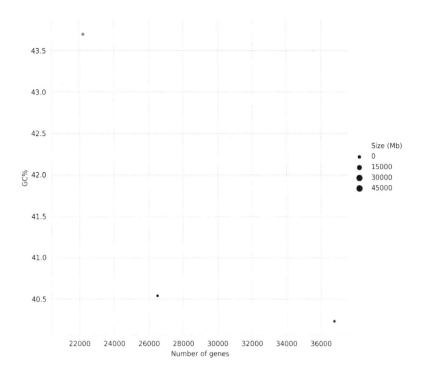

Notice how the sizes displayed on the legend are much bigger than those on the plot. The reason for this is because seaborn is using all of the sizes to figure out the range for the legend - including genomes like *Ambystoma mexicanum* which will not actually be plotted. So for this dataset, the legend is scaled to accommodate a size of over 30,000 megabases, despite the fact that the largest genome which will actually be plotted is only 6,000 megabases.

We see the same phenomenon if we map the size column to hue:

```
# amphibian_hue.py

g = sns.relplot(
    data=amphibians, x="Number of genes", y="GC%", hue="Size (Mb)", height=7
)

g.fig.suptitle("GC% vs number of genes for amphibians", y=1.1)
```

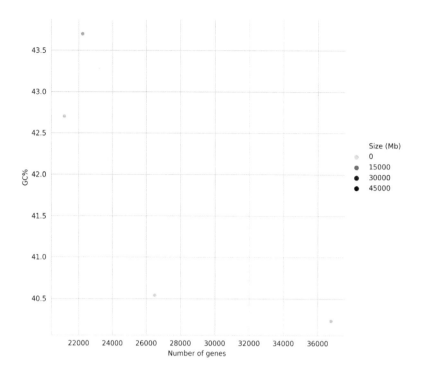

GC% vs number of genes for amphibians

The color range is chosen to show up to 30,000, so the points which are actually plotted are all squeezed into the low end of the scale, making color useless.

18.3.1 Fixing the problem

The workaround for this is to explicitly drop rows containing missing data for any of the columns that we are planning to use in our plot:

```
# skip_missing.py

non_missing = amphibians.dropna(subset=["Number of genes", "GC%", "Size (Mb)"])

g = sns.relplot(
    data=non_missing, x="Number of genes", y="GC%", size="Size (Mb)", height=7
)

g.fig.suptitle("GC% vs number of genes for amphibians", y=1.1)
```

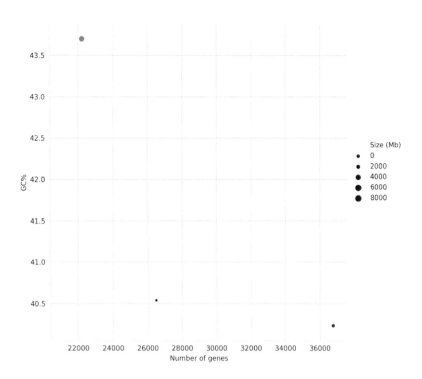

which allows the sizes to be appropriately scaled.

This behaviour is documented here:

https://github.com/mwaskom/seaborn/issues/1761

19 High performance Pandas

One of the main reasons for using a data analysis stack like pandas + seaborn is to get answers quickly. As we've seen, once we are familar with the tools we are able to very quickly explore large datasets with a small amount of code. You might have noticed that in previous chapters we have studiously avoided mentioning issues of performance. There are a number of reasons for this.

Firstly, in introducing new tools and concepts, we generally want to favour clarity over performance. In other words, we want to concentrate on writing code that is as clear as possible, rather than code that runs as fast as possible. Secondly, the tools that we are using are already well optimized. Since pandas uses numpy for most numerical calculations, we generally don't have to go to any great effort to get good performance.

And finally, in many problems that we encounter with biological data, the datasets are so small that even inefficient code runs fast enough. Consider our daily temperature dataset:

```
# read_weather.py

weather = pd.read_csv("weather.csv")

from pandas.api.types import CategoricalDtype

months = ["January", "February", "March", "April", "May", "June", "July",
    "August", "September", "October", "November", "December"]

weather["Month"] = weather["Month"].astype(
    CategoricalDtype(categories=months, ordered=True)
)

weather
```

	City	Year	Month	Day of year	Day of month	Mean temperature
0	Berlin	1960	January	1	1	6.4
1	Berlin	1960	January	2	2	8.1
2	Berlin	1960	January	3	3	5.4
3	Berlin	1960	January	4	4	3.9
4	Berlin	1960	January	5	5	6
...	...	...	...	...	...	...
63711	London	2018	October	300	27	4.9
63712	London	2018	October	301	28	7.4
63713	London	2018	October	302	29	5.8
63714	London	2018	October	303	30	6.6
63715	London	2018	October	304	31	7

This is the largest dataset we've used, with around sixty thousand rows. Suppose we want to find the warmest day for each year in Berlin. The approach that we've been using in this book - filter the dataframe, then group by year and take the max temperature of each group - takes around 3 milliseconds on my desktop:

```
# quick_filter.py
weather[weather["City"] == "Berlin"].groupby("Year")["Mean temperature"].max()
```

```
Year
1960    25.0
1961    27.2
1962    23.1
1963    28.4
1964    27.4
          ...
2014    27.6
2015    30.1
2016    28.2
2017    25.6
2018    28.9
Name: Mean temperature, Length: 59, dtype: float64
```

A less efficent way, that uses an explicit loop for the year - and will hence end up filtering the dataset multiple times - takes around 70 milliseconds:

```python
# slow_filter.py

maxes = {}

for year in weather["Year"].unique():
    this_year = weather[weather["Year"] == year]
    just_berlin = this_year[this_year["City"] == "Berlin"]
    year_max = just_berlin["Mean temperature"].max()
    maxes[year] = year_max
```

In relative terms that's a big difference; the more efficient code is over twenty times faster. But from the perspective of human experience, the difference is not noticable. Both pieces of code run effectively instantly, and in either case it will certainly take us far longer to write the code than to run it!

So, in many cases, worrying about performance is unnecessary when using pandas. The cases where it is necessary tend to fall into a few categories: when we have very large datasets, when we have a piece of code that needs to run very frequently, or when we have very computationally intensive work to do. In this chapter we'll take a look at a few performance considerations that can make sure our code is as fast as reasonably possible.

19.0.1 A note on timing

For the examples in this chapter, we'll be using the python `timeit` module, which we can do inside Jupyter notebook or iPython by adding the `%%timeit` code at the start of the code. If you end up running these examples in a different environment, just omit the `%%timeit` line. In the example files, the preamble code that imports modules and loads the files comes first, so to run these examples in iPython put that code in a separate cell.

If you try running these examples yourself, you will obviously get different absolute measurements depending on a bunch of factors: most significantly the hardware on which you're running. So in the text, we will concentrate on relative times rather than absolute times.

19.1 Looping vs vectorization

The most important rule when considering pandas performance is one that should feel natural if you've followed the examples in this book: avoid writing `for` loops. To take an example that we've seen before - turning all of our genome sizes into bases by multiplying by 1,000,000 - carrying out an expression on the entire column:

```python
%%timeit
# fast_broadcast.py

sizes = euk["Size (Mb)"] * 1_000_000
```

```
74.7 µs ± 1.32 µs per loop (mean ± std. dev. of 7 runs, 10000 loops each)
```

is much faster than using a loop to process one element at a time:

```
%%timeit
# slow_loop.py

sizes = []
for size in euk["Size (Mb)"]:
    sizes.append(size * 1_000_000)
```

```
853 µs ± 10.1 µs per loop (mean ± std. dev. of 7 runs, 1000 loops each)
```

For our purposes we don't have to worry too much about why the vectorized approach is faster. All of the optimizations happen at the `numpy` layer.

The same argument applies to vectorized numpy functions. For example, to take the log of all the genome sizes this:

```
%%timeit
# fast_np.py

np.log(euk["Size (Mb)"])
```

```
178 µs ± 5.37 µs per loop (mean ± std. dev. of 7 runs, 10000 loops each)
```

is much faster than using a loop, even using the exact same `np.log` function:

```
%%timeit
# slow_log.py

logs = []
for size in euk["Size (Mb)"]:
    logs.append(np.log(size))
```

```
5.71 ms ± 262 µs per loop (mean ± std. dev. of 7 runs, 100 loops each)
```

In the above examples, we are iterating over a single series so we can just put it in the `for` loop as we would a list, or any other iterable type. In contrast, if we try to iterate over the dataframe, the results might not be what we expect:

```
for x in euk:
    print(x)
```

```
Species
Kingdom
Class
Size (Mb)
GC%
Number of genes
Number of proteins
Publication year
Assembly status
```

Iterating over a dataframe just gives us a list of the column names. To iterate over rows we have to us the `iterrows` method. This will give us a list of tuples where the first element is the index and the second element is the row represented as a series. We normally write a loop that uses tuple unpacking to specify two variable names:

```
for index, row in euk.iterrows():
    pass
```

We can access individual columns for each row by using the `row` series, so to calculate the gene density we may write something like this:

```
%%timeit
# slow_row_iteration.py

densities = []
for index, row in euk.iterrows():

    # calculate number of genes per megabase
    gene_density = row["Number of genes"] / row["Size (Mb)"]

    densities.append(gene_density)
```

```
583 ms ± 12.3 ms per loop (mean ± std. dev. of 7 runs, 1 loop each)
```

This works, but the way that we learned to do this calculation earlier in the book is both shorter and far faster:

```
%%timeit

euk["Number of genes"] / euk["Size (Mb)"]
```

```
130 µs ± 5.42 µs per loop (mean ± std. dev. of 7 runs, 10000 loops each)
```

19.2 Looping vs `apply`

Sometimes, we run into situations where vectorization isn't possible. Often that's because we need to work with an existing function that only works on a single input. Such situations are likely to be very specific to the problem that we're working on, so rather than try to come up with a convincing example we'll look at an obviously contrived one. Let's say that we want to take our genomes and check whether they were published in a leap year. The maths for determining whether a given year is a leap year is not too tricky, but conveniently it's already implemented in Python's standard library:

```
import calendar

calendar.isleap(1992)
```

```
True
```

Because `calendar.isleap` is not a vectorized function, we can't simply pass it a list of values. We have to explicitly run the function on each value. We can iterate over the column:

```
%%timeit
# leap_with_loop.py

leaps = []
for year in euk["Publication year"]:
    leaps.append(calendar.isleap(year))
```

```
1.61 ms ± 27.2 µs per loop (mean ± std. dev. of 7 runs, 1000 loops each)
```

or over the dataframe with `iterrows`:

```
%%timeit
# leap_with_rows.py

leaps = []
for index, row in euk.iterrows():
    leaps.append(calendar.isleap(row["Publication year"]))
```

```
490 ms ± 3.17 ms per loop (mean ± std. dev. of 7 runs, 1 loop each)
```

For this calculation, iterating over the column is fastest as it doesn't require pandas to package up each row into a new, temporary Series object. Faster yet, though is to use `apply` on the series:

```
%%timeit
# leap_with_apply.py

euk["Publication year"].apply(calendar.isleap)
```

```
1.14 ms ± 11.8 µs per loop (mean ± std. dev. of 7 runs, 1000 loops each)
```

19.3 Applying with multiple columns

For some calculations, we need multiple columns, so the only way to do it with a loop is to use `iterrows`. Here's another silly example; we want to find genomes where the number of genes and proteins are both prime numbers. To accomplish this we'll need a function that can take a number and tell us if it's prime. Here's the simplest one:

```
# check_prime.py

def is_prime_number(x):
    x = int(x)
    if x >= 2:
        for y in range(2, x):
            if not (x % y):
                return False
    else:
        return False
    return True
```

The logic isn't too hard to follow: for numbers greater than 2, return **False** as soon as we find a smaller integer that divides our number exactly. If we don't find one, return **True**. And for numbers smaller than 2 (i.e. 0 and 1), return **False**. Becuase this function isn't a simple expression, but instead involves a loop and some logic, it isn't easy to vectorize, so we'll have to run it once for each genome.

Let's compare the various ways that we might use our function to create a list of boolean values for our genomes. Becuase some of our genomes don't have numbers of predicted genes and proteins, we'll use `dropna` before processing them:

```
# drop_missing.py

both_present = euk.dropna(subset=["Number of genes", "Number of proteins"])
```

Using `iterrows`:

```
%%timeit
# prime_rows.py

result = []
for index, row in both_present.iterrows():
    result.append(
        is_prime_number(row["Number of genes"])
        and is_prime_number(row["Number of genes"])
    )
```

```
389 ms ± 5.16 ms per loop (mean ± std. dev. of 7 runs, 1 loop each)
```

is much slower than using `apply` on the dataframe:

```
%%timeit
# prime_apply.py

both_present.apply(
    lambda row: is_prime_number(row["Number of genes"])
    and is_prime_number(row["Number of proteins"]),
    axis=1,
)
```

```
307 ms ± 3.3 ms per loop (mean ± std. dev. of 7 runs, 1 loop each)
```

Notice that we have to use a lambda expression to run the function on both numbers for each row.

Another approach is to `apply` the function separately to each column, then combine them using `&`, just like we do when carrying out complex conditions:

```
%%timeit
# prime_lambda.py
(
    both_present["Number of genes"].apply(is_prime_number)
    & both_present["Number of proteins"].apply(is_prime_number)
)
```

```
274 ms ± 6.46 ms per loop (mean ± std. dev. of 7 runs, 1 loop each)
```

In this case, that approach turns out to be slower - the overhead of running `apply` twice outweighs that of creating `Series` objects.

19.4 Caching a slow function

For calculations on categorical data in particular, we can often use our knowledge of the structure of our dataset to help improve performance. Consider the case where we want to add a new column based on an input that has a small number of unique values. For instance, let's try to add a new column that counts the number of papers in pubmed that refer to each class in our dataset.

We can begin with a function that will take the name of a class and return the number of papers that mention it:

```
# count_papers.py

from urllib.request import urlopen
import re
import time

def count_papers(classname):
    link = f"https://eutils.ncbi.nlm.nih.gov/entrez/eutils/esearch.fcgi?db=pubmed&term={classname.replace(' ', '+')}&
    ↪ rettype=count"
    f = urlopen(link)
    myfile = f.read()
    count = re.search(r"<Count>(\d+)</Count>", str(myfile)).group(1)
    time.sleep(1)
    return int(count)
```

The details of how this function works are not important. It uses the EUtils system to construct a search URL based on the class name, then uses a regular expression to parse the result. For our purposes, there are two things to note. Firstly the signature: we put in a class name as the argument, and get back an integer:

```
count_papers("Ascomycetes")
```

```
211403
```

Secondly, the timing - this function takes a very long time to run. Not only does it have to wait for the pubmed server to respond, but we also have a call to `time.sleep` to make sure that the function won't be called more frequently than once per second. This is a common situation when we are using an API over the web.

So in contrast to the previous examples, we are unlikely to notice any systematic difference in performance between the various methods of running this function on our class names. We can do an experiment with the first 5 rows:

```
%%timeit
# count_papers_loop.py

counts = []
for classname in euk.head()["Class"]:
    counts.append(count_papers(classname))
```

```
7.29 s ± 92.7 ms per loop (mean ± std. dev. of 7 runs, 1 loop each)
```

```
%%timeit
# count_papers_apply.py

euk.head()["Class"].apply(count_papers)
```

```
7.23 s ± 34.5 ms per loop (mean ± std. dev. of 7 runs, 1 loop each)
```

The running time is dominated by the function itself, so any improvements in looping will be minimal. In the above experiment, it took around 7 seconds to run the function on five rows, so to run it on the whole dataset:

```
(7 / 5) * len(euk)
```

```
11622.8
```

is expected to take over ten thousand seconds, or more than 2 hours.

This is where our knowledge of the data can come in handy. We know from our previous explorations that there are only a small number of unique class values:

```
euk["Class"].nunique()
```

```
19
```

And since the function always gives the same output for the same input, there's no need to count the number of papers for the same class multiple times. Instead we can construct a dictionary by calling the function on each unique class name:

```
# build_dict.py

count_dict = {}
for classname in euk["Class"].unique():
    count_dict[classname] = count_papers(classname)
```

This takes about half a minute, and leaves us with a dictionary where the keys are class names and the values are the numbers of papers:

```
print(count_dict)
```

```
{'Other Protists': 1052, 'Land Plants': 617686, 'Ascomycetes': 211403, 'Basidiomycetes': 28734, 'Kinetoplasts': 162, '
Apicomplexans': 558, 'Other Fungi': 296445, 'Roundworms': 77970, 'Insects': 314692, 'Fishes': 194516, 'Other Animals':
947466, 'Mammals': 22174438, 'Other': 3622674, 'Amphibians': 111993, 'Birds': 240807, 'Green Algae': 24973, 'Flatworms':
51140, 'Reptiles': 43226, 'Other Plants': 153909}
```

Now we can simply use **replace** to look up the counts for each row:

```
%%timeit

euk["Class"].replace(count_dict)
```

```
4.85 ms ± 37.3 µs per loop (mean ± std. dev. of 7 runs, 100 loops each)
```

Even including the 30 seconds it took to build the dictionary, that's a significant time saving on our baseline of 2 hours!

For large datasets, **replace** itself is inefficient. Using **apply** and passing in the **get** method of our dictionary gives us a four fold speed up:

```
%%timeit

euk["Class"].apply(count_dict.get)
```

```
1.29 ms ± 11.1 µs per loop (mean ± std. dev. of 7 runs, 1000 loops each)
```

In recent versions of Python, we can actually be lazier than this; the **functools** module has a decorator called **lru_cache** which, if we apply to it a function, will take care of "remembering" the output when we run it with identical inputs. So this:

```
# cache_decorator.py

from functools import lru_cache

@lru_cache(maxsize=None)
def count_papers(classname):
    link = f"https://eutils.ncbi.nlm.nih.gov/entrez/eutils/esearch.fcgi?db=pubmed&term={classname.replace(' ', '+')}&
    ↪ rettype=count"
    f = urlopen(link)
    myfile = f.read()
    count = re.search(r"<Count>(\d+)</Count>", str(myfile)).group(1)
    time.sleep(1)
    return int(count)

euk["Class"].apply(count_papers)
```

```
0          1052
1        617686
2        617686
3        617686
4        617686
        ...
8297     211403
8298     211403
8299     211403
8300     211403
8301     211403
Name: Class, Length: 8302, dtype: int64
```

is about as efficient as using a dict, and certainly less work to write.

19.5 Using `sample` before analysing a whole dataset

Remember that it's very easy to grab a subset of the rows from a pandas dataframe using `sample`. This trick comes in useful any time we want to run an operation on a small number of rows to check that it works, before running it on the whole dataset. The paper counting function from above provides a good example. What if, instead of counting papers for each class name, we instead want to count papers for each species name? Unlike classes, most species names are unique, so we'll need to run the function on many inputs and it'll take a long time.

But there are many oppourtunities for errors in the function itself, so before we start it running on all four thousand unique species names, we'll run it on a subset to make sure it works. One way to do this is simply to use `head` to take the first few rows:

```
euk["Species"].head().apply(count_papers)
```

```
0            6
1        74885
2        27266
3         2477
4        14941
Name: Species, dtype: int64
```

but in many datasets this will run into problems with structure. If the data are ordered in any way, then taking the first few rows might not be a good test. Using `sample` we can get random rows from throughout the dataframe:

```
# random_samply.py

euk["Species"].sample(10).apply(count_papers)
```

```
3662         1
3451         5
696       4475
6636       320
2045         9
8104    129543
6141       586
3195        25
6180         8
2012       172
Name: Species, dtype: int64
```

and get a more representative sample of species names to feed into our function.

Another situation in which `sample` is useful is when drawing complex charts. Let's read in the combined weather dataset that we created in the chapter on merging:

```
# read_weather.py

all_weather = pd.read_csv("all_weather.csv")
all_weather
```

	City	Year	Day of year	Month	Day of month	Rainfall (mm)	Temperature (°C)
0	Berlin	1960	1	January	1	4	6.4
1	Berlin	1960	2	January	2	25	8.1
2	Berlin	1960	3	January	3	0	5.4
3	Berlin	1960	4	January	4	0	3.9
4	Berlin	1960	5	January	5	104	6
...	...	...	...	...	...	...	...
65281	London	2019	208	July	27	20	NaN
65282	London	2019	209	July	28	0	NaN
65283	London	2019	210	July	29	0	NaN
65284	London	2019	211	July	30	42	NaN
65285	London	2019	212	July	31	0	NaN

We will attempt to draw a contour plot showing the relationship between temperature and rainfall in each city. The code to do this is quite complicated, but we can more or less copy the example that we saw in the chapter on using facet grids directly. To aid visualization we'll exclude any outlier days with more than 100mm of rain:

```
# kde_grid_weather.py

# first lay out the grid
g = sns.FacetGrid(
    data=all_weather[all_weather["Rainfall (mm)"] < 100],
    col="City",
    aspect=1,
    height=4,
)

# then plot the charts
g.map(
    sns.kdeplot,
    "Temperature (°C)",
    "Rainfall (mm)",
    shade=True,
    shade_lowest=False,
    cmap="OrRd",
)

g.fig.suptitle(
    "Density plot of temperature vs. rainfall for three cities", y=1.05
)
```

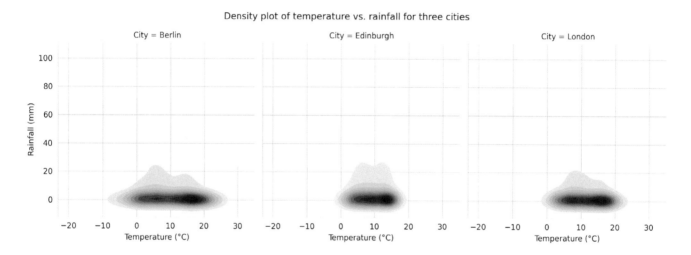

Because drawing contour plots involves a lot of resampling, this figure takes a long time to generate. In order to tweak the various properties of the chart, we'd like to have a faster way of drawing it. In this case, the problem with using `head` is readily apparent:

```
# kde_grid_head.py

# first lay out the grid
g = sns.FacetGrid(
    data=all_weather[all_weather["Rainfall (mm)"] < 100].head(1000),
    col="City",
    aspect=1,
    height=4,
)

# then plot the charts
g.map(
    sns.kdeplot,
    "Temperature (°C)",
    "Rainfall (mm)",
    shade=True,
    shade_lowest=False,
    cmap="OrRd",
)

g.fig.suptitle(
    "Density plot of temperature vs. rainfall for three cities", y=1.05
)
```

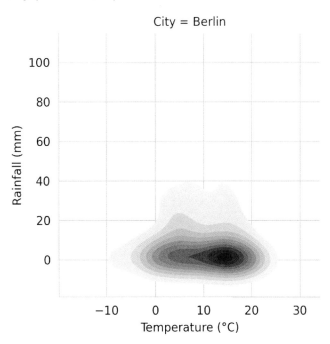

Because the dataset is ordered, all of the data for Berlin comes first, so even plotting the first 1000 rows gives us only a single plot. In contrast, using **sample**:

```
# kde_grid_sample.py

# first lay out the grid
g = sns.FacetGrid(
    data=all_weather[all_weather["Rainfall (mm)"] < 100].sample(1000),
    col="City",
    aspect=1,
    height=4,
)

# then plot the charts
g.map(
    sns.kdeplot,
    "Temperature (°C)",
    "Rainfall (mm)",
    shade=True,
    shade_lowest=False,
    cmap="OrRd",
)

g.fig.suptitle(
    "Density plot of temperature vs. rainfall for three cities", y=1.05
)
```

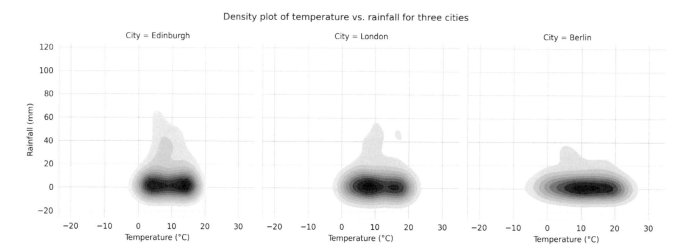

gives us a random selection of rows, so all three cities are represented and our figure looks much more like the one that uses the whole dataset.

19.6 Categories and performance

We've seen in a previous chapter that changing the data type of a column to a categorical type makes a big difference in terms of memory. It can also make a modest difference in performance. To select just the rows for Berlin from our weather dataset takes around 3 milliseconds when the city column is a string:

```
%%timeit

weather[weather["City"] == "Berlin"]
```

```
3.05 ms ± 19.6 µs per loop (mean ± std. dev. of 7 runs, 100 loops each)
```

but after changing to a category:

```
weather["City category"] = weather["City"].astype("category")
```

the same operation takes less than 1 millisecond.

```
%%timeit

weather[weather["City category"] == "Berlin"]
```

```
983 µs ± 2.99 µs per loop (mean ± std. dev. of 7 runs, 1000 loops each)
```

19.7 Indices and performance

If we know that we're planning to filter rows based on a particular column frequently, then it might be worth turning that column into an index. If, like our weather data, the column is a category - i.e. contains a small number of values - then we must sort the index to gain any performance benefit:

```
# city_index_weather.py

weather = weather.set_index("City").sort_index()
weather
```

City	Year	Month	Day of year	Day of month	Mean temperature	City category
Berlin	1960	January	1	1	6.4	Berlin
Berlin	1960	January	2	2	8.1	Berlin
Berlin	1960	January	3	3	5.4	Berlin
Berlin	1960	January	4	4	3.9	Berlin
Berlin	1960	January	5	5	6	Berlin
...	...	...	...	...	...	...
London	2018	October	300	27	4.9	London
London	2018	October	301	28	7.4	London
London	2018	October	302	29	5.8	London
London	2018	October	303	30	6.6	London
London	2018	October	304	31	7	London

After doing this, the time required to look up the rows for Berlin falls to under 200 microseconds:

```
%%timeit

weather.loc["Berlin"]
```

```
217 µs ± 1.86 µs per loop (mean ± std. dev. of 7 runs, 1000 loops each)
```

Whether or not this improvement will be offset by the time required to build and sort the index in the first place will depend on how many times we will need to run a filter like this.

For situations where we can supply an index with unique values, the performance increase can be dramatic. Let's read our weather data again, and see how long it takes to find the row for a specific day in a specific city:

```
weather = pd.read_csv("weather.csv")
```

```
%%timeit
# weather_complex_filter.py

weather[
    (weather["City"] == "Berlin")
    & (weather["Year"] == 1989)
    & (weather["Month"] == "November")
    & (weather["Day of month"] == 9)
]
```

```
5.12 ms ± 32.3 µs per loop (mean ± std. dev. of 7 runs, 100 loops each)
```

This is a fairly slow operation, since it involves checking each of 60,000 rows individually. If, however, we make a multi index with the four columns we want:

```
# weather_complex_index.py

weather = weather.set_index(["City", "Year", "Month", "Day of month"])
```

then looking up the same day (using `loc` to select rows by index) becomes much faster:

```
%%timeit
# weather_filter_index.py

weather.loc["Berlin", 1989, "November", 9]
```

```
143 µs ± 1.45 µs per loop (mean ± std. dev. of 7 runs, 10000 loops each)
```

Notice that in this case, we don't have to sort the index, since the values are unique.

Unique indices have a very useful property: the time required to select a single row is constant regardless of the size of the dataset. To illustrate this, we will read two versions of the weather dataset: a small one, with just the first 6000 rows, and a large one, with ten times as many rows. We'll set the same index as above on both datasets:

```
# small_large_weather.py

small_weather = pd.read_csv(
    "weather.csv",
    nrows=6000,
    index_col=["City", "Year", "Month", "Day of month"],
)
large_weather = pd.read_csv(
    "weather.csv",
    nrows=60000,
    index_col=["City", "Year", "Month", "Day of month"],
)
```

Now we will use the index to look up a single day in both datasets (being careful to pick a day near the start, so that it will be present in both):

```
%%timeit

small_weather.loc["Berlin", 1965, "November", 9]
```

```
141 µs ± 560 ns per loop (mean ± std. dev. of 7 runs, 10000 loops each)
```

```
%%timeit

large_weather.loc["Berlin", 1965, "November", 9]
```

```
140 µs ± 427 ns per loop (mean ± std. dev. of 7 runs, 10000 loops each)
```

Notice that even though the large dataset is ten times larger, there's no difference in the performance of this query.

20 Further reading

As this book has hopefully made clear, the packages that we've been exploring - chiefly pandas, seaborn and matplotlib - are large and complex. Attempting to discuss them comprehensively would result in an unreadably long book, so we've tried to concentrate on just the most useful parts. Complex tools like pandas generally follow a kind of Pareto principle where 20% of the features account for 80% of what we need to do our work, and it's this 20% that we have focused on.

The same can be said of the wider field of data visualization - there is a whole discipline devoted to understanding the ways that we see and process visual information. We have taken the most useful insights - for example, best practice when using color - as our topics for this book.

There are a few topics that, although we don't have space for a comprehensive discussion, are worth mentioning as starting points for further reading. The purpose of this chapter is to provide a few pointers to techniques that are more rarely needed, but which may prove very useful for specific problems.

20.1 Dates and times

In a way, we have been working with dates throughout this book. Every time we refer to the **Publication year** column in our eukaryone genome dataset, or any of the year/month/day columns in our weather datasets, we are obviously working with dates. However, we have been manipulating these values as integers, rather than actual dates. Pandas has tools for working with dates and times directly, with a rich suite of functions.

A couple of examples from the weather dataset will make the point. Let's start by taking our weather dataset and just selecting London:

```
london = weather[weather["City"] == "London"]
```

If we now take our filtered dataset and make a new series by concatenating our date columns:

```
dates = (
    london["Day of month"].astype(str)
    + " "
    + london["Month"]
    + " "
    + london["Year"].astype(str)
)
dates.head()
```

```
42227    1 January 1960
42228    2 January 1960
42229    3 January 1960
42230    4 January 1960
42231    5 January 1960
dtype: object
```

we get a series of strings containing dates in a fairly human readable format.

If we then pass that series to `pd.to_datetime`:

```
pd.to_datetime(dates).head()
```

```
42227    1960-01-01
42228    1960-01-02
42229    1960-01-03
42230    1960-01-04
42231    1960-01-05
dtype: datetime64[ns]
```

we get a series with a new data type that we've not seen before: a date/time. We can store this as a new column:

```
london["date"] = pd.to_datetime(dates)
london.head()
```

	City	Year	Month	Day of year	Day of month	Mean temperature	date
42227	London	1960	January	1	1	10.6	1960-01-01
42228	London	1960	January	2	2	6.1	1960-01-02
42229	London	1960	January	3	3	8.4	1960-01-03
42230	London	1960	January	4	4	9.4	1960-01-04
42231	London	1960	January	5	5	8.9	1960-01-05

then use it to answer questions that would be tricky with our original columns. For example, it's easy to get the day of the week using a `dt` accessor that reminds us of the `str` accessor for string columns:

```
london["date"].dt.dayofweek
```

```
42227    4
42228    5
42229    6
42230    0
42231    1
         ..
63711    5
63712    6
63713    0
63714    1
63715    2
Name: date, Length: 21489, dtype: int64
```

Then we can verify that there's no real difference between the temperature during the working week and at the weekend, even though it might seem that way:

```
(london.groupby(london["date"].dt.dayofweek)["Mean temperature"].mean())
```

```
date
0    11.141075
1    11.100326
2    11.140717
3    11.154383
4    11.158762
5    11.115765
6    11.129870
Name: Mean temperature, dtype: float64
```

Notice that pandas takes care of all the awkward calculations to figure out the day of the week for us.

We can also group in ways that would be difficult with the date split over multiple columns. For example, finding the warmest day in each month is easy using our original columns:

```
london.groupby(["Year", "Month"])["Mean temperature"].max()
```

```
Year   Month
1960   April        13.3
       August       19.4
       December     10.8
       February     13.0
       January      10.8
                    ...
2018   June         22.1
       March        11.1
       May          21.3
       October      21.3
       September    21.4
Name: Mean temperature, Length: 706, dtype: float64
```

but what if we wanted to do the same for each 2 week period? With a datetime column, this is easy:

```
london.resample("2W", on="date")["Mean temperature"].max()
```

```
date
1960-01-03    10.6
1960-01-17     9.4
1960-01-31    10.8
1960-02-14    10.0
1960-02-28    12.0
              ...
2018-09-09    19.6
2018-09-23    21.4
2018-10-07    17.1
2018-10-21    21.3
2018-11-04    14.2
Freq: 2W-SUN, Name: Mean temperature, Length: 1536, dtype: float64
```

Notice that we can use this very convenient `2W` shorthand to tell pandas that we want to divide our dataset into 2 week chunks.

We can use a similar syntax to do a rolling window calculation (in biology we might call this a *sliding window*). For example, if we plot the mean daily temperature for a given year we see quite a bit of day to day noise:

```
sns.relplot(
    data=london[london["Year"] == 1981],
    x="date",
    y="Mean temperature",
    kind="line",
    ci=None,
    aspect=3,
    height=4,
)

plt.title("Mean daily temperature for each day in London in 1981")
```

20 Further reading

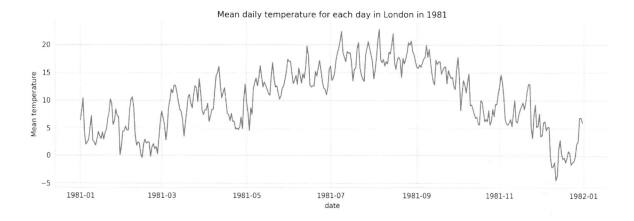

Mean daily temperature for each day in London in 1981

We might wish to smooth out the noise by taking a rolling average - for each day, taking the mean of the temperature in the 7 days before and after. We do this with `rolling`:

```
london.rolling("14D", on="date")["Mean temperature"].mean()
```

```
42227    10.600000
42228     8.350000
42229     8.366667
42230     8.625000
42231     8.680000
            ...
63711    11.992857
63712    11.514286
63713    11.078571
63714    10.342857
63715     9.864286
Name: Mean temperature, Length: 21489, dtype: float64
```

and plotting these values makes it easier to see periods of warm and cold weather:

```
london["rolling_mean"] = london.rolling("14D", on="date")[
    "Mean temperature"
].mean()
sns.relplot(
    data=london[london["Year"] == 1981],
    x="date",
    y="rolling_mean",
    kind="line",
    ci=None,
    aspect=3,
    height=4,
)

plt.title("14 day rolling mean temperature for London in 1981")
```

```
Text(0.5, 1.0, '14 day rolling mean temperature for London in 1981')
```

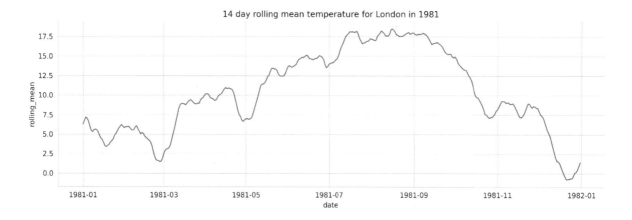

If these features sound useful, there's a comprehensive section in the pandas tutorial devoted to working with times and dates:

https://pandas.pydata.org/docs/user_guide/timeseries.html

20.2 Pandas alternative syntax

One of the features of pandas that we've actively avoided in this book is the fact that there are often several different types of syntax that we could use to accomplish a given goal. The most basic example is simply selecting a column from a dataframe. We have consistently used square brackets:

```
weather["Year"].head()
```

```
0    1960
1    1960
2    1960
3    1960
4    1960
Name: Year, dtype: int64
```

but for column names that are valid Python identifiers we can simply use a dot:

```
weather.Year.head()
```

```
0    1960
1    1960
2    1960
3    1960
4    1960
Name: Year, dtype: int64
```

The reason that we've chosen to use the square brackets approach is that the dot shorthand only works for column names without spaces, and as soon as we want to select multiple columns we'll need square brackets anyway. However, it's worth knowing about the dot notation as it's sometimes used in documentation.

Another example arises when we want to filter a dataframe to select some rows, then select some columns. In this book, we have generally done it like this:

```
weather[weather["City"] == "Berlin"]["Mean temperature"]
```

20 Further reading

```
0            6.4
1            8.1
2            5.4
3            3.9
4            6.0
        ...
21484        7.9
21485        6.1
21486        4.6
21487       13.3
21488        9.0
Name: Mean temperature, Length: 21489, dtype: float64
```

but it's also possible to do it using the `loc` accessor:

```
weather.loc[weather["City"] == "Berlin", "Mean temperature"]
```

```
0            6.4
1            8.1
2            5.4
3            3.9
4            6.0
        ...
21484        7.9
21485        6.1
21486        4.6
21487       13.3
21488        9.0
Name: Mean temperature, Length: 21489, dtype: float64
```

You may recall that we have occasionally used the `loc` syntax when we need to update some cells.

Even the process of filtering itself has an alternative. There's a `query` method where we pass a string containing an expression to be evaluated on each row:

```
weather.query('City == "Berlin"').head()
```

	City	Year	Month	Day of year	Day of month	Mean temperature
0	Berlin	1960	January	1	1	6.4
1	Berlin	1960	January	2	2	8.1
2	Berlin	1960	January	3	3	5.4
3	Berlin	1960	January	4	4	3.9
4	Berlin	1960	January	5	5	6.0

This works well for simple filters; however we've avoided using it in this book because it becomes cumbersome for more complicated ones.

All of these alternative syntax forms are described in detail in the pandas user guide:

https://pandas.pydata.org/docs/user_guide/index.html

If you see any syntax in examples or real life code that you don't recognize from this book, you should be able to find a description there.

20.3 Pandas plotting functions

Another feature of pandas that we've completely ignored in this book is its build in plotting capabilities. Hopefully the reason for this is obvious: we have concentrated on using seaborn for plotting, so learning two different plotting systems would be confusing. However, for very simple plots it might be useful to know that we can take a pandas series and call `plot` on it:

```
# pandas_plot.py

(
    weather[(weather["City"] == "Edinburgh") & (weather["Year"] == 1990)]
    .set_index("Day of year")["Mean temperature"]
    .plot()
)

plt.title("Mean daily temperature in Edinburgh in 1990")
```

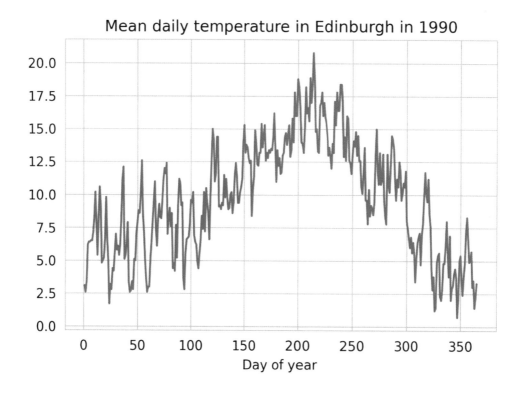

With wide format data:

```
year_summary = (
    weather[weather["Year"] == 1990]
    .groupby(["Day of year", "City"])["Mean temperature"]
    .mean()
    .unstack()
)

year_summary.head()
```

City Day of year	Berlin	Edinburgh	London
1	-1.7	3.1	4.5
2	-1.4	2.6	5.2
3	-0.4	3.4	4.0
4	-1.4	6.2	5.3
5	-0.2	6.4	6.6

we can even make slightly more complicated plots:

```
year_summary.plot()
plt.title("Mean daily temperature in three cities in 1990")
```

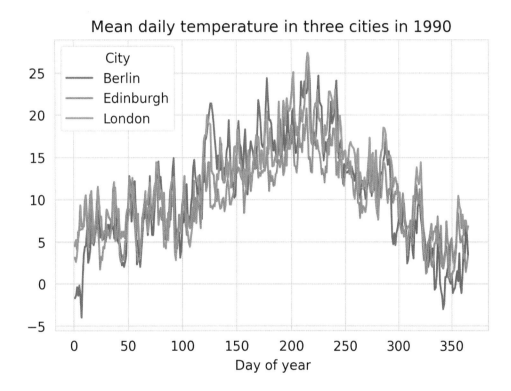

But as we've already seen, using seaborn is easier as it doesn't require reshaping the data, and as a bonus results in a better looking plot:

```
sns.relplot(
    data=weather,
    x="Day of year",
    y="Mean temperature",
    hue="City",
    kind="line",
    ci=None,
    aspect=3,
    height=3,
)

plt.title("Mean daily temperature in three cities in 1990")
```

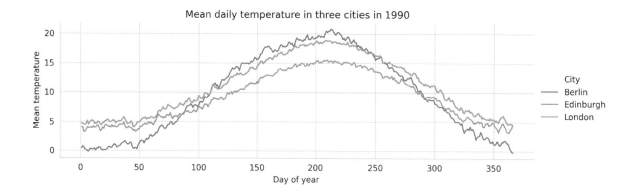

Mean daily temperature in three cities in 1990

If you want to read all about pandas' build in plotting tools, take a look at this page:

https://pandas.pydata.org/docs/user_guide/visualization.html

20.4 Jupyter widgets and interactive charts

If you're running your pandas/seaborn code in Jupyter notebook (which is highly recommended) then it may be useful to take a look at **Jupyter widgets**:

https://ipywidgets.readthedocs.io/en/latest/#

This is a system for adding small interactive controls to a Jupyter notebook, which allow the user to change parameters using familiar interface elements like sliders, dropdown menus and text boxes. Although Jupyter widgets are not associated with any of the packages we've been using, in practice they work very well for making interactive charts. For example, we might implement a slider to let the user select a range of years for plotting the weather, or a text box to filter our eukaryotic genomes by species name.

For a higher degree of interactivity, take a look at the **Bokeh** package:

https://docs.bokeh.org/en/latest/index.html

This is currently one of the best ways to build interactive visualizations with Python. It's well beyond the scope of this book, but a quick look at the user guide should help you decide if it is likely to be useful for your work.

20.5 Machine learning and statistics

The modern explosion of interest in machine learning is making steady inroads into biological topics. If you're interested in using machine learning in Python, your first visit should be to **scikit-learn**:

https://scikit-learn.org/stable/

which is an excellent package for getting started with various machine learning tasks. If it turns out that you want to build deep neural networks in Python, take a look at **PyTorch**:

https://pytorch.org/

For statistical testing, we have touched on a few examples in this book, but many others are implemented in the `scipy.stats` module:

https://docs.scipy.org/doc/scipy/reference/stats.html

Machine learning and statistics are both, of course, huge fields and well beyond the scope of this book.

Index

alpha, 65
applymap, 281, 284
between, 39
comment, 305
decimal, 302
distplot, 54, 55, 136, 221, 340, 348
dodge, 167
facetgrid, 339, 346, 347, 351, 352
fastcluster, 287
figsize, 263, 292
filter, 196
first, 268
groupby, 183, 184, 193, 195, 196, 209, 223, 225, 231, 236, 262, 357
inplace, 32
isin, 37
iterrows, 374
loc, 256, 257, 386, 393
math.log, 27
mean, 41, 265
melt, 247, 251
merge, 318
nlargest, 24
np.abs, 332
pd.concat, 310
pd.cut, 224, 274
pdist, 286
plt.savefig, 54, 137
rename, 129
sample, 25, 380, 381
skipfooter, 301
split, 46
transform, 207
unstack, 244, 262, 272, 295
usecols, 300, 326
vmax, 263
vmin, 263

aggregation, 25, 187, 189, 202, 268, 364
alias, 13, 53
annotation table, 282

bandwidth, 108
bar plot, 114, 122
bin boundaries, 224, 225, 227, 231
binning, 228, 234, 273, 276
box plot, 103, 107, 112, 148, 152, 154
broadcasting, 26

categorical palette, 81
center point, 268
color map, 71, 72, 263, 264
color scale, 263, 291, 355
comparison operators, 36

confidence intervals, 74
consistent colors, 154
contour plot, 71, 381
custom qualitative palettes, 154

data type, 15, 33, 224, 235, 239, 306, 307, 325, 328–331, 384, 389
dendrogram, 288, 289, 292, 294
descriptive statistics, 20
distance matrix, 285, 287
dot syntax, 23

error bars, 120, 126
excel files, 22
explicit order, 175, 253

filtering, 9, 33–36, 40, 42–44, 49, 195, 196, 198, 256, 335, 348, 373, 393

gene density, 26, 27, 375
genus, 46, 47
group labels, 357
grouping, 126, 180, 183–185, 187, 188, 193–195, 209, 223, 357

heatmap, 262, 265, 272, 281, 285, 289, 351–353
hexadecimal color, 139
hexbin, 69, 70, 90

indices, 184, 188, 243, 244, 254, 258, 314, 386
intercept, 75
interquartile range, 103

joint distribution, 216
jupyter, 7, 8, 14, 54, 373, 396

kernel density estimation, 107

legend labels, 131
line width, 66
long form, 242, 244, 245, 248, 262

marginal histograms, 69
mask, 34, 38, 40
memory usage, 323–325, 327, 328, 330, 331, 333, 334
merging, 316, 321
metadata, 11, 242
missing data, 18, 27, 31, 40, 58, 73, 272, 304, 305, 307, 321, 361, 364
multi index, 257, 386

naming columns, 20, 21
normalization, 202, 277
number of bins, 227

ordered category, 240
outliers, 58, 64, 154, 291

pivot, 253

point estimate, 90, 127
point plot, 124, 126
point properties, 61
polynomial regression, 79

regression lines, 73
rolling window, 390

scatter plot, 90, 154, 180, 190, 236, 345, 367
selecting multiple columns, 29
sequential palettes, 146, 263
series objects, 14, 24
slice syntax, 49, 258, 259
slope, 78, 122
small multiples, 86, 89, 90, 103, 346

step size, 259
string methods, 28
strip plot, 92, 97, 124
summary tables, 244, 278
swarm plot, 97, 101

t-test, 123
tabular, 8, 13, 360
timing, 378
transparent, 65, 66

vectorization, 375
violin plot, 107, 112

wide form, 245, 249, 262

Made in the USA
Las Vegas, NV
21 December 2024

14920895R00238